Dictionary of Health and Medicine

JOHN O. E. CLARK

Viva Books

New Delhi | Mumbai | Chennai | Kolkata | Bengaluru | Hyderabad | Kochi | Guwahati

This edition published
in 2012 by

Viva Books Private Limited
4737/23, Ansari Road, Daryaganj
New Delhi 110002
Tel: 011-4224 2200, Fax: 011- 422 2240
E-mail: vivadelhi@vivagroupindia.net
http://www.vivagroupindia.com

ISBN: 978-81-309-1253-0

Printed and bound in India by India Offset Private Limited, New Delhi.

Contents

A

abdomen Lower body cavity, separated from the chest (*thorax*) by the *diaphragm* and containing the digestive and excretory organs: bladder, gall bladder, intestines, kidneys, liver, pancreas, spleen and stomach. In men it also contains the prostate, and in women the ovaries and uterus.

ablation Removal of tissue, usually by surgery.

abortion Termination of pregnancy. The term is usually used to refer to deliberate or induced abortion as a medical procedure, most often carried out for medical or social reasons before the embryo/foetus is capable of independent survival (up to the 24th week). In the UK, induced abortions after this time are allowed only on special grounds (risk of grave injury to the mother or of serious foetal handicap). Medical staff may use the term to refer to accidental or spontaneous pregnancy loss, also called *miscarriage*, or, in later pregnancy, stillbirth. An induced abortion may be brought about medically using drugs such as mifepristone and sometimes *prostaglandins* (hormones), or surgically with techniques such as vacuum *aspiration* (sucking out the womb contents through a thin tube or cannula), *dilatation and curettage*, commonly referred to as a D and C (in which the opening in the cervix or neck of the womb is slightly enlarged and the womb lining is scraped out), and, rarely, *hysterectomy* (removal of the womb).

abrasion Medical name for a graze, a skin injury caused by scraping which results in oozing of blood and serum. Abrasions are easily infected and treatment includes removing any foreign matter, cleaning (with an antiseptic) and applying a dry sterile dressing. An antitetanus injection may also be recommended.

abreaction Reliving of emotionally painful experiences, often associated with repressed memories, either spontaneously or deliberately induced by using drugs (such as thiopentone, a barbiturate used in anaesthesia), hypnosis or psychotherapy, as part of the treatment for a *neurosis*.

abscess Accumulation of pus anywhere in the body, where it is walled off by inflamed tissue. Usually caused by bacterial infection, examples include *boils*, *carbuncles* and tooth abscesses (gumboils). Abscesses may also occur within the body. They usually cause pain and often visible swelling or other symptoms depending on the site. Release of the pus, as when a boil bursts, or is lanced, is necessary for healing. In the case of abscesses within the body, surgery may be required to drain the pus. Antibiotics may also be prescribed.

accommodation Ability of the lens of the *eye* to change shape to focus light rays on the retina. Lack of accommodation, caused by loss of flexibility of the lens, is a common defect in later life, easily corrected with *glasses* or *contact lenses*. See also *sight, sense of*.

acetabulum Medical term for the socket part of the *hip* joint, located at each side of the pelvis.

acetone Organic chemical compound, a type of ketone formed in various biochemical processes. Accumulation of ketones in the blood (*ketosis*) is symptomatic of certain disorders, and the smell of acetone on the breath (which resembles that of nail varnish remover) may indicate *diabetes* mellitus.

acetylcholine (ACH) Chemical *neurotransmitter* which passes impulses between the ends of *neurones* (nerve cells).

acetylsalicylic acid Chemical name of *aspirin*.

achalasia Muscular defect of the *oesophagus* (gullet) that interferes with swallowing, usually treated by surgical enlargement of the circular sphincter muscle (cardia) at the entrance to the stomach.

ache Usually a dull persistent pain, often caused by minor muscular strains. The term is also part of the name of more painful conditions, such as *headache*, stomach ache and *toothache*.

Achilles tendon Tendon at the back of the ankle that joins the calf muscles to the heel bone (calcaneus).

achondroplasia Inherited genetic disorder of cartilage and bone that prevents normal growth of the limb bones. It results in *dwarfism* in which the head and body grow to normal size but the arms and legs remain short. Intelligence is unaffected.

acid Chemical substance characterized by a sour taste (technically a compound that releases hydrogen ions in solution). Strong acids are corrosive, causing burns on the skin if not washed off immediately with copious amounts of cold water. Some acids occur naturally in the body. For example, *hydrochloric acid* is a component of digestive juice, and lactic acid is a breakdown product of glucose (blood sugar) when it is converted into energy in the muscles (where an accumulation of it causes *cramp*). A stomach upset, usually *indigestion*, is commonly called an "acid stomach", and for this reason some drugs that prevent indigestion are called *antacids*. "Acid" is also a slang term for the hallucinatory drug LSD (lysergic acid diethylamide).

acidaemia Abnormally high acidity (or low alkalinity) of the blood, caused by a failure of the body to maintain the correct *acid-base equilibrium*. See also *acidosis*.

acid-base equilibrium Balance between the amount of acidic and alkaline substances in the blood. Normally blood is very slightly alkaline, resulting from an excess of bicarbonate (alkaline) over carbonic acid (dissolved carbon dioxide, which is acidic) in the *plasma*. The balance is maintained chiefly by the actions of the kidneys and lungs. An imbalance leads either to *acidosis* or *alkalosis*.

acidosis Abnormally high acidity of the fluids and tissues of the body because of a failure to maintain the correct *acid-base equilibrium* (chemical balance). It occurs if respiration is impaired and the lungs cannot remove sufficient carbon dioxide from the blood (as in cases of near drowning), or if the kidneys fail to retain sufficient bicarbonate in the blood. It may also be a complication of *diabetes* mellitus, liver failure, shock or prolonged *diarrhoea*. The patient will usually be, and feel, extremely ill and may have difficulty breathing. Treatment depends on the cause. Restoration of normal breathing, where this is the problem, is a matter of urgency. In other cases treatment aims to correct the disturbance of blood chemistry, often by giving fluids through a drip, then dealing with the underlying problem.

acne Skin disorder, common in adolescence, resulting in pimples and *blackheads*, mostly on the face, neck and back, which are unsightly and may be irritating. It is caused by hormonal changes that stimulate overactivity of the sebaceous glands, whose oily secretion (sebum) blocks the pores, particularly at hair follicles. A plug of *keratin* (the protein that forms hair and nails and adds protection to the skin) in the pores forms pimples or darkens. Mild cases can be treated by skin lotions such as benzoyl peroxide. More severe cases are often treated with antibiotics, which must be taken for long periods, or sometimes isotretinoin (a drug related to vitamin A). In women a special form of the contraceptive pill may be used.

acoustic Pertaining to sound or hearing.

acquired immune deficiency syndrome Full term from which the name *AIDS* was coined.

acrania Gross deformity of a foetus in which the skull is missing.

acrocyanosis Blueish colour of the skin of the hands and feet caused by poor circulation in the blood vessels just below the surface.

acromegaly Enlargement of body tissues, and especially bones of the face, hands and feet, resulting from an excess of *growth hormone* (somatotropin) in an adult. It is usually caused by a tumour on the *pituitary gland*, which may be removed by surgery or radiotherapy.

ACTH Abbreviation of *adrenocorticotropic hormone*.

actin Protein in the form of strands that, together with those of *myosin*, are responsible for the contraction of skeletal (striated) *muscle*.

actinomycin Anti-cancer (cytotoxic) drug. Dosage is carefully controlled to prevent possible side-effects, which include damage to the bone marrow and, with one form of the drug, vomiting and diarrhoea.

actinomycosis Disorder that causes multiple abscesses, usually in the jaw, lungs, brain or intestines. It is caused by a bacterium that is normally present in the mouth but which can turn pathogenic after a tooth abscess (gumboil) or tooth extraction. It is treated by draining the abscesses if possible and with a long-term course of antibiotics.

acuity Medical term for the degree of sharpness of *vision*.

acupuncture Form of *complementary medicine*, originating in China, which usually involves the insertion of long thin needles into the skin. The needles may be rotated, heated or connected to an electric current. The method is used as a form of anaesthesia, to treat symptoms, or to promote the health of the whole body. It is thus a holistic approach to medicine. One theory is that stimulation of deep-seated sensory nerves causes the brain to release natural painkillers called *endorphins*.

acute Describing a symptom or disorder that arises suddenly and may be severe, but brief (as opposed to *chronic*).

Adam's apple Projection of the thyroid cartilage of the *larynx* at the front of the neck, more prominent in men than women (because men usually have a larger voice box).

adaptation Gradual reduction in the response to stimulation by a sense organ. There are many everyday examples, including the way touch receptors in the skin fail to "feel" the presence of clothes soon after one gets dressed, and the way the eyes slowly adapt to very dim light after being in bright light.

addict Somebody who is physically or psychologically dependent on a substance, such as the nicotine in tobacco (see *smoking*), alcohol in alcoholic drinks (see *alcoholism*) or various drugs (see *dependence*), which is taken habitually.

addiction Physical or psychological *dependence*, usually on a drug.

Addison's disease Group of symptoms caused by failure of the *adrenal gland* to secrete *corticosteroid* hormones. They include weight loss, lethargy, low blood pressure (*hypotension*) and dark pigmentation of the skin and mucous membranes, sometimes as a complication of *tuberculosis*. It is named after the English physician Thomas Addison (1793–1860), who first described it. Treatment is by *hormone replacement therapy* (HRT) with corticosteroids.

adenitis Inflammation of a *gland* or *lymph node*.

adenocarcinoma Malignant (cancerous) *tumour* in a *gland* or glandular tissue, classified according to the secretion it produces (for example, mucus or sebum). See also *carcinoma*.

adenoids Areas of lymphatic tissue at the rear of the nasal cavity in children (which tend to disappear in adulthood). Repeated infection causes inflammation and enlargement, and if the swollen adenoids obstruct breathing they may be surgically removed (adenoidectomy), often also with the tonsils (*tonsillectomy*).

adenoma Benign (non-cancerous) *tumour* in a *gland* or glandular tissue, which may become malignant (*adenocarcinoma*). Even a benign tumour on a gland such as the *pituitary* can produce profound hormonal changes – as in *Addison's disease* – and is therefore removed or destroyed if possible using surgery or radiotherapy.

adenosine diphosphate (ADP) Chemical remaining when *adenosine triphosphate* (ATP) releases metabolic energy.

adenosine triphosphate (ATP) Energy-storing chemical consisting of a base (adenosine), a sugar (ribose) and three phosphate groups, which occurs in body cells. In the tissues during muscle contraction, for example, ATP releases energy to form *adenosine diphosphate* (ADP, with only two phosphate groups). Energy from the breakdown of carbohydrates (or other foods) causes ADP to be changed back into ATP.

adenovirus Any of a group of *viruses* that cause cold-like infections of the upper respiratory tract or *conjunctivitis* of the eye.

ADH Abbreviation of *antidiuretic hormone*.

adhesion Part of the normal healing process that causes the edges of a wound to knit together, or an abnormal fusion of membranes or organs with fibrous tissue following inflammation, injury or surgery.

adipose Fatty, usually describing connective tissue with a preponderance of fat cells. Most people have a layer of adipose tissue beneath the skin and a layer around the kidneys. It acts as insulation against cold and serves as a store of energy. For this reason, somebody who eats too much – takes in more energy (calories) than required – gets fat. See also *obesity*.

adjuvant Substance that stimulates the effect of another. For example, *vaccines* prepared from toxins of diphtheria or tetanus contain aluminium hydroxide as an adjuvant.

Adler, Alfred (1870–1937) Austrian psychiatrist and friend of Sigmund *Freud*, from whom he split in 1911 to form his own movement called "individual psychology" which placed less emphasis on sex as a driving force.

adolescence Period in a personís development between the onset of *puberty* and the end of physical *growth*. Hormonal activity during adolescence accounts for the physical changes that take place and probably also for many of the emotional problems as well.

ADP Abbreviation of *adenosine diphosphate*.

adrenal gland One of two triangular *endocrine glands* located on top of each *kidney*. Each consists of a central medulla and an outer cortex. Under stimulation of the *sympathetic nervous system*, the adrenal medulla produces various hormones, the most important of which are *adrenaline* and *noradrenaline*. The adrenal cortex is under the control of the *pituitary gland*, whose hormones (such as ACTH) stimulate it to secrete *corticosteroids*, which are also hormones that control various body functions (such as metabolism and the sex glands).

adrenaline One of the two principal hormones secreted by the medulla (central part) of the *adrenal glands* (hormone-producing glands situated on top of the kidneys within the abdomen). The other is *noradrenaline*. Its presence in the bloodstream prepares the body for "fight or flight" – increasing the heartbeat and rate and depth of breathing, while diverting blood away from the intestines and to the muscles. Adrenaline may be injected as a drug to constrict blood vessels, for instance, during surgery or dental procedures, or to relieve asthma or treat anaphylaxis (severe allergic reactions). In the United States it is known as epinephrine.

adrenocortical Pertaining to the cortex (outer layer) of the *adrenal glands*.

adrenocorticotropic hormone (ACTH) Also called corticotropin, a hormone produced by the anterior (front) part of the *pituitary gland*. Its main function is to control the activity of the *adrenal glands*, and may be injected as a drug to compensate for underactivity of these glands. It is also used to treat rheumatic conditions and asthma.

adverse reaction Undesirable and potentially dangerous reaction to a drug or vaccine, usually by only a small proportion of patients and part of the calculated risk of administering such medication.

aerobic Requiring free oxygen, as do most living organisms and as do carbohydrates (from food) when they are oxidized in the tissues to produce energy – a process known as aerobic respiration.

aerosol Technically a form of colloid consisting of tiny liquid droplets or solid particles suspended in a gas. Many *inhalants* consist of drugs in aerosol form.

Aesculapius Also known as Asclepius, Greek god of medicine whose priests practised healing using herbs.

aetiology Scientific study of the causes of disease. The american spelling is etiology.

affect In psychiatry, someoneís predominant emotional state (such as sad or angry), or the specific emotional effect of a particular idea.

affective disorder Disorder of mood or emotion, such as deep *depression* or *mania*.

afterbirth *Placenta* and membranes delivered as the third stage of *labour.*

agar Gelatinous substance derived from seaweed, used as a *culture* medium for growing bacteria. Blood agar also contains animal blood and is used for various laboratory procedures.

agglutination Clumping together of suspended matter in solution, such as blood cells or bacteria. It occurs when blood of incompatible blood groups is mixed (but is different from *coagulation*), and is used in the laboratory to identify bacteria.

agglutinins *Antibodies* present in blood serum that cause *agglutination.*

aggression Hostility towards others, usually associated either with a desire for dominance or a need for defence.

aging Natural effects that take place in the body as one gets older. Obvious external effects include loss of pigment from the *hair* or loss of hair altogether (*baldness*) and loss of elasticity in the *skin* leading to the formation of wrinkles. Gradual loss of calcium from the bones causes them to shrink slightly, giving a curvature to the spine and a stooped posture. Loss of *accommodation* (focussing ability) and other changes in the eyes may affect vision, and the senses of hearing and taste may also deteriorate. There is usually also a gradual loss in the sex drive (*libido*). Degenerative changes in the body may result in *arthritis* and *rheumatism*, but, although a person as a whole may "slow down", there is usually no change in intellectual capacity. The study of the disorders of the elderly is the province of *geriatrics.* The cellular changes that accumulate during the aging process, and possible ways of arresting or even reversing them, remain the subject of intensive research.

agnosia Inability to interpret correctly information from the sense organs, caused by a disorder of the parietal lobes of the *brain.* For instance, somebody may have perfectly good hearing but be unable to interpret speech (auditory agnosia), or be able to see but unable to interpret letters and words (visual agnosia or *alexia*).

agonist Muscle that contracts to cause bodily movement, associated with relaxation of a corresponding *antagonist* muscle.

agoraphobia Unreasonable fear of open spaces or public places. See *phobia.*

agranulocytosis Serious disorder characterized by a deficiency of a type of white blood cell (*neutrophils*), caused by poisoning of the bone marrow by drugs or other chemicals. Its symptoms include fever, ulcers in the mouth and throat, and unconsciousness leading to death. A possibly life-saving treatment is transfusion of white blood cells, followed by massive doses of antibiotic drugs.

ague Old name for a *fever*, especially if accompanied by shivering, applied most commonly to *malaria.*

AID Abbreviation denoting *artificial insemination* using sperm from a donor.

AIDS (acquired immune deficiency syndrome) Viral disease that causes failure of the bodyís normal *immune response* (defence system) by destroying a vital type of lymphocyte (white blood cell) called helper T-cells. The virus (human immunodeficiency virus, or *HIV*) is passed on in body fluids including semen, so AIDS is a *sexually transmitted disease* that may be contracted through both heterosexual and homosexual intercourse. HIV can also be passed on in contaminated blood. In Western countries where sterile needles are used in medical procedures and blood or blood products are carefully screened, transmission of HIV by this route is only a risk for drug users who share hypodermic needles. However, in many countries such precautions are inadequate and travellers who need medical treatment abroad may still be at risk. HIV can also be transmitted from a mother to her baby, either at birth or during breast-feeding. Someone who has HIV may have no symptoms yet still be infectious to others. Symptoms, which may not develop for years, include loss of weight, fever, diarrhoea and swelling of the *lymph nodes*. AIDS itself involves failure of the body to combat infections, especially a type of pneumonia called pneumocystic pneumonia, which can be fatal. People with AIDS are also at risk of *tuberculosis* and of tumours, especially an otherwise rare cancer called *Kaposi's sarcoma*, which causes pigmented nodules on the skin. Treatment with a combination of antiviral drugs can slow the progression of symptoms of AIDS, sometimes considerably so, and new drugs are continually being developed. Considerable research efforts are also being expended to find an effective vaccine against HIV.

AIH Abbreviation of *artificial insemination* using sperm from the womanís husband.

air embolism Obstruction (*embolism*) to the flow of blood from the heart caused by a bubble of air in an artery. The symptoms are pain in the chest and breathlessness. An embolism may lead to sudden *heart failure*. Causes of an air embolism include injury, intravenous injection or surgery if any of these allows air to enter the bloodstream.

air sickness See *motion sickness*.

airway Passages that carry air to the lungs, particularly the *trachea* (windpipe) and *bronchi*. Blockage of the airway causes *choking* and ultimately *asphyxia*.

albino Somebody whose skin, hair and eyes lack any pigment and who consequently appears very pale with white hair and "pink" eyes (because the blood vessels are visible). Albinism is a genetic condition inherited as a *recessive* trait which results in the absence of an enzyme that normally controls the production of the pigment *melanin*.

albumin Soluble protein that occurs in blood plasma (as serum albumin), where it carries various substances (such as drugs and hormones) and helps to maintain the bloodís osmotic pressure. It is produced in the *liver*. Its presence in the urine is known as *albuminuria*.

albuminuria Also called proteinuria, the presence of albumin in the urine. It sometimes occurs after vigorous exercise or prolonged standing, but may be a symptom of kidney disease or heart disease.

alcohol Organic chemical compound containing a hydroxyl group, commonly used to mean *ethanol* (ethyl alcohol). See also *methanol*.

alcoholism Physical *dependence* on (addiction to) alcohol. It affects mental functions such as judgement and memory, and causes physical skills to deteriorate. Other organs affected include the heart (*cardiomyopathy*), liver (*cirrhosis*) and nerves (*neuritis*). Sudden deprivation of alcoholic drinks causes withdrawal symptoms of anxiety, tremor ("the shakes"), hallucinations and delusions (*delirium tremens*, the "DTs"). The main treatment for alcoholism is psychiatric, possibly including *group therapy* and the use of drugs such as disulfiram (Antabuse), which makes the patient vomit if he or she drinks alcohol.

aldosterone Corticosteroid hormone produced by the cortex (outer layer) of the *adrenal glands*. Its chief function is to control the level of salt in the blood by making the kidneyís filtration system retain sodium and water but excrete potassium. Overproduction of the hormone causes high blood pressure (hypertension) and swelling of the tissues (oedema) because of fluid retention – a group of symptoms known as Connís syndrome. Underproduction results in low blood sodium, low blood pressure (hypotension) and loss of fluid from the tissues.

alexia Commonly called word-blindness, an inability to understand anything printed or written, caused (in a right-handed person) by a disorder to the left-hand side of the brain. An alexic person who can speak and write normally is suffering from a type of *agnosia*. Somebody who can neither read nor write, and who often has a speech impediment, is suffering from a type of *aphasia*. See also *dyslexia*.

alienation Psychological disturbance in which the patient believes that somebody else is able to share or control his or her thought processes, a symptom of *schizophrenia*.

alimentary canal Medical term for the gut, the passage from the mouth to the anus through which food passes to be digested and from which waste products of digestion are eliminated. It consists of the *mouth*, *oesophagus* (gullet), *stomach*, small intestine (*duodenum*, *jejunum* and *ileum*) and the large intestine (*colon* and *rectum*).

alkalaemia Abnormally high alkalinity of the blood, caused by an increase in alkaline constituents (bicarbonate) or decrease in acidic ones (carbonic acid) through an imbalance in the *acid-base equilibrium*. See also *alkalosis*.

alkali Also called a base, a substance that produces hydroxyl ions in solution or is capable of neutralizing an *acid*. Strong alkalis are caustic and can cause "burns" on the skin if not washed off immediately with copious amounts of cold water. The usual alkaline substance in the body is bicarbonate. See also *antacid*; *alkalosis*.

alkaloid Nitrogen-containing plant product or substance made from one that can have narcotic or poisonous effects on the body. Some alkaloids are (or were) used as drugs, including atropine, codeine, digitalis, heroin, morphine, quinine and strychnine.

alkalosis Condition in which body fluids have an abnormally high alkalinity, because of a failure of the mechanism that maintains *acid-base equilibrium* (chemical balance). It may be caused by an excessive intake of alkali (in the form of bicarbonate or other *antacid*) or loss of acidic digestive juices through excessive vomiting, by overbreathing (as occurs in certain diseases) and occasionally by drugs. Symptoms include inappropriately deep breathing and muscle weakness or cramp. Treatment depends on the cause. It may include correcting the disturbance of blood chemistry by giving fluids through a drip, drug treatment for particular symptoms, or counteracting overbreathing, plus treatment of the underlying problem.

allergen Substance (an *antigen*) that triggers an *allergy* in somebody who is sensitive to it. It may be eaten, inhaled, injected or merely touched. Common allergens include foods and materials derived from plants (pollen, fungus spores and moulds), animals (feathers, fur, house mites) and materials (dust, metals, cosmetics, various chemicals and drugs). Allergens may be identified by means of a *patch test*.

allergy Bodily reaction, because of hypersensitivity, to an *allergen* (a substance – such as food, medicine, animal products, dust or pollen – which the body treats as foreign, provoking a form of immune reaction). Symptoms range from *hay fever* and skin rashes to *asthma* and *anaphylactic shock* (potentially fatal collapse). Most involve an abnormal antibody response to the presence of an allergen, with the formation of a type of antibody (IgE) that binds to special cells within tissues, causing the release of *histamine* and serotonin (chemicals that provoke inflammation) when the body next encounters the allergen. Various creams and drugs, particularly *antihistamines*, which counteract the effects of histamine, are used to treat minor reactions. With an established allergy, the best course of action is to avoid the allergen where possible. In severe allergic reactions causing collapse with anaphylaxis, emergency treatment with adrenaline may be life-saving.

allopathy Use of drugs to relieve the symptoms of disorder. It is an orthodox medical approach, unlike that of some forms of *complementary medicine* such as homoeopathy.

alopecia Medical name for *baldness*, although more often applied to the unusual loss of hair caused by disease, injury or the puzzling disorder alopecia areata (in which hair falls out in patches for no known reason) than to natural hair loss with *aging*. Wigs and hairpieces may be used to disguise hair loss. For male-pattern balding, various forms of hair "transplants" have been attempted, and the drug minoxidil may be applied to the scalp to prevent further loss and stimulate regrowth.

alphafetoprotein (AFP) Protein that occurs in *amniotic fluid*, produced mainly by the liver of a foetus. It may be detected in the motherís blood around the 16th week of pregnancy, when tests may show increased levels associated with various foetal abnormalities, including *anencephaly* or *spina bifida* (defects in the nervous system); or reduced levels, associated with *Down's syndrome*. Blood tests, however, are not definitive, and abnormal results usually lead to further tests, such as *amniocentesis* (where foetal cells are sampled and their chromosomes analysed) or ultrasound scanning. If these confirm an abnormality, the parents have the opportunity to consider terminating the pregnancy.

ALS Abbreviation of *antilymphocyte serum*.

alternative medicine Older term for *complementary medicine*.

altitude sickness Also called mountain sickness, effects of sudden exposure to altitudes of 4,500 metres (15,000 feet) or more, where the pressure and oxygen content of the air are much lower than at sea-level. Symptoms include rapid deep breathing (*hyperventilation*), which may lead to *alkalosis*, exhaustion and nausea. Fluid may accumulate in the lungs (*pulmonary oedema*), leading to shortness of breath. Treatment involves a return to a lower altitude, with diuretic drugs for any oedema.

aluminium hydroxide Commonly used *antacid* and *laxative*.

alveolus One of the millions of microscopic air-sacs in the lungs, in which oxygen from inhaled air is exchanged for the waste product carbon dioxide in the blood. It resembles a miniature bunch of grapes surrounded by a network of capillary blood vessels in which gas exchange takes place. Inhalation of dust or spores can cause inflammation of the alveoli (alveolitis), as in *farmer's lung*.

Alzheimer's disease A form of *dementia* occurring in middle age or later. Its cause is unknown but various changes in brain structure and function have been found, including alterations in transmitter chemicals, and some forms may be inherited. Symptoms include memory loss, especially for recent events; impaired intellectual performance and learning capacity; behaviour changes and defective judgement. There is no cure, but drugs that maintain levels of brain chemicals reduced as a result of the disease may improve symptoms.

amalgam Alloy of mercury and other metals (often silver and tin), used by a dentist to fill holes in a drilled tooth.

ameba American spelling of amoeba.

amenorrhoea Absence of *menstruation*. Normal before the *menarche* and after the *menopause*, its most common cause among women of child-bearing age is pregnancy (or lactation). Primary amenorrhoea, in which menstruation fails to bĕgin when expected at puberty, may be a symptom of a congenital disorder. There are many possible causes of secondary amenorrhoea – the stopping of menstruation in an adult woman – including hormone deficiencies (of the ovaries, pituitary or thyroid glands, or associated with *diabetes* mellitus), malfunction of the *hypothalamus*, undernourishment or *anorexia nervosa*, or emotional problems.

amentia Lack of intellectual development. See *mental deficiency*.

amino acid Nitrogen-containing building-block of *protein*, about twenty of which are needed by the human body. All but eight amino acids can be synthesized in the body; the eight so-called essential ones have to be supplied by proteins in food.

ammonia Poisonous, pungent alkaline gas, once commonly used in aqueous solution as a disinfectant. The restorative effect of smelling salts is caused by ammonia.

amnesia Loss of memory, which may be total or only partial, caused by drugs (including *alcohol*), injury, or an organic brain disease. It may also be a symptom of a *mental disorder*, or merely a natural consequence of growing old. In amnesia caused by a psychological trauma, retrograde amnesia is loss of memory for events that happened before the traumatic experience, anterograde amnesia for events after it. Such conditions may benefit from *psychotherapy*.

amniocentesis Technique, used after the sixteenth week of pregnancy, which involves taking a sample of *amniotic fluid* surrounding the embryo. A hypodermic needle is inserted through the abdominal wall into a pregnant womanís womb, and some fluid withdrawn and analysed for chromosomal or other abnormalities. If such evidence is found, the parent can be given an opportunity of choosing to terminate the pregnancy.

amnion Double-membrane "sac" that encloses an embryo in the womb. It forms the amniotic cavity, which is filled with *amniotic fluid.*

amniotic fluid Liquid that surrounds and protects an embryo or foetus in the amniotic cavity within the womb. It consists mainly of urine excreted by the kidneys of the foetus, and contains cells and chemicals (such as *alphafoetoprotein*) that can be analysed using *amniocentesis*.

amoeba Microscopic single-celled organism which lives in moist places and resembles a tiny shapeless lump of jelly. Some amoebae cause diseases in humans, such as *amoebic dysentery*.

amoebiasis Infestation with amoebae, another name for *amoebic dysentery.*

amoebic dysentery Type of *dysentery* (severe gut infection) caused by infestation with *amoebae* (a type of parasitic organism), common in tropical regions and usually caused by drinking water contaminated with human faeces. The chief symptom is repeated attacks of diarrhoea containing blood and mucus; anaemia, liver abscess or *hepatitis* may be complications. Treatment is with tetracyclines or other drugs to kill the amoebae.

amphetamine Potentially addictive *stimulant* drug, sometimes used as an appetite suppressant by people who are trying to lose weight.

ampulla Enlarged ending of a canal or tube, such as the ampullae in the *semicircular canals* of the ear, concerned with the sense of *balance.*

amputation Surgical removal of a limb or part of a limb, usually following an injury or destruction of tissue by *frostbite* or *gangrene.* The operation is generally planned to facilitate the subsequent fitting of an artificial limb (prosthesis).

anabolic steroid Any drug, usually a synthetic form of androgen (male sex hormone), that promotes protein synthesis (manufacture) and therefore growth. They have been prescribed for seriously underweight patients, such as elderly people or those with serious illnesses featuring weight loss, and for promoting blood cell formation. Anabolic steroids have also been taken by athletes wishing to gain weight, although they can cause masculinization in women.

anabolism Building up of complex substances (such as fats and proteins) from simpler compounds in the body. Its opposite is *catabolism.*

anaemia Blood disorder involving a deficiency of *haemoglobin* (the oxygen-carrying pigment in red blood cells) or red blood cells (erythrocytes). Symptoms include pallor, tiredness, and breathlessness or fatigue after exertion. Among the many causes are blood loss (through *haemorrhage*), deficiency of *iron* (essential for the production of haemoglobin), over-rapid destruction of red blood cells (haemolytic anaemia, usually caused by *Rhesus factor incompatibility*), damage to the bone marrow where red cells are produced (*aplastic anaemia*), distorted red cells (as in *sickle-cell anaemia*) and deficiency of vitamin B_{12} (*pernicious anaemia*). Anaemia is thus a symptom of another disorder. Treatment depends on the cause; severe cases may require blood transfusion.

anaerobic In the absence of free oxygen, an environment necessary for certain organisms (such as the bacterium that causes *botulism*).

anaesthesia Deadening of sensation in all or part of the body caused by a disorder or by the administration of an *anaesthetic.*

anaesthetic Drug used to deaden sensation (usually to pain). The term may also be used to describe any effect causing loss of sensation, for instance, due to disease or other therapeutic techniques such as acupuncture or hypnosis. General anaesthetics used in surgery affect the central nervous system (brain) and produce unconsciousness; they include drugs given by injection and various anaesthetic gases. A mixture of *nitrous oxide* with oxygen (laughing gas) may also be given to relieve pain and produce euphoria without causing unconsciousness, as is often used during childbirth ("gas and air"). Local anaesthetics deaden sensation in a specific area; they may be given by injection for minor operations or dental procedures, or applied to the skin or mucous membranes to numb the surface. A local anaesthetic injected into the space round the spinal cord, called a spinal or *epidural anaesthetic*, blocks sensation in the whole of the body below the point of injection (as is sometimes used in *childbirth*).

anal phase Stage in the *psychosexual development* of a child in Freudian theory.

analgesia Suppression of pain, using a drug called an *analgesic*, without causing loss of consciousness or deadening of sensation (which is the function of an *anaesthetic*).

analgesic Pain-killing drug which does not cause loss of consciousness, although the term is usually taken to include *narcotics*, which also act as *sedatives*. Common non-narcotic analgesics include *aspirin* and *paracetamol* (although aspirin is no longer recommended for children under twelve years old); narcotic analgesics include *heroin* and its derivatives codeine and *morphine* (which are potentially addictive).

analysis Examination of a substance, or sample of a substance, to determine its composition. In psychology, it is any method of investigating mental processes, particularly those of somebody suffering from a *mental disorder*.

anamnesis Medical term for the act of remembering.

anaphylaxis Sudden, severe allergic reaction to substances such as animal *venom* or certain drugs (particularly antibiotics) in somebody who has an unusual sensitivity to them. Symptoms include an asthma-like attack with a dramatic fall in blood pressure; because of the latter symptom the condition is also called anaphylactic shock. Urgent treatment is required, which may include injections of *adrenaline* and *antihistamines*.

anastomosis Connection between two vessels or tubes in the body. It may occur naturally (for example, between two blood vessels), or be created surgically (for example, to join two sections of the intestine or coronary arteries to by-pass a diseased or obstructed part). See also *shunt*.

anatomy The study of the structures of humans and animals, including the bones, joints, muscles, organs and other tissues. The study of how they function is the province of *physiology*.

androgen Male *sex hormone* (normally present also in small amounts in the bodies of women and girls). In men they include the steroids androsterone and testosterone, produced mainly in the testes. At *puberty* they are responsible for the development of *secondary sexual characteristics*.

androgyny Possession of female sex organs, but the outward appearance (*secondary sexual characteristics*) of a man. See also *hermaphrodite*.

anemia American spelling of anaemia.

anencephaly Major developmental fault of a foetus in which part of the skull and brain are missing.

anerobic American spelling of anaerobic.

anesthetic American spelling of anaesthetic.

aneurine Another name for *thiamine*, one of the B complex of vitamins.

aneurysm Swelling in the wall of an artery, associated with a congenital defect or a disorder (such as *arteriosclerosis* or *syphilis*). The layers of tissue that form the wall separate, and blood seeps in and causes the swelling. Common in the *aorta*, an aneurysm may press on adjacent blood vessels and restrict the flow of blood in them. Aneurysms also occur in the brain and heart; the internal *haemorrhage* that results if one bursts can be fatal. Some can be repaired by surgery.

angiitis Inflammation of a (usually small) blood vessel. Symptoms vary widely depending on the site, and include *arthritis*, rashes and even kidney failure, associated with *polyarteritis*, *serum sickness* or *nephritis*. Treatment is usually with *corticosteroid* drugs. See also *phlebitis*.

angina Spasmodic pain, often causing a feeling of suffocation. The term is also often used as a short form of *angina pectoris*.

angina pectoris Also called angina of effort, a pain in the chest that comes on during exertion, or sometimes emotional excitement or upset, and goes away when the person rests, or calms down. It is caused by an inability of the coronary arteries to supply enough blood to the heart muscle during periods of increased demand. This is usually due to *arteriosclerosis* within the coronary arteries but may also result from spasm (sudden narrowing) of the arteries. Nitrate drugs such as glyceryl trinitrate – taken by mouth spray or by dissolving a tablet under the tongue – usually relieve an established attack rapidly. Longer-acting forms can be taken as prevention, and tablets, ointments or patches are available. Other drugs may also be used. In more severe cases, surgery may be required to widen the narrowed arteries (coronary angioplasty) or to replace them (coronary artery bypass graft).

angiogram X-ray photograph of a blood vessel, which is made visible by the introduction of a *radio-opaque* substance.

angiology Study of the function, diseases and disorders of blood vessels.

angioma Benign (non-cancerous) tumour consisting of a knot of blood vessels. It may form in an organ such as the brain, where pressure from it can cause a type of *epilepsy* or it may burst to cause a *subarachnoid* haemorrhage (resulting in a stroke). An angioma just under the skiní s surface causes a purple birthmark (*naevus*), usually on the face. Small angiomas may be removed by surgery or cauterization.

angio-oedema Unusually severe allergic reaction causing raised, red swellings (weals) on the face, commonly around the eyes or mouth. It is a form of *urticaria*, and may be dangerous if the swelling involves the lips, tongue or throat, as the air passages may become narrowed, impairing breathing. The *allergen* (allergy-provoking substance) is usually something the person has eaten, or in some cases is a reaction to a drug or other substance such as an insect sting. Treatment is similar to that for urticaria and may involve *antihistamine* drugs (to counteract chemicals released in the allergic reaction) and sometimes emergency medical treatment to restore normal breathing.

ankle Joint between the leg and the foot, consisting of the *talus* (ankle bone) which articulates with the ends of the *tibia* and *fibula* in the lower leg. These are surrounded by tendons and ligaments, which may be twisted in a fall (sprained ankle). The resultant swelling is best treated with cold compresses for several hours; strapping the ankle with tape or bandages may also help. Swelling of the ankles (*oedema*) without injury may be a symptom of poor circulation, especially in somebody with *varicose veins* or who is pregnant or taking oral *contraceptives* (the Pill). Or it may be a symptom of a more serious disorder such as *heart disease*, *kidney disease* or *toxaemia* of pregnancy. Treatment then depends on the cause.

ankylosing spondylitis Disorder of the spine in which the vertebrae gradually fuse together, creating pain and stiffness. It is caused by inflammation of the synovial joints (*synovitis*) and may result in curvature of the spine (*kyphosis*). There is no cure, but symptoms may be eased with drugs, rest or a spinal support.

ankylosis Fusing of the bones in a joint, so that the joint becomes rigid. It is often a complication of *arthritis* or an infection such as *tuberculosis*.

ankylostomiasis Disorder resulting from infestation with the hookworm ankylostoma, common in tropical regions with poor sanitation. The worm larvae live in the soil and penetrate the skin of humans. They travel in the bloodstream to the lungs, and from there via the windpipe and oesophagus through the stomach to the small intestine. Symptoms include pain in the abdomen, diarrhoea and weakness. Damage to the intestinal wall results in *malnutrition* (because food absorption is impaired), bleeding and hence *anaemia*. Treatment with drugs is rapidly effective.

anodyne Old name for an *analgesic* (pain-killing) drug.

anorectic Suffering from loss of appetite.

anorexia nervosa Psychological disorder, usually of adolescent girls, in which those affected falsely believe themselves to be fat, or have a morbid fear of becoming fat. Usually their body image is distorted and they often develop an obsessive desire to lose weight. Family problems are common and there is often an underlying anxiety about developing sexuality. Those affected either eat little or no food, or attempt to counteract what they do eat by means such as inducing vomiting or abusing laxatives. Sometimes they will have periods of binge eating interspersed with such purging (*bulimia*). Symptoms include severe weight loss and cessation of menstruation (*amenorrhoea*). Without treatment, the resultant *malnutrition* can lead to death. Treatment, which is difficult, is by psychotherapy to address underlying emotional disturbances and attempt to persuade the person to eat.

anosmia Loss of the sense of *smell*, either temporarily (for example, because of a cold), or permanently because of a skull fracture or tumour affecting the centre for smell reception in the brain.

anoxia Condition resulting from lack of oxygen. It may be caused by insufficient oxygen in the air (*altitude sickness*), an insufficiency of haemoglobin or red blood cells (as in *anaemia*), or a respiratory disorder that interferes with lung function (such as *pneumonia*). Treatment depends on the cause.

antacid Alkaline substance taken to neutralize excess acidity in the stomach, typically to treat *indigestion* or a *peptic ulcer*. Antacids include hydroxides of aluminium and magnesium, calcium carbonate, magnesium trisilicate and sodium bicarbonate, either alone or in combination in various proprietary preparations. Overuse of antacids may lead to *alkalosis*, and anybody who finds the need to take them regularly should seek medical advice.

antagonist Muscle whose contraction complements that of another (the *agonist*), or a drug whose action opposes that of another drug or substance in the body.

antenatal Also called prenatal, describing *pregnancy*, the time before childbirth.

anthelmintic Drug used to treat infestation with *worms*.

anthracosis Lung disorder, a type of *pneumoconiosis*, caused by long-term breathing of coal dust.

anthrax Bacterial infection of farm animals, which can be transmitted to humans by contact with the animals or their hides or meat. Symptoms are fever, swelling of the lymph nodes and pneumonia or ulceration of the skin. Treatment is with large doses of antibiotics; untreated it can be fatal.

anthropology Scientific study of the human race, either its evolution (physical anthropology) or behaviour (social anthropology).

anthropometry Measuring the human body, usually to establish norms and detect faulty growth.

antiarrythmic Drug used to treat *arrhythmia* (irregular heartbeat).

antibiotic Drug used to kill or prevent the growth of micro-organisms. Themselves originally derived from microscopic organisms (such as the Penicillium mould), antibiotics are most effective against *bacteria*; they are mostly ineffective against *virus* infections. Some modern antibiotics are entirely synthetic, or modified versions of natural substances. Apart from penicillin, they include the tetracyclines and streptomycin. Long-term use of antibiotics (or their use to treat only minor infections) may cause side-effects by destroying useful bacteria and weaken the bodyís defences or encourage the development of antibiotic-resistant strains of bacteria.

antibody Protein substance (a *globulin*) produced in the lymph nodes as part of the bodyís natural *immune system* in response to the presence of an *antigen* – a disease-causing organism (pathogen), "foreign" material such as bacterial *toxins* or transplanted tissue, or an *allergen* such as pollen grains. Antibodies destroy or neutralize antigens, and may persist in the bloodstream and confer *immunity* against subsequent infection. The action of *vaccines* is to stimulate the formation of antibodies.

anticoagulant Substance that prevents or slows the clotting of blood. Some anticoagulants, such as coumarin, heparin and warfarin, are used as drugs to treat circulatory disorders associated with *arteriosclerosis* or to prevent or break up blood clots in *thrombosis* and *embolism*.

anticonvulsant Drug that acts on the brain to prevent or reduce convulsions in disorders such as *epilepsy*. Dosage has to be carefully monitored to prevent undesirable side-effects.

antidepressant Drug used to treat *depression*. There are several different types, including tricyclic antidepressants, which reduce several symptoms of depression with comparatively minor side-effects such as a dry mouth, difficulty in urination, and constipation, but which may cause troublesome sedation. A newer group of antidepressants called serotonin-specific reuptake inhibitors (SSRIs) act on specific brain chemicals involved in depression and are less sedative. Older drugs include *monoamine oxidase (MAO) inhibitors*, which are now rarely prescribed as they may have serious side-effects including potentially dangerous interactions with certain foods or other medicines.

antidiuretic hormone (ADH) Also called vasopressin, a hormone produced by the *pituitary gland* that controls the reabsorption of water by the kidneys (and so helps to maintain the correct water balance in the body). It is also used to treat *diabetes* insipidus.

antidote Drug used to counteract the effects of a *poison* or of another drug.

antiemetic Drug used to treat disorders that cause nausea and vomiting, such as *morning sickness*, *motion sickness* and *vertigo*.

antifungal drug Drug used to treat fungal infections (see *fungus*).

antigen Any substance (usually a protein) regarded by the body as foreign and stimulating the production of *antibodies*. Antigens include bacteria, viruses (or their products), fungal spores and *allergens*.

antihistamine Drug used to counteract the effects of *histamine* (a chemical found in many body tissues that has several functions and is released during allergic reactions) in the body. It acts by blocking histamine receptors (points on cells at which histamine acts), of which there are two types: H_1 receptors, which are involved in allergic reactions, and H_2 receptors, found in the stomach. Antihistamines that block H_1 receptors are used mainly to treat *allergies*, but also have strong *antiemetic* properties (stopping nausea and vomiting), so may also be given to prevent *motion sickness*. They tend to cause drowsiness, so are sometimes also used as a *hypnotic drug* to aid sleep. Drugs that block H_2 receptors reduce stomach acid secretion so are used to treat *peptic ulcer* and related conditions.

anti-inflammatory Drug used to reduce *inflammation*, generally by suppressing one or more of the body chemicals involved. Many anti-inflammatory drugs also act as analgesics (pain-killers), including *aspirin* and non-steroidal anti-inflammatory drugs (NSAIDs), often used to treat joint pains. *Corticosteroid* drugs are also anti-inflammatory, as are *antihistamines*.

antilymphatic serum (ALS; or ALG, antilymphatic-globulin) Preparation containing *antibodies* that reduce the action of the scavenging white blood cells called *leukocytes*. Such cells form part of the bodyís *immune system*, and their action has to be suppressed to prevent rejection following transplant surgery. ALS is therefore a type of *immunosuppressive drug*.

antinauseant Another name for an *antiemetic*.

antineoplastic Drug that suppresses the formation of cancer cells, an anti-cancer or *cytotoxic drug*.

antipruritic Drug used to treat itching (*pruritis*).

antipyretic Drug that lowers body temperature, used to treat *fever*. Antipyretic properties are shared by some analgesics, such as *aspirin* and *paracetamol*.

antirheumatic Drug used to treat *rheumatism* and other rheumatic disorders.

antisepsis Elimination of disease-causing organisms (pathogens) using chemicals. Modern antiseptics are powerful enough to kill such organisms without damaging the tissues to which they are applied, unlike carbolic acid (phenol), the first antiseptic introduced by

Joseph *Lister*. They are used to clean wounds or flush out body cavities (such as the bladder and intestines) to combat infection.

antiseptic See *antisepsis*.

antiserum Preparation, usually obtained from the blood of animals, that contains *antibodies* against a specific disease or toxin (such as tetanus or botulism). It may be used to treat various diseases or to give temporary protection by passive immunity (meaning that the individual is protected by the antibodies in the antiserum, rather than by stimulating the body to manufacture its own, as with a vaccine). Antisera are also used in some blood tests for infections (see *agglutination*).

antispasmodic Drug used to treat muscular *spasms*.

antitoxin Antibody produced in the body to counteract the effect of poisonous *toxins*, most often those released by infective micro-organisms, usually bacteria. Antitoxins produced in the blood of animals may be used as *antiserum*.

antitussive Drug that acts on the coughing centre in the brain to suppress a *cough*. Antitussive properties are shared by some analgesics, such as codeine.

antivenin Type of *antiserum* containing *antibodies* that neutralize the *venom* of animals such as arachnids (including scorpions and spiders) and poisonous snakes.

antrum Cavity, particularly in bone (as in the *mastoid* bone or a *sinus*), or part of the stomach near the *pylorus*. An operation to remove part of either type is an antrectomy.

anuria Serious disorder in which the kidneys fail to produce urine, usually caused by conditions that result in very low blood pressure. It is different from retention, in which the flow of urine from the bladder is obstructed (usually by an enlarged prostate gland). In anuria, toxins build up in the blood and the patient rapidly becomes very ill. Urgent treatment by *dialysis* (to filter out harmful waste products from the blood) is often necessary.

anus Opening of the bowel, at the lower end of the *rectum*. It has two circular sphincter muscles, which control bowel movements. It can be affected by such disorders as *fissure* and *haemorrhoids* (piles).

anxiety Feeling of fear for no apparent reason or as an over-reaction to a situation most people could cope with. Deep, lasting anxiety is a form of *neurosis*. Anxiety that interferes with a personís lifestyle can be treated with *tranquillizers* or *psychotherapy*.

aorta Major artery that carries oxygenated blood from the left ventricle of the heart and, through its branches, to all parts of the body.

aortic regurgitation Also called aortic incompetence, a backflow of blood from the *aorta* into the left ventricle of the heart, usually because of scarring of the aortic valve caused by *rheumatic fever*. There may be no symptoms, or breathlessness, *angina pectoris* and a heart *murmur*. Severe cases may be corrected by surgically replacing the disordered valve with a synthetic one.

aortic stenosis Narrowing of the aortic valve (thus obstructing the flow of oxygenated blood from the left ventricle of the heart), caused by scarring of the valve (often following *rheumatic fever*). Symptoms and treatment are similar to those of *aortic incompetence*.

apathy General lack of interest in oneself or oneís surroundings, normal in all people occasionally but in an extreme form a possible symptom of *depression*.

aperient Another name for a mild *laxative*.

Apgar score Assessment of the general health of a newborn baby, based on assigning a score of 0, 1 or a maximum of 2 points for the quality of heart beat, breathing, muscle tone, skin colour and responses to stimuli. Thus a "perfect" Apgar score is 10; babies with low scores need immediate attention.

aphasia Also called dysphasia, an inability to speak, and commonly to read or write, caused in a right-handed person by damage to the left side of the brain (often resulting from a *stroke*). Treatment is by *speech therapy*. See also *aphonia*; *dyslexia*.

aphonia Inability to speak caused by a disorder of the *larynx* (such as laryngitis) or possibly as a symptom of *hysteria*. Speechlessness caused by brain damage is *aphasia*.

aphrodisiacs Foods, drinks or drugs that are supposed to increase sexual desire. Some substances placed in this category are irritants, such as cantharidin (Spanish fly), which is poisonous and can cause fatal kidney damage; alcohol initially releases inhibitions, but soon acts as a depressant; and others, such as caviar and oysters, are harmless.

aphtha A harmless form of *ulcer*, also called an aphthous ulcer, in the mucous membrane of the mouth. Causes are unknown but most resolve spontaneously in a short time. Soothing lozenges may relieve discomfort in the meantime.

aplastic anaemia Severe type of *anaemia* in which insufficient red blood cells (erythrocytes) are produced because of damage to the bone marrow. Symptoms include bleeding from the nose and mouth, dark spots on the skin and lack of resistance to infection. Bone-marrow damage may be caused by poisonous chemicals or as an over-reaction to certain drugs, overexposure to *radiation*, or bone *cancer*. Immediate treatment is with blood transfusion, followed by the identification and elimination of the cause.

apnoea Temporary cessation of breathing, for any reason. Attacks are common in newborn babies, and usually harmless, but should nevertheless be medically investigated. In adults, especially men who snore heavily, breathing may stop for short periods while the person is asleep (sleep apnoea); this may be linked with an increased risk of heart disease.

apocrine gland Type of *sweat gland* that occurs in parts of the skin with copious hair, such as the armpits.

apoplexy Another name for a *stroke* caused by a *cerebral haemorrhage*.

appendectomy American name for an *appendicectomy*.

appendicectomy Surgical operation to remove an inflamed appendix (see *appendicitis*).

appendicitis Inflammation of the vermiform *appendix*, a blind-ended sac leading off the *caecum*. The main symptom is pain in the abdomen, first near the centre and then in the lower right side, often accompanied by diarrhoea and vomiting, and fever in a child. It may result from blockage of the appendix by compacted faeces or a swollen lymph node. The preferred treatment is surgical removal of the appendix (*appendicectomy*), although if surgery cannot be performed for any reason antibiotics may be prescribed. Without treatment, there is a danger that the appendix will burst and cause *peritonitis*.

appendix Full name vermiform appendix, an apparently functionless blind-ended tube, about 7–12 cm (3–5 inches) long, that branches off the lower part of the ascending colon (*caecum*) of the large intestine. Inflammation of the appendix is *appendicitis*.

apperception In psychology, the way somebody perceives the qualities of something by comparison with existing knowledge.

approved name Preferred medical name of a drug, also called its *generic name*, as opposed to a proprietary name chosen (and usually trade-marked) by a manufacturer.

aqueous humour Watery fluid that fills the front part of the *eye* between the lens and the cornea.

arachnoid mater The central of the three membranes (*meninges*) that cover the brain and spinal cord.

areola Pigmented skin that surrounds a nipple, or part of the iris of the eye bordering the pupil.

arm Upper limb, articulated at the shoulder, consisting of three bones – the *humerus* (upper arm bone) jointed at the *elbow* with the *ulna* and *radius* (in the lower arm) – and their associated muscles, tendons and ligaments. At the lower end, the *wrist* provides a joint with the hand.

armpit Medical name axilla, the hollow where the upper arm joins the side of the chest. In adults it is plentifully supplied with *apocrine glands* and hair follicles. Lymph nodes in the area may swell as a symptom of various disorders.

arrhythmia Irregular heartbeat, caused by malfunctioning of the heartís natural pacemaker (*sinoatrial node*). The usual symptoms are chest pain, breathlessness and palpitations, accompanying heart conditions such as *fibrillation, heart block* or *tachycardia* and in severe cases leading to *cardiac arrest* or *Stokes-Adams syndrome*. Drugs may be used in treatment. A harmless condition called sinus arrhythmia sometimes occurs in healthy young people (in which the heart beats faster when breathing in than when breathing out).

arteriogram X-ray photograph of an artery taken after a *radio-opaque* dye has been injected into it.

arteriole Small *artery*.

arteriosclerosis Commonly called hardening of the arteries, a condition in which the walls of arteries become narrowed or less elastic, impairing blood flow to the areas they supply. The most common form occurs when fatty deposits accumulate, damage the arterial wall and seriously impede blood flow (atherosclerosis). A major component of the fatty deposits is *cholesterol*, found in animal fats and dairy products. People with a high risk of atherosclerosis include those with high cholesterol levels or who are obese, smokers, those who take little exercise and those with a family history of the disorder. Arteriosclerosis may also occur due to minerals such as calcium being deposited in the arterial walls over time, or to general thickening and loss of elasticity in the small arteries with age or as a reaction to high blood pressure. There are no symptoms from arteriosclerosis itself, but if the coronary arteries supplying part of the heart muscle are affected, it can lead to *angina* due to poor circulation at times of increased demand, or may cut off blood flow altogether and cause a *myocardial infarction* or *heart attack*. A similar situation affecting the arteries supplying blood to the brain may lead to a *stroke*. Arteriosclerosis in an artery supplying blood to the legs may cause pain on walking and even gangrene due to impaired blood supply. A healthy diet, containing low levels of animal fats and sugar but plenty of fruit and vegetables, combined with avoiding smoking and taking regular exercise, can help prevent the disorder or avert complications. Drug treatment to lower high cholesterol levels may be recommended. Once symptoms have developed, drug treatment or surgery may be needed to attempt to restore blood flow.

artery Blood vessel that transports blood from the heart. All arteries except one carry blood that has been oxygenated in the lungs. The exception is the pulmonary artery, which takes deoxygenated blood from the left side of the heart to the lungs. Walls of arteries are elastic and consist of three layers; they are thicker and stronger than those of *veins* to withstand higher blood pressures. Disorders that affect arteries include *aneurysm*, *arteriosclerosis* and *atheroma*.

arthritis Inflammation of a joint, which causes pain, swelling, and warmth and restricted movement in the joint. It is a feature of many diseases, some of which also affect other body tissues. Causes include wear and tear, an inherited tendency and sometimes infections. The most common form is *osteoarthritis*, also called osteoarthrosis, in which joint linings degenerate either spontaneously or following trauma or overuse. The cartilage lining the joint is first eroded, typically in the hip, knee or thumb, followed by damage to the bone. It gives a characteristic appearance on X-ray pictures. The next most common form is *rheumatoid arthritis*, an autoimmune disorder (where the body attacks its own tissues) occurring more often in women than in men. This typically first affects the ankles, feet, fingers, and wrists, then later the hips, knees and shoulders. It is diagnosed with a blood test, and damage to the bone in the joint may show up on X-rays. Usually rheumatoid arthritis has periods of remission and relapse during which progressive joint damage accumulates. Sometimes it resolves spontaneously but may leave deformity. A similar joint disease accompanied by fever and other symptoms in children is known as Stillís disease. Arthritis may also occur as a complication of *gout*, *psoriasis* and some forms of *tuberculosis*. The pain of most forms of arthritis may be eased with pain-killers (*analgesics*) and anti-inflammatory drugs. In osteoarthritis, weight loss often helps by reducing the load on joints, and surgery is sometimes carried out, including the use of artificial replacement joints, particularly for the hips and knees. Rheumatoid arthritis may be treated by drugs, injections or surgery.

arthrodesis Surgical technique to fuse the bones at a joint, making it rigid, usually to treat instability or deformity.

arthroplasty Surgical treatment to remodel the bones of a disordered joint.

articulation Normal movement between the bones of a *joint*.

artificial heart A pump implanted into the body to maintain the heartís pumping action when the natural version fails through heart disease. They are usually made of titanium and nowadays can be small enough to be implanted into the heart cavity itself. However, the artificial heart must still be powered by batteries, connected through wires leading to the outside, which must be strapped to the patientís chest.

artificial insemination (AI) Introduction of semen into a womanís reproductive tract to allow conception without sexual intercourse. The semen may come from the womanís partner, if there are difficulties with natural conception (caused, for example, by *impotence*), or from a donor (artificial insemination by donor, or AID) if the partnerís sperm is deficient or defective, or if a woman wishes to have a child without a partner.

artificial kidney Also called a kidney machine, a machine that fulfils the function of the kidneys in a patient with *kidney failure* using a technique known as renal *dialysis* or haemodialysis. Blood taken from an artery in a patientís arm or leg is pumped through a dialyser, in which a semi-permeable membrane separates the blood from a dialysing fluid (which contains salts and other *electrolytes* similar to those in blood). Waste products in the blood pass through minute holes in the membrane, which are too small to allow the passage of blood cells. The filtered (and purified) blood is pumped back into the patientís circulation through a vein. Portable kidney machines have been developed, which allow the patient complete freedom of movement, but even so a machine is usually only a temporary expedient until a donor kidney suitable for a *transplant* operation becomes available.

artificial limb Type of *prosthesis*.

artificial pneumothorax Injection of air into the pleural cavity (space between the *pleura*) to collapse a lung, once used as a treatment for pulmonary tuberculosis.

artificial respiration Any method of forcing air in and out of the lungs of somebody who has stopped breathing. The simplest emergency technique is mouth-to-mouth resuscitation (the kiss of life) in which, after making sure that the victimís air passages are unobstructed, the rescuer blows regularly into the victimís mouth (or nose and mouth of a young child). See also *respirator*.

asbestosis Form of *pneumoconiosis* caused by long-term inhalation of asbestos fibres. It causes a predisposition to *lung cancer*, especially in smokers.

ascariasis Disorder caused by infestation with parasitic roundworms, which occurs mainly in regions with poor sanitation. Larval worms may lodge in the lungs, causing *pneumonia*. Adult worms live in the intestines, causing symptoms of pain in the abdomen, vomiting and diarrhoea or constipation. Possible complications include *appendicitis* and *peritonitis*. Treatment is with anthelmintic drugs.

ascites A type of *oedema* caused by the accumulation of fluid in the abdominal cavity, associated with a serious disorder such as *cirrhosis* of the liver, *heart failure*, *kidney failure*, *tuberculosis* or abdominal *cancer* (of the liver or ovary).

ascorbic acid Chemical name of *vitamin C*.

asepsis Total absence of micro-organisms that can cause disease (pathogens). For example, *sterilization* techniques are used to ensure aseptic conditions in an operating theatre.

aspergillosis Disorder in which a *fungus* (Aspergillus) multiplies in the lungs, and may attack mucous membranes elsewhere in the body.

asphyxia Suffocation, caused by choking, drowning or inhaling poisonous gases. It causes death if respiration cannot be restored within a very few minutes (using *artificial respiration* or a *respirator*).

aspiration Suction, used to withdraw fluids from the body (such as from a cyst, the lungs or the mouth during dentistry), or the contents of the womb in an *abortion*.

aspirator Device used for *aspiration*.

aspirin Chemical name acetylsalicylic acid, analgesic (painkilling) drug that blocks production of *prostaglandins* (chemicals produced in the body especially during inflammation), and also acts to reduce fever (antipyretic) and inflammation (*anti-inflammatory*). It is useful for treating minor aches and pains, particularly those of arthritis, and for lowering temperature in minor infections. It is also used in regular low doses to protect against heart attacks and strokes in people at risk, and may offer protection from other diseases including colon *cancer*. Side-effects include bleeding from the lining of the stomach and an asthma-like reaction. Aspirin has been linked with the development of a serious condition, *Reye's syndrome*, in children, so should not be given to anyone under twelve years old; *paracetamol* or ibuprofen (a non-steroidal *anti-inflammatory* drug) are recommended instead.

assay Analytical test.

asthma Disorder of the bronchial tubes that carry air to the lungs, which go into spasm and cause difficulty in breathing, coughing or wheezing. It usually begins in childhood and is often part of a hereditary tendency (atopy) to allergic reactions including asthma, eczema and hay fever. Asthma may be provoked by foods, drugs, pollen, dust, animal dander, infections, exercise or emotional stress. Whatever the cause, *histamine* is released into the suffererís bloodstream, causing swelling of the mucous membranes that line the airways. This in turn causes tightness of the chest, with wheezing and coughing. Immediate treatment is usually with drugs that expand the air passages, sometimes including corticosteroids, inhaled through an inhaler or nebulizer. In severe cases *corticosteroid* drugs may be given by mouth and attacks may require hospital treatment. Avoiding known allergens (triggers) may help to prevent attacks.

astigmatism Disorder of the *eye* which results in distorted vision because not all light rays are brought to the same focus on the retina (usually caused by imperfect curvature of the lens or cornea). It is easily corrected with *glasses* or some types of *contact lenses*.

astringent Preparation that causes cells to shrink, and thus used as a *styptic* (to stop bleeding) and in lotions to harden the skin.

asylum Old name for a mental hospital.

ataxia Lack of control of limb movements, leading to shaking arms and unsteady gait, caused by a disorder of the brain or nervous system. Speech may also be affected. It may be hereditary (Friedreichís ataxia) or a symptom of advanced *syphilis* (tabes dorsalis or *locomotor ataxia*).

atelectasis Condition (usually in newborn babies) in which the lungs fail to expand properly, either because of immaturity or the absence of a surfactant (wetting agent) on the inside surface of the lungs. In an adult, atelectasis may accompany *pneumothorax*.

atheroma Thickening and degeneration of the inner wall of an *artery* caused by the build-up of scar tissue and fatty deposits. The roughened wall interferes with blood flow and may provide a site for *thrombosis*. Cigarette smoking, being overweight (obesity) and eating a diet rich in animal fats (which contain *cholesterol*) are all contributing factors. The symptoms and treatment are as for *arteriosclerosis*.

atherosclerosis Circulatory disorder caused by the accumulation of fatty deposits on the inner wall of an artery (atheroma). See *arteriosclerosis.*

athlete's foot Medical name tinea pedis, highly contagious type of *ringworm* (fungal infection) that affects the skin between the toes, which blisters, splits and scales. Treatment is with antifungal drugs in the form of powders or creams, together with scrupulous drying between the toes after bathing.

atlas Uppermost bone of the spine (the first cervical vertebra), which supports the skull and pivots on the *axis* (the second cervical vertebra).

atopy Inherited tendency to develop allergic reactions in the form of *eczema, asthma* and *hay fever.* Which of these conditions develops, and how severe it is, varies between affected individuals, and the pattern may change over the course of someoneís life. Symptoms often first develop in childhood with atopic eczema, a weeping skin rash that can be intensely itchy and unsightly and is difficult to treat. Asthma may develop alone or following eczema earlier in childhood, featuring attacks of wheezing with difficulty breathing; in children, persistent coughing may be the first sign. Attacks may be provoked by foods, drugs, pollen, dust, animal dander, infections, exercise or emotional stress; severe attacks may require hospital treatment. Atopic individuals often have attacks of hay fever, with a streaming nose, sneezing and watering eyes due to an allergic response to pollen, grass or other plant material, most often in the spring and early summer.

ATP Abbreviation of *adenosine triphosphate.*

atrial fibrillation Erratic muscular contractions of one or both atria (upper chambers) of the heart. See *fibrillation.*

atrial flutter Less severe form of *atrial fibrillation.*

atrium Also called auricle, one of the two upper chambers of the *heart.* The right atrium receives deoxygenated blood from the bodyís main vein (vena cava) and the left atrium receives oxygenated blood from the lungs and passes it into the left *ventricle.*

atrophy Wasting away of a tissue or organ through disorder or disuse, such as the atrophy of leg muscles in *poliomyelitis.*

atropine *Alkaloid* drug obtained from deadly nightshade (belladonna) that is used as a muscle relaxant (for example to treat colic or dilate the pupil of the eye) or as *premedication* (to dry up bodily secretions). Its side-effects therefore include blurred vision and a dry mouth.

attention deficit disorder A recently recognized condition, often abbreviated to ADD, that may include a range of symptoms such as poor concentration, impaired learning ability and behavioural problems, usually in children. It is often accompanied by extreme overactivity and an inability to sit still (*hyperactivity*), so the two together are sometimes called attention deficit hyperactivity disorder (ADHD). Such children need little sleep and are prone to continual fidgeting, impulsiveness and poor appreciation of risk. They are hard to parent and difficult to teach, and may themselves become frustrated and sometimes aggressive. In some cases, affected children have impaired intelligence or mild brain damage but usually the label is applied to disruptive children with learning problems. Diagnosis should be made by an expert. Behaviour or family therapy can help in many cases. Increasingly, stimulant drugs such as methylphenidate (Ritalin) are given, which, paradoxically, calm the childís behaviour. Affected families sometimes report dramatic improvements by eliminating food additives from the childís diet, although few doctors suggest this approach.

auditory nerve Nerve that carries impulses concerned with hearing from the inner *ear* to their respective centres in the brain.

aura Warning sensation felt by somebody before an attack of *epilepsy* or *migraine*.

auricle Another name for an *atrium*.

auscultation Diagnostic technique that involves listening, usually with a *stethoscope*, in order to interpret the sounds produced. It is most often used by doctors to listen to heart sounds, movements of air in the lungs during respiration, or gas in the bowels. Medical staff also listen to the sounds produced in arm arteries when a cuff is inflated to measure blood pressure (see *sphygmomanometer*).

autism Severe mental disorder that usually begins in early childhood in which the patient has difficulty communicating, appears unable to understand other peopleís feelings, and cannot form normal relationships. Language development is usually delayed. Affected children develop stereotyped behaviour patterns, with repetitive movements and fierce resistance to any change of surroundings. They often seem to live in a world of their own, may develop behavioural problems and become extremely isolated, having little normal contact with others. Some affected children have learning disabilities, but others are of standard intelligence or even gifted in a specific area. Treatment may involve special educational measures, and intensive family support is usually required. Behaviour therapy may modify particular behavioural problems, and drugs may be given to help symptoms such as anxiety.

autoantibody *Antibody* formed against tissues of oneís own body, an aspect of *autoimmune disease*.

autoclave Equipment for sterilizing medical equipment that works like a pressure cooker using high-temperature steam.

autograft Tissue *graft* (usually of skin) taken from the patientís own body, and therefore not subject to the problems of *rejection*.

autoimmune disease Disorder probably caused by *antibodies* (called autoantibodies) that act against the bodyís own tissues. The many examples include haemolytic and *pernicious anaemia*, rheumatoid *arthritis*, and some kidney and thyroid disorders. Such disorders are said to confer autoimmunity.

autolysis Cell destruction caused by the bodyís own *enzymes*.

automatism Usually repetitive movements that are a symptom of a type of *epilepsy*.

autonomic nervous system Part of the *nervous system* that controls "automatic" (unconscious) body functions such as breathing, heartbeat, glandular secretions and the movement of food through the digestive tract. It consists of the *sympathetic nervous system*, which prepares the body to meet an emergency ("fight or flight"), and the *parasympathetic nervous system*, which relaxes it after the emergency is over.

autopsy Another name for a *post mortem.*

autosuggestion Psychotherapeutic technique involving repetitive self-*suggestion* in order to change attitudes or habits.

axilla Medical name for the *armpit.*

axis Bone in the upper neck (the second cervical vertebra) that pivots with the *atlas* (first cervical vertebra) and allows rotation of the head.

axon Nerve fibre, a strand that extends from a *neurone* (nerve cell) and carries nerve impulses. It may have an insulating sheath of *myelin,* containing gaps (nodes of Ranvier) at axon branches.

B

Babinski reflex *Reflex* in children up to the age of 2 years, in which the big toe bends up when the outer side of the foot is stroked. In older children the *plantar reflex* occurs, bending the foot down.

bacillus Rod-shaped type of *bacterium*, of which most are harmless to humans. However, bacilli are responsible for some serious diseases, including *tuberculosis*, *diphtheria*, *tetanus* and typhoid fever.

bacillus Calmette-Guérin (BCG) Artificially prepared type of tuberculosis-inducing *bacillus* that no longer has the potency to cause the disease but retains enough to evoke the formation of antibodies in the bloodstream. It is thus used as a *vaccine* against tuberculosis. Its name derives from its French creators, Léon Calmette and Camille Guérin, who first used it in 1906.

backache Common condition with a multitude of possible causes. Most backache results from strain, either of the ligaments or the muscles, or related to some derangement of an *intervertebral disc* (the discs between the vertebrae of the spine). Occasionally, a nerve is pinched and may cause fibrositis or more severe symptoms. *Arthritis* may occur. Persistent or sharp pain should be referred to a doctor for diagnosis. Often rest, or adjustment of posture, may relieve mild pain. Pain-killers, massage or gentle exercises can also help with short-term strains. Some forms of *complementary medicine* (such as *chiropractic* or *osteopathy*) are especially competent at treating long-term backache. In severe cases of slipped disc, surgery may be offered if other methods do not control the pain.

backbone Informal name for the *spine*.

bacteraemia Presence of bacteria in the blood, a form of *blood poisoning*.

bacteria A group of tiny micro-organisms whose cells are less complex than those of either animals or plants. They are widely distributed in nature, being found in human beings, animals, plants, soil, water and air; only a few types cause human disease and most of the bacteria encountered by the human body are harmless *commensals*, meaning that they live on or in the body without doing any damage – indeed some, such as many gut bacteria, are helpful, aiding in the breakdown of foods for digestion or protecting the body against colonization by more dangerous organisms. Most bacteria are unicellular (have only one cell), and are broadly classified according to the shape and form of the cell: the most common are spherical *cocci*; rod-shaped *bacilli*; comma-shaped vibrio and corkscrew-shaped *spirochaetes*; the spirochaetes are able to use their shape to move around, whereas most other forms have no independent motion. All of these forms themselves appear in variations of size or of combination. A few types of bacteria cause human disease, either by their presence in vast numbers (overwhelming the bodyís defence mechanism, the *immune system*) or through the *toxins* (poisons) or *enzymes* (chemicals that affect the bodyís metabolic reactions) they produce in the body. Bacterial infections are treated with *antibiotics*, some of which have broad activity against many types of bacteria, while others attack certain forms preferentially. Some bacteria are able to develop resistance to certain antibiotics, so that the drugs are no longer effective – such bacterial resistance has increased considerably over the past few decades. Treatment of some infections therefore requires laboratory identification of the type of bacteria, often depending on the affinity of certain forms for specific dyes (staining), and on determining the sensitivity (susceptibility) to specific antibiotics.

bacterial endocarditis Most common form of the potentially dangerous disorder *endocarditis*.

bacteriology Study of bacteria and their effects on and in the human body. Considerable research is presently being carried out by bacteriologists on discovering new techniques and uses for *genetic engineering*.

bacteriophage Type of *virus* that attacks and destroys a specific type of *bacterium* by attaching to it and injecting its own genetic material (*deoxyribonucleic acid*). It then grows and replicates inside the bacterial cell. The term is frequently shortened to "phage".

bacterium The singular form of *bacteria*.

bad breath Informal name for *halitosis*.

balance Vital sense provided by a combination of organs in the *inner ear* (or labyrinth). They are the *utricle* and *saccule*, and the *semicircular canals*. The utricle and saccule are small chambers both filled with fluid; when the head moves, the fluid swirls across a sensitive spot from which hair cells send sensory information to the brain about the changed position of the head. The three semicircular canals are aligned in three different planes; hair cells within them also detect the movement of fluid corresponding to directional and attitudinal positions of the body. Infection of the inner ear (*otitis* interna) generally affects the senses of balance and of *hearing*.

baldness Partial or total loss of hair from an area where it is normally found, usually the top of the head. The most common form is male-pattern baldness, which is hereditary; other causes include aging (in men and women), hormonal factors (in women), certain infections of the scalp, and autoimmune disease (where the immune system attacks the bodyís own tissues). Hair loss also sometimes occurs in response to certain types of head injury, serious illness, pregnancy and drug treatment, especially chemotherapy (anticancer drugs). Wigs, hairpieces and various minor operations to transfer hair follicles from elsewhere have been used in attempts to conceal baldness; the drug minoxidil when rubbed into the scalp promotes hair regrowth and prevents further loss, but is not a complete cure.

bandage Strip of soft material used to bind a *dressing* onto a wound, to form a protective casing around a sensitive limb or area, or to support a damaged limb by holding it in a fixed position. Many forms of bandage are produced, some in sizes or shapes that correspond to specific types of wound (those on the head, for example), some in elasticated material, and some in material that encourages the flow of air through them. Plaster *casts* represent a form of bandage that is impregnated with plaster of Paris and wetted for application over a fractured limb.

Banting, Frederick G. (1891–1941) Canadian scientist who with Charles Best researched into the secretions of the pancreas and in 1921 derived *insulin*. The discovery meant prolonged life for many sufferers of *diabetes* mellitus. Banting, and the head of his university department, John Macleod, received the Nobel Prize in 1923.

barbiturate Any of a group of *hypnotic* (sleep-inducing) *drugs* derived from barbituric acid.

All barbiturates are potentially addictive and have potentially serious side-effects, hence their use as tranquillizers or sedatives has been largely discontinued. Certain types are still used in anaesthesia and in the treatment of *epilepsy* (convulsions).

barefoot doctor Popular term for a minimally equipped, usually indigenous rural medical worker in a developing country. Such medical workers are trained mostly to give first aid and assist in the basic medical education of the local community.

barium Metallic element, one salt of which (barium sulphate) is used as the *radio-opaque* medium in X-rays of certain parts of the stomach and intestines.

barium enema Introduction of *radio-opaque* barium sulphate through the anus into the colon, in order to take an X-ray of the colon.

barium meal Oral administration of *radio-opaque* barium sulphate (a thickish, white, virtually tasteless gruel) and water, in order that X-rays may be taken during its progress through the alimentary canal. The substance is impervious to digestive processes.

Barnard, Christiaan N. (1922–) South African surgeon who at the end of 1967 surprised the world by performing the first heart transplant at Groote Schuur hospital near Cape Town, at which he was professor of surgery.

baroreceptor Small aggregation of nerve endings that monitor the local pressure of the blood in the bloodstream, and constantly relay information to the brainstem. Major baroreceptors (or baroceptors) are located near the heart and in the neck. Internal adjustment of the blood pressure can to some extent be made by the *autonomic nervous system*.

barotrauma Injury caused by a rapid change in environmental atmospheric pressure, as in flying or diving. It mainly affects the *Eustachian tube* and the *middle ear*, although in severe cases the *eardrum* may burst, the *sinuses* around the nose may be damaged, and the tissues of the lungs may be stretched.

basal ganglia Areas of *grey matter* buried within the *white matter* that forms the inner core of each *cerebral hemisphere*. Forming a connection between the grey matter of the *cerebral cortex* and the *thalamus*, the basal ganglia are responsible for the unconscious aspects of voluntary movements.

basal metabolic rate (BMR) Measure of the amount of energy used by the body to maintain vital functions such as breathing, digestion and blood circulation, expressed as a minimum (corresponding to a body at rest). As a statistic it can be represented in Calories (or kilojoules) per hour or per day, or as a percentage of what might be expected in relation to body height and weight. BMR is influenced by factors such as age, sex, body temperature and level of thyroid activity. For research purposes it is determined by placing the subject in a special chamber that measures the amount of heat given off; medical assessment is usually indirect, through measuring the ratio of oxygen taken up and carbon dioxide excreted by the lungs.

base In chemistry, either a compound that reacts with an acid to form a salt, or a molecule or ion that can take on a proton or has an available pair of electrons. In genetics the term is used in the latter sense specifically of adenine, thymine, guanine and cytosine which are linked in pairs by hydrogen bonds to form the helical strands of the *deoxyribonucleic acid* (DNA) molecule.

basement membrane Thin layer of membrane that underlies the surfaces of *epithelium* (chiefly of the skin, but also those surfaces lining many of the hollow organs) in the body.

basophil One of the three types of *granulocyte*; the others are neutrophils and eosinophils. Like the other granulocytes, basophils ingest foreign particles as part of the *immune system*; uniquely, however, they contain *histamine* and *heparin*.

battered baby syndrome Old term for *non-accidental injury*.

battle fatigue Set of symptoms amounting to an anxiety *neurosis* experienced by armed servicemen and policemen who have faced constant danger of violent death. There may be tremor, sensitivity to sudden light or noise, selective loss of memory, and other minor manifestations of *hysteria*. During World War I such symptoms were ascribed to "shell shock"; during World War II they were accurately ascribed to battle fatigue.

BCG vaccine *Vaccine* made from *bacillus Calmette-Guérin*.

Beaumont, William (1785–1853) American physiologist who, as an army doctor, had the opportunity to study the workings of the stomach through a permanent fissure that developed in the side of a wounded patient. Later, to much acclaim, he published a classic description of the gastric processes.

bedbug Small, ovoid, dun-coloured wingless insect that sucks the blood of humans as they sleep at night. Bedbugs may infest beds, but just as commonly live in corners and crevices of walls and nearby furniture. Bites are painful and may itch. Treatment is with antiseptics, and disinfestation of the room.

bedpan Container for faeces and urine used by a bedridden patient.

bedsore Painful ulceration of the skin and damage to the underlying tissues caused by constant pressure, as occurs in bedridden patients so ill or old that they cannot move independently in bed, or among unconscious patients. The blood supply to the area may be seriously reduced, and the nerves affected, so that the patient may not even be aware of the condition – which can in severe cases lead to *gangrene*. The condition is known technically as a decubitus ulcer or a pressure sore. Treatment is primarily by prevention: patients should be turned regularly and be well cushioned. If a sore develops, dressings and good nursing care are vital.

bed-wetting Involuntary passage of urine at night (the technical term is enuresis). This is abnormal only after a child has definitely learned bladder control: on average this occurs around the age of four, but there are wide variations and many children are not dry at night until the age of seven or later. Persistent bed-wetting often runs in families. Occasionally there is an underlying urinary tract problem, such as infection; more often the problem is behavioural. It usually settles with age. Treatment is with parental patience and avoidance of criticism. Practical aids include a mattress cover and avoiding fluid intake before bedtime, with encouragement to pass urine just before sleeping. Behaviour techniques such as rewarding dry nights, or alarm systems (a bell and pad), which wake the child just as urination starts, can be very successful. Occasionally drug treatment is offered for persistent enuresis.

behaviourism School of psychology that suggests that the events of the mind correspond only to organic functions of glands and nerves, and thus that the study of behaviour should be restricted specifically to what can be physically observed or measured. This approach tends towards relating behaviour to *conditioned reflexes*, and away from accepting any unconscious elements.

behaviour therapy Forms of *psychotherapy* based on the premise that *neurosis* (and other minor forms of mental disorder) is a matter of learning, and can be unlearned by a patient. Treatment is directed personally towards each patientís specific problem, generally to confront and change behaviour in the presence of the disordering stimulus. Elements of behaviour therapy include *aversion therapy*, *desensitization* and *conditioning*.

Békésy, Georg von (1899–1972) American otologist who discovered that vibrations of sound are registered according to their pitch at different points along the basilar membrane that runs the length of the spiral *cochlea* in the *inner ear*.

Bell, Charles (1774–1842) Scottish surgeon who claimed to have been the first to distinguish between motor and sensory functions of the nerves. He certainly made that distinction in his classic work on the brain (published in 1811) – but the claim was forcefully disputed by the French dietician Francois *Magendie*.

Bell's palsy Temporary paralysis of the facial nerve, causing a characteristic drooping of the features on one side of the face; the eyelid on the affected side may fail to blink. The nerve affected is a motor nerve only: there is no loss of sensory function, so the patient is usually quite unaware of any difference from normal. The cause is generally unknown – although the condition can follow infection of the inner ear (*otitis* interna), *shingles*, or the experience of an extremely cold environment. It was first described by Charles *Bell* (1774–1842). Recovery usually occurs without treatment, but can take many months.

bends Common name for *decompression sickness*.

benign In medicine, describing a growth (*tumour*) that is not destroying the tissue on which it is based, and not spreading through the body. In these respects it is the opposite of *malignant*. But because of their eventual size, benign tumours may occasionally require surgical removal. In more general terms, the word may describe any disorder that is temporary and harmless.

benzodiazepines Group of drugs used as *hypnotic* (sleep-inducing) *drugs* and tranquillizers as replacements for *barbiturates*. Some benzodiazepines are also used as *muscle relaxants*, *anticonvulsants* (to treat *epilepsy*) or premedication agents before surgery. In high dosages they tend to have a depressant effect on breathing and with prolonged use may become addictive.

beriberi Deficiency disorder caused by lack of *thiamine* (vitamin B_1). It occurs most commonly in areas where the diet consists mainly of polished rice; in the Western world it is prevalent among alcoholics. Symptoms are those of muscle disorders, especially of the heart muscle, accompanied by the degeneration of nerves (peripheral neuritis), causing numbness and weakness. This condition by itself is dry beriberi; wet beriberi involves the additional accumulation of fluid in the tissues, causing swelling (*oedema*). Treatment is to make up the deficiency.

Bernard, Claude (1813–1878) French physiologist who investigated and explained many of the functions of the body's metabolic processes. He discovered the roles of the liver and the pancreas; of the red blood cells in transporting oxygen (and the effect of carbon monoxide on that process); of the nerves in contracting or dilating the blood vessels; and of the glands and kidneys in the secretions they produce. Of at least equal significance was his concept of the "milieu intérieur" - of an unchanging internal equilibrium in contrast to the ever-changing external world.

Bert, Paul (1833–1886) French physiologist who pioneered methods for surviving in environments of different atmospheric pressure. It was due to his study of the causes of *decompression sickness* that deep-sea diving (and, incidentally, space travel) became possible for human beings.

Best, Charles (1899–1978) Canadian physiologist and partner of Frederick Banting in the initial isolating of *insulin* from the pancreas. But it was the head of the university department, John Macleod, who was awarded a Nobel Prize with Banting in 1923, although Banting insisted on sharing the financial proceeds of his Prize with Best.

bestiality Sexual activity with an animal.

beta-blocker Drug that slows the heartbeat by acting upon the *sympathetic nervous system* to block stimuli that might otherwise cause a rise in heart rate and pressure. Beta-blockers are thus used to treat *hypertension* (high blood pressure) and *angina pectoris*. High dosage may have a depressant effect upon breathing.

bezoar Accumulated mass of discrete, indigestible items in the stomach, usually due to swallowing non-food material. This may occur in children, particularly hair-chewers, or among people with mental illness. The resulting ball of foreign material may cause abdominal pain or obstruction of the gut, and often requires surgery to remove it.

bicarbonate of soda (sodium bicarbonate) Salt used as an *antacid* to combat indigestion and other stomach disorders because of its alkaline properties. Administered orally or by injection, it may also be used to make up a sodium deficiency. High dosages may themselves cause stomach upset or *alkalosis*.

biceps Name of two large muscles, both with two "heads" or attachments (via tendons). The biceps of the arm is doubly attached to the shoulder blade (scapula) and singly to the radius bone of the forearm; it bends both shoulder and elbow, and rotates the forearm. The biceps of the thigh is one of the *hamstrings*; based on the fibula (of the lower leg), its two "heads" are attached to the pelvis and the back of the thigh bone (femur).

Bichat, Marie François Xavier (1771–1802) French anatomist and research scientist in Paris at the time of the French Revolution. A competent surgeon and lecturer, Bichat put most of his energies into a masterly reference work on anatomy that reflected his own pioneering study of the various types of tissue within the human body; he thus founded the science of *histology*.

bifocals Pair of *glasses* with special *lenses*; each lens has an upper area which is suitable for focusing objects at a distance, and a lower area for focusing objects that are closer.

bile Viscous yellow-brown or green alkaline fluid secreted by the *liver* and stored in the *gall bladder* (where it becomes slightly more concentrated). The presence of fats as they enter the *duodenum* from the stomach causes a contraction in the gall bladder that forces bile down the common *bile duct* into the duodenum. There, bile emulsifies the fats – so enabling the fat-soluble *vitamins* to be absorbed through the intestinal wall – and activates other digestive *enzymes*. The waste products of these reactions, and those of the liver carried by the bile (such as the bile pigment *bilirubin* and excess *cholesterol*), are excreted down the intestine and eventually form a constituent of the *faeces*.

bile duct Any of a number of ducts that convey *bile*. Ducts that collect bile from the *liver* join as one large duct underneath – the hepatic duct. From this, the cystic duct leads to the *gall bladder* where bile may be stored until required. When it is required, bile returns down the cystic duct to the junction with the hepatic duct, and is there conveyed down a third major duct – the common bile duct – to the *duodenum*.

bilharziasis See *schistosomiasis*.

biliary colic Form of *colic* caused by an obstruction in the common *bile duct* or the *gall bladder*, especially by a *calculus* (gallstone). Severe waves of pain are felt in the centre of the upper abdomen (or perhaps just to its right), commonly after meals, and may last for several hours; there may also be vomiting. Treatment may be with antispasmodic drugs until the gallstone passes into the duodenum of its own accord, or with lithotripsy (use of a special machine that sends out shock waves to shatter the stones); sometimes surgery may be necessary.

bilirubin One of two major *pigments* in *bile*, representing breakdown of the blood pigment *haemoglobin* (the other is biliverdin). Bilirubin is orange-yellow, as is evident when it becomes visible within the blood through the skin in a patient with *jaundice*.

Billroth, Theodor (1829–1894) Austrian professor of surgery who standardized practical and antiseptic surgical methods in many fields of surgery – but notably of the stomach – that are now considered classic.

bioassay Test of the effect of a drug or therapy by reference to its effect on living organisms as compared with the effect of a known, measured rival. Such estimation is particularly used of *hormones* when chemical or physical experimentation is not practicable.

biochemistry Study of chemistry and chemical factors in relation to living organisms. In recent decades, one major topic of study has been *enzymes*.

bioengineering Use of engineering expertise to create and apply devices and machines towards medical assistance for or within the human body. It includes, for example, the design and manufacture of *prostheses*.

biofeedback Experimental process of showing information concerning somebodyís metabolic functions from monitoring machines and devices immediately to the person, so that he or she may attempt to influence those internal activities that are not usually subject to voluntary control. It is possible, for example, through concentration and practice to slow the heartbeat at will – which can be very useful for a person with a particularly rapid heartbeat.

biomechanics Study of the structure and operation of the moving parts of living organisms.

biomedical engineering See *bioengineering*.

bionic limb Mechanically – and even electronically – operated *prosthesis* that looks and moves like a real part of the body.

biopsy Collection of a small number of cells, or a small amount of tissue, taken from a part of the body for laboratory examination. For example, a biopsy is taken of the tissue from a tumour in order to discover whether the growth is *benign* or *malignant*. Biopsies of tissue from internal cavities are made using a long hollow needle or an *endoscope*.

biotin Vitamin of the B complex important in the metabolism of fats, and in the secretion of certain hormones. Biotin is present in most foods, and produced by bacteria that normally reside in the intestines; deficiency is therefore virtually unknown.

birth See *childbirth*.

birth canal Passage through which a baby travels from the uterus to emerge into the world, consisting of the expanded *cervix* and the *vagina*.

birth control Any method of *contraception* or *sterilization*.

birth rate One of the measures of a populationís growth per year, expressed usually as the number of live births per thousand inhabitants, or per thousand women of child-bearing age.

birthmark Congenital skin blemish. There are two main types. The major form (also called a naevus) represents a network of tiny blood vessels under the skin, and is unusual but harmless, and sometimes only temporary. Categorized by location and prominence of appearance, naevi include the strawberry mark (which is reddish, slightly raised, and generally temporary) and the portwine stain (which is purplish, flat, spread over an area, and generally permanent). Treatment is inadvisable for these: cosmetic surgery may in fact make things worse. The second type of birthmark is the *mole*, treatment for which is sometimes possible – and necessary if it changes colour or spreads.

bisexuality Practice or desire for sexual activity with members of either sex.

bite Bites from animals, including domestic pets, may carry disease and should, as a matter of prudence, be referred for medical diagnosis and possible precautionary measures (such as an antitetanus vaccination). In northern latitudes, bites from insects are usually harmless (if temporarily painful), although in tropical climates they may carry the risk of disease. In dentistry, the bite is a less formal term for dental *occlusion* (the closing together of the teeth of both jaws).

Black Death Old name for bubonic *plague*, especially the epidemic of 1346–1349.

black eye Severe bruising around the eye, caused by a hard blow in the area or at the top of the nose. There may be considerable swelling caused by the escape of blood into the tissues, which may weigh down the eyelid and make opening it impossible. Rarely, these symptoms mask a fractured skull. Treatment is with ice-packs, applied with pressure.

blackhead Medical name comedo, a fatty plug (comprising *sebum* and *keratin*) in the short duct that connects a *sebaceous gland* with the skin surface, commonly associated with *acne*. The top turns black as the keratin oxidises.

blackout Sudden, temporary loss of consciousness for whatever reason. Causes include *fainting*, head injury, blood loss, disease and intoxication. The term is also used to describe loss of vision without loss of consciousness among military pilots subject to extreme acceleration forces.

blackwater fever Rare complication of the *tertian fever* form of *malaria*. The major symptom is the presence of the red blood pigment *haemoglobin* in the urine (turning it blackish) caused by destruction in the body of many red blood cells; other symptoms are very high temperature, enlargement of the spleen, vomiting and jaundice; kidney obstruction may occur (requiring emergency treatment). Treatment is rest, copious drinks of alkaline liquids, and infusions of plasma and glucose.

bladder Term for any of several reservoirs for fluids in the body. Most commonly refers to the urinary bladder, a flexible, muscular, bag-like reservoir in the lower abdomen that collects *urine*, the waste product from the *kidneys*, received through the *ureters* and passed out through the *urethra*. The urge to urinate arises when nerve endings sense the bladderís muscular walls to be stretching. By training from early in life, the reflex to empty the bladder can be suppressed for a time until socially more convenient. The average volume of a full bladder is about 500 ml (just over a pint). Inflammation of the bladder is called *cystitis*; other bladder disorders include the presence of *calculi* (stones) or *polyps*, other forms of obstruction, and *cancer*. Other bladders in the body include the *gall bladder*.

bland diet Dietary regimen in which, for reasons of health, somebody eats only food that is easily digestible, and that is likely to cause no acidity or rise in blood pressure. Both texture and flavour are also considered, and must be soothing. This need not necessarily mean, however, that the diet is truly and tediously bland.

blastocyst Hollow ball of cells that represents the initial stage of an *embryo* and the *amnion*. It is in this form – developed first from a *zygote* (the fertilized combination of sperm and ovum), then from a *morula* (a solid ball of dividing cells) – that *implantation* occurs in the lining of the *uterus* (womb). Where it implants, the *placenta* is created. Within the hollow ball of cells there is already a thickening on one wall that represents what is to become the actual embryo.

blastomycosis Fungal infection that occurs mainly in the Americas. Internally, the fungi affect mainly the lungs, causing a disorder resembling *pneumonia*, but may attack other organs. Externally, the fungi can cause serious skin warts and growths. Treatment for both types is with antifungal drugs.

bleeding Common term for *haemorrhage*.

blepharitis Inflammation of one or both eyelids. The cause is mostly unknown, although the condition can stem from the presence of dust, fumes or dandruff, or result from an allergic reaction. Symptoms are redness, pain and watering of the eye; a *stye* may form, or the edges of the eyelid may ulcerate (matting the eyelashes). Treatment involves cleaning the eyelids; an antibiotic ointment may be prescribed for a short time.

blindness Partial or complete inability to see through one or both eyes. The most common causes globally are trachoma (a tropical eye infection), onchocerciasis (an infestation with tiny worms, common in tropical countries) and severe vitamin A deficiency; in the West common causes are *glaucoma*, *cataract* or degeneration of the retina or cornea, and retinal damage due to *diabetes*. Other causes include congenital disorders (resulting from hereditary factors, perhaps, or infection of the mother during pregnancy). The underlying cause of some forms of blindness may be treatable. Temporary blindness may be caused by high or low blood pressure (*hypertension* or *hypotension*), *migraine*, *fainting*, or more serious conditions of blood insufficiency. Most blind people become extremely competent in leading a relatively independent life; the extra acuteness of their other senses is legendary. Many aids are available. Other forms of blindness are *colour blindness* and *night blindness*.

blind spot Small area on the *retina* of the eye at which the nerve fibres from the *rods* and *cones* leave it to form the *optic nerve*. At this point there are no rods or cones – and so no vision is registered from it.

blister Small fluid-filled swelling on the surface of the skin, caused most commonly by friction or heat. The fluid inside is generally watery *serum* – occasionally there may also be blood. Treatment is with antiseptics; if a blister is lanced to release the fluid, it should be done with a sterilized point. Other forms of blistering, such as *urticaria*, may be an allergic reaction.

blood Vital fluid pumped by the *heart* in the *circulation* all round the body to convey oxygen and other nutrients to the tissues and to remove waste products (such as carbon dioxide). It is in blood that the products of digestion are conveyed to the liver and the kidneys for extraction and disposal, and it is factors in the blood that begin the process of healing a wound. In composition, blood is made of straw-coloured *plasma* (which itself comprises *serum* and the blood *clotting* factors) in which many different types of cells are suspended. Principal among the cells are *erythrocytes* (red blood cells), which contain the pigment *haemoglobin* responsible for oxygen transport, and *leukocytes* (white blood cells), which are major components of the bodyís defence mechanism, the *immune system*. In an average adult there is about 4.8 litres (10 pints) of blood, 90% of which passes through the heart every minute when the body is at rest. Disorders of the blood correspond to infections, disruption of the blood-forming organs and tissues, abnormalities in the clotting mechanism, abnormalities of the blood cells, and the results of incorrect matching of the *blood group* during blood *transfusion*.

blood alcohol Level of ethanol (ethyl alcohol) in the blood following its consumption. Alcohol is absorbed through the stomach wall (most other fluids have to wait until later in the alimentary canal), and so has a much quicker effect in the bloodstream. In many countries, it is illegal to drive a motor vehicle on public roads with blood alcohol greater than a specified level.

blood bank Form of *tissue bank* in which blood is stored, carefully categorized according to blood group. Blood donors are thoroughly screened and the blood itself tested to ensure it is free from contamination, particularly by *hepatitis* viruses and HIV (the virus that causes AIDS). Blood may be kept under controlled conditions for up to four weeks after it is given. Various blood products may also be stored.

blood cells Cells suspended in the *plasma* of the *blood*. There are two main types: *erythrocytes* (red blood cells) and *leukocytes* (white blood cells). Leukocytes are further subcategorized as *granulocytes*, *lymphocytes* and *monocytes*. Red blood cells by far outnumber white blood cells. Also in the blood are the partly cell-like *platelets*.

blood clot Medical name *thrombus*, a ball of congealed blood, formed by the bloodís *clotting* mechanism. Normal at sites of healing, it is abnormal and potentially dangerous if it occurs in the bloodstream.

blood count Numbers of the various cells in 1 litre of blood. The blood count calculated from a small sample of blood taken from a patient, if abnormal, may indicate the presence of a disorder.

blood donor Somebody who donates blood under medical supervision to a tissue bank for storage until needed.

blood group Any of several categories within the various classification systems of *blood*. All classification systems identify the presence or absence of specific antigens adhering to *erythocytes* (red blood cells). Blood of one group contains *antibodies* likely to react against elements in the blood of other groups. In this way, the ABO classification system categorizes blood as of groups A (with specific antigen A), B (with antigen B), AB (with both antigens), and O (with neither antigen). Conversely, therefore, blood of group A contains antibodies against antigen B; blood of group B antibodies against antigen A; blood of group AB antibodies against neither antigen; and blood of group O antibodies against both antigens. In practice this means, for example, that individuals with the most common blood group, group O, can donate blood to any other group without causing a reaction, but can themselves receive only blood of group O without experiencing a reaction. The other major blood classification system is that which depends on identification of the absence or presence of the *Rhesus factor*.

blood poisoning Presence of bacteria in the blood (bacteraemia), and the resultant damage to tissues, fragments of which are then carried as blood pollutants (septicaemia); or the presence in the blood of the toxins emitted by bacteria (toxaemia). All these disorders produce very similar severe symptoms. See *septicaemia*.

blood pressure Pressure within the arteries of the blood flowing through them. It occurs in waves corresponding to the rhythmic contraction of the heart muscle as it pumps; measurements of blood pressure thus represent a maximum (during the pumping phase of the heartbeat) and a minimum (during the resting phase). Traditionally these were measured on a scale of millimetres of mercury, as calibrated on a column of a device called a *sphygmomanometer*, on which blood pressure can be read while a cuff is inflated and deflated around the upper arm; modern devices may give a digital read-out. Normal blood pressure at rest is about 120/80. A pressure measured at considerably higher than this (at rest) is *hypertension*, at considerably lower (at rest) is *hypotension*. Exertion, emotion and certain drugs strongly affect blood pressure.

blood sugar Level of sugar (glucose) in the blood, usually measured as a concentration in millimoles per litre. High or low levels (*hyperglycaemia*, *hypoglycaemia*) are important diagnostic indicators to certain disorders, particularly *diabetes* mellitus.

blood test Any test of blood to analyse its contents. Small samples may be taken by pricking a fingertip or earlobe; more often a hypodermic syringe is used to draw a quantity from a large blood vessel in the arm. Blood tests may be used to assess quantities of normal blood constituents, such as red cells, blood chemicals or hormones; to check for the presence of drugs (including alcohol) or infectious agents; to establish the blood group; to screen for various diseases that may not as yet display symptoms; or to attempt to establish paternity.

blood transfusion See *transfusion*.

blood vessel Any of the many tubes and ducts belonging to the *cardiovascular system*.

blue baby Newborn baby with one of several *congenital heart diseases*, resulting in poor oxygenation of the blood and a consequently bluish tinge (cyanosis) to the skin. Most forms can be immediately rectified by surgery; babies with severe malformations of the heart are not likely to survive.

blushing Medically the same as flushing. See *flush*.

BMR Abbreviation of *basal metabolic rate*.

body odour Medical name bromhidrosis, an offensive smell, caused generally by a failure to wash frequently enough to remove the products of the breakdown of sweat by bacteria on the skin surface. How rapidly this situation comes about depends not just on regular bathing, however, but on a personís skin condition (including the rate at which dead cells accumulate), the level of perspiration, the constituents of the perspiration, and on his or her diet. Treatment is by washing; frequent changes of underwear may help, as may the use of a deodorant.

body temperature Generally, the *temperature* of the blood, as measured by a *thermometer* in the mouth (or in the rectum). The temperature actually varies slightly all over the body, as is evident from pictures taken by *thermography*.

boil Rounded red and painful swelling on the skin (medical name, furuncle), containing *pus*, thus representing a smaller version of an *abscess*. Boils occur when *Staphylococcus* bacteria infiltrate the hole in the skin through which a hair emerges, a sebaceous duct, or an open wound. In general, boils heal spontaneously, but they may heal more quickly if the pus is released in antiseptic conditions. Local heat may encourage them to "come to a head" and release the pus. Lancing a boil without antiseptic preparations or squeezing it tends merely to spread the infection, however.

bone Any of the 206 or so hard, densely constructed units of the skeleton. In composition it represents a form of *connective tissue*, comprising a matrix of strands of *collagen* permeated by calcium salts. The outer surface of bone is the *periosteum*. Inside it, the first layer is made up of concentric cylinders of bony tissue (Haversian systems); within this compact layer there is a central, trellised honeycomb of bone filled with *bone marrow* (the medullary cavity). Bones are categorized as long, short, flat or irregular. Growth is regulated by *growth hormone* (somatotropin) produced and secreted by the *pituitary gland*; the parathyroid glands are also significant in controlling a balance in the body of the calcium and phosphorus levels. Bone disorders may thus result from hormone deficiencies, and from infections, vitamin D (calciferol) deficiency, and tumours. Injuries (such as *fractures*) are not uncommon and bones may also be affected by degenerative disorders (such as osteoarthritis and osteoporosis).

bone graft Operation to replace part of a bone with a piece of bone either from elsewhere in the patient or from a donor. If the graft is from a donor, the tissue has to be matched as closely as possible in order to minimize tissue *rejection*. Even with bone from the patient, there may be difficulties in effecting a strong union.

bone marrow Soft tissue within the central core of the bones. In early life the tissue is mostly the blood-forming red marrow (myeloid tissue); as growth and physical development finishes, the long bones are gradually filled instead with the fatty yellow marrow. It is possible to obtain samples of bone marrow for laboratory examination, but only at the expense of minor bone damage.

booster *Vaccination* administered as the effect of the previous vaccination comes to an end, or as an extra precaution in a time or area of *epidemic*.

borborygmus Rumbling or gurgling sound emanating from the large intestine, as fluid (and flatus) is squeezed along it by *peristalsis*.

Bornholm disease An acute viral infection caused by a type of *Coxsackie virus*, sometimes called epidemic pleurodynia. Symptoms include chest pain, high temperature, headache and muscular tenderness. These recede gradually to leave lassitude and depression for some time afterwards. There is no effective treatment other than to relieve symptoms by drugs and high fluid intake. Recovery is spontaneous.

bottle-feeding Feeding of a baby with milk through a teat on a bottle. A breast-fed baby should be accustomed gradually to a bottle, so that on weaning the bottle is not an unwelcome surprise. Many types (formulas) of milk are available. How much milk is fed to the baby depends on the babyís weight: a general rule is about 75 ml (2 fluid oz) of milk for every 450 gm (1 lb) weight – the milk should be warmed to blood temperature. Feeding should take place in a chair in which the mother is comfortable and relaxed, the baby held at about 45°, the bottle held from underneath and removed from the babyís mouth from time to time in order to allow air in. Afterwards, the bottle should be sterilized, not just washed. See also *breast-feeding*.

botulism Serious form of *food poisoning* caused by swallowing a bacterial *toxin* found especially – but not solely – in tinned raw meats. (The toxin is neutralized by cooking.) The result is damage to parts of the central nervous system. Initial symptoms include visual disturbances, weakness and abdominal pain; there may also be nausea and diarrhoea. Finally there may be heart and lung failure, causing death. Medical treatment early enough is effective, although intensive care may be required.

bougie Cylindrical instrument inserted into body passages – such as the urethra or rectum – usually in order to dilate some form of constriction.

bovine spongiform encephalopathy (BSE) A rapidly fatal neurological disease of cattle apparently linked with the appearance of a new form of *Creutzfeldt-Jakob Disease* (CJD), a fatal human brain disease. BSE was first recognized in 1986 and is believed to have been introduced by the use in the early 1980s of cattle feeds containing infected animal tissues. Animal ingredients in cattle feeds have now been banned, and controls introduced to stop highly infectious tissue such as brain, spinal cord, glands and intestines entering the human food supply. The use of cattle material in drugs, vaccines or other medical products has also been stopped. Cases of BSE in cattle have been reduced. However, because symptoms of CJD take many years to show, it remains uncertain how many people who ate potentially contaminated beef products in the 1980s, or were perhaps infected by other routes, could be liable to develop CJD. There is no treatment for BSE. Infected cattle are destroyed.

bowel Another term for the (large or small) *intestine*.

bow legs Curvature of the legs such that when the feet are together the knees are apart (the medical name is genu varum). Normal in young children, in others the condition may result from bone disease or deformity. Treatment depends on the cause; surgical correction is sometimes possible.

Bowman, William (1816–1892) English eye surgeon and physiologist who made his reputation mostly by describing the function of the kidney.

Bowman's capsule Cup-like end of a single *nephron*, the unit of filtration in the *kidney*. Each capsule surrounds a *glomerulus*, a network of tiny blood vessels that is one element within the larger blood system that brings blood to and takes blood away from the kidney. From the glomerulus, the capsule drains the impure fluids of the blood; these products are then conveyed down the length of the nephron, through the *loop of Henle*, to the *renal tubule*.

brace Metal binding to hold a part of the body rigidly in place. Braces are used particularly in *orthopaedics* and *orthodontics*, in order that growth should be normalized. Less often, they are used for support.

brachial plexus Network of nerves, stemming from the spine, that together supply the whole of a shoulder and an upper arm. From it branch the nerves that supply the forearm and the hand. The plexus may be subject to damage during birth, or as a result of pressure from a prolapsed *intervertebral disc*.

bradycardia Slow heartbeat. It is a feature of certain infections (such as influenza), but occurs more seriously with *hypothyroidism*, *hypothermia* and *heart block*. Treatment depends on the cause.

Braille Tactile alphabet used for reading by the blind. The alphabet – in which there are not only letters but phonemes and whole words – corresponds to a code formed of raised dots within a fixed matrix of two vertically parallel lines of three dots. (The letter A is represented as a single dot at top left; the word "for" is all six dots.) The system is named after its inventor, the French scholar Louis Braille (1809–1852), who was himself blind from the age of 3.

brain Large soft mass of nerve tissues that comprises one of the two elements of the *central nervous system* (the other is the *spinal cord*). There are very few aspects of the functions of the human body for which the brain is not responsible or does not control. Enclosed within the three *meninges* membranes, and surrounded by and containing weight- and shock-reducing *cerebrospinal fluid*, the brain is made up of many relatively independent elements. The forebrain comprises the vast dome of the *cerebral hemispheres*, together with the *thalamus* and *hypothalamus*. The midbrain represents the connection between the forebrain and the hindbrain. And the hindbrain consists of the *cerebellum*, *medulla oblongata* and the *pons*. Disorders of the brain may have physical or psychological symptoms, or both. Many such disorders represent a form of congenital abnormality. Despite the protection of the skull, the brain is susceptible to injury – it is also susceptible to infections. Cardiovascular disorders may affect the brain and cause a stroke. With regard to psychological disturbances, however, a proper understanding of many forms of mental illness has yet to be achieved.

brain death Cessation of all brain activity, specifically in those areas in the brain that normally control vital functions, as determined by medical tests by at least two independent practitioners. Once brain death has been declared, the person is legally dead and organs may be removed for transplantation. Brain death leads automatically to cessation of heartbeat and respiration over the ensuing days; in some circumstances, however, a patient may be declared brain dead while heart and lung function are being sustained artificially on a ventilator: this may allow organs to be removed in a healthier condition. In some countries or states organs may only be removed for transplant with the prior permission of the deceased or of relatives; in others "opt out" legislation has been introduced in which doctors may remove organs unless there is evidence that the person expressed a prior objection.

brainstem Part of the *brain* that is the final element of the *spinal cord*. It comprises the *medulla oblongata*, *pons* (or pons Varolii) – together known collectively as the bulbar area – and the *midbrain*.

brainwaves Waves representing patterns of electrical energy in the brain, traceable as specific rhythms on an *electroencephalograph*. Interpretation of these rhythms is controversial. However, an alpha rhythm represents a patientís electrical activity measured when awake but with the eyes closed; a beta rhythm represents the activity when the patient is awake with eyes open; a delta wave occurs in deep sleep.

bran Fibrous food made from the husks of cereals, often recommended as part of the diet of people with various intestinal disorders. See *fibre in the diet.*

breast Front part of the chest. The paired breasts of a woman contain the mammary glands and consist of fatty tissue surrounding milk ducts leading to the nipple. They develop as *secondary sexual characteristics* in a girl at puberty, under the influence of *sex hormones* produced by the ovaries. After childbirth, a hormone (prolactin) secreted by the *pituitary gland* stimulates the production of milk, triggered by the baby suckling on the nipple. The breasts should be supported by a well-fitting brassiere; large breasts can be remodelled by *cosmetic surgery*. Disorders of the breast include inflammation of the breast (mastitis) or nipple, abscesses, cysts and tumours (*breast cancer*). Any lump in the breast, detected by self-*palpation*, should be reported to a doctor. The enlargement of the breasts in a pubescent boy or in a man is called *gynaecomastia.*

breastbone Common name for the *sternum.*

breast cancer Malignant tumour in the breast. The most common form of *cancer* in women, its cause is unknown, although some cases are hereditary. The usual symptom is a lump in the breast, or, rarely, bleeding or discharge from the nipple. Undetected it may spread to adjacent *lymph nodes*, causing a lump in the armpit. The earlier treatment is given, the better the chances are of a complete recovery. For this reason, women are encouraged to feel their breasts regularly (*palpation*) for lumps between menstrual periods and to consult a doctor immediately if any are found. The usual treatment is surgery to remove the tumour (lumpectomy) or the whole breast (*mastectomy*), sometimes also with *radiotherapy* and *cytotoxic* (cancer-killing) drugs. A woman who has had a mastectomy may be fitted with an artificial breast (*prosthesis*) or have reconstructive surgery to construct a new breast mound.

breast lump The texture of a womanís breasts often changes slightly during the menstrual cycle. But any persistent lump (felt by self-*palpation* carried out routinely after each menstrual period) should be reported to a doctor, who may recommend tests in case there is a tumour. Most lumps, however, are not cancerous.

breast-feeding Lactation, the production of milk by a womanís breasts following childbirth, is stimulated by secretion of a hormone (prolactin) by the *pituitary gland*, itself triggered by the suckling of the baby. For the first two or three days after the birth, the breasts produce a watery fluid (*colostrum*), which is rich in proteins and contains *antibodies* that give the baby temporary immunity to various infections. Then the true milk comes in (see *milk*). Motherís milk has exactly the correct formulation and is available at the right temperature and in convenient containers. Also the act of breast-feeding helps to establish a bond between the mother and the baby. Nevertheless, if a woman cannot or prefers not to breast-feed, modern milk substitutes (formulas) provide all the nourishment the baby needs.

breathing See *respiration.*

breathlessness Medical name dyspnoea, breathlessness or laboured breathing (except normal lack of breath following physical exertion or a severe fright) is usually a symptom of a disorder. It may be caused by a lung disorder (such as *emphysema*, *lung cancer*, *pleurisy*, *pneumoconiosis*, *pneumonia* or *tuberculosis*), a disorder affecting the airways (such as *asthma* or *bronchitis*), a blood disorder (*anaemia*) or *heart disease*. Anybody who experiences shortness of breath for no obvious reason should consult a doctor.

breech birth Birth of a baby buttocks-first. See *presentation*.

Bright, Richard (1789–1858) English physician best-known for describing the group of kidney diseases characterized by protein in the urine (albuminuria), usually forms of *nephritis* (Brightís disease).

Broca, Paul (1824–1880) French surgeon who gave his name to several disorders, including Brocaís aphasia (inability to speak) and various body structures (such as Brocaís area, the speech centre of the brain).

bromhidrosis Medical term for *body odour*.

bronchiectasis Widening of the airways to the lungs (bronchi), usually caused by an infection, obstruction or pressure from a growth (tumour). An infection (usually associated with *bronchitis*) may lead to an accumulation of pus, which is coughed up in the sputum. Treatment is with antibiotics and physiotherapy; severe cases may need surgery to remove part of the lung.

bronchiole One of the many branches of the airways to the lungs (bronchi), which do not contain mucus glands.

bronchitis Inflammation of the bronchi (the main airways that lead to the lungs), often also affecting the bronchioles (smaller airways) as well as the throat and larynx. The acute form of the disorder is caused by infection by bacteria or viruses, and results in a fever with narrowing of the airways and coughing up of pus-containing sputum. Chronic bronchitis, associated with a disorder of the upper respiratory tract, heavy cigarette smoking or breathing of polluted air, also causes a persistent cough and possibly breathlessness. Bacterial infection may be treated with antibiotics, and an *expectorant* (cough medicine) may be prescribed to loosen the mucus; steam inhalations may also help.

bronchodilator Drug that relaxes the bronchial muscles and so dilates the airways, used to treat disorders such as *asthma* and *bronchitis*. It is often dispensed in the form of an *aerosol* inhalant.

bronchopneumonia Form of *pneumonia* that affects the terminal airways (bronchioles) and surrounding tissue of the lungs.

bronchoscopy Technique for examining inside the windpipe (trachea) and airways to the lungs (bronchi). It uses a bronchoscope, which may be a rigid tube or a flexible fibre-optic instrument fitted with a light and lenses. The bronchoscope may also be used to extract a small sample of tissue for analysis (*biopsy*).

bronchospasm Difficulty in breathing due to narrowing of the respiratory passages in conditions such as *bronchitis* or *asthma*. Wheezing may be heard as the patient breathes out. Some forms such as asthma are reversible, and the narrowing can be relieved with drugs that dilate the air passages (bronchodilators); in other cases these drugs have no effect and the condition may be irreversible, as in chronic *bronchitis*.

bronchus Any of the airways to the lungs that branch off the lower end of the windpipe (trachea) and themselves branch into narrower *bronchioles*. The bronchi are strengthened by circular rings of cartilage, have glands that secrete *mucus* and are lined with hair-like *cilia* (which move in waves to transport mucus and any entrapped foreign particles). Disorders that can affect the bronchi include inflammation (*bronchitis*) and muscular spasm (as in *asthma*).

brucellosis Also called undulant fever, a bacterial disease of cattle that can be passed to human beings by contact or by drinking unpasteurized milk. Human symptoms include fatigue, weakness and headache leading to alternating fever and chills with enlargement of the spleen and lymph nodes (in the neck and armpits). Treatment is with prolonged courses of antibiotics; untreated, the disorder may persist for years.

bruise Medical name contusion, discoloration of the skin and swelling caused by a blow or pressure. The colour, caused by leakage of blood from damaged blood vessels, is pink at first, turning blue then yellowish. A minor bruise can be relieved with cold compresses and will resolve spontaneously. Severe bruising should be examined by a doctor in case there is internal injury (such as a bone fracture) that may need treatment.

BSE See *bovine spongiform encephalopathy*.

bubo Swollen lymph node, especially in the armpit or groin, caused by inflammation resulting from a disease such as bubonic *plague*, *kala-azar* (leishmaniasis) or various *venereal diseases*.

bubonic plague Type of *plague*, so called because one of its symptoms is the formation of *buboes*.

bug Insect that feeds by sucking juices from a plant or animal. Some bugs carry diseases that can be passed to humans in their bites (for example, in some countries mosquitoes transmit *malaria*).

bulimia Compulsive overeating, caused by damage to the *hypothalamus* (the appetite control centre) of the brain, or as a factor in *anorexia nervosa* (in which the patient may eat excessively and then deliberately induce vomiting). If the condition is due to brain damage, specialized neurological assessment and treatment is needed. Treatment of bulimia associated with anorexia is with psychotherapy.

bulla Medical name for a large *blister*; a fluid-filled swelling on the skin. The term is also used to mean one of the thin-walled, air-filled spaces that may develop within the lung in the disease pulmonary *emphysema*.

bunion Painful swelling of the joint between the big toe and the foot, often displacing it sideways towards the other toes. A *bursa* and bony growth may form, adding to the deformity. Almost always caused by badly fitting shoes, severe bunions can be treated by orthopaedic surgery.

burn Damage or destruction of tissue caused by extreme heat, caustic chemicals, radiation or high-voltage electricity. Similar damage caused by hot liquids or steam is called a scald. Burns are classified as first, second or third degree. A first-degree burn damages only the outer layer of skin (the epidermis), causing reddening but no blisters; a second-degree burn is accompanied by blistering and may damage the second layer of skin (the dermis); and a third-degree burn penetrates deeper and destroys all the skin and possibly the tissues below – although, because nerve endings are also destroyed, it may be less painful than the other types. The seriousness of a burn, however, depends more on the extent of the area affected than the depth of the burn. Any burn that involves more than a tenth of the bodyís surface needs emergency treatment for *shock* (preferably in a specialist hospital burns unit) and to reduce the risks of infection. A skin *graft* may also be required. Minor burns are best treated by being placed under cold running water (to remove heat) for at least ten minutes and being covered by a dry antiseptic dressing; creams or ointments should not be used.

bursa Small liquid-filled pouch, occurring at parts of the body subject to friction, such as the knees or elbows. Abnormal bursae may also form on body surfaces subjected to pressure or rubbing.

bursitis Inflammation of a *bursa* (a fluid-filled sac located in areas subject to friction, such as joints), caused by infection, pressure or injury. Prepatellar bursitis (housemaidís knee), for example, affects the bursa of the knee. The bursa becomes swollen, causing pain and tenderness, and restricting movement of the joint. Prepatellar bursitis is prevented by avoiding kneeling for long periods, particularly on hard surfaces. Once symptoms arise the patient should avoid kneeling at all. In any sort of bursitis, resting the affected joint, and taking painkilling drugs, may help. In severe cases, a doctor may drain off the excess fluid or inject *corticosteroid* drugs. Bursitis due to infection may be treated with antibiotics.

by-pass Tube (or shunt) introduced to divert the flow of a fluid round an infected or obstructed part. See *cardiopulmonary by-pass*.

C

cachexia Effect of long-term illness involving weight loss and deterioration in muscle and skin tone. There may also be increasing lethargy.

cadaver Corpse, a dead body that may or may not be used for medical purposes before disposal.

caduceus Rod or wand carried by the god Mercury (Hermes), which has two snakes entwined around it and two wings behind it. It is often used as a symbol of professional medical care.

caecum Rounded pouch or pocket that forms the junction of the small intestine (*ileum*) and the large intestine (*colon*). At the opening from the coils of the ileum there is a strong dual-membraned valve (the ileocaecal valve); the colon leads directly off it upwards. From the underside of the caecum hangs the *appendix*.

Caesarean section Surgical delivery of a baby through the abdominal wall. It was originally performed only when there was some reason why *childbirth* through the vagina was judged hazardous or difficult, such as the position of the baby or the *placenta*, or ill-health in the mother. However, increased use of foetal monitoring has led to more Caesareans being undertaken when there are signs of apparent foetal distress; the use of epidural *anaesthesia* may also have contributed to the increase. Rates of Caesarean section vary widely between hospitals and between types of patient (particularly paying versus non-paying patients), and many commentators have criticized unnecessary use of the operation. It is generally now carried out with an epidural anaesthetic, so that the mother remains fully conscious throughout (although she may not observe the surgical procedure) but feels no pain; she may also see the baby immediately after birth. Recovery time is prolonged compared with a normal birth and the complications of any major abdominal surgery may ensue.

caesium Metallic element, an artificial radio-isotope of which (caesium-137) is used in *radiotherapy*.

caffeine Mildly stimulant alkaloid drug that occurs in coffee and tea, and which also has minor diuretic and analgesic effects. It is combined with aspirin or paracetamol in various proprietary pain-killers. Taken late at night it may prevent or disturb sleep.

caisson disease Another name for *decompression sickness*.

calamine Liquid suspension of zinc oxide or zinc carbonate and ferric oxide used, in the form of lotion or cream, to soothe itching (especially in infections that cause a rash) or sunburn, or as a mild astringent.

calcaneus Thick, strong heel bone, on which the entire weight of the body rests when walking. It articulates with the talus bone of the ankle and the cuboid bone of the foot.

calciferol Vitamin D, a fat-soluble *vitamin* important for the uptake of calcium and phosphorus in the diet – deficiency leads to bone weakness or deformity. Food sources include eggs, fish oil, liver and dairy products, but a major proportion is synthesized in the body by the action of sunlight on the skin. Deficiency of vitamin D causes *rickets* in children and *osteomalacia* in adults. A higher intake is necessary during the years of growth or during pregnancy and lactation; excess, however, may cause damage to the kidneys.

calcification Depositing of calcium salts on or in body tissues. This occurs normally as part of the formation of bones and teeth. As a disorder, however, it may occur following excess intake or synthesis of vitamin D (*calciferol*) or following a bone fracture. There is sometimes a build-up of calcium on a torn ligament which may further damage the ligament.

calcitonin *Thyroid hormone* that decreases the amount of calcium and phosphates in the blood, and thus works in opposition to *parathormone* in order to maintain a balance between these substances.

calcium Metallic element vital to the body for normal development (specifically of the bones and teeth) and everyday functioning (specifically of muscle contraction, nerve action and blood conditioning). It is found in the body mostly in the form of calcium phosphate; its level in the blood is regulated by the combined actions of *calcitonin* and *parathormone*. Principal food sources are dairy products, especially milk, from which its absorption in the body is facilitated by *calciferol* (vitamin D). Deficiency of calcium in the body leads to bone weakness or deformity, and the muscle disorder *tetany*. Excess in the body may lead to the formation of *calculi* (stones) and areas of abnormal *calcification*.

calculus "Stone" formed by gradual accretion of normally soluble calcium salts and other substances within a body vessel or duct. Calculi are not uncommon anywhere in the urinary tract (*kidneys, ureters, bladder* or *urethra*), and may also be found in the *gall bladder* and *bile ducts*. If they become large enough to hinder the passage of fluid or obstruct it altogether, there is pain in waves (colic) and other symptoms depending on the location. Treatment may be by *litholapaxy* or lithotripsy. The term is used also for a calcium accretion on the teeth or in a *salivary gland*.

calliper Either a metal brace that supports the leg, taking the weight of the body and keeping the leg rigid; or a measuring device like a large pair of geometrical dividers, used mostly in obstetric measurement of the pelvis.

callisthenics Exercises carried out to improve strength and smoothness of movement, without the use of any apparatus. Most forms concentrate on developing specific groups of muscles.

callus Also known as a callosity, an area of thickened, hardened skin, generally the result of constant friction and pressure. A common site for a callus is on the soles of feet unused to shoes. A callus is also the formation of blood and special tissues that develops on the "ends" of bones that are fractured, as part of the healing process.

calorie Unit of heat, equivalent to the energy required to raise the temperature of 1 gram of water 1°C. The dietary calorie, more accurately called a kilocalorie (or Calorie), is used as a measure of the energy content of foods. It is defined as the amount of heat required to raise the temperature of one kilogram of water through 1°C, and is equal to 4,185.5 joules.

cancer Presence of a *malignant tumour* formed by the abnormal and uncontrolled replication of cells; the cells then attach to other tissues, and may destroy them in the process. A cancer can form in any organ of the body, particularly in *connective tissue*, including bone and cartilage (sarcoma), or in the *epithelium* (membrane) that lines many internal organs and is present in quantity in the skin (carcinoma). Another form of cancer is *leukaemia*, which affects the blood-producing bone marrow, and leads to the formation of cancerous white blood cells. Genetic (hereditary) factors increase the risk of many cancers, and influences such as smoking, radiation and some viral infections are linked with the development of certain tumours. Such cancer-promoting factors are called carcinogens. Part of the condition of malignancy is that cancers may spread around the body (by *metastasis*), conveyed by the blood or lymphatic system. Initial symptoms of cancer depend on the body site, but may include skin ulceration, unexpected haemorrhage (bleeding) or discharge, a palpable lump under the skin, unusual difficulty in swallowing or defecating, an increase in the size of a skin marking (such as a mole), or blood in the sputum. Treatment depends on the body site, but often includes surgery, *radiotherapy* and *chemotherapy* (cancer-killing drugs). In general, the earlier the treatment, the more likely it is to be successful. Prevention of some forms of cancer is to some extent possible by avoidance of substances (and associated activities) known to be potential *carcinogens* (substances that promote cancer formation).

candidiasis Also called moniliasis or thrush, an infection by a yeast-like fungus, some species of which live normally (and harmlessly) on the body. It occurs in moist, enclosed areas (such as the mouth, bronchial passages and vagina, and in folds of skin) and appears as white blotches on red, inflamed tissue, and may itch. The fungus causes infection mainly when there is some change or abnormality in the external or internal environment, for example, fluctuating hormonal levels, a course of antibiotics or an impaired immune system. As an infection it can also be transmitted fairly easily to others by direct contact. Treatment is with antifungal drugs given as creams, tablets or vaginal pessaries.

canine Any of the four fang-like *teeth* at the corners of the mouth, between the *incisors* and (in adults) the *premolars*.

cannula Thin tube that can be inserted into a vessel or cavity of the body in order to draw off or infuse fluid.

cap Common abbreviation of Dutch cap, another name for the diaphragm used in *contraception*.

CAPD Abbreviation of *continuous ambulatory peritoneal dialysis*.

capillary Narrowest type of blood vessel, its walls only one cell thick (enabling the exchange of gases and liquids through it). Most tissues of the body contain large networks of capillaries, connected with the smallest arteries and veins.

capsule Membranous sheath that encloses an organ or an area of tissue, especially the *synovial* capsule that surrounds the moving parts of joints in the limbs. The term is used also for the type of pill that consists of a powdered drug enclosed in a soluble gelatine casing.

carbohydrate Organic substance rich in energy, that is one of the three major components of food (the others are *fats* and *protein*). In the body it is broken down to *glucose* in order to use its energy potential; any excess is converted to *glycogen* for storage in the liver and the muscles. Food sources include sugar (in fruit and sweets) and starch (in cereals and potatoes).

carbolic acid Common name for *phenol.*

carbon dioxide Gas that occurs as a waste product in the body, is conveyed in solution in the blood of the veins to the lungs, and is there exchanged for oxygen and exhaled. A small amount is also excreted in urine or sweat. Its concentration in the blood is monitored by the respiratory centre of the brain: a high level causes the breathing rate to increase. Carbon dioxide is also produced, as a suffocating gas, when carbon or any of its compounds burns in a plentiful supply of air.

carbon monoxide Odourless, colourless, poisonous gas that when inhaled is easily absorbed by the red pigment *haemoglobin* in the blood, preventing the haemoglobin from absorbing oxygen. Asphyxiation swiftly follows, resulting quite quickly in permanent brain damage or death. It is produced when carbon or any of its compounds burns in a restricted supply of air (and is a major component of car exhaust fumes and cigarette smoke).

carbuncle *Pus*-filled swelling on the skin surface, caused by a bacterial infection. It has multiple heads or is formed in a cluster of swellings, and effectively represents a collection of *boils* with several drainage channels. Common sites are the back of the neck, buttocks and thighs. Treatment is with antibiotics; occasionally, lancing of the swelling to release pus is necessary.

carcinogen Substance (or an activity associated with a substance) that has the potential to cause *cancer.*

carcinoma *Cancer* of epithelial tissue.

cardiac Pertaining to the *heart* or upper part of the stomach.

cardiac arrest The cessation of a personís heartbeat and therefore the heartís pumping action. The blood stops where it is, and the person immediately loses consciousness and stops breathing. It may occur abruptly or following a brief period of *ventricular fibrillation.* Without emergency treatment (*cardiopulmonary resuscitation, defibrillation, artificial respiration*), permanent brain damage or death may quickly follow. The most common of many causes is *myocardial infarction* (a heart attack).

cardiac cycle Operation of the heart from one heartbeat to the next. It thus comprises the events of one *systole* (contraction of the heart muscle in order to pump blood away from the lower chambers of the heart) followed by those of one *diastole* (relaxation of the muscle so that the upper chambers refill with blood).

cardiac massage Massage of the heart performed from outside the chest; it is an essential part of *cardiopulmonary resuscitation.*

cardiac muscle Specialized type of fibrous *muscle* of which the walls of the heart are made. Inside the heart, the muscle is lined with *endocardium*; outside the heart, it is enclosed by the dual *pericardium* membrane.

cardiac output Also called the minute volume, the volume of blood pumped through either of the ventricles (lower chambers of the heart) in one minute, equivalent to the flow of blood through the lungs.

cardiac pacemaker Natural or artificial *pacemaker* of the heart.

cardiogram Another name for an *electrocardiogram.*

cardiology Study of the operation, structure, diseases and disorders of the heart.

cardiomyopathy Any chronic disorder of the heart muscle. Causes include infection, alcoholism, hereditary factors, deficiency disorders, and unknown factors. Potential complications include *heart failure, arrhythmia* and enlargement of the heart. Treatment depends on the cause, if known.

cardiopulmonary by-pass Use of a *heart-lung machine* to take over the functions of the heart while the heart is stopped for surgery.

cardiopulmonary circulation Shorter circuit of blood pumped by the heart, taking venous blood from the heart to the lungs (via the pulmonary artery), where it is reoxygenated through the thin alveolar walls, before being returned (via the pulmonary vein) to the heart. The reoxygenated blood is then pumped through the much larger circuit of arteries and veins in the body - the systemic circulation.

cardiopulmonary resuscitation Technique for restarting the *heartbeat* and breathing of somebody who has just suffered a *cardiac arrest*. It thus combines heart massage (to restart the heart) and the kiss-of-life method of *artificial respiration* (to restart the breathing). Ideally there should be one person for each technique, although a single person can do both adequately. Heart massage is performed by using the ball of one fist gently but firmly to depress the lower half of the breastbone (sternum) by about 4 cm (1 in) in a sharp movement – but not violently enough to break ribs – at a rate of about once a second. For the kiss of life, first the patientís head must be tilted back to check that the air passages of the mouth and throat are clear, and the tongue offers no obstruction. Then, holding the patientís nostrils closed, the assistantís mouth is placed tightly against the patientís mouth, and air is gently but firmly breathed in over about two seconds. The patientís chest may rise, and should fall as the rescuer removes the mouth to take another breath. An ideal rate for this operation is one breath every 5 seconds (3 seconds in children). In combination, however, the most practical timing with two rescuers is 5 chest compressions for every 1 kiss of life; with a single rescuer, 15 chest compressions followed by 2 kisses of life. The technique should be repeated continually until resuscitation occurs (or until medical help arrives).

cardiothoracic surgery Surgery in the area of the chest cavity occupied mainly by the heart.

cardiovascular system Entire network of blood vessels (arteries, arterioles, capillaries, veins and venules) which, together with the heart, pass the blood around the body to deliver nutrients to the tissues and to carry away waste products. It thus includes both the systemic circulation and the cardiopulmonary circulation. See also *circulation.*

caries Medical term for *tooth decay*.

carminative Drug intended to remedy *flatulence*. Most work only by distracting the sufferer with spicy flavours, so fooling the stomach and intestines into the normal preparatory actions for receiving food.

carotene Pigment within many plants, one form of which (beta-carotene, an antioxidant) can be converted by the body into *vitamin* A (retinol). Food sources include carrots, egg yolk, liver (especially of fish) and milk products.

carotid artery Either of two large arteries in the neck, which branch to supply blood to the head and neck. Smaller branches penetrate the skull and supply various areas of the brain; disease or obstruction in any of these may cause a *stroke*.

carpal tunnel syndrome Set of symptoms caused by the compression of the median nerve between the carpal bones of the wrist and the band of strong fibrous tissue over them. The nerve normally serves the muscles of the ball of the thumb and transmits sensory information from all the fingers except the little finger; when it is compressed it results in tingling and numbness in all the areas served. It may occur for no apparent reason, or following trauma, overuse of the wrist, in pregnancy or hypothyroidism. It is sometimes associated with arthritis. Treatment may include rest, splinting or *hydrocortisone* injections; in persistent cases, surgery may be undertaken to loosen the fibrous band. Treatment of any underlying condition may be necessary.

carpus Eight bones of the *wrist*, over which the strong ligament that forms the carpal tunnel is located. For movement, the bones at the wrist slide over each other; they articulate with the metacarpal bones of the hand, and with the *radius* and the *ulna* bones of the forearm.

Carrel, Alexis (1873–1944) French surgeon and pioneer in some of the most difficult forms of surgical technique. He made what were probably the first attempts at organ transplants, and greatly improved methods for stitching together damaged blood vessels. He was awarded a Nobel Prize in 1912.

carrier Somebody who – without suffering from a disease to which he or she has been exposed – transmits it, either as an infection (such as *diphtheria*) or as a hereditary condition (such as *haemophilia*). In this sense, animals which transmit infections are also carriers; animals which transmit *parasites* (in any form) that then cause disorders are also known as vectors.

car sickness A kind of *motion sickness*.

cartilage Commonly called gristle, a dense form of *connective tissue* without blood vessels that occurs in three main forms. Fibrocartilage makes up much of the *tendons* and the *intervertebral discs*; elastic cartilage forms the outer ear flap (pinna); and hyaline cartilage is the rigid tissue that forms the *larynx* and the upper respiratory tract, much of the nose and the connections between the ribs and the breastbone or other ribs, and covers the ends of bones in the joints of the limbs. A large proportion of the cartilage in a babyís body turns into bone within the first ten years of life.

caruncle Small red lump as, for example, at the inner corner of the eye (a lacrimal caruncle). As a disorder, a caruncle may appear on the urethral opening or the vagina of women. Treatment, when necessary, is by minor surgery to remove it.

case In medical statistics, one specific disorder in comparison in any way with another (in prevalence, fatalities, duration of symptoms, for example), or one individual patient compared with others (in social background, method of contracting the disorder, effectiveness of treatment, for example).

cast Rigid bandage, made of gauze impregnated with plaster of Paris, used to immobilize and support a limb following a bone *fracture*.

castration Removal of a manís *testes* (with or without the surrounding scrotum). The term emasculation means much the same, except that in that operation the penis may also be removed. Performed before puberty, castration prevents the normal development of *secondary sexual characteristics*. After puberty, there may be visible effects of the lack of male *sex hormones* (no facial hair, rounding of the body frame) although the voice, once broken, stays deep. Reasons for castration include certain types of cancer or severe infection. The term is sometimes applied to the surgical removal of the ovaries from a woman, which may be required in treatment of cases of hormone-dependent cancers.

catabolism Chemical breakdown of large, complex molecules into smaller, simpler constituents, with the simultaneous release of energy. It occurs in the body both during the metabolic processing of ingested food, and in the muscles in order to contract. The reverse process is *anabolism*.

catalepsy Symptom of some forms of *catatonia* in which a patient, seemingly in a trance or under hypnosis, remains immobile – like a statue – in any position. The personís limbs can be moved by someone else without resistance, but they then remain where they are put (so-called "waxy flexibility"). The cause is some form of mental disturbance, such as *schizophrenia*, or it may result from *encephalitis* (inflammation of brain tissues). Treatment is usually with sedatives and tranquillizers, but may also include hypnotic suggestion.

cataract Formation of an opaque area within the *lens* of an *eye*, sometimes progressive, causing blurring of vision and, if left untreated, eventual near-blindness. Causes include hereditary factors, aging, injury, diabetes mellitus, and certain blood disorders. Treatment is by surgical removal (or replacement) of the lens, and the use of corrective *glasses*.

catarrh Condition of excessive mucus in the nose and throat, caused by infection (such as a common cold) or any other source of inflammation of the mucous membranes (such as smoking or irritation by nasal sprays).

catatonia Term for a condition in which the symptoms of mental disturbance are manifested as aberrations in physical movement. Such symptoms usually consist of immobility, as with *catalepsy* (maintaining abnormal postures) or *stupor* (unresponsiveness), often accompanied by *mutism* (lack of speech); in some cases there may instead be violent and uncoordinated activity. Catatonia used to be a common manifestation of *schizophrenia*, but is now rare; other causes include *conversion disorder* or *encephalitis* (inflammation of brain tissues). Treatment depends on the cause but may include sedatives and tranquillizers.

catecholamines Group of hormones and other organic secretions that are important to specific nerve functions, some simply by being *hormones* (such as *adrenaline*), others as *neurotransmitters* (such as *noradrenaline*), and yet others as intermediate stages between the two that have their own special functions (such as dopamine). They all have a similar chemical composition.

catgut Chemically toughened fibre made from the intestine of a sheep. In medicine it is used as the material for sutures (*stitches*) because it is rapidly biodegradable; having held the two edges of a wound together long enough for healing, it gradually disappears.

catharsis Bringing of relief through causing an emission – either of faeces through the use of *laxatives*, or of the emotive key to a psychological condition through *psychotherapy*.

cathartic Drug that causes *catharsis* – usually a *laxative*.

catheter Thin tube made of rubber or plastic and used to convey body fluids to or from a site in the body (commonly the bladder).

cathode-ray tube Principal mechanism of a television or video screen, as used in many of the modern medical techniques for *scanning* parts of the body.

cat-scratch fever Generally minor infection contracted through a scratch (perhaps caused by a catís claw, but equally perhaps by some other sharp object). Symptoms are an abscess over the scratch, and enlargement of the lymph nodes throughout the body; there is usually also high temperature. These symptoms vanish fairly quickly; general malaise may, however, persist for about two weeks afterwards. There is no treatment.

Cattell, James M. (1860–1944) American psychologist who investigated what the mind was capable of. His initial experiments categorized different responses to a single stimulus presented in varying intensities; later he became more interested in measuring intellectual and practical mental capacity.

cauda equina Great sheaf of nerve roots stemming from the end of the *spinal cord* (resembling a horseís tail). In evolutionary history, the spinal cord would once have run the length of the spinal column, right down to the tail; in humans, however, that length has shrunk, so that the cord ends at the second lumbar vertebra – all the nerves that used to stem in neat pairs from the final portion now derive together from the last segment of the cord.

causalgia Sharp burning or tingling pain in a limb, caused by nerve damage. Such damage is usually the result of injury that has caused thinning (or some other deformity) of the skin surface and abnormal sensitivity of the sensory nerves within it. Long-term pain from the condition may be highly distressing. Treatment is with analgesics and, occasionally, surgery to sever the nerves altogether.

cauterizing Deliberate destruction of tissue using heat. With modern instruments such as lasers, the heat used in the process can at the same time seal up minor blood vessels that have been incidentally severed.

cavity Hollow area within the body. The two major cavities of the body are the thoracic (chest) and abdominal cavities.

cecum American spelling of *caecum.*

celiac American spelling of *coeliac.*

cell Basic structural unit of the body. Humans have approximately 10 billion of them. Most cells comprise a nucleus, within its own membrane-like envelope, and a mass of *cytoplasm* in which there are several *organelles* (such as the mitochondria and ribosomes), all bounded by an outer double-membrane "skin". The nucleus contains the genetic information for replication and regulation of the specific function of the cell in the form of *deoxyrobonucleic acid* (DNA), represented in most human cell nuclei by 23 pairs of *chromosomes* made up of a multitude of *genes* all in a specific order. The sex cells (*sperm* and *ova*) have only half that number of chromosomes, however; at *fertilization* one complete cell is formed. Cell division and replication is by *mitosis* (of ordinary cells) or *meiosis* (to form sex cells).

cellulitis Inflammation of *connective tissue.* Both the structure and abundance of connective tissue throughout the body encourage such an inflammation to spread, especially if – as is usual – it is caused by bacterial infection of a wound. The lymphatic system may become involved. Treatment is with antibiotics.

cellulose Plant matter that is indigestible to humans, but that generally makes up a large proportion of the normal (and useful) *fibre in the diet*. It is found particularly in green vegetables.

Celsius Temperature scale derived from one devised by the Swedish scientist Anders Celsius (1701–1744). On it the freezing point of water is 0° and the boiling point 100°; normal blood temperature is measured at 37° (as opposed to 32°, 212° and 98.6° on the now less customary *Fahrenheit* scale). The scale is also sometimes called the centigrade scale.

central nervous system (CNS) *Brain* and the *spinal cord*, together the major anatomical elements involved in monitoring and controlling all human activity. From those two elements stem the rest of the *nervous system*, which is called the *peripheral nervous system*.

centrifuge Machine that whirls a tube horizontally around a central pivot. In this way, constituents of different densities within a liquid in the tube (such as blood) can be separated out by centrifugal force.

cephalic Of or like the head.

cerebellum Major part of the *hindbrain*, occupying virtually all the area between the *brainstem* (the medulla oblongata and the pons) and the overhanging lobes of the rear of the *cerebral hemispheres*. Like the hemispheres, there are two lobes, both composed of (outer) *grey matter* and (inner) *white matter*. Its function is concerned mainly with the co-ordination of muscular activity for smoothness of movement and maintenance of muscle tone; it has no conscious sensory or intellectual function.

cerebral cortex Outer layer of the *cerebral hemispheres*, made up of tightly convoluted folds of *grey matter* (consisting of more than 12,000 million *neurones*). With neural connections to every part of the body, the cerebral cortex fulfils almost all of the intellectual and voluntary functions. It is responsible for consciousness – including memory recall, perception and deduction – and for all voluntary activity. Specific areas of the cortex are known to have specific functions (such as the motor cortex, responsible for actuating movement; or the sensory cortex, responsible for interpreting sensory information). Beneath the cortex is the cerebral medulla, consisting of *white matter*, which connects the cortex to the rest of the nervous system.

cerebral haemorrhage Leakage of blood from one of the arteries that supply the *cerebral hemispheres*, into the tissue of the brain. The cause is generally either the degenerative disintegration of a blood vessel through disease, or the bursting of a blood vessel through high blood pressure (hypertension). Symptoms and effects depend on the volume of the haemorrhage and, to a lesser extent, its location: they range from temporary numbness to the potential total paralysis of a *stroke* or coma and death.

cerebral hemispheres Two great, rounded areas of nervous tissue that make up the major part of the *brain*. The outer, very convoluted layer (the *cerebral cortex*) is composed of *grey matter*; inside there is the *white matter* that in turn encloses a chamber (*ventricle*) containing *cerebrospinal fluid*, beneath which is the *thalamus*. Each of these elements has its own function. Together the hemispheres are called the cerebrum; they are connected along the midline by the thick bundle of nerve fibres called the *corpus callosum*. For anatomical purposes, each hemisphere is described as being made up of a number of lobes.

cerebral palsy Congenital failure of the brain to develop normally, caused by neural damage before or about the time of birth (perhaps by infection of the mother during pregnancy, by hereditary factors, by poor oxygen supply through the placenta, or by injury during birth). The classic symptom is involuntary spasms of the muscles (spasticity); there may be corresponding muscle deformity. The sense of balance, and the other senses, may be impaired; speech may be laboured; and there may also be a degree of mental retardation. Treatment is to alleviate these symptoms as far as possible, and may thus include physiotherapy and speech training.

cerebral thrombosis The formation of a blood clot (thrombus) in an artery that supplies blood to the brain. It is one of the three major causes of a *stroke* (the others are *cerebral haemorrhage* and *embolism*). Treatment for this kind of stroke may be with *anticoagulants*, or through surgical removal of the clot.

cerebrospinal fluid Watery liquid consisting mainly of a solution of sugars and salts that bathes some of the tissues of the *brain* and *spinal cord*. It is contained within four inter-linked chambers (*ventricles*) of the brain, down the central channel of the spinal cord, and in the *subarachnoid* space between two of the three *meninges*. The brain thus has fluid all round it and inside it, which provides it with shock-reducing protection because the brain virtually "floats" in the pressurized fluid. Diagnosis of certain conditions is made through examination of cerebrospinal fluid (by means of a *lumbar puncture*).

cerebrovascular accident Sudden onset of any condition caused by damage to the blood vessels in the brain or supplying the *meninges*. Causes and symptoms are thus those of a *stroke*.

cerebrum Term for the part of the brain consisting of the two *cerebral hemispheres*.

certification Creation of an official medical document, signed by a doctor, declaring what the doctor considers to be a medical fact – that, for example, an individual is too ill to go to work, that immunization against a specific disease has been administered, that a person has died, or that a person requires admission to a mental hospital.

cerumen Medical name for the *wax* that forms in the *ears*.

cervical cancer *Cancer* in the *cervix* (neck of the uterus) at the top of the *vagina*. In this region, cancer may be detected at an early stage of development, before it becomes truly *malignant* (spreading through the body); diagnosis may follow a regular *cervical smear test*, allowing treatment to be carried out immediately. The development of cervical cancer is linked with the presence of certain types of *human papillomavirus* (HPV), as found in genital warts, a common *sexually transmitted disease*; tests for HPV may suggest a higher risk of cancer and the need for frequent investigations to look for changes in the cervix. Undiagnosed, cervical cancer may cause a vaginal discharge with or without blood and pain. Treatment at the precancer stage may include the use of a laser or other method of removing layers of tissue, and is almost always successful. Cancer may be treated through *radiotherapy* or by surgical removal of the uterus (*hysterectomy*), or both, sometimes with chemotherapy (anticancer drugs).

cervical erosion An area of damaged and inflamed tissue on the surface of the cervix (the neck of the uterus that projects down into the vagina), prompted usually by infection in the *vagina* or by hormonal imbalance (as sometimes occurs through the use of the contraceptive "pill"); it may also follow childbirth or abortion. The condition may cause a vaginal discharge and some bleeding, and tends to be persistent because natural healing is problematic in this area. Treatment is not always necessary unless these symptoms have become troublesome, and then may include antibiotics or laser *cauterization* of the blood vessels in the area.

cervical smear test Removal of a sample of cells from the surface of the cervix (neck of the uterus) at the top of the *vagina*, for laboratory examination and analysis. If the sample is found to contain cells showing evidence of *cervical cancer* or precancerous changes, these can then be treated as early as possible. Traditionally the sample was taken by scraping the cervix with a wooden spatula and transferring the sample to a glass slide; this is also known as a Papanicolaou or Pap smear. Modern testing methods being introduced are simpler and also allow the detection of *human papillomavirus* (HPV), some strains of which are linked with an increased risk of cervical cancer.

cervical vertebrae Seven *vertebrae* of the spinal column in the neck, from the junction with the skull (at the *atlas*) to the thoracic vertebrae at the level of the shoulder.

cervix Neck, particularly of the womb (*uterus*) at the top of the *vagina*. It is structured of muscle that is capable of extraordinary dilation during childbirth, and its narrow channel is normally lined with mucus that changes its composition according to the *menstrual cycle*. Inflammation of the cervix is cervicitis; its cause is generally infection or unknown factors, and treatment corresponds to diagnosis. *Cervical cancer* is a relatively common form of cancer.

Cestoda Group of *worms* comprised mainly of *tapeworms*.

chalazion Small, inflamed swelling in an eyelid, caused by a blockage in the duct from a sebaceous gland. The gland itself changes composition either into a jelly-like mass or a hard lump. There is usually no pain. Treatment, if necessary, is with antibiotic creams and, as a last resort, surgery to open the gland and remove the lump.

chancre Painless ulcer that represents an initial symptom of *syphilis*. It appears at the site of infection – usually on the genitals, but sometimes on the mouth or eyelid. After some three weeks the ulcer fades – but it is essential that a full medical diagnosis is made. (Rarely, a similar form of ulcer is an initial sign of one form of *trypanosomiasis*.)

chancroid Bacterial infection transmitted as a *sexually transmitted disease*. It is most common in hot climates. Symptoms begin with a small, red, ulcerous sore at the site of infection. Enlargement of many of the *lymph nodes* in the groin follows, and there is usually also general malaise with high temperature. Diagnosis may require several skin tests. Treatment – for the patient and sexual partner(s) – is with antibiotics.

Charcot, Jean-Martin (1825–1893) French nerve specialist who pioneered several innovatory aspects of neurology. His work included descriptions of *multiple sclerosis* and tertiary *syphilis*, and he also contributed considerably to the contemporary understanding of mental disorders.

cheiropompholyx Condition similar to *eczema* in the thick skin of the palms of the hands. Piedopompholyx affects the soles of the feet. In these areas, the rash that forms the eczema cannot break the surface of the skin, and remains itching fearsomely below. Eventually the skin peels and the condition clears – but infection at this stage is common.

chelating agent Chemical that can bind to molecules of heavy metals (such as lead or mercury). Used as an antidote to treat poisoning by such metals, a chelating agent permits the metals to be excreted in the normal way.

chemoreceptor One or more cells that initiate a sensory nerve impulse upon detecting the presence of a specific chemical stimulus. The senses of taste and smell both rely on chemoreceptors (in the taste buds and the nose).

chemotherapy Treatment of disease or disorder with drugs intended to destroy an invading micro-organism or an area of tissue without harming the patient. Against *cancer*, such a combination includes *cytotoxic drugs*, some of which have unpleasant side-effects, and may be combined with *radiotherapy*; chemotherapy may additionally be used in treatments for cancer in areas where radiotherapy is not appropriate.

Cheyne-Stokes breathing Variation in the breathing rate – slowing down to a temporary halt (for some seconds) before speeding up to an abnormally fast rate, and slowing again – that is characteristic of impairment or suppression of the respiratory centre in the brain, as may occur in *coma* or under sedation. The condition is named after the Scottish doctor John Cheyne (1777–1836) and the Irish doctor William Stokes (1804–1878).

chiasma Crossing-over. Chiasma occurs at the exchange of genetic material during the form of cell division called *meiosis* or *mitosis*. The term also describes the crossing-over in the brain of fibres from one side of each of the *optic nerves*, so that part of the vision in each eye is interpreted by the opposite side of the brain.

chickenpox Highly infectious disease caused by a *herpes* virus and transmitted by airborne droplets (in coughing or sneezing). The initial symptoms are those of a cold, with a high temperature, followed, a day later, by a characteristic rash of watery vesicles on a red base, appearing first on the chest and back, and then all over the body. The itchy vesicles turn into scabs, which last for up to a fortnight before dropping off; scratching them may occasionally leave scars. Chickenpox is infectious from the start of symptoms until all the spots disappear. The patient may feel tired and unwell for a week or so afterwards. Sometimes the spots become infected from scratching, and rarely there are more general complications. In patients with vulnerable immune systems, such as those with *AIDS*, chickenpox can be very serious. The same virus (herpes zoster) causes *shingles* in adults, which may occur when the virus reactivates in later life. Treatment is to alleviate the symptoms, and may include soothing lotions and plenty of liquids. Patients at risk of complications, such as those with AIDS, may be given antiviral drugs.

chilblain Painful, reddened, swollen area of tissue on the ears, toes or fingers, accompanied by sensations of itching and burning. It represents an extreme response of the body to cold, caused by an abnormally strong contraction of the blood vessels of the skin in order to conserve heat, strong enough to deplete the flow of oxygen and nutrients in the blood to the areas affected. A tendency to chilblains often runs in families. The best treatment is prevention: keeping warm. In severe or persistent cases, drugs to improve blood flow to the extremities may be given.

childbirth Delivery, at the end of pregnancy, by a mother of a child through the process of *labour* or a *Caesarean section*. In natural childbirth, the birth itself constitutes the second stage of labour (the third and last is the delivery of the *afterbirth*). The babyís head (or other part of the body, with any other *presentation*) appears at the end of the *cervix* and the contractions become strongly rhythmic. There is an increased urge in the mother to "bear down" and push the baby out. Rapidly, the baby reaches the vaginal opening and, with or without assistance, makes its way into the world. Any membranous debris and blood is wiped away, and the *umbilical cord* is cut and tied.

chill Sudden feeling of cold that may or may not be associated with shivering (the bodyís attempt to warm itself when feeling cold). A *fever* may be accompanied by chills because the blood heat is inappropriate to the environmental temperature. Persistent chill is an indication of an impending infection, of malnutrition, or of strong anxiety.

Chinese restaurant syndrome Mundane group of symptoms that may follow the consumption of excessive amounts of monosodium glutamate (a common ingredient of Chinese dishes). The symptoms resemble those of *indigestion*, with heartburn and a high temperature. Treatment is as for indigestion.

chiropody Study of the structure, functioning, disorders, diseases and care of the feet.

chiropractic Also known as chiropractice or cheiropraxis, form of *alternative medicine* in which the basic precept is that disorders are caused mostly by the displacement of bones and their associated nerves. Therapy thus consists mainly of spinal manipulation, concentrating on the *vertebrae* of the spine and the muscles of the back (which most of the major nerves are connected to).

chirurgy Old form of the word *surgery*.

Chlamydia Group of tiny bacteria-like micro-organisms that cause disease (pathogens). One form causes the eye disease *trachoma*; another causes the lung disease psittacosis, transmitted from birds, while other strains cause sexually transmitted diseases – inflammation of the urethra (*urethritis*) or vagina (*vaginitis*). If vaginal infection spreads it may lead to *pelvic inflammatory disease* with blockage of the Fallopian tubes, a common cause of infertility in women. Episodes of infection can be treated with antibiotics. If vaginal infections remain untreated and lead to pelvic inflammatory disease, surgery may be needed.

chloasma Condition affecting women, in which there is an increase in the skin of the dark pigment *melanin*, resulting in brown or yellow blotches on the face, that occurs during pregnancy or while taking the contraceptive pill, caused by a disturbance of the normal hormonal balance. The condition fades altogether in the absence of these hormonal factors. See also *melasma*.

chlorine Poisonous, choking gas that is nevertheless useful in weak solution as an antiseptic and bleach. In the human body it is a constituent of hydrochloric acid in *gastric juices* of the stomach and of salt (sodium chloride) in cellular fluids.

chloroform Early *anaesthetic*, used well into the twentieth century but now regarded as too toxic. A very volatile liquid, its use could cause *arrhythmia* of the heart and damage to the liver.

choking Inability to breathe because of an obstruction in the throat that prevents the *epiglottis* from opening the air channel through the *larynx*, or because the obstruction itself prevents air from passing in or out. There are several methods for assisting somebody who is choking; one of the best is the *Heimlich manoeuvre*.

cholangiogram X-ray photograph of the *bile ducts*, taken after the introduction of a radio-opaque medium into the ducts. It is usually made to assess the location of a *calculus* (gallstone), or to investigate any other obstruction in the ducts.

cholecystectomy Surgical removal of the *gall bladder*. The most common reason is inflammation (*cholecystitis*) or *gallstones*.

cholecystitis Inflammation of the *gall bladder*. The two main causes are bacterial infection – acute cholecystitis, causing pain and a high temperature (treatment is bed rest, and antibiotics) – and *gallstones*. Treatment of either cause is, in the last resort, surgical removal of the gall bladder (*cholecystectomy*).

cholelithiasis Presence of *gallstones* in the *bile ducts* or the *gall bladder*.

cholera Potentially dangerous bacterial infection of the small intestine, contracted through eating or drinking material contaminated by the faeces of an infected person: it is thus common only in areas of poor sanitation. Symptoms are massive loss of fluid from the body through vomiting and diarrhoea, and the consequent effects of dehydration (cramp and shock), which may be serious enough to cause death. Treatment with tetracycline can speed recovery and reduce dehydration, but the most important treatment is to replace lost fluids by copious drinking of solutions of salted sugar or rice water. A vaccine is available, but is effective for less than a year.

cholesterol Substance much like *fat*, synthesized in the body mainly by the *liver* and present in the blood and most tissues. An important contributor to the structure of cell membranes and an element in the production of certain essential hormones, cholesterol is also a major constituent of the fatty deposits (*atheroma*) that may clog the blood vessels in the potentially serious condition *atherosclerosis*, and a normal constituent too of *bile* although it may contribute to the formation of *gallstones* in the bile duct.

choline Organic compound significant in some chemical reactions in the body, specifically in producing the *neurotransmitter* acetylecholine. Sometimes likened to a B vitamin – except that it is synthesized in the body and most vitamins are not – it is also important to the transport of fats in the body.

chord In medicine, generally referring either to the *spinal cord* or the *vocal cords* of the larynx.

chorea Either of two major diseases that cause uncontrolled jerky movements of the limbs and sometimes of the muscles of the face, caused by a disorder of the *basal ganglia* within the *white matter* of the brain. *Sydenham's chorea* is an allergic response to bacterial infection, commonly a delayed complication of rheumatic fever; it occurs mostly in children, and is known alternatively as St Vitusí dance. *Huntington's chorea*, on the other hand, is an inherited disorder accompanied by progressive *dementia*, caused by degeneration of the nerve cells in the brain. A third, and minor, form of the disorder may accompany extreme old age.

chorion Membrane that surrounds and protects the *blastocyst* at *implantation*, and the *embryo* and *foetus* thereafter. It is from the chorion, which is particularly well supplied with blood vessels, that the *placenta* is initially formed, through which is effected the exchange of oxygen and nutrients from the motherís blood wastes from that of the foetus.

chorionic gonadotrophin Hormone produced and secreted in women by the *placenta* during pregnancy. It takes over the function of the *gonadotrophin* hormones normally secreted each *menstrual cycle* by the *pituitary gland* to stimulate the production of *progesterone* by the *corpus luteum* in one *ovary* (the effects of the pituitary gland are not felt during pregnancy). The excess produced is excreted in the urine – the presence of which is the basis of most pregnancy tests. As a drug, chorionic gonadotrophin may be used in women to treat *premenstrual syndrome* or infrequency of *ovulation*; or in men to treat delayed puberty.

chorionic villus sampling Method of testing for abnormality of a foetus early in pregnancy. It involves the collection of one or more of the tiny finger-like extrusions (villi) of the *chorion* – the membrane that surrounds the *embryo* or *foetus*, and constitutes much of the *placenta*. Laboratory tests can then determine if there is any cause for worry.

choroid Middle layer of the three layers of the eyeball. The inner layer is the *retina*, which is present in any significant depth only towards the back of the eyeball. The outer layer is the *sclera*, which at the front turns into the *cornea*. The choroid thus has to insulate the retina from the sclera and to act as the body from which the muscles of the iris and the lens both derive their basis. Inflammation of the choroid is *choroiditis*.

choroiditis Inflammation of the *choroid* of the eyeball, usually without further inflammation of other layers of the eye. The symptoms include blurred vision, with flashes of light. The cause is generally unknown, and treatment is fairly standard – with *corticosteroids* – but there may be serious complications such as *glaucoma* and *detached retina*.

choroid plexus Network of tiny blood vessels originating from the *pia mater* and ending in the *ventricles* of the brain, where it is the source of the *cerebrospinal fluid*. The fluid is eventually reabsorbed within the *subarachnoid* space.

chromatic aberration Defect in a simple lens because of its inability to bring all wavelengths of white light to the same focus; as a result, optical images are surrounded by a rainbow-hued "halo". It can be overcome by making compound lenses from two or more different types of glass (with different refractive indices).

chromatin Substance of which *chromosomes* are formed, consisting of the material that makes up the major *genes* (euchromatin) and the substance that either makes up the lesser genes or represents a supporting or controlling factor (heterochromatin). In both materials one essential constituent is *deoxyribonucleic acid* (DNA).

chromatography Separation of two or more constituents of a liquid or gas mixture by their absorption to different extents in an absorbent medium. There are two major methods of liquid chromatography: one uses filter paper, the other a column of absorbent powder (such as aluminium oxide). In gas chromatography, the mixture is transported in an inert carrier gas and the analysis usually presented as a graph on a chart recorder or computer printout. It is capable of detecting minute quantities of substances and is used to analyse samples of blood and other body fluids.

chromosome Major unit of heredity – one of 46 in the nucleus of most body cells – composed of *deoxyribonucleic acid* (DNA) in the form of a strand of many *genes*. The sex cells (the *sperm* and the *ova*), however, have only 23 chromosomes each, so that every human inherits 23 chromosomes from one parent and 23 from the other; the 46 come together initially at *fertilization*, thus forming a new individual with characteristics inherited from both parents. In women, the 46 chromosomes may be distinguished as 23 matching pairs; in men, however, there are 22 pairs and an odd couple with one much smaller (the *Y-chromosome*) than the other (the *X-chromosome*). Cell division for the purpose of replication – necessary to form new tissue for growth or replacement – is ordinarily by *mitosis*, but in the process of forming sex cells it is by *meiosis*; in either case, the chromosomes also divide and replicate so that the correct number is always present within any new daughter cell. On the rare occasions when there is an absent or extra chromosome within the cell nuclei, the result is most commonly foetal death; very few with this type of anomaly survive to birth – an exception being people with *Down's syndrome* (in which there is an extra 21st chromosome).

chronic Describing a condition that lasts for a long time (as opposed to a short-term or *acute* problem), usually beginning gradually and changing only slowly. The severity of the condition is immaterial.

chronic fatigue syndrome A condition of disabling fatigue that may last many months or even years. Slight exertion may make the person exhausted. Other symptoms include muscle weakness and aching, joint pains, intermittently raised temperature, swollen lymph nodes, sore throat and depression. The cause is unknown but it often follows a viral infection, so is sometimes known as postviral fatigue syndrome. It has also, wrongly, been called myalgic encephalomyelitis (ME). There is no specific treatment. Various medicines may be given to improve symptoms such as sore throat or depression.

chyle Milky product of fat absorption that occurs within the *lymph* vessels serving the lining of the small *intestine*. Consisting of a suspension of tiny droplets of fat (chylomicrons) within lymph, it is conveyed by the *lymphatic system* through the thoracic duct to the bloodstream.

chylomicron Tiny droplet of fat which, with others in suspension (as *chyle*), is conveyed to the bloodstream by the *lymphatic system* after absorption from the small *intestine*. In the bloodstream it is available for use as a source of energy.

chyme Partly digested food that is passed through the *pylorus* from the *stomach* to the duodenum for further *digestion*. After the action of the stomach acids and gastric juices, and the normal churning by the stomach muscles, the food is mostly in liquid form except for fibrous elements.

cicatrix Medical name for a *scar* in which failure of a wound to heal completely results in *scar tissue* remaining visible.

cilia Hair-like projections from a surface, particularly the tiny processes on the surface of the bronchial passages which move in waves to transport mucus (together with any entrapped inhaled dust and foreign bodies).

circadian rhythm Pattern of body processes attuned to the average dayís routine – including hunger at mealtimes and tiredness at night, but also variations in blood pressure, body temperature, levels of consciousness (especially during sleep), and the timing of regular glandular secretions and alimentary functions. Disturbance in this rhythm – as in *jet lag* – may cause some uncomfortable symptoms while the body readjusts its internal "clock".

circle of Willis Circular system of arteries on the underside of the *brain*, around the *optic chiasma* and the stalk of the pituitary gland. As a closed circuit, into which and from which many vessels lead, it represents a guarantee of flow to all the other vessels if one should become blocked.

circulation System in which the *blood*, pumped by the *heart*, flows around the body. In effect there are two circulations: one from the heart to the *lungs* and back (during which the blood is reoxygenated), and the other from the heart to all the tissues of the body and back (during which the oxygen is transported to the tissues and waste products are carried away for disposal, or back to the heart for going on to the lungs). Vessels leading away from the heart are *arteries*, which branch into narrowed arterioles and very fine capillaries; those leading back to the heart are capillaries, venules and *veins*. Diseases and disorders of the heart naturally affect the circulation, as do any of the many diseases, disorders and injuries of the arteries and veins. The term circulation may be used also of the *lymphatic system*, and of the flow of *cerebrospinal fluid* through the chambers (ventricles) of the brain.

circumcision Surgical removal of most or all of the *prepuce* (foreskin), usually during very early childhood. The reasons for circumcision include religion or tradition, or disorders affecting the prepuce. The latter include malformation or abnormal tightness of the foreskin (*phimosis*) and persistent inflammation (*balanitis*).

cirrhosis Condition in which strands of fibrous tissue and abnormal nodular growths form in the *liver*, which loses its colour and is characteristically misshapen. Liver function gradually fails as more of its cells are incapacitated and die. Causes include unknown factors (in more than half of all cases), *heart failure*, *alcoholism*, viral *hepatitis*, blockage of the common *bile duct* (draining bile from the gall bladder), and *autoimmune disease* (where the immune system attacks the bodyís own tissues). Liver damage is irreversible; treatment is to halt the damaging process, according to diagnosis of the cause, and may include drugs, a special diet or surgery.

claudication Medical term for painful limping or lameness. Disease of the arteries in the legs may cause *intermittent claudication*.

claustrophobia Abnormal terror of being confined or contained in an enclosed, windowless room (or any area that might represent one). As with many *phobias*, *behaviour therapy* may help.

clavicle Medical name for the collarbone, either of two thin bones that connect the breastbone (*sternum*) with a scapula (*shoulder blade*) at the point of the shoulder. The muscular connections at either end are extremely strong, with the result that a violent blow on the light bone in between – or on the breastbone or on the shoulderblade – tends all too easily to snap it: the clavicle is the most commonly broken bone in the body. The usual treatment for a broken collarbone is to keep the arm on the affected side in a sling until it heals.

claw foot Malformation of the foot, in which the foot is permanently as arched as possible, with only the heel and toe-tips touching the ground (known medically as pes cavus)). The cause is almost always unknown, but in some cases may bear upon some imbalance in the position or length of the muscles that flex and extend the toes. The condition occasionally occurs as a result of a neuromuscular disorder. Treatment with surgery may or may not be successful.

claw hand Condition of the hand in which the middle joints of all the fingers remain permanently flexed, forming a sort of claw. Causes include injury, and nerve or muscle disorders; treatment depends on the cause.

cleft palate Failure of the two sides of the roof of the mouth to close and meet each other in the developing foetus, resulting in a fissure at birth. The cleft may penetrate the gums at the front, disrupting the *dentition* (in which case there is generally also a *hare lip*); or it may affect only the central portion of the palate or extend to the back of the palate. Surgery (often requiring a series of operations during childhood) can generally make an effective and neat repair.

climacteric Another name for the *menopause*, and its accompanying effects, in women. The term is also sometimes used to refer to the decline in libido experienced by men in middle age.

climax Peak of excitement or effect; in medicine generally of sexual excitement, and thus the equivalent of the term *orgasm*.

clinic Part of a hospital or a health centre devoted specifically either to one type of patient or to one form of treatment or care. Medical staff at clinics may include senior specialists and medical instructors.

clinical Pertaining to the treatment of patients, as opposed to studying disease in the laboratory or in experimental environments. Clinical medicine is thus practised by any doctor (a clinician) who sees patients for diagnosis and treatment, whether in a hospital, clinic, GPís surgery or family doctorís office, or elsewhere.

clinical trial Initial use of a form of therapy (particularly a drug) on patients. To be licensed for general use, any new drug must successfully undergo clinical trials for a number of years without untoward effects or disadvantages becoming apparent.

clitoris Small, sensitive organ in a womanís genitalia. Part of the *vulva*, enfolded between the forward junction of the labia minora (the inner lips), it is made up of erectile tissue (in the same way as the penis of a man) and is thus subject to sexual arousal by either physical or psychological stimulation.

clone Cell or organism replicated (asexually) from a single original cell, and thus genetically identical with the original. In animal cloning a single cell of the parent is manipulated to produce an "embryo" without the usual input of genetic material from a second parent; a cloned animal is thus genetically identical with its parent. The use of cloning methods to obtain a large number of identical cells is useful in *genetic engineering*; a gene clone is the production of identical genes, usually obtained by inserting a single gene into a *bacterium* where it replicates (reproduces itself). The term is also used as a verb to describe the action of cloning.

clot Small area or ball of congealed blood, formed by *clotting*. Within a blood vessel, a clot may travel (as an *embolus*) and become an obstruction (*thrombus*) that may have dangerous consequences.

clotting Process of coagulation, congealing and drying of the blood, most commonly at the site of a wound as part of healing, but sometimes – in special circumstances – as a condition of the blood. The process involves a number of chemical reactions, all relying on the presence of specific factors in the blood *plasma*, and is triggered by contact between the blood and damaged tissue or a foreign surface. The result of the chemical reactions is the localized appearance of the enzyme thromboplastin, the function of which is to convert soluble *fibrinogen* in the plasma to insoluble strands of *fibrin*. The strands then act as the matrix for the collection and accumulation of other blood elements, especially the blood *platelets*, before contracting (squeezing out *serum*) and leaving a dry clot. Blood clots that occur without external cause most often result from very slow circulation (as may be caused by long-term use of certain drugs) or from arterial damage (as with *arteriosclerosis*). Lack of any of the blood-clotting factors in the blood plasma results in failure of the blood to coagulate (as with *haemophilia*).

clubbing Deformity of the tissues at the tips of the fingers and toes that is a symptom of certain specific conditions, mostly relating to serious disorders of the heart or the lungs. The skin at the base of the nails thickens, and the nails themselves pad out to become completely convex, so that the digits all seem to end in bulbs. Rarely, the condition is found as a congenital abnormality unrelated to any medical problem.

club foot Congenital malformation of one or both feet. The sole of the foot cannot be placed on the ground because it is twisted downwards and inwards (talipes equinovarus – in which the patient walks on the outside rim of the upper part of the foot), inwards (talipes varus – in which the patient walks on the outer ankle) or outwards (talipes valgus – in which the patient walks on the inner ankle). Treatment with physiotherapy, strapping or the use of a plaster cast may be sufficient; if not, surgery may be required.

CNS Abbreviation of *central nervous system*.

coagulation Thickening of a liquid, preparatory to congealing; the first part of the process of *clotting*. In blood, coagulation requires the presence in the *plasma* of specific chemical factors. Drugs to "thin" blood and reduce the tendency to clot are called *anticoagulants*.

coarctation Narrowing of a vessel, particularly as a congenital defect of the *aorta* (the artery from the heart through which blood is pumped to all the tissues of the body). The result is high blood pressure (hypertension) in the upper part of the body, and low blood pressure (hypotension) in the lower. Treatment is through surgical replacement of a section of the artery.

cobalt Metallic element, of which an artificial isotope (cobalt) is used in *radiotherapy* to treat cancer.

cocaine Alkaloid drug, of which the possession and use by unauthorized persons is illegal in most countries. It is rarely used for medical purposes – very occasionally, in synthetic form, as a local anaesthetic in minor operations on the face – because it is a strong, potentially hallucinogenic stimulant and repeated doses can lead rapidly to (psychological) *dependence*.

coccus General term for the spherical types of *bacteria*. They include gonococcus (responsible for *gonorrhoea*), pneumoeoccus (responsible for *pneumonia*), *Staphylococcus* and *Streptococcus*.

coccyx Final four *vertebrae* of the spinal column, fused together as a single unit, representing a vestigial tail. It articulates with the *sacrum*. Fracture, by a blow between the buttocks, is uncommon and painful, but generally not serious.

cochlea Spiral-shaped organ, located in the *inner ear*, that is the main sensory organ of *hearing*. Three chambers run the length of the tubular spiral, separated by two membranes. The floor of the middle chamber is the basilar membrane, on which sits the *organ of Corti* (also running the length of the spiral); when sound vibration causes reverberation in the basilar membrane, tiny hair cells that attach the organ of Corti to the overlying membrane (tectorial membrane) are stretched and pulled accordingly, and transmit those movements to the auditory nerve (which sends the information on to the brain for interpretation). High-pitched sound is registered at the beginning of the coil; low-pitched sound at the centre. Infection of the inner ear (*otitis* interna), congenital malformation or injury may prevent the full functioning of the cochlea and cause perceptive *deafness*.

coeliac disease Malabsorption of food (medical name, gluten enteropathy), caused by an abnormal sensitivity of the lining of the small intestine to the protein *gluten* (which is found in wheat, rye and barley). The condition occurs mostly in young children; symptoms are all the signs of *malnutrition*, including *deficiency disorders*. In adults (in whom the condition is also called *sprue*), symptoms are fatigue, cramps and breathlessness. A strict diet with no gluten must be followed, with further treatment to alleviate any deficiency symptoms.

coenzyme Organic compound that acts as a catalytic agent in reactions which are themselves catalysed by *enzymes*. Their presence is required before the enzymes –most often very powerful digestive enzymes – can function, and their absence in sensitive areas of intestinal tissue thus represents a means of protecting those areas from the effect of the enzymes.

cognition Combination of consciousness, perception and memory, which enables us to experience and learn.

coil Another name for an *intrauterine device*, used for *contraception*.

coitus *Sexual intercourse* between a man and a woman.

coitus interruptus Frustrating and inefficient method of *contraception*. Undertaken during *sexual intercourse*, it involves the withdrawal of the manís erect penis from the womanís vagina before *ejaculation*.

cold Known medically as coryza, a very common viral infection of the mucous membranes of the nose, throat and bronchial passages. Any of more than 40 viruses can cause the common cold. They are transmitted by droplets coughed or sneezed into the air or by direct contact with infected secretions (for example, by shaking hands with an infected person) that are readily transferred to the face. Initial symptoms are generally a sore throat and a cough, followed by a stuffy nose or painful breathing, and then a running nose; there may also be headache, high temperature and watering eyes. Treatment is usually to alleviate the worst symptoms.

cold abscess Slow-forming *abscess* associated with *tuberculosis*, that can appear virtually anywhere on the skin surface. The warmth and inflammation that normally accompanies an abscess is in this instance scarcely noticeable, represented only by local surface tenderness on pressure.

cold sore Characteristic blister occurring on the skin or mucous membranes due to infection with a type of *herpes* virus. The virus type that causes cold sores around the lips and nose is closely related to the one causing genital herpes, and occasionally either type may cause blisters in their nonpreferred area. Cold sores on the face are highly infectious and may be painful or itchy. They tend to recur. Occasionally they may infect the conjunctiva and cause eye complications. Treatment with antiviral drugs can speed healing but does not affect the tendency to recur.

colic Intense abdominal pain that occurs in short cycles that peak and fade. In adults, causes include constipation, intestinal obstruction, menstruation, gallstone in the bile duct and kidney stone (which is especially painful). In babies, so-called infantile colic is common in the first three or four months. The baby has periods of prolonged crying, often in the evenings, which are not related to the usual causes of crying such as hunger or discomfort. It is thought that this may be caused by wind in the intestines or emotional upheaval. In adults medical assessment is advisable if colic persists. Sometimes drugs can help ease the pain, but in some cases surgery may be required to treat the underlying cause. Infantile colic may be soothed by walking around with the baby, and episodes usually fade spontaneously after about four months of age.

colitis Inflammation of the large intestine (*colon*). Its two major forms are *mucous colitis* and *ulcerative colitis*, but it may also occur with *Crohn's disease*.

collagen Major component of the fibrous type of *connective tissue* (present, for example, in tendons), in which the molecular structure itself is in fibre-like strands. It is an inelastic but strong form of protein, found not just in skin, cartilage and ligaments but also in bone.

collagen diseases Old term for *connective-tissue diseases*.

collapse Inability to continue in activity. Collapse may be physical – of the whole body (as with fatigue), or of part of it (as for example a lung) – or mental.

collarbone Common name for the *clavicle*.

Colles' fracture Fracture of the *radius* bone at the wrist, generally caused by falling on to one hand. The fracture is normally reduced (set) under anaesthesia, and takes about six weeks to heal. A fracture similar – but not identical – was first described by the Dublin physician Abraham Colles (1773–1843).

colloid Material that consists of very fine particles of one substance evenly dispersed in another. A common type is a gel or jelly, in which a substance does not form a true solution in a liquid but remains dispersed in molecular form evenly within it. Other examples include *aerosols* and emulsions. Colloid chemistry, in medicine, refers to the study and preparation of atomized liquids, foams, emulsions and other forms of colloidal suspension.

coloboma Defect within the tissues of the eyeball (or, rarely, in the eyelid), caused by a failure of development before birth. There may be malformation of the iris, lens, choroid or retina, resulting in corresponding deficiencies of vision.

colon Greater part of the large *intestine*, from the *caecum* (where the small intestine – the ileum – ends) to the *rectum*. It has three major sections: the ascending colon (from the caecum – which includes the *appendix* – up the right side of the body), the transverse colon (across the body) and the descending colon (down the left side of the body to the sigmoid colon and the rectum). Its purpose is the absorption of water and various salts from the relatively solid waste material (faeces) passing through it – for by the time the material reaches the colon, digestion has been completed. The passage is continuous, and the material moved within it by strong *peristalsis*. Inflammation of the colon is *colitis*; serious disease of the colon may require surgery to effect a *colostomy*.

colonic irrigation Thorough washing out of the *colon* (or much of it) through the use of multiple *enemas*.

colostomy Surgical operation to cut the *colon* (usually above an area of disease or injury) and bring it to the abdominal surface to form a false anus there. Faeces may then be collected at the new orifice (stoma) in a renewable hermetic bag. The colostomy may represent a temporary measure while the original disease or injury heals, or it may be permanent (if the rest of the colon has to be removed altogether).

colostrum Initial form of *milk* produced by a womanís breasts immediately before and after childbirth. Yellowish, it contains a higher proportion of white blood cells and antibodies (for defence against infection) – and less fats and carbohydrates – than the true milk which follows a few days afterwards.

colour blindness Congenital defect in the *cone* cells within the *retina* of the eyes, causing an inability to distinguish between certain colours, or to distinguish more than one colour at all. The condition is 200 times more common (in any form) in Caucasian men than in Caucasian women, indicating that it is an *X-linked disorder*. The most common form (Daltonism) is one in which the nerve endings that detect the colour red are absent – so that both red and green are identified as green, nerve endings for which are present. Blue-yellow colour blindness occurs less commonly; totally monochromatic vision is rare. Diagnosis of colour blindness makes use of the *Ishihara tests*.

colour vision Colours are distinguished by sensory nerve endings in and around the *cone* cells of the *retina* of the eyes. The colours they detect are red, green and blue (which, with the light and dark contrast provided by the *rod* cells are all that is required for full colour vision), represented in the cones as pigmented areas. Absence for any reason of sensory information from nerve endings relating to cones with a specific type of pigmentation results in *colour blindness*.

colposcopy Examination of the *vagina* by a specialist using an instrument called a colposcope. Gently inserted through the vaginal opening, the instrument allows inspection of the walls of the vagina and the neck of the uterus (cervix).

coma Prolonged state of *unconsciousness* from which a patient cannot be roused; in deep coma there may also be an absence of response to painful or reflex stimuli. Constant supervision of such patients is thus essential, not least to ensure that the respiratory passages are kept clear (for there is no reflex to cough out saliva entering the trachea). Causes include head injury and brain damage, poisoning (either by chemicals, drugs or by failure of internal metabolism), serious infection of the brain, or hypoglycaemia (through *diabetes* mellitus). Occasionally, an epileptic seizure may also result in coma.

comedo Medical name for a *blackhead*.

commensal Any organism that lives in or on another organism, but causes neither harm nor benefit by its presence. Many bacteria residing in the skin or intestines of humans are commensals. A similar relationship, but one in which both organisms derive benefits essential to each, is *symbiosis*. An organism that lives totally at the cost of another (host) is a *parasite*.

comminuted fracture Type of bone *fracture* in which there is splintering of the bone into more than two fragments.

common cold Another name for what many people simply call a *cold*.

communicable disease General term for an *infectious* or contagious disease that can be transmitted by one person to another and may thus be the principal factor in an *epidemic*. The most serious forms are *notifiable infectious diseases*.

community medicine Branch of medicine aimed at studying and treating the diseases and disorders of entire sections of the population (as opposed to individual patients). It involves many aspects of social health care, and includes such disciplines as *public health*, *preventive medicine*, *epidemiology* and the planning and organization of health care services.

community nurse General term for *district nurses*, health visitors and community midwives.

compatibility In surgical practice, the degree of matching between two *tissues*. The greater the compatibility, the less likely that there will be tissue *rejection* (involving harmful reactions by the bodyís *immune system* and the formation of *antibodies*) if they are grafted together. Blood and other forms of tissue are most compatible between close relatives, and especially siblings (and closest of all between identical twins). For most forms of *graft* (or *transplantation*), the tissue of relatives is thus sought. It is in circumstances when no relative is available that *tissue banks* – containing carefully maintained and categorized tissues – come into their own. See also *Rh factor incompatibility*.

complementary medicine Methods of therapy involving techniques that are not traditionally taught as part of standard or orthodox medicine. Formerly known as alternative medicine, many of these techniques have been shown to be of benefit and are increasingly accepted as having a role to play alongside orthodox medicine; some doctors have additional training in the more widely accepted techniques, although many doctors remain sceptical. Therapies range from physical and manipulative methods such as *acupuncture*, *chiropractic* and *osteopathy* to the use of "natural" drugs and diet, as in *herbalism*, *homoeopathy* and naturopathy, diagnostic techniques such as iridology, and mystical therapies such as *faith healing*. Complementary therapies tend to take a holistic approach to medicine – that is, they are concerned with treatment aimed at restoring a healthy balance in the whole body, not merely relieving symptoms or treating a specific area or organ.

complex In *psychoanalysis*, the result in an individualís behaviour of a group of repressed emotive thoughts and desires; sometimes the effects are contrary to the normal behaviour and expectations of the individualís conscious mind. According to Sigmund *Freud*, at least one form of complex is normal during every personís *psychosexual development*. See *Oedipus complex*.

complication Second, and possibly worse, disorder occurring during (and often as a result of) a first disorder.

compound In medicine, a substance (usually a drug) that is a mixture of ingredients. In chemistry, it is a substance that contains more than one chemical element.

compound fracture Type of bone *fracture* in which one or both "ends" of the bone at the break penetrate the skin surface.

compressed air illness Another name for *decompression sickness*.

compulsion In psychology, an irresistible urge to carry out a specific action, often many times over. It represents one form or symptom of an *obsession*.

computerized tomography (CT scanning) Method of deriving a computer-enhanced three-dimensional X-ray picture of a part of the body. The method involves multiple X-raying of the part from many measured angles within a special X-ray machine (CAT scanner), and analysis and interpretation by a computer to form an image on a video screen that can be set to show specific depths from specific angles, as cross-sections. It is particularly useful in examining the structure of the brain.

conception Moment and process of the *fertilization* of an *ovum* (egg cell) by a *sperm*, following *sexual intercourse*. The result is the formation of a *zygote* (a combined cell with 23 pairs of *chromosomes* in its nucleus), representing the beginning of *pregnancy*. Conception most often takes place in a *Fallopian* tube, from which the zygote – becoming next a *morula*, then a *blastocyst* – travels down to the *uterus* (womb) for *implantation*.

concretion Gradual formation of a *calculus* (stone) or of a hard coating of calcium salts around an organ (or foreign body).

concussion Effect of a blow to the head (or, technically, anywhere on the body) that results in unconsciousness or semiconsciousness for any period, even if only seconds. Return to full consciousness may be only gradual, however, and accompanied by headache, blurred vision and slight mental confusion; there may also be loss of memory for the events before or after the trauma. Symptoms may be due to bruising within the brain, and generally fade, but medical advice should still be sought (in case there is a skull fracture, for example); in a few cases symptoms persist for a long period (postconcussion syndrome). Repeated concussion may result in brain damage, as in the "punch-drunk syndrome" that may occur in boxers after repeated blows to the head, featuring tremor, *dementia* and sometimes *epilepsy*.

conditioned reflex Type of *reflex* action that can be produced in a person merely by an accompanying factor of the original stimulus, because the stimulus and the accompanying factor are so firmly associated in the individualís experience. (*Pavlovís* original experiment centred on dogs who eventually salivated on hearing a bell, knowing that the bell usually signalled the imminence of food.)

conditioning Modification of behaviour by engendering new responses to stimuli. There are two methods. Classical conditioning involves the establishing of a *conditioned reflex*: a stimulus that produces a specific response is accompanied so often by another independent stimulus that eventually the second stimulus also produces the specific response. Operant conditioning relies on *reinforcement*: on rewards or punishments accompanying a response so often that eventually the response itself becomes the reward or punishment, and occurs more often or less often accordingly.

condom Latex sheath fitted over the penis during *sexual intercourse*, used as a means of barrier *contraception* or as a precaution against contracting a *sexually transmitted disease*; condoms do not, however, provide complete protection against either. The use of condoms is an important aid to safer sex practices, helping to protect both sexual partners against infections, including HIV, the virus that causes *AIDS*; use is recommended for this purpose even if the contraceptive effect is not required, and particularly with new, frequent or homosexual partners. A female condom that fits inside the vagina to function in a similar manner is also available.

condyle Rounded lobe that forms part of the end of certain bones, particularly those of the jaws, limbs and digits. The lateral and medial condyles together form the lower end of the femur (thigh bone), for example.

cones Type of cells in the *retina* of the eye that effectively provide colour vision. (The cells that provide light and dark contrast are the *rods*.) Of the six or seven million cones in each retina, one third are (probably) responsible for sensing red, one third for sensing blue, and the last third for sensing green – from which (with the contrast) all vision is made up. The cones are particularly concentrated at the *fovea* on the retina.

congenital abnormality Malformation or disorder that is present at birth. Most are of unknown cause; some result from hereditary factors; a few from disease or disorder in the mother during pregnancy. Some can be detected in the foetus well before birth (using *amniocentesis*). Conditions such as *cleft palate*, *congenital heart disease* (such as *Fallot's tetralogy*) or *dislocation* of the hip can be rectified quickly by surgery. For most congenital abnormalities, however, there is no curative treatment, only long-term alleviation of the symptoms or lifelong care and precautions. Such disorders range from lack in the body of certain enzymes or hormones, to *haemophilia*, *spina bifida* and *Down's syndrome*. Parents of children born with such disabilities may benefit from *genetic counselling* before deciding to have another child.

congenital dislocation of the hip (CDH) Condition of a newborn baby born with a hip joint out of its socket or readily displaceable from the acetabulum (the "cup" in each pelvic bone into which the head of the femur or thigh bone fits). If undetected, the joint will be damaged with use and *arthritis* may result. All babies are examined for signs of this uncommon (but not rare) condition during the neonatal period; if examination suggests CDH the diagnosis may be confirmed by ultrasound scanning or X-rays. Treatment is to reduce (reset) the dislocation – possibly under anaesthesia – and to immobilize or support the joint for a while in a harness or plaster cast.

congenital heart disease Any disorder of the heart and its major blood vessels that is present at birth. Many are relatively minor and not diagnosed until later in life; some, however, are potentially life-threatening and may require surgery. Of the latter type is the defect in the septum (wall) between the *ventricles* that affects the blood circulation to the lungs and causes difficulty in breathing and a bluish tinge to the skin ("blue baby"). *Fallot's tetralogy* may have the same effect. More commonly, there is abnormal narrowness of the opening from the heart into the main artery (aorta), or a failure of the *ductus arteriosus* to close. Even in the case of the latter, there may be no symptoms at first. Hereditary factors are implicated in most forms of congenital heart disease.

congenital syphilis Condition of a newborn baby who, before being born, contracts *syphilis* from the bloodstream of the infected mother through the placenta. Symptoms may then appear at any time of life, but do so most commonly shortly after birth. They include blisters on the hands and feet, raised areas of skin around the genitals, nosebleed, and muscle weakness; there may also be serious complications, such as meningitis or mental retardation. Following an initial appearance later in childhood, symptoms may also include eye disorders, deformed dentition, and progressive deafness. Treatment with penicillin halts the progress of the disease at any stage.

congestion Accumulation of blood within a vessel or an organ, causing swelling. It results from an increased supply from the heart (as may occur with inflammation following infection) or from the partial or complete obstruction of a vein (as may occur with *thrombosis* or *heart failure*), and may or may not be associated with *oedema* (the accumulation of other fluids within the tissues).

conjunctiva Thin layer of mucous membrane that lines the *eyelids* (where it is well supplied with blood vessels) and covers the front of the eyeball (where it has very few, and is transparent) over the *cornea*.

conjunctivitis Inflammation of the *conjunctiva* (the delicate membrane covering the front of the eyeball) of one or both *eyes*. Causes are local infection (when the disorder is commonly called pink eye), irritation by fumes or dust, or allergic reaction. Symptoms are a red and swollen eyelid, watering of the eye, and discomfort; there may also be a discharge of pus. Vision, however, is usually undisturbed. Most cases get better spontaneously within a week or two. If infection is responsible, antibiotic eyedrops may be given.

connective tissue Generalized cellular tissue in the body which supports the organs, vessels and more specialized cells, retaining them in their places and minimizing friction between them. It basically consists of mucopolysaccharides, forming a "ground substance" in which there are fibres of *collagen* and other materials, and various large cells such as *macrophages*.

connective-tissue diseases Various conditions in which there is inflammation of *connective tissue* (the tissue that forms many of the supporting structures of the body, including bone, cartilage, ligaments and tendons), caused mainly by (or involving) the disruptive degeneration of the molecular structure of *collagen* (the strong, fibrous protein element of connective tissue). Aging by itself produces certain distortions in the three fibre-like strands that make up the collagen molecule, and – correspondingly – some of the effects of aging are thought to be caused by these distortions. They may also be associated with certain skin diseases and rheumatic disorders (including rheumatoid *arthritis*), in some of which the molecules are regarded as "foreign" by the immune system and attacked by the bodyís own defensive mechanisms (*autoimmune disease*). An example is *lupus* erythematosus.

consanguinity Closeness of a familial blood relationship over three or fewer generations.

consciousness State of somebody when awake, aware of the immediate environment, and able to use his or her intellect. In psychology, the term also includes the faculty of recalling past experiences and associations from the memory.

constipation Difficult, infrequent or painful *defecation*, or abnormal hardness of the *faeces* within the colon or rectum. Causes range from disruption of the *circadian rhythm* (normal daily rhythms) or lack of dietary *fibre*, to intestinal disorders or the use of certain drugs. If constipation represents a definite change in bowel habit, or if simple measures fail to ease the problem, medical advice should be sought. In general the condition is temporary and, if necessary, can be remedied by taking a *laxative* (a food or drug that promotes defecation). Increasing the amount of fibre in the diet often helps in persistent cases. Treatment in cases of intestinal disorders depends on the underlying cause.

constitution General word for the composition of the body, applied not only to body shape but also to overall health in relation to diet, exercise or any other factor.

consultant Doctor who, in a hospital or clinic (including an out-patients clinic), has the ultimate responsibility for the patients and their treatments. Consultancy is by appointment, following a number of years of hospital experience and successive passes in examinations, and a corresponding rise in status. Many consultants have additional private appointments in an advisory capacity.

consumption Old term for a disease that causes wasting of the muscles or noticeable loss of body weight, particularly *tuberculosis* of the lungs.

contact lens Form of *lens* used to correct visual defects that is placed on the front of the eyeball, in contact with the conjunctival membrane (and thus the *cornea*) except for a thin film of tear fluid. Some lenses also overlap the *sclera*. All move with the eyeball, and thus give better peripheral vision than ordinary *glasses*. They may be made of hard or soft material, some of which are gas-permeable, thus allowing more oxygen to pass through to the cornea and reducing the discomfort that some people find with contact lens wear. Ordinary reusable lenses require daily removal and sterilization; extended-wear lenses and disposable lenses are also available.

contagion Any disease that can be contracted by physical contact with an infected person (as opposed to diseases which are, for example, contracted only by breathing in airborne droplets exhaled by the person, by touching articles the person has touched, or by eating food contaminated by the person in some way).

continuous ambulatory peritoneal dialysis (CAPD) Method of *dialysis* (taking over the normal functions of the kidney), following permanent failure or surgical removal of the *kidneys*, that uses the *peritoneum* (the membrane that lines the abdominal cavity) as the membrane through which blood is filtered. It is used when, for whatever reason, the use of an *artificial kidney* (kidney machine) is not suitable. The patient is given a surgically implanted abdominal valve, through which filtration medium is infused to the peritoneal cavity to act as dialysing fluid and left for several hours (if necessary overnight), before being drained out. This performs a similar function to a kidney machine in ridding the blood of impurities, and allows considerably more freedom, but there is a risk of infection and possible peritonitis.

contraception Any method or device – including natural means, mechanical devices, drugs and surgery – that prevents *conception* following *sexual intercourse*. Natural methods include *coitus interruptus* (in which the man withdraws his penis from the womanís vagina before *ejaculation* – an unreliable method that is frustrating to both partners) and the rhythm method, which relies on assessing fertility, and avoiding sexual intercourse just before and during the probable time of peak fertility between menstrual periods. Since this is variable, this is a relatively unreliable method by itself, but the addition of more sophisticated means to predict ovulation – such as fertility thermometers and assessment of cervical mucus – can make it relatively efficient for people who are well-motivated and prepared to take the trouble. Contraceptive devices tend to represent either a barrier between *sperm* and *ovum*, or a means of preventing *implantation* of a fertilized ovum in the uterine wall. A common barrier device is the *condom* (or sheath), consisting of a rubber sheath for the manís penis (which must be withdrawn from the vagina before becoming completely flaccid or the condom may fall off); in combination with a spermicide, this method is quite reliable. Another barrier method is the diaphragm, fitted round the womanís *cervix* at the top of the vagina; it too is effective with a spermicide. A method of contraception thought to prevent implantation in some way is the intrauterine contraceptive device (IUCD, also known as the coil or loop), consisting of a thin, coiled length of plastic or metal-and-plastic sometimes impregnated with copper or hormones (and thus needing periodic renewal). This is inserted by a doctor into the womanís uterus. Although effective in many cases, some women find an IUCD causes heavy or painful periods; it is also linked with an increased risk of *pelvic inflammatory disease* and *ectopic pregnancy* (pregnancy outside the womb, often in a *Fallopian tube*), and the IUCD may be naturally expelled from the womb. The most common means of contraception, however, is with a *contraceptive drug*, particularly the contraceptive pill (popularly called "the Pill") and also injections, implants and skin patches. These alter the womanís hormonal balance so as to prevent *ovulation* (as though the woman were pregnant). There are many forms of contraceptive pill. All contain the hormone *progesterone*, and some also contain *oestrogen*. Prescription by a doctor for one or the other type depends on the womanís age and other factors. The Pill is the most reliable method of contraception (other than surgical *sterilization* of the man or the woman) provided it is taken regularly and extra precautions are used if for any reason its efficacy is likely to be reduced, such as while taking a course of antibiotics. As with all methods, there are sometimes individual reactions (particularly overall weight gain). Side-effects include a small increased risk of blood clotting (*thrombosis*) and heart disease and reduced fertility later on; against this, the Pill offers protection against various diseases including some types of *cancer*. Emergency postcoital contraception may be used after unprotected intercourse or following, say, condom failure. Special formulations of the contraceptive pill or a drug called mifepristone are effective up to 72 hours after intercourse, as is insertion of an IUCD up to five days afterwards.

contraceptive Method or device for *contraception*.

contraceptive drug Either the hormone *progesterone* (with or without the hormone *oestrogen*) as used in the method of *contraception* commonly called "the Pill"; or other more recently introduced forms of hormonal contraception including injections, implants, skin patches and hormone-impregnated devices inserted into the uterus or vagina. Injections, usually of a synthetic form of progesterone (a progestogen), have the same effect as the Pill over a much longer period; they need to be repeated every two or three months. An implant involves inserting a tiny rod under the skin, where it slowly releases progestogen into the body; it can last for up to three years before needing replacement. An intrauterine system, similar to an *intrauterine contraceptive device* (IUCD) and containing a progestogen designed for slow release, lasts for at least five years and has greater efficacy and fewer side-effects than traditional IUCDs.

contracture Permanent flexing (contraction) of a muscle because its tissues have shortened or shrunk. Causes include thickening and scarring through injury or disease, disuse of the muscle, and unknown factors. Treatment depends on the cause but may include remedial surgery. See also *Dupuytren's contracture*.

contrecoup Form of injury to the brain that results from a blow on the opposite side of the head.

contusion Medical term for a *bruise*.

convalescence Period of relaxed healing and recovery after an acute illness or a surgical operation. Convalescent patients may need considerable reassurance and mental support, as well as physical assistance. Eating and exercise may be monitored.

conversion In psychiatry, the manifestation of physical symptoms representing a mental disturbance. It is believed to result from inner conflict or repressed drives, and in extreme forms can lead to conversion disorder (formerly known as hysteria), in which severe physical dysfunction – for example, paralysis or blindness – is present despite a lack of physical factors or disorders to account for it.

convulsion Muscle spasm involving many of the bodyís muscles, actuated by the brain. Generally, there is a whole series of such spasms that cause jerking of limbs and contortions of the face; there may also be loss of consciousness (which, if the convulsions continue, may be dangerous to the patient). Causes include grand mal *epilepsy*, *meningitis* (or other infection of the brain and surrounding tissues), very high temperature, poisoning, *toxaemia of pregnancy*, brain injury, *diabetes* mellitus, and *arteriosclerosis*.

coprolàlia Mental disorder in which somebody continually speaks obscenely.

copulation *Sexual intercourse* between a man and a woman.

cordotomy Severing of the nerve fibres within the spinal cord that transmit sensations of pain from the pelvis and lower limbs, performed in order to spare the patient further suffering.

corium Another name for the *dermis*, the outer layer of the skin.

corn Type of deep, painful *callus* on the skin on top of the joint of a toe, usually caused by ill-fitting shoes that rub the toe and force it to bend. Eventually, the tissue becomes dead and horny. Treatment in the early stages is to soak the corn in hot water or apply softening agents – and to wear larger shoes. A persistent corn may be treated by a chiropodist.

cornea Transparent outer layer of the front of the eyeball, attached to the *sclera* at its edges, and in turn covered by the thin coating of the *conjunctiva*. The *iris* and the *pupil* are visible through them. The cornea refracts incoming light through the eyeís aqueous humour to the *lens* (which then further refracts it towards the retina). Although it has no blood vessels it is surprisingly sensitive to pain – so much so that even an implied threat to it closes the eyelids by reflex action. Also because it has no blood vessels (and there is thus very little chance of tissue rejection) it is a very successful subject of transplant surgery (*corneal graft*).

corneal graft Lay term for *keratoplasty*.

coronary artery Either of two arteries that branch from the *aorta* to supply the muscle of the heart itself with blood. Unlike any other arteries, they are responsive to the amount of carbon dioxide or oxygen they contain. If there is insufficient oxygen, they dilate; if they dilate their furthest and there is still not enough oxygen, the pain of *angina pectoris* is felt. Damage or obstruction in them causes *coronary artery disease*.

coronary artery disease Effects of damage to the heart muscle that results from a reduction in the supply of blood by the *coronary arteries*. The most common cause is disease of the arteries (*arteriosclerosis* or atherosclerosis), giving rise to narrowing, which impairs blood flow. This may be symptomless at first, or may cause *angina pectoris* (chest pain on exertion) due to poor circulation at times of increased demand or – particularly if *thrombosis* (blood clotting) also occurs at the site of damage within the artery wall – may cut off blood flow altogether and cause a *myocardial infarction* or *heart attack*. Treatment depends on severity of the disease. Angina may be relieved or prevented with drugs, and reducing risk factors (for example, by stopping smoking, modifying the diet or taking exercise under supervision) may keep the condition manageable. If not, surgery may be required. Sometimes narrowed segments of artery can be dilated (expanded) by a special catheter (tube) passed through a blood vessel into the heart, where a tiny balloon is inflated within the coronary artery, a procedure known as coronary angioplasty. In other cases a coronary artery bypass graft may be required to replace a diseased segment of coronary artery with a non-essential blood vessel grafted from elsewhere in the body; this generally involves major surgery to open the chest wall, although new techniques are being developed to avoid this. If a heart attack does occur, emergency treatment is essential, and may include drugs to dissolve the blood clot (*thrombolysis*). Once the patient is stable, subsequent management is as for angina.

coronary by-pass Surgical operation to replace a section of part of one of the *coronary arteries* that has become inefficient (because of *arteriosclerosis*), or to replace a *valve* in either of the heartís *ventricles*.

coronary heart disease Another name for *coronary artery disease*.

coronary thrombosis Presence of a blood clot (thrombus) in one of the two *coronary arteries* that supply blood to the heart muscle. The resultant obstruction of the blood flow causes the death (infarction) of part of the heart, with the correspondingly serious effect of a heart attack (*myocardial infarction*). The cause is usually the gradual build-up of fatty tissue (*atheroma*) in the blood vessels, which may have been indicated by bouts of *angina pectoris*. Emergency treatment is essential. Recovery may be slow, but careful monitoring of diet and exercise is often beneficial.

coroner Official appointed by government authority to preside over all *inquests* in a particular region. The coroner must be a lawyer or a medical practitioner of at least five years standing.

cor pulmonale Swelling of the right *ventricle* of the *heart* because of a backflow of blood from the lungs or from the artery taking blood to the lungs. Causes include *emphysema* of the lungs, *obesity*, *congenital heart disease* or other forms of heart disease. Treatment depends on the cause.

corpus callosum Thick bundle of about 300 million nerve fibres in the brain that lies in the gap between the two *cerebral hemispheres* and acts as the connection between them.

corpuscle Any small, relatively independent body within a tissue or organ – especially a (red or white) *blood cell*.

corpus luteum Specialized tissue that forms at the site of a ruptured *ovarian follicle* after a mature *ovum* has been released from an ovary at *ovulation*. The tissue produces and secretes the hormone *progesterone*, which prepares the uterus (womb) for the possible implantation of a *blastocyst* following *conception*. If conception does not occur, the corpus luteum ceases to produce the hormone and degenerates. If it does occur, the corpus luteum continues producing progesterone until the fourth month of pregnancy, at which time the *placenta* takes over this function.

cortex Outer layer of an organ or area of tissue; the inner layer is the *medulla*.

Corti, Alfonso (1822–1888) Italian anatomist who specialized in research into the ear. Named after him are the *organ of Corti* – the major sensory organ of *hearing* – and the canal, membrane and tunnel of Corti, all in the ear.

corticosteroid Any of several *steroid hormones* produced by the cortex (outer part) of the *adrenal glands*, which are located on top of the kidneys. There are two main types: *glucocorticoid hormones* (which contribute to stress responses and assist in the metabolism of food) and mineralocorticoids (which monitor and control the balance of water and salt in the body). Examples of glucocorticoids, many of which are now synthesized as drugs, are *cortisone* and *hydrocortisone*; an example of a mineralocorticoid is *aldosterone*.

corticotrophin Abbreviation of *adrenocorticotropic hormone*.

cortisol A steroid hormone produced by the adrenal cortex (the outer part of each adrenal gland, which sits upon the kidney on each side). It is involved in carbohydrate metabolism and is released particularly during stress; long-term raised levels may be damaging. The drug *hydrocortisone* is a manufactured version of cortisol.

cortisone *Glucocorticoid hormone* produced and secreted by the cortex (outer part) of the *adrenal glands*. It remains inert in the body, however, until converted into *hydrocortisone* in the liver. Synthesized in a laboratory and administered as a drug, it therefore has the same effects as hydrocortisone. Long-term use – especially if taken to improve athletic performance – may cause serious side-effects.

coryza Medical term for the common *cold*.

cosmetic surgery *Plastic surgery* undertaken to improve the appearance. It may be performed to repair or conceal a congenital malformation (such as a hare lip or a particularly prominent birthmark) or deforming injury (as after serious burns); or it may merely be an attempt at rejuvenation.

costal Pertaining to, or in the area of, the *ribs*.

cot death Another name for *sudden infant death syndrome*.

cough Expulsion of *mucus* and irritant particles from the bronchial passages and the *larynx* through (or at least as far as) the throat, using air from the lungs previously built up to pressure behind the *vocal cords*. It is most commonly voluntary, but as an involuntary reflex a cough may also be stimulated by inflammation of the air passages, or by pressure from the adjacent *lymph nodes* if they are swollen (as with whooping cough), even when there is no mucus or dust to expel. Treatment may be with drugs to promote the formation of mucus (*expectorants*), to soothe irritation or inflammation (syrups and *linctuses*), or to suppress the coughing centre in the brain (*antitussives*).

Cowper's glands Two small glands, situated below a manís *prostate gland* and connected by a short duct to the *urethra*, that contribute to seminal fluid (*semen*). They are named after the English anatomist William Cowper (1666–1709).

cowpox Viral infection of cows that can be transmitted through direct contact with their udders to humans. It is caused by an organism so similar to the one that causes smallpox that an attack of cowpox confers immunity to smallpox, a fact that led Edward *Jenner* to discover *vaccination*. Symptoms are a mild rash of pus-filled blisters, which quickly fade.

Coxsackie virus Any of a type of about 30 viruses that infect and multiply within the cells of the intestine. For many years their effect was unknown, and they were called "orphans", as reflected in their older name, echo viruses, standing for enteric cytopathic human orphan (virus). It is now known that some types may cause infections, ranging from severe throat infections or the chest pain of *Bornholm disease* to *meningitis* (inflammation of the membranes around the brain) or *encephalitis* (inflammation of the brain), as well as damage to heart muscle and other effects; they are also suspected of involvement in childhood *diabetes* and *motor neurone disease*.

CPR Abbreviation of *cardiopulmonary resuscitation*.

crab louse Type of *louse* that attaches itself to body hair, particularly in the pubic region. Crab lice live on cellular debris on the skin surface; their bites are occasionally mildly irritant, but they do not transmit disease. The lice themselves may be transmitted by close body contact or by contact with hairs that have been shed. Infestation with the lice is known medically as *pediculosis*.

cramp Tingling, painful spasm of a muscle or group of muscles. Causes include a low level of sodium (salt) in the body, overexertion, reduced blood supply, and unknown factors. The condition usually wears off fairly quickly, especially if the affected muscle is stretched. Cramp in the leg that passes away after rest (*intermittent claudication*), or similarly in the heart muscle (*angina pectoris*), requires medical diagnosis to investigate and treat any underlying cause.

cranial nerves Twelve pairs of nerves that lead from the brain out through apertures in the skull, nearly all to parts of the head and neck. They are referred to by a Roman numeral or name, as follows: I, *olfactory nerve* (sense of smell); II, *optic nerve* (sense of vision); III, *oculomotor nerve* (eye movements); IV, trochlear nerve (eye movements); V, *trigeminal nerve* (sensory nerve of the face); VI, abducens nerve (eye movements); VII, *facial nerve* (motor and sensory nerve of the lower face, tongue and salivary glands); VIII, *auditory nerve* (hearing and balance); IX, *glossopharyngeal nerve* (tasting and swallowing); X, *vagus nerve* (supplying the *parasympathetic nervous system*); XI, spinal accessory nerve (rotation of the head on the neck); and XII, hypoglossal nerve (tongue movements). Disorder in any of the nerves produces symptoms in the organs they serve.

cranium Eight fused bones of the *skull* that together enclose the brain.

creatine Nitrogen-containing product of the metabolism of proteins, important in the functioning of muscles. The formation of creatine phosphate in a muscle produces energy in a form that can be stored; muscle contraction removes the phosphate, leaving creatine once more. The waste product of this process (creatinine) is excreted in the urine.

cremation Incineration of a corpse.

crepitation Crackling or grating noise heard through a stethoscope placed over inflamed lungs, produced either by air bubbles in fluid or by the *alveoli* (tiny air sacs) opening forcibly as air is inhaled. The noise, known medically as a rale, may be used as an aid to diagnosis.

crepitus Either the grating noise of two bones rubbing together in an arthritic joint, or the same as *crepitation*.

cretinism Set of symptoms that result from congenital *hypothyroidism*. They consist of restricted growth (*dwarfism*), *mental retardation*, and coarse facial features and skin; the expression is generally vacant, with drooling. Treatment with supplements of the *thyroid* *hormone* thyroxine, initiated within the first six weeks of life, may allow the patient to grow and develop normally.

Creutzfeldt-Jakob Disease (CJD) A fatal brain disease, formerly rare and occurring mostly in older people, but recently appearing in young people and linked with a similar disease, *bovine spongiform encephalopathy* (BSE), in cattle. Both conditions are caused by newly recognized infectious agents called prions, which survive normal methods of decontamination by heat, chemicals or radiation. Cattle became infected through the use of animal ingredients in their feedstuffs in the 1980s, a practice that has now been stopped. However, it is believed that material from infected cattle may have entered the human food supply, or have been used in the production of drugs, vaccines and cosmetics, before controls were introduced to stop this. Because the incubation period (the time between infection and symptoms) of CJD can be many years, scientists are still unsure how many people may be at risk of developing the disease. Symptoms include twitching, loss of balance and coordination, and rapidly progressing *dementia* that is ultimately fatal. There is no treatment other than to keep patients as comfortable as possible.

crib death American term for cot death. See *sudden infant death syndrome*.

Crick, Francis H.C. (1916–) English biophysicist who with James *Watson* used the X-ray crystallographic studies of Maurice *Wilkins* to determine the molecular structure of the nucleic acids, specifically *deoxyribonucleic acid* (DNA). All three men were awarded a Nobel Prize in 1962 for their work.

crisis Peak in the intensity of symptoms, which may constitute a turning point for the better or for the worse.

Crohn's disease Serious disorder of the small intestine, particularly of the *ileum* where it joins the caecum. Parts of the intestinal wall become inflamed and may ulcerate; where folds of the intestine touch each other, small fissures break through from one fold to another. In an acute form, the condition may appear similar to appendicitis; in a chronic form, there may be partial intestinal obstruction, leading to diarrhoea, pain and the malabsorption of food. The cause is unknown but may be an infectious agent related to the mycobacterium that causes *tuberculosis*. The condition is named after the American gastroenterologist Burrill B. Crohn, who first described it in 1932. Treatment is to relieve the symptoms, and generally includes antibiotics and other drugs, sometimes corticosteroids, and bed rest; surgery may be necessary to remove the affected segment of intestine.

cross-eye Common name for a *squint*.

cross-infection Infection in a clinic or hospital ward of one patient by another.

croup Inflammation of the *larynx* (the part of the throat containing the vocal cords), which, in young children (aged between six and thirty months), leads to partial obstruction of the air passages. Breathing becomes laboured and noisy; there is a high temperature and a barking cough. The cause is usually a viral infection, but this may be complicated by secondary bacterial infection. Treatment is generally by humidifying the environment. In cases of secondary infection, antibiotics may be required. Very rarely, obstruction of the airways may necessitate surgery to restore proper breathing.

crutch Wooden or metal support that helps the arms to take the weight off an injured (or missing) leg when walking; or the part of the body between the legs (medical name *perineum*).

cryosurgery Method of tissue destruction that involves very localized freezing. The instrument used is a cryoprobe; its tip is so fine that one of the most common sites for its use is in the lens of the eye (to remove cataracts).

cryotherapy Use of cold, but not freezing cold, as a form of treatment. Hypothermia may be deliberately induced during surgery, for instance, to decrease a patientís oxygen requirement.

cryptorchidism Congenital abnormality that involves the retention of a boyís *testes* (testicles) within the abdominal cavity, leaving the *scrotum* virtually empty at birth. The condition does not really matter much until close on puberty (by which time, in many cases, the testes have descended of their own accord), but normal development at that time requires the testes to be properly sited, and surgery may be performed to do this if the testes can be located. The possession of only one testis is called monorchidism.

CT scan Abbreviation of *computerized tomography*.

culture Laboratory growth of *bacteria* (or another kind of micro-organism) in a special environment. Long used in the preparation of vaccines and antibiotics, bacterial cultures are now important for experiments into the commercial and medical applications of *genetic engineering*. A tissue culture is the similarly produced growth of living tissue (such as skin) taken from a patient.

cupping Medical practice of former centuries, involving the placing of a heated cup over the skin near a wound or inflamed organ, leaving it to cool, and so causing a partial vacuum within the cup that drew the skin upwards underneath it, also drawing an increased blood supply to the area.

curette Spoon-shaped scraping instrument, used to peel off cells from a surface for medical analysis or as a treatment (as in *dilatation and curettage*).

Cushing's syndrome Disorder of the *adrenal glands* (endocrine, that is, hormone-producing glands sitting on top of the kidneys), which makes them produce excessive amounts of corticosteroid hormones. Causes include prolonged use of steroid drugs, unknown factors, a benign or cancerous tumour in the adrenal glands, or a tumour in the pituitary gland (which secretes the hormones that stimulate the adrenal glands into production). Symptoms include fatness of the face, neck and torso (although the limbs remain thin), increased hair growth, weakness and fatigue; there are also usually striations (stripes) on the skin and a reduced sexual drive. Complications include high blood pressure, bone thinning and sometimes mental changes. The condition is named after the American surgeon Harvey Cushing (1869–1939). Treatment depends on the cause. If a tumour is responsible, this is usually removed by surgery, sometimes also with radiotherapy and hormone supplements.

cuticle Outer layer of the skin (epidermis) in all its forms, including the hardened skin that surrounds a nail, and the outer layer of cells on a hair or tooth.

cyanocobalamin Vitamin B_{12}, a water-soluble *vitamin* important to the functioning of nerve cells and to the maintenance of red blood cells. Deficiency of it in the diet results in *anaemia* and nerve disorders. Good dietary sources include meat, eggs, fish and dairy products. Absorption of the vitamin in the body, however, requires what is known as the "intrinsic factor" to be present as a stomach secretion; a person born without this factor develops *pernicious anaemia*.

cyanosis Bluish coloration of the skin and lips caused by lack of oxygen in the blood. It is a symptom of many disorders, particularly of the lungs and heart. Treatment depends on the cause.

cyclothymia Fluctuations of mood that are abnormal in their decisiveness, yet not as exaggerated as those of *manic-depressive illness*. The condition represents a form of *personality disorder* that often responds to psychiatric counselling.

cyst Fluid-filled sac or swelling. There are many types, some forming spontaneously (as in the skin or ovaries) or through irritation (as by broken teeth), some through blockage of ducts (as with *sebaceous cysts*), some containing various forms of parasitic organisms, and some corresponding to a type of cancer. Treatment, when required, depends on diagnosis.

cystic duct Another name for the *bile duct*.

cystic fibrosis Hereditary disease that causes *exocrine glands* (mucus- and sweat-producing glands) to produce abnormally thick *mucus*. The cause is a recessive gene, meaning both parents must carry the gene to produce an affected child. Only those with two defective genes, one from each parent, have symptoms; those with one defective gene are symptomless carriers of the condition. Organs affected include the liver, lungs, gut and pancreas, with the result that passages in which mucus is normally present may then become congested. Symptoms include the malabsorption of food and recurrent respiratory problems. Treatment is to relieve the symptoms as far as possible, and may include replacement pancreatic enzymes and physiotherapy to clear mucus from the lungs. Genetic counselling is offered to carrier parents. In severe cases, a heart-lung transplant may be offered. In future, gene therapy may be able to correct the underlying problem.

cystitis Inflammation of the (urinary) *bladder*, most commonly caused by bacterial infection and less common in men than in women (who have a shorter *urethra* – the passage from the bladder to the outside – for bacteria to penetrate). Symptoms are increased frequency of urination, cloudy urine, and usually pain or a burning sensation on passing urine; there may also be a high temperature, abdominal cramp and blood in the urine. Treatment may consist solely of flushing the infection out by drinking large volumes of water; alternatively, *antibiotics* or *sulphonamide* drugs may be prescribed. While the condition lasts, special care with hygiene should be observed.

cytoplasm Jelly-like contents of a cell, in which the organelles "float".

cytotoxic drugs Drugs that destroy or prevent the replication of cells. They are used mainly to treat *cancer*. Most may also affect normal cells in the body, and so dosage has to be very carefully controlled and monitored.

D

dacryocystitis Inflammation of the lacrimal sac, the reservoir under the inner corner of each eye, in which the fluid that constantly bathes the eyes and forms tears accumulates before draining into the *nasal cavity*. The cause is usually an infection from the eye or nose. Symptoms are pain and inflammation at the corner of the eye, watering, and sometimes a discharge of pus. Treatment is with antibiotic eye drops.

D and C Abbreviation of *dilatation and curettage*.

dandruff Greasy scaling of the scalp in which flakes of dead skin accumulate among the hairs and may brush or fall off. About half of all individuals have troublesome dandruff, which has been linked with the presence of a yeast, *Pityrosporum ovale* (a type of fungal infection), on the scalp. The medical name is pityriasis capitis. Treatment is with antidandruff lotions or shampoos containing tar, selenium sulphide or antifungal drugs.

Darwin, Charles R. (1809–1882) English naturalist and biologist who first publicly suggested the theory of natural selection ("survival of the fittest") as the major means of the evolutionary adaptation of species. Controversial as this was at the time, it virtually refounded the study of biology on a scientific basis.

day hospital Form of clinic or sanatorium in which medical care and therapy is given only during normal working hours; patients do not stay overnight. Most patients of day hospitals are those suffering the problems of old age or mental illness, in which perhaps care and supervision are more important than medical treatment.

deafness Serious impairment, or total failure, of the sense of *hearing*. There are two main types of deafness. Conductive deafness arises when there is a blockage or failure in the conduction of sound vibrations from the outer ear to the auditory nerve (which leads from the *inner ear* to the brain), as may be caused by *otitis* media (infection of the *middle ear*) or certain degenerative conditions of the inner ear. Perceptive (or nerve) deafness (also called sensorineural deafness) is caused by damage to the *cochlea*, auditory nerve (the inner ear or nerve from the ear to the brain), or to the interpretive centre in the brain, as may be caused by infection with *rubella* (German measles) before birth, injury, long-term noise, or disease (such as *Ménière's disease*). Diagnosis of the type of deafness is by means of various tests using tuning forks; testing of severity is by means of an audiogram that measures the ability to hear different sound frequencies. Both types of deafness can be alleviated with a *hearing aid*. In some types of severe deafness, hearing can now be partially restored by means of a cochlear implant, an artificial hearing device surgically inserted into the ear.

death Cessation of life, traditionally defined as permanent cessation of heartbeat and respiration. In law a diagnosis of *brain death* (when no brain activity is detectable, especially in the areas of the brain that normally control vital functions) now allows death to be certified (and organs to be taken for donation, if appropriate) even if the heart is still beating and the personís breathing is maintained artificially. When death is unexpected, violent, or of unknown cause, a *post mortem* may be conducted by a pathologist, the findings of which may be presented at an *inquest*. Usually, however, the cause of death is known or unsuspicious, and the deceasedís own doctor signs a death certificate.

DeBakey, Michael (1908–) American surgeon and practical pioneer of new techniques in the field of cardiovascular disorders. He was the first to use synthetic materials successfully to replace diseased arteries, and he invented an auxiliary pump system to help the heart function during convalescence.

debility Abnormal physical weakness affecting the whole body.

decibel Unit of power or intensity, particularly of sound (and thus understood as a measure of sound volume). It is usually abbreviated to dB. Silence is 0 dB; ordinary speech is generally rated at 50 dB. Long-term exposure to sound at more than 100 dB can cause perceptive *deafness*.

deciduous teeth Also called milk teeth, the first set of *teeth* which erupt during the first two-and-a-half years of life. There are twenty: eight *incisors*, four *canines*, and eight *molars* (no premolars, as with the permanent dentition). The second set of teeth begin to appear about the age of six, but may not have completed eruption until the age of thirteen or so; *wisdom teeth* (the third molars) appear later still. In rare cases, there is no second set, and the deciduous teeth remain functional well into adulthood and perhaps into old age.

decompression sickness Painful and potentially dangerous disorder caused when somebody who has been breathing air at high pressure (such as a deep-sea diver) returns too rapidly to normal atmospheric pressure. The nitrogen in solution in the bloodstream expands and forms bubbles that may hinder or even block the circulation in the small arteries. Joint pain and paralysis may occur, and permanent damage may be caused to the brain, heart or lungs. Decompression sickness is also known as "the bends", caisson disease, and compressed-air illness. Treatment is an immediate return to the former high-pressure environment (or its equivalent in a pressure chamber) so that the nitrogen redissolves. Slow depressurization ("decompression") should then allow the person to return gradually and comfortably to normal.

decongestant Drug or other agent taken – often in the form of a spray or drops – to clear mucus from a passage or cavity (such as the *nasal cavity*). Long-term use of a decongestant may be harmful to the mucous membranes.

decubitus ulcer Medical name for a *bedsore*.

deep vein thrombosis (DVT) A blood clot that forms in the calf veins when blood flow is sluggish or the bloodís tendency to clot is increased. The medical term is phlebothrombosis. Causes include impaired circulation to the legs from prolonged immobility, resulting from a surgical operation or a period of bed rest, as well as heart failure, pregnancy and the contraceptive pill. The leg becomes swollen and sore, and there is a risk that the clot may break off, travel through the bloodstream (embolize) and become lodged in the lungs (pulmonary embolus, see *thromboembolism*), which can be fatal. Anticoagulant drugs are given to treat an established thrombosis, and occasionally surgery may be required to remove a large clot. Drugs to reduce clotting may be given before prolonged operations to reduce the risk, and recovering patients are encouraged to become mobile or to do leg exercises to stimulate blood flow.

defecation Process and action of evacuating *faeces* from the *rectum* through the *anus* (or, when the intestine has been brought surgically to the surface elsewhere in the abdomen, at the site of an *ileostomy* or *colostomy*). The normal process relies on *peristalsis* within the *colon*, the use of voluntary muscles in the pelvic floor, and the relaxation of the tight muscular ring (sphincter) of the anus. Impaction of faeces causing difficulty in defecation is *constipation*; frequent defecation of rather liquid faeces is *diarrhoea*.

defibrillation Restoration of the heartís natural heartbeat rhythm after the chaotic heartbeat of ventricular *fibrillation*. A *defibrillator* is used to give an electric shock through the chest wall.

defibrillator Device that administers electric shocks to the heart in order to achieve *defibrillation*. Electrodes may be placed on the skin over the heart or, during a surgical operation, on the heart itself.

deficiency disorders Disorders caused either by the lack of one or more essential dietary constituents – such as fats (and particularly fatty acids), carbohydrates (sugars), proteins, vitamins or trace elements – or by a failure of the body to metabolize one or more of these constituents correctly. Deficiency disorders caused by inadequate diet include *anaemia, beriberi, goitre, malnutrition, osteomalacia, rickets* and *scurvy*. In all cases, treatment is to make up the deficiency. Failure of metabolism may be due to hereditary factors (absence of specific *enzymes*), inappropriate excretion in wastes (urine or faeces), parasitic infestation, or vómiting. Treatment depends on the cause. See also *vitamin deficiency*.

deformity Abnormality of the tissues, especially of the bones. The term is used mainly of the results of injury or disease; a congenital structural abnormality is more often described as a *malformation*.

degeneration Progressive deterioration of a cellís capacity for fulfilling its function. Rather than disintegrating, most cells in a state of degeneration are unable to get rid of cell products such as fat or calcium salts, and so expand as the products accumulate. Fats and fibrous tissues may thus build up in the body, and the cells eventually become inert. Causes of degeneration include reduced blood supply, disease, inadequate or inappropriate diet, alcoholism and anaemia.

dehydration Insufficiency of water in the body. Causes include excessive sweating in unaccustomedly high temperatures or through fever, diarrhoea or vomiting, diseases that promote urination (such as diabetes), and fluid loss following injury or surgery. Symptoms are thirst, possibly followed by nausea, muscle cramps, constipation and lethargy. Treatment is with small quantities of water at frequent intervals; the addition of a little salt is often beneficial. Treatment of any underlying cause is essential.

déjà vu Strong impression that an event being witnessed has happened before, down to precise details. A common illusion, experienced at one time or another by most people, it is sometimes said nevertheless to be a symptom of certain forms of epilepsy.

delirium State of confusion and excitement that accompanies high fever and other forms of organic disorders that affect the brain. Mental activity is completely disorganized: there is no sequence of thought, and there may be *hallucinations*. Causes include serious infections, heart failure, malnutrition, and overdoses of drugs (such as alcohol).

delirium tremens Potentially dangerous form of *delirium* that mostly affects patients who are or have been alcoholics; it also affects heroin addicts. It occurs particularly at times when, through injury or disease, patients are not supplied with what they have become dependent on – but the symptoms are no longer thought to be entirely due to *withdrawal*. The symptoms include extreme anxiety, tremor, high temperature, nausea, insomnia, and vivid and terrible *hallucinations*. Treatment is with sedatives, bed rest, and therapy to lessen the patientís *dependence*.

delivery Another name for *childbirth*. Technically, however, the term refers solely to the third stage of *labour* – the delivery of the *afterbirth*, consisting mostly of the *placenta*, finally expelled from the uterus (womb) within half an hour or so after childbirth.

deltoid muscle Large triangular muscle firmly rooted on the collarbone (clavicle) and attached to the shoulderblade (scapula), that stretches from the point of the shoulder half-way down the outer side of the upper arm bone (humerus). Its function is to lift the arm out from the body.

delusion Belief and insistence that something exists when it plainly does not nor could ever exist. It differs from an *illusion*, which is an impression that something exists but is quickly corrected if it is not so. And it differs again from a *hallucination*, which is an impression that something exists because there is sensory evidence of it (although that evidence may be faulty). Delusions tend to centre on a patientís anxieties or hopes about what other people think of him or her, and may thus be delusions of persecution or of grandeur. They are symptoms of *psychosis*.

dementia Complete disruption of the mental processes so that rational thought is no longer possible. The condition is generally reached gradually but progressively as a result of organic changes in the brain tissue, usually in the form of cell *degeneration*. Such changes may be caused by "old age" (senile dementia) at any age from about 60, or by unknown factors before that age (presenile dementia, including *Alzheimer's disease*) from about age 40, or by injury, infection, poisoning, or any disease that results in a reduced blood supply to the brain over a long period. In a few cases the condition is reversible. Most of those affected will undergo progressive decline, although modern drug treatments may slow this and alleviate some of the symptoms.

demography Statistical study of a population or a community. Specific subjects for statistical investigation include birth rates, death rates, racial composition and social factors.

demyelination Structural damage to the *myelin* sheath surrounding the *axon* of a *neurone* (nerve cell). In major nerves, demyelination may result in loss of motor or sensory function. The cause may be serious disease of the nervous system (such as *multiple sclerosis*), a stroke, or head injury. Treatment depends on the cause.

dendrite Any of a number of "arms" branching from the cell body of a *neurone* (nerve cell), all of which receive nerve impulses. Each dendrite is in near-contact with the *axon* of another cell at a *synapse*.

denervation Loss of motor or sensory function in a nerve supplying the muscles or the skin. The result is immobility and numbness in the area, and the replacement of the wasting muscle tissue with fat. Causes include injury and serious disease of the nervous system; treatment depends on diagnosis.

dengue Potentially dangerous viral disease of tropical regions, carried by a mosquito. Symptoms are high temperature, an irritating skin rash, severe pain in the joints (giving the condition its alternative name of "breakbone fever"), headache and watering eyes. They last for about three days, fade and then recur in a milder form. Treatment is to alleviate the symptoms as much as possible. Convalescence may take several weeks.

dental brace A device used in *orthodontics* consisting of a metal binding attached to the teeth for a period of time in order to realign them.

dental caries Medical name for *tooth decay*.

dental clinic Another name for a *dental surgery*.

dental hygienist Medical auxiliary who, under the supervision of a fully qualified dentist, carries out the process of scaling patientsí teeth of *plaque* and other debris following (or sometimes before) dental treatment, and assists the dentist in various other ways. A dental hygienist may also advise patients on the importance of oral hygiene.

dental surgery Specially prepared room or rooms – or a department in a hospital – in which a dentist examines and treats patientsí teeth (and possibly gums). Equipment includes hand tools, water supply and drainage, a variety of drilling equipment (also used for polishing and scaling), and usually an X-ray machine.

dental technician Operative in a dental laboratory or hospital (especially the *orthodontics* department) who constructs crowns, bridges, *dentures* and *dental braces* – first making wax impressions and plaster models – or fits new teeth on existing dentures.

dentine Main substance in a tooth, covered by enamel at the top (crown) and sides of the tooth and by cementum at the root. From the pulp at the centre there are short nerve endings inset into the hard dentine.

dentist Medical and surgical specialist in the care and treatment of teeth, gums, jaws and other structures of the mouth. A fully qualified dentist is registered as a practitioner by the countryís dental authority – in the UK the General Dental Council. Specialties within dentistry include *orthodontics*.

dentition Number and arrangement of *teeth* in the upper and lower jaws. The *deciduous teeth* (milk teeth), a maximum of twenty, are the first set of temporary teeth, erupting from about six months of age. The permanent teeth, totalling thirty-two after the eruption of the *wisdom teeth*, come through at any age from about six years. The manner in which the teeth of the upper and lower jaws meet is called *occlusion* (and a misaligned bite is a malocclusion).

dentures False teeth. The teeth are made of very hard plastic and attached either to a series of metal bands that wrap around individual adjacent (real) teeth, or to a plastic "plate" that may cover a larger area around the gums. Most dentures are removable for daily cleaning.

deoxyribonucleic acid (DNA) Basic substance of the *genes* in the nuclei of the *cells* that thus is also the basic unit of life. Of the two nucleic acids – *ribonucleic acid* (RNA) is the other – DNA is in human beings by far the more significant. The genetic information that the genes carry is represented by specific sequences of the four bases (adenine, guanine, thymine and cytosine) linked by hydrogen bonds in the two strands of DNAís double-helix molecular structure. This *genetic code* forms the purpose of each cell – to replicate, to produce protein, to generate a nerve impulse – whatever the code directs. Very rarely, there are faults or anomalies in the code, which may result in a *mutation*.

dependence Effects of addiction. Physical dependence produces a mental compulsion to continue taking the addictive substance – often in increasing dosage as tolerance builds up

– and *withdrawal* symptoms (some of which may be extremely unpleasant) if the supply is not available. This kind of dependence may result from taking "hard drugs" such as cocaine and heroin, and from excessive alcohol consumption. Treatment is notoriously difficult. More common is psychological dependence, in which there is still a mental compulsion (generally because the addictive substance produces such a euphoria that ordinary life pales by comparison) but there are no withdrawal symptoms if supply dries up. This type of dependence is produced by "soft drugs" such as amphetamines and barbiturates, and by cigarette smoking. Treatment, as with physical dependence, depends on the patientís own motivation, but may also include psychiatric counselling or hypnosis.

depersonalization State of anxiety in which an individual feels as if the mind is separating from the body, or that one of the two is unreal. If this state becomes more than mere (temporary) anxiety brought on by stress, it may indicate a psychological disorder.

depilatory Substance or method for removing unwanted hair either temporarily (generally using creams) at the skin surface, or permanently (using *electrolysis*) by destroying the follicles.

depressant Drug or agent that acts to reduce the level of function of any part of the body. Many such drugs act on specific centres of the brain (to produce anaesthesia, for example, or analgesia).

depression State of mind dominated by feelings of despair and worthlessness. This may be accompanied by lethargy and disinterest in eating or sleeping. The condition is natural in certain circumstances (such as recent bereavement, or the final frustration of long-held hopes) but is abnormal in the absence of such circumstances or if it is prolonged for an undue time. Untreated, it may lead to suicide. Other effects may include neurotic behaviour and even *manic-depressive illness* (where periods of depression alternate with manic phases during which the person is elated, impulsive and sometimes takes irrational risks). Treatment is with *antidepressant* drugs; psychiatric counselling and particularly cognitive therapy may be beneficial; occasionally a patient may undergo *electroconvulsive therapy* (ECT).

dermatitis Inflammation of the skin surface, with redness and itching, caused by external agents (unlike eczema, in which similar skin changes occur as a result of an internal tendency; both terms are, however, often used interchangeably). Primary irritant dermatitis is due to substances that irritate the skin, such as detergents or caustic substances, to which anyone exposed to a sufficient degree is vulnerable. Allergic contact dermatitis is due to individual sensitivity to particular substances, for example, nickel. The best treatment is to cease exposure to the cause. Where this is not possible, scrupulous drying of hands and the use of barrier creams may avoid flare-ups.

dermatology Study of the composition, diseases and disorders of the skin.

dermatome Area of the skin supplied by any one of the major spinal or cranial nerves. (It is most commonly only one of these areas that is affected by *shingles*, producing a "stripe" of inflamed skin). Such bands of skin represent the progressive method of tissue growth in the early embryo. The term is used also for a special kind of surgical knife employed in tissue grafts.

dermis Second of the two layers of skin, under the *epidermis* but lying on top of the thin basal membrane. In its thick single stratum of connective tissue lie sensory nerve endings, blood capillaries, lymph vessels, tiny muscle fibres, sweat glands, sebaceous glands and hair follicles. An alternative (but rarely used) name for it is the corium.

desalination Loss of salt in the body through sweating. It is an effect of *heat exhaustion.*

desensitization Method of treatment in which a patient is exposed repeatedly to something to which he or she is particularly sensitive, until a degree of tolerance is established and built up. The method is effective with both physical sensitivity (as with *allergies*) and mental (as with *phobias*, in *behaviour therapy*), although patients may find the process punishing.

detached retina Dislodgement of part or all of the *retina* of the eye from the backing stratum of the *choroid.* It most commonly occurs after a hole has been formed in the retina, through which some of the vitreous humour (the jelly-like substance between the lens and the retina) seeps in to cause a separation. Vision is lost from the eye according to the proportion of the retina separated. Treatment is surgery to reattach the retina by promoting scar tissue formation between the detached layer and the choroid; this may be achieved using extreme cold (cryosurgery) or heat (photocoagulation).

detoxification Natural function of the liver that separates out and removes toxic substances in the blood. The term is used also for the "drying out" of somebody who is dependent on alcohol or other drugs, generally within a sanatorium specifically dedicated to the rehabilitation of addicts.

diabetes Either of two serious disorders, both of which cause excessive thirst and frequent urination (the symptoms give the conditions their name, from the Greek: dia-bet- "passing through"). Diabetes insipidus is caused by failure of the *pituitary gland* (the gland in the brain that controls the actions of most other glands) to produce or secrete enough *antidiuretic hormone* (ADH), which normally controls the amount of water reabsorbed by the kidneys. But by far the more common disorder is diabetes mellitus, in which the hormone *insulin* – which is normally produced by the *islets of Langerhans* (special cells in the pancreas) in order to reduce the level of sugar (glucose) in the blood – is central. Either no insulin is produced, or the tissues fail to respond to its presence. The first condition, type I diabetes, occurs most frequently in children and is consequently known as juvenile-onset diabetes; the second, type II diabetes, arises more often in adults and is thus often known as adult-onset diabetes. The cause is generally unknown, although there may be a family tendency to diabetes; sometimes an infection or alcoholism seems to contribute to its development in an adult. In either case, diet and blood sugar levels must be carefully controlled, as the latter can quickly become too high (*hyperglycaemia*), leading to chemical changes in which the blood may contain ketones (which can sometimes be smelled on the breath); coma may follow. However, coma may also follow a too-rapid lowering of blood sugar levels, from an imbalance between the diet and insulin dose. Long-term complications of diabetes includes damage to small arteries, including those in the back of the eye, which can cause blindness. Treatment of diabetes insipidus is to make up the deficiency of antidiuretic hormone. Juvenile-onset diabetes is treated with daily doses of insulin, usually by self-administered injection; treatment for adult-onset diabetes may require only dietary change, or drugs taken by mouth to help reduce blood sugar levels (oral hypoglycaemics).

diagnosis Provisional identification by a medical practitioner of the cause of a disorder or condition, generally by noting the signs and symptoms exhibited by the patient. Tests may then be carried out to confirm (or disprove) the diagnosis.

dialysis Process of cleansing the blood by filtration through a semi-permeable membrane. In effect, this is what happens normally and naturally in the *kidneys*. Blood supplied by the renal artery is filtered by the *nephrons* and *glomeruli* in the kidneys; purified blood and useful products are allowed to flow on, and waste products are siphoned off to the ureter and bladder for disposal as *urine*. When the kidneys are not working, however, the process may have to be undertaken by an *artificial kidney* or kidney machine (a dialysis machine or dialyser) which uses exactly the same mechanism. Alternatively, the process can be carried out internally (following a surgical operation to make it possible) by using the membrane that normally lines the abdominal cavity (*peritoneum*) as the filtration membrane; the technique is called peritoneal dialysis.

diaper American name for a *nappy*.

diaper rash American term for *nappy rash*.

diaphragm Strong, thin, domed sheet of muscle tissue that separates the chest cavity (containing the heart and lungs) from the abdominal cavity (containing the liver, gall bladder, spleen, kidneys, bladder, internal sex organs, stomach and intestines). Through it pass the oesophagus (gullet) and several major nerves and blood vessels. Contraction of the diaphragm causes the inhalation of air into the lungs, as part of the process of *respiration*; relaxation allows exhalation. Rupture of the diaphragm is called *hiatus hernia*.

diaphragm (contraceptive) Method of *contraception* comprising a domed rubber cap that fits over the neck of the womb (cervix) at the top of the vagina. In combination with a spermicide, the method is generally very effective.

diarrhoea Abnormally frequent *defecation*, or passing abnormally liquid *faeces*. The urge to defecate may continue even after the rectum is empty. Loss of liquids in this fashion – especially in young children – may lead to *dehydration*. Causes of diarrhoea range from stress, over-rich diet and mild *gastritis* (inflammation of the stomach) and *gastroenteritis*, to food poisoning, *otitis* media, chemical poisoning, infection of the intestines or of the lungs, infestation with *worms*, and (rarely) cancer. Treatment depends on diagnosis of the cause, but should include fluids to replace liquid lost. A medicine containing *kaolin* may give immediate relief.

diastole Phase of the *heartbeat* during which the heart muscle relaxes and the chambers of the heart are filled with blood. The phase ends as the heart once again contracts (*systole*) to pump the blood out.

diathermy Technique in which heat is applied to the body by the generation of a high-frequency electric current between two electrodes attached to the skin or inserted into the body. The method is used both to apply heat as therapy, and to destroy unwanted tissue in a process (sometimes called fulguration) in which the heat simultaneously cauterizes minor blood vessels.

diet Composition and nutritive value of the foods somebody regularly eats. A balance is required between the *fats, proteins, carbohydrates, vitamins* and *trace elements* (minerals) consumed; imbalance may cause *malnutrition, obesity, vitamin deficiency* or any of various metabolic disorders. For this reason, foods are classified in several ways according to different aspects of nutrition. The main method is in terms of their heat energy content, for which the unit is the *calorie*. The symptoms of many disorders can be controlled or modified by careful dietary intake. With some, specific foods must be avoided altogether (as with *coeliac disease* and allergies, for example); with others, diet must be planned not to aggravate conditions but if possible to soothe and heal (as with *peptic ulcers, heart disease* and *kidney disease*). The study of diets for all purposes is dietetics, and an expert in the subject is a dietitian (or dietician).

dietary fibre Parts of the diet (roughage) that cannot be absorbed or used by the body, but which are thought to be helpful in preventing (or at least inhibiting) the occurrence of *constipation, diverticulosis, appendicitis* and certain other conditions. High-fibre foods include wholemeal cereals, nuts and fruit. The main constituent of many of these is *cellulose*.

digestion Absorption of useful products ingested as food in the *digestive tract*. The process is one basically of breaking down large molecules into smaller constituents that can be transported within the bloodstream either to the *liver* or to the *kidneys*, and is carried out almost entirely in the *stomach* and the small *intestine*. *Enzymes* secreted within the acidic environments of the stomach, *duodenum* and *ileum* catalyse most of the required chemical reactions. *Fats* and *carbohydrates* are used or stored for energy; *proteins* are broken down into *amino acids*; *vitamins* and *trace elements* are assimilated as required, and waste products are excreted. The whole complex process may be disrupted by disorder or disease in any of the contributory organs.

digestive tract Major part of the *alimentary canal*, a long tube and associated organs that process food (*digestion*). It is generally considered to begin at the stomach – although in fact the processing of food actually begins with its breakdown in the mouth by the teeth, and its mixing with *saliva*, before being swallowed down the *oesophagus*. In the stomach, food comes into contact with hydrochloric acid, other gastric juices and enzymes; protein breakdown begins. In the *duodenum*, the food encounters *bile* and other juices from the *pancreas*; breakdown of proteins, sugars and fats occurs. More enzymatic secretion is added in the *ileum*, where most absorption of food products takes place. In the large *intestine*, processing is largely a matter of the absorption of water, leaving waste products to continue along to the *rectum*. In most of the intestines, food is squeezed along by the muscular contractions of *peristalsis*; absorption of useful products is into blood vessels that lead to the *liver* or *kidneys*. The whole complex process may be disrupted by disorder or disease in any of the contributory organs.

digitalis Extract from the dried leaves of the foxglove plant, source of several drugs that increase the efficiency with which the heart muscle contracts. Such drugs include digoxin (which is quick-acting but short-lived in effect) and digitoxin (which is slow-acting but works for a long time).

dilatation and curettage (D and C) Minor operation on women, carried out usually under local or general anaesthetic, to dilate the cervix (neck) of the *uterus* (womb) and insert an instrument that then peels off part or all of the *endometrium* (lining of the womb, normally shed at menstruation). It is a normal procedure for investigating the condition of the reproductive organs, but may also be carried out to remove cysts or extraneous material in the womb, or to procure an *abortion*.

dioptre Measure of the focal power of a *lens*: 1 dioptre is the power that refracts parallel rays of light to a focus 1 metre from the lens (and is equal to the reciprocal of the focal length in metres). Dioptre is positive for a converging lens, negative for a diverging one.

diphtheria Potentially dangerous – but now rare – contagious bacterial infection that generally affects the throat but may also attack other areas of mucous membrane (such as in the nasal cavity and larynx) or the tissues of the skin. Some (human) carriers of the disease are not themselves affected. Symptoms are sore throat, general malaise and high temperature; weakness, and the appearance of a painful white "crust" at the back of the throat follow. Breathing may become laboured. Treatment is isolation and bed rest in hospital, with antibiotics and antitoxin. A vaccine is available (and usually administered during the first year of life).

diplopia Medical term for *double vision*.

dipsomania Form of extreme *alcoholism*, in which the craving for drink is insatiable.

disc Flattish, rounded structure. Discoid structures in the body include the *intervertebral discs* of the spinal column, and the *platelets* in the blood.

disease Disorder or malfunction in part or all of the body, caused by specific factors (not by injury but especially by infective organisms) and giving rise to specific and recognizable symptoms.

disinfectant Substance or agent used to rid tissues or instruments of infective micro-organisms. See also *antiseptic*.

dislocation Violent and painful dislodging of a bone at a joint from the socket, tendons and ligaments that normally hold it in place. Dislocation of the shoulder, hip and elbow are perhaps the most common forms. First aid is to treat as a *fracture*. Remedial treatment is to reduce (reset) the bone by manipulation back into its normal position – which may require general anaesthesia – and to rest the joint. The tendons and ligaments remain sore and stiff for up to a month afterwards.

disorientation Condition in which somebody becomes suddenly aware that the environment (in location and time) is utterly different from what had been the last recollection of it. It is a state found mostly in anxiety and stress, or with fever or dementia, but can be caused also by drugs or by a mental disturbance. In the latter cases, there may also be a loss of memory (*amnesia*) in regard to identity.

dispensary Room or department in which drugs and medical creams, lotions and equipment are stored, put together, and distributed as required.

dissection In pathology, the cutting open of an organism to reveal its various tissues and organs. Anatomical classes may feature the dissection of corpses of animals and humans for educational purposes; *post mortems* use dissection for investigative purposes.

disseminated sclerosis Alternative term for *multiple sclerosis*.

dissociation In psychology, a state in which somebody has one or more additional and separate personalities (which may exist only in sketchy detail) in order to be able to accommodate mentally contradictory notions and desires.

distal Farthest from the source; outermost from the mid-line. The distal surface of a tooth, for example, is on the outside of the mouth.

district nurse Trained and qualified nurse specializing in visits to the homes of patients to give advice or therapy, and employed by local health authorities. Many are also trained as a *midwife*. Most district nurses (or home nurses, or community nurses) are allocated their patients by local general practices or hospitals, and work only during normal business hours. Some are available in special circumstances for medical responsibilities outside those times.

diuretic Drug that promotes the production and elimination of *urine*, so decreasing the amount of liquid in the body. The effect is achieved most often by stimulating the normal filtration process of the *kidneys* so that extra salts and water are excreted. Such drugs are particularly useful in treating *oedema* (in which fluids accumulate in the tissues), even when the oedema is caused by partial kidney failure. Other conditions treated effectively are high blood pressure (*hypertension*) and *glaucoma*.

diurnal Of the daytime (as opposed to nocturnal), daily.

diverticulitis Inflammation of a small out-pouching (diverticulum) in the wall of the gut, usually in the colon (the last part of the large intestine leading to the rectum and then the anus). Diverticula form in areas of weakness of the gut wall and become increasingly common with age. Usually they cause no symptoms, but when infected and inflamed can cause lower abdominal pain with constipation or diarrhoea, and sometimes bleeding from the rectum. There may be a high temperature and other signs of infection. Sometimes an *abscess* may form. Treatment is to alleviate symptoms, often with laxatives or antidiarrhoeal drugs, and rest until acute symptoms subside, followed by a high-fibre diet. If the condition recurs, or if an abscess forms, surgery may be necessary.

diverticulosis Presence in the outer wall of the *colon* (the last part of the large intestine leading to the rectum and then the anus) of little pockets or pouches (diverticula). Causes are either pressure on a weak area within the colon, or the drawing out of tissue from outside the colon by tissues in the abdominal cavity. Most often there are no symptoms other than a tendency to constipation or diarrhoea (which may be treated by a high-fibre diet or antidiarrhoeal drugs) and sometimes abdominal pain due to spasm. However, a diverticulum may become inflamed (*diverticulitis*) or infected, requiring treatment with antibiotics or, sometimes, surgery. Occasionally, diverticula appear elsewhere in the alimentary canal but outside the colon they do not cause symptoms.

diverticulum Small pocket or pouch that may form in the intestines. See *diverticulitis*; *diverticulosis*.

diving injuries Injuries sustained in a swimming pool through diving are mostly *concussion* or *fractures* (although an extremely clumsy belly-flop from the top diving-board could rupture the diaphragm or burst the stomach or a lung). In deep-sea diving the most common injuries are caused by *decompression sickness* (the bends).

dizziness Inability to retain balance involving unsteadiness, together with a light-headed feeling. Causes include low blood pressure (*hypotension*) and drugs; treatment, if required, corresponds to the cause. See also *vertigo*.

DNA Abbreviation of *deoxyribonucleic acid*.

Domagk, Gerhard (1895–1964) German pathologist and pioneer in *antibacterial drugs*, whose research into how to destroy bacteria without at the same time killing the patient led both to the discovery of sulphonamides (*sulfa drugs*) and, indirectly, to *Fleming*ís discovery of penicillin. He was awarded a Nobel Prize in 1939.

dominance Individuals are the results of *genes* inherited from their parents – half from one parent, half from the other – paired together (as *alleles*). Each pair comprises two dominant genes, two *recessive* genes, or one of each. In each of the pairs that includes a dominant gene, the effect that gene has on hereditary traits is manifested in the individual.

donor Somebody who contributes tissues or organs to be grafted on or into another. Sometimes the donor is a close relative (so that tissues are fairly well matched) and the tissue is of a sort that allows both donor and recipient a reasonable quality of life afterwards (as with the donation of one kidney out of two, or of bone marrow); at other times, the donor is matched with a prospective recipient only immediately after the donorís death (as with the donation of corneas or a heart).

dorsal Of, on or at the back.

dose Prescribed measure of a drug, to be taken or administered at regular intervals. The measure, representing the least that is sure to have the desired effect, may vary according to the patient (and particularly if a known tolerance level has already been established) or according to the diagnosed seriousness of the symptoms.

double vision Medical name diplopia, an effect that results when both eyes independently transmit a slightly different image to the brain, or the brain fails to combine the images from the two eyes. The cause is usually lack of co-ordination in the muscles that turn the eyeballs, as may result from fatigue, excessive consumption of alcohol or, much more rarely, concussion (or other head injury) or a stroke. In most cases, the condition is temporary and may be endured if one eye is covered.

douche Jet of water used for washing a body orifice, most commonly the vagina. (It is ineffective as a method of contraception.)

Down's syndrome Also called trisomy 21 or mongolism (now obsolete), a congenital abnormality that results from the presence of an extra chromosome – a triad of the 21st chromosome instead of the normal pair – in the cell nuclei. The result is characteristic formations of the skull and face, the tongue and the hands, and often mental retardation; stature may be squat. The condition may be accompanied also by other congenital disorders, particularly heart malformations and deafness. Affected people may need special care all their lives. Statistically, the chances of giving birth to a Downís syndrome child grow with increasing maternal age. There is no treatment other than to correct associated deformities where possible. Various tests are offered to older mothers that can help to predict the risk of Downís syndrome, including ultrasound scanning, a blood test (the triple marker test), chorionic villus sampling and amniocentesis (where foetal cells are sampled and their chromosomes analysed), which may be followed by abortion of affected pregnancies.

DPT vaccine Form of *immunization* against *diphtheria, tetanus* and *whooping cough* (pertussis), usually administered by injection on three separate occasions to babies in their first year of life. There may then be booster shots to follow at ages 5 and 10. Reactions to the vaccine are rare, although the doctor usually ascertains first if the family has any history of allergy or convulsions.

dreaming As with sleep, there is no known reason for people to dream – but without it, there are physical symptoms of deprivation. Dreaming takes place during the relatively short periods of *rapid eye movement (REM) sleep*, and may represent the brainís way of classifying the information and events of the previous day in with various aspects of memory. It is said that only a minority of dreams are in colour, however.

dressing Aseptic covering for a wound, with or without medication on or in it, and generally held in place by a *bandage* or plaster. Most are simple pads of lint or gauze; some are made instead of modern fibres for extra absorbency or "breathing". Special forms include *tampons*, *swabs* and eye pads.

drip Method and action of infusing blood, saline solution, plasma, or other body fluid (or its equivalent) into a vein by gravity through a tube from a bottle (or sachet). The rate of infusion can be monitored and controlled by regulating the flow of drips passing through a transparent valve in the tube.

dropsy Old term for *oedema* (particularly of the abdomen).

drowning Death through inhaling a liquid into the lungs (especially water). It occurs generally in two stages. On first plunging into a liquid somebody may, if unable to reach the surface, inhale some and begin to choke – but not all air escapes from the lungs because a reflex snaps the *epiglottis* shut over the *larynx*, and the effect is then of *suffocation*. The victim quickly loses consciousness. If at this stage the person is rescued – and especially if all body processes are slowed by cold –breathing may be restored. However, soon after consciousness is lost, the epiglottis relaxes and liquid does enter the lungs.

drug abuse Use of self-administered drugs to provide a state of temporary *euphoria* or other *psychedelic* effect (and thus for no medical purpose). Almost all drugs abused in such a way (including nicotine and alcohol) eventually produce *dependence* (physical or psychological need to continue taking the drug), even if only indirectly. Treatment is extremely difficult, relies on the person wanting to stop the drug habit, and is based on psychological support during withdrawal and afterwards. Sometimes drugs are used to alleviate symptoms, to replace the drug of abuse with a less harmful substitute, or to enforce abstinence by causing unpleasant symptoms should the patient lapse.

drug addiction State of *dependence*, usually following *drug abuse* but sometimes caused by long-term medical treatment with drugs.

drugs Chemical compound or solution which, when taken into the body, has a specific effect – generally one that is beneficial in relieving medical symptoms or in assisting with recovery from a disorder. Some are substances found naturally in the body (such as hormones) and are administered mostly to make up for a deficiency; others are obtained from plants or synthesized, and affect the operation of specific organs or areas of tissue, or promote specific chemical reactions in the body. All have to be used carefully (as prescribed by a doctor) and in specific doses, for an overdose of almost any drug can lead to harmful side-effects; a few drugs can provoke an allergic reaction; certain drugs in combination can also have serious consequences. Drug types include *analgesics* (pain-killers), *anaesthetics, antacids, anthelmintics* (against worm infestations), *antiarrhythmics* (to regulate the heartbeat), *antibiotics, anticoagulants, anticonvulsants, antidepressants* (against depression), *antifungal drugs, antihistamines, antinauseants, antipruritics* (against itching), *antipyretics* (against fever), *antirheumatics, antispasmodics, antitussives* (against coughs), *antivenins* (against venom), drugs for *contraception, corticosteroids* (a type of *hormone*, to regulate body processes), *cytotoxic drugs* (against cancer cells), *diuretics* (to eliminate fluids from the body), *emetics* (to promote vomiting), *expectorants, hallucinogens, hypnotic drugs* (to encourage sleep), hypotensive drugs (to lower blood pressure), *immunosuppressive drugs, laxatives, muscle relaxants, narcotics* (such as *morphine*), *sedatives, stimulants* (such as *amphetamines*), vasoconstrictors (to narrow blood vessels), *vasodilators* (to widen them), *vaccines* and, as supplements, *vitamins*. All new drugs are rigorously tested before being licensed for public use.

drunkenness State of alcoholic *intoxication*; the term implies consumption of alcohol on a habitual and excessive basis that may or may not have already resulted in *dependence*.

Duchenne, Guillaume (1806–1875) French doctor who popularized the use of electricity to diagnose and treat patients with neurological conditions. In particular, he investigated and explained the condition of *locomotor ataxia*, a symptom of tertiary syphilis. He was also the first to describe the operation of the *diaphragm* during respiration. The most common form of *muscular dystrophy* is sometimes called after him.

duct Tube, particularly one that conveys a glandular secretion away from a gland.

ductless gland Another term for an *endocrine gland*.

ductus arteriosus Relatively small blood vessel near the heart of an unborn child that until birth allows the blood circulation to by-pass that part of the *cardiovascular system* which normally conveys blood to the *lungs* and back for reoxygenation. It thus confines the blood circulation simply to the main circuit around the body. At birth – at the first breath of life – the vessel normally closes, and the pulmonary circulation begins. (If it does not close in childhood, surgery to close it is often necessary.)

duodenal ulcer Form of *peptic ulcer* (an eroded area within the gut lining) located in the wall of the *duodenum*. Affected individuals (people with blood group O seem to be at increased risk) usually have excess acid production from the stomach, and infection of the stomach with a type of bacteria called *Helicobacter pylori*, which is believed to contribute to the formation of ulcers. Symptoms include intermittent episodes of upper abdominal pain, often precisely located and worse if the person has not eaten for a while, and sometimes vomiting. Treatment is with a combination of drugs, often including antibiotics to treat the infection; surgery is rarely necessary unless complications, such as bleeding, obstruction or perforation, develop.

duodenum Section of the small *intestine* immediately following the *stomach*. Partly digested food that enters through the pyloric sphincter is further processed in the duodenum, the wall of which contains glands that secrete *enzymes*. Also in the wall are the openings of ducts from the *pancreas* (conveying pancreatic juice) and the *gall bladder* (conveying *bile*). The duodenum is a major site for the breakdown of fats, sugars and proteins for absorption in the veins that connect directly with the liver.

Dupuytren's contracture Condition in which the little finger (and often the finger next to it) remains immovably bent over towards the palm. It is caused by a fibrous overgrowth around the tendon in the palm of the hand that normally flexes the finger. Why the overgrowth occurs, however, is not known. Treatment is generally by surgical separation of the fibres so as to release the tendon. The condition is named after the French military surgeon Guillaume Dupuytren (1777–1835).

dura mater Outermost of the three *meninges* membranes that surround and protect the brain and spinal cord. (The other two are the *arachnoid membrane* and the *pia mater*.) It is also the thickest of the three, and itself comprises two layers, the outer of which – in the head – represents the lining of the skull (periosteum). A fold of the dura mater separates the cerebral hemispheres.

dwarfism Abnormally restricted growth of the body. The most common cause is *achondroplasia*, a genetic disorder affecting the growth of bones and cartilage in the limbs only (although the trunk and head are of normal size). In other people, restricted growth occurs because of a deficiency of *growth hormone* (somatotropin), normally produced and secreted by the *pituitary gland*. Such people are of fairly normal proportions, but small. A rarer variant of this condition occurs in people whose bodies are genetically incapable of reacting normally to growth hormone. In all these types of dwarfism, mental development is ordinarily normal. Restricted growth caused by *hypothyroidism*, however, results also in mental subnormality.

dysentery Severe form of infection in the *intestines* (the guts) and possibly spreading from there to elsewhere in the body. The main symptom is violent diarrhoea, passing blood and mucus. Dysentery has two main forms: *amoebic dysentery* (amoebiasis) and bacillary dysentery. The infective organisms of both forms – a protozoan in the first case, a bacterium in the second – are spread in food or water contaminated with the faeces of a carrier, and thus occur mostly in areas of poor (or no) sanitation. Bacillary dysentery has much milder symptoms – diarrhoea, nausea, high temperature and cramps; there may also be intestinal haemorrhage. It lasts only for about ten days. Treatment is with fluid replacement and antibiotics.

dysfunction Abnormal difficulty of a part of the body in operating normally, perhaps resulting in inefficient or insufficient action.

dyslexia Abnormal difficulty in learning to read, write and spell despite usually standard intellect. More boys are affected than girls and the condition often runs in families; it is believed to be due to some defect in specific language centres in the brain, although it can be exacerbated by poor educational facilities and unsympathetic teaching. Specialized assessment and tuition are important to help overcome the serious educational difficulties that may otherwise result.

dysmenorrhoea Difficulty or pain experienced on *menstruation*. There are two forms. Primary dysmenorrhoea occurs when the periods first start (at the *menarche*), when cramping abdominal pain during menstruation may be accompanied by general feelings of being unwell, nausea and headache. This is believed to be due to hormonal disturbances. Secondary dysmenorrhoea occurs in older women, who may experience aching or cramping pains from before menstruation starts. This form may be a symptom of *endometriosis*, *fibroids* or pelvic inflammatory disease (a result of infection ascending from the vagina to the uterus and Fallopian tubes); it can also be a result of an intrauterine contraceptive device (IUCD). In primary dysmenorrhoea treatment aims to alleviate symptoms, and the problem usually settles down with age. In the secondary form, treatment is directed towards the cause of the pain.

dyspareunia Difficulty or pain experienced during *sexual intercourse*; the term is usually applied to women, who are more subject to the problem than men. The difficulty may centre on physical problems, including abnormal dryness of the vagina or any of many forms of inflammation of the reproductive organs, or on psychological factors such as involuntary contraction of the vaginal muscles impeding penetration (*vaginismus*), which may, in turn, be due to physical problems in the area or fear of sex, or may precipitate attempts at penetration by an inexperienced male partner. Pain on intercourse in men is most often due to inflammation (balanitis) or tightness (*phimosis*) of the foreskin.

dyspepsia Another word for *indigestion*.

dyspnoea Medical term for *breathlessness*.

dystrophy Effect in tissues of the body (generally of a muscle) of an insufficient supply of nutrients. It varies depending on the tissues involved, but in *muscular dystrophy* there is wasting of the muscle fibres, which are eventually replaced by fat.

E

ear Organ responsible for the senses of *hearing* and *balance*. Located on each side of the head, within a cavity of the temporal bone of the skull, it consists of the outer ear (the ear flap or pinna, earlobe and auditory canal) up to the *eardrum*; the *middle ear* (containing three tiny bones called ossicles: the malleus, incus and stapes); and the *inner ear* or labyrinth (containing the *cochlea*, utricle and saccule, and the *semicircular canals*). Sound vibrations are funnelled along the auditory canal to the eardrum, relayed through the ossicles, and received by the cochlea for transmission via the cochlear nerve to the brain. Balance is achieved by the sensory nerves of the semicircular canals. Inflammation of the ear – *otitis* – may affect both hearing and balance.

eardrum Delicate septum of skin and membrane that separates the outer ear from the *middle ear* (medical name: tympanic membrane). Sound vibrations are transferred from the eardrum to the *malleus*, the first of the three ossicles of the middle ear. Outside the eardrum, accumulating dirt is trapped by hairs and *wax* (cerumen) produced by special sebaceous glands lining the auditory canal.

earwax Cerumen, *wax* produced by glands in the outer ear canal.

Ebola virus Virus responsible for a serious infectious disease in parts of Africa, possibly transmitted from animals as well as by contact with infected body fluids of a human sufferer. Symptoms may include a high temperature, headache, diarrhoea, vomiting and bleeding from the mouth; early treatment can avert complications but without it those affected may develop severe haemorrhaging (bleeding) from internal organs. The disease tends to occur in outbreaks, and may be fatal in more than half of those affected.

ecchymosis Medical term for a haemorrhage in the skin, a *bruise*.

eccrine gland Gland that secretes directly on to the outside skin surface – unlike apocrine glands which secrete to the surface through short ducts (usually in association with hair follicles). All are *sweat glands*, and are most common on the palms of the hands and soles of the feet.

ECG Abbreviation of *electrocardiogram*.

echocardiography Means of monitoring how well the chambers of the heart are functioning, using ultrasound. Ultrasound signals are bounced off the heart, and the returning signals recorded and interpreted. The analytical record produced is an echocardiogram.

echovirus Old name for *Coxsackie virus*.

eclampsia Dangerous condition that represents a complication of *toxaemia of pregnancy*, and affects a woman either in the last weeks of pregnancy or shortly after childbirth. Symptoms are high blood pressure, oedema (swelling of the tissues because of accumulated fluid), protein in the urine (*albuminuria* or proteinuria), and convulsions leading to coma. If still pregnant at this stage, the mother is in danger of losing both the baby and her life. Treatment is to relieve the symptoms – to prevent further convulsions and to lower blood pressure – but may include precautionary induction of labour or a Caesarean section to deliver the baby.

ecology Study of the relationship between humans (and their activities) and the environment (and its maintenance), animate and inanimate.

Ecstasy Common name for an illegal drug that produces feelings of euphoria in users. Its chemical name is methylenedioxymethamphetamine (MDMA), and its greatest danger is that it can cause *hyperthermia* (dangerously high body temperature), which may be exacerbated – sometimes with fatal results – by the common conditions of its use, while engaged in strenuous dancing.

ECT Abbreviation of *electroconvulsive therapy.*

ectoderm Outermost of the three distinct types of tissue that make up the very early form of an *embryo*. (The other "germ" layers are the *mesoderm* and *endoderm.*) It is from the ectoderm that the nervous system, organs of the mouth, and entire outer surface of skin (and nails and hair) are eventually formed.

ectomorph Somebody who has a body shape that is taller than average and thinner than average – and who is therefore neither a *mesomorph* nor an *endomorph.*

ectopic pregnancy Potentially dangerous condition resulting from the implantation of a *blastocyst* (the earliest form of *embryo*) not in the *uterus* (womb) as normal but in a *Fallopian tube* (or even, in very rare cases, on the surface of an *ovary* or in the abdominal cavity). The cause may be blockage or inflammation in the Fallopian tube. Growth of an embryo in the tube commonly results in death of the embryo and subsequent reabsorption of the tissues back into the womanís body. But in some cases, growth continues and the embryo eventually bursts the tube, causing massive bleeding and severe pain, leading to shock. Treatment is surgical removal of the embryo and, generally, the Fallopian tube.

eczema Inflammation of the outer layer (epidermis) of the skin, causing a reddish itching rash with blisters that may weep and crust over. Marks or different textures in the skin may be left afterwards. Unlike *dermatitis*, eczema is mainly due to an internal, often inherited, tendency and need not involve a reaction to external substances; both terms are, however, often used interchangeably. Atopic eczema, which can appear anywhere on the body, is the most common form, usually starting in childhood and linked with a family tendency to eczema, asthma and hay fever (*atopy*). Seborrhoeic eczema is also common, involving the face and scalp, and linked with a yeast organism and with *dandruff.* Other forms are discoid eczema, with round skin lesions in adults, *pompholyx*, which occurs on the hands and feet only, and gravitational eczema in areas of poor venous circulation. Treatment depends on diagnosis, but includes emollient skin lotions and often *corticosteroids*, usually as skin creams but sometimes as tablets, and in some cases other drugs or special light therapy.

edema American spelling of *oedema.*

EEG Abbreviation of *electroencephalogram.*

efferent Conveying or flowing away from a source. The term thus describes nerves that transmit information from – but not to – the central nervous system (brain and spinal cord), and vessels that drain fluid from an organ.

effusion Escape of a body fluid from its normal area into another body cavity, where it then accumulates. Causes include an excess of the body fluid in its normal area, and inflammation.

egg In medicine, a mature *ovum* released by an *ovary* at *ovulation*.

ego In *psychoanalysis*, the consciously aware mind that is interactive with the outside world and influenced by both the instinctual desires of the *id* and the moral goals of the *superego*.

Ehrlich, Paul (1854–1915) German bacteriologist and specialist in the use of drugs and *antitoxins* to achieve *immunization*. It was for his researches into the mechanisms of antigens and antibodies that he was awarded a Nobel Prize in 1908. He also produced a drug to treat syphilis, and marketed it as Salvarsan.

ejaculation Emission of *semen* from a manís erect penis at and just after sexual climax (orgasm). The process involves the discharge of secretions from four sources – *Cowper's glands, prostate gland, testes* and *seminal vesicles* – in that order.

EKG American abbreviation of *electrocardiogram*.

elbow Hinge joint at the middle of the arm, where the *humerus* (bone of the upper arm) meets the *radius* and the *ulna* (bones of the forearm). Bending of the arm is effected by the biceps muscle; straightening by the triceps. The joint is protected by a synovial capsule and by the olecranon process (the bony projection of the ulna). Over the end of the humerus lies the ulnar nerve, the combination of the two forming the *"funny bone"*.

electrocardiogram (ECG) Record of the electrical activity of the heart through electrodes placed on the skin of the chest wall and limbs, and occasionally elsewhere. Leads from the electrodes attach to the recording device, with each lead making its own trace on the record; since the most usual type of test uses 12 electrodes, it may be known as a 12-lead ECG. Tracings from the various leads show a characteristic pattern; changes in these during exertion or in various disease states aid diagnosis of problems such as chest pain or heart rhythm disturbances.

electroconvulsive therapy (ECT) Momentary passing of an electric current through the brain, via electrodes on the scalp. Once a common form of treatment for patients with mental disorders, it is now used on a much smaller scale and with some preliminary precautions against the effects of the convulsion and brief period of unconsciousness (or other side-effects) that the electric shock inevitably causes. In particular, only one side of the brain is now usually subjected to the current. The method is surprisingly effective in treating severe depression, but in many countries has been entirely superseded by the use of drugs.

electroencephalogram (EEG) Record of the electrical activity of the brain ("brain waves"). Electrodes are placed on the skin of the scalp. Leads from them attach to the recording device, and each lead makes its own trace on the record. The pattern created by the traces – representing the state of the brain and level of consciousness of the patient – forms the basis for analysis and diagnosis.

electrolysis In medicine, the destruction of cells by passing an electric current through them. The method is used particularly to destroy hair follicles and so permanently remove unwanted hair.

electrolyte Solution (usually of salt) that can conduct an electric current. In medicine, the term is used of any mineral-containing fluid within the body.

electron microscope Instrument for viewing objects smaller than the wavelength of light. It is a *microscope* that uses a beam of electrons (instead of light) as a radiation source by which to examine a specimen, focused either on to a fluorescent screen or on to a photographic plate. The object has to be placed in a vacuum. A scanning electron microscope views the surface of an object.

electrotherapy Treatment of muscles and the nerves that supply them with stimulation by an electric current. The method is used mostly in an attempt to improve sensation and mobility in patients with *paralysis*.

elephantiasis Form of *filariasis* (infestation by parasitic *roundworms*) that causes inflammation and obstruction of the *lymphatic system*, so that lymph vessels fail to drain into the blood system and instead become massively congested and bloated, and associated tissues of the skin become drastically thickened. The result is gross enlargement of the area of the body affected – most commonly the legs, but sometimes alternatively or additionally the breasts, hands or scrotum. Treatment is support of the affected parts, and with drugs.

elixir Base for a medicine – especially one that does not taste pleasant by itself or has immediate unpleasant effects – consisting of a sweetened alcohol or glycerine solution.

emaciation Wasting of the bodyís muscles through using up all its store of energy in the form of fat. The condition is caused primarily by *malnutrition*, but the cause of the malnutrition (if not simply dietary insufficiency) may be *worms*, *tuberculosis* or *cancer*.

emasculation In common usage, the same as *castration*, including any consequent manifestations of *feminization* – or an emotional shock that may temporarily seem to have similar effects. But the term can technically also mean the surgical removal of the penis.

embolism Blockage of the blood circulation by some extraneous matter in the bloodstream (an *embolus*). Symptoms are usually serious, but depend on the site of the embolism – the most common site is the pulmonary artery (which conveys blood from the heart to the lungs), which can result in sudden death. In the brain, embolism causes a stroke; in a limb, the result may be gangrene.

embolus Matter – generally a blood clot caused by *thrombosis*, but also possibly a ball of fat, foreign body or even air bubble – that causes a blockage in the blood circulation (*embolism*).

embrocation Alternative name for *liniment*.

embryo Early stage of development of an unborn child, representing *gestation* between initial implantation as a *blastocyst* and the end of the second month of pregnancy. During this period all the major organs appear in rudimentary form. After this period the embryo is known as a *foetus*.

embryology Study of the developmental factors and disorders of an unborn child from conception to childbirth.

emesis Medical term for *vomiting*.

emetic Drug (or any substance) that induces vomiting. Some emetics work by irritating the stomach lining; others by acting on a reflex centre in the brain. (The latter type is sometimes used in *aversion therapy* for alcoholism.)

emotion Temporary and subjective mental disposition that is different from the normal equilibrium, and is the focus of mood. With most emotions there are also accompanying physiological and behavioural variations from normal. Emotions may be pleasant or unpleasant, and may result in considerable stress or comfort. Inappropriate emotion – or evident lack of emotional development – may indicate a mental disorder that requires treatment.

emphysema Presence of air in the tissues. This normally does not matter much – it occurs during surgery, and the air is usually gradually absorbed by the body. Sometimes leakage of gas from the lungs or air passages accumulates in tissues, leading to a characteristic crackling feeling on touching the affected area (surgical emphysema), and the leak must obviously be stopped. In the condition known as pulmonary emphysema, tissue degeneration in the *lungs* results in the overexpansion of the air sacs (alveoli), and further degeneration of the thin alveolar walls through which the respiratory exchange of gases takes place. Breathing becomes laboured and difficult, especially if the patient contracts a respiratory infection. The precise cause of pulmonary emphysema is uncertain, but it occurs mostly in men, is increasingly common with age and is linked with chronic *bronchitis* and smoking. The only treatment for pulmonary emphysema is oxygen therapy to aid breathing.

empyema Presence of *pus* in a body cavity, particularly in the small space between the two layers of membrane (*pleura*) between the *lungs* and the chest wall. There, the condition arises generally as a complication of lung infection (such as *pneumonia*) or direct injury. Symptoms include high temperature, chest pain and coughing, and in addition to the effects of any original infection may endanger life. Treatment is surgical drainage of the pus, and antibiotics.

enamel Hard outer coating on the exposed part (crown) of a tooth, consisting of a more crystalline form of the material that makes up bone. Its hardness can be enhanced by the use of *fluorides*.

encephalins *Two peptides* (complex molecules formed from two linked amino acids) belonging to a group of naturally occurring substances called *endorphins*. They are found in the brain and other parts of the nervous system, as well as in parts of the intestinal tract, and have effects similar to those of morphine and other *opiate* drugs, so function as a natural *analgesic* when released at times of injury or trauma. They may have further functions in regulating some of the endocrine glands and co-ordinating the bodyís response to emotion.

encephalitis Inflammation of brain tissue, a dangerous condition caused by bacterial or viral infection, or by allergic reaction (especially to certain vaccines). The form caused by viruses is more common in the tropics, and may occur as a complication of several other viral diseases (particularly *herpes* infections). Symptoms are high temperature, vomiting, headache and neck stiffness; there is mental confusion that may lead to coma (in which breathing may become severely laboured) and sometimes death. A worldwide epidemic of encephalitis lethargica, or "sleeping sickness", occurred in the 1920s, characterized by headache, drowsiness and coma, for which no specific cause has been found. Treatment follows diagnosis of the specific cause and includes supportive measures and sometimes antibiotics, antiviral drugs or antiallergic medication.

encephalomyelitis Inflammation of both the brain (as in *encephalitis*) and the spinal cord. It may be due to a viral infection or to a type of delayed allergic response following a week to 10 days after an immunization, when it is known as acute disseminated encephalomyelitis. Treatment depends on the cause and includes supportive measures during the acute illness.

endemic Arising frequently, if not continually, within a specified region and its population.

endocarditis Inflammation of the *endocardium* (the lining of the heart cavity) and the heart valves, almost always caused by the presence of bacteria carried there in the bloodstream. It is sometimes a complication of *rheumatic fever* in childhood, but occurs especially after minor surgery (such as a tooth extraction) or childbirth. Symptoms are fatigue and bouts of fever; *anaemia* and weight loss follow, and "blood spots" may appear on the skin, representing small clots (emboli). The heart valves may be damaged, sometimes leading to long-term problems. Treatment involves hospitalization, rest and antibiotic therapy for several weeks; surgery may be required to repair or replace damaged heart valves.

endocardium Membranous layer that lines the chambers of the heart and the associated blood vessels; it also forms the flaps (cusps) of the heart valves. Inflammation of the membrane is called *endocarditis.*

endocrine gland Gland that emits its *hormone* secretions directly into the bloodstream – unlike *exocrine glands*, which use ducts to convey their secretions to specific sites. Major endocrine glands include the pituitary, adrenal, thyroid and parathyroid glands, and the gonads; many secrete their hormones only in response to the presence of other hormones in the bloodstream.

endocrinology Study of the functions, secretions (*hormones*) and disorders of the *endocrine glands*.

endoderm Innermost of the three distinct types of tissue that make up the very early form of *embryo*. (The other layers are the *ectoderm* and the *mesoderm.*) It is from the endoderm that the digestive system – and all its associated glands and organs – develops, as do the urinary apparatus and the lining of the respiratory passages.

endometriosis Presence of small areas of tissue of the same type as the *endometrium* (womb-lining), not lining the womb as normal, but elsewhere in the abdomen (such as on an *ovary*). The tissue goes through the same cycle as the rest of the endometrium, including bleeding at *menstruation*, and if there is no immediate escape for the blood, the pain that follows may be severe for several days. The cause is usually a retrograde (backwards) displacement of endometrial cells along a *Fallopian tube* (connecting the womb with each ovary) into the abdomen at *menstruation*. Treatment is with drugs such as danazol, which alters the levels of pituitary hormones, although severe cases may require surgery. The condition usually resolves during pregnancy and ceases after the *menopause*.

endometrium Membranous lining of the *uterus* (womb) that changes significantly during each episode of the *menstrual cycle* of a woman between the menarche and the menopause. Following each *menstruation*, the endometrium gradually thickens and increases its blood supply. If, following sexual intercourse, *conception* occurs, it is in the endometrium that the resultant *blastocyst* implants to form a *placenta* and begin development as an embryo. If no conception occurs, the thickened endometrium is shed, with blood, through the vagina at the end of the cycle as the menstrual flow. Inflammation of the endometrium is called endometritis, almost always caused by bacterial infection.

endomorph Somebody who has a body shape that is shorter and more rounded than the average – and who is therefore neither an *ectomorph* nor a *mesomorph*.

endoplasmic reticulum Organelle within the cytoplasm of a *cell* that is made up of a network of membranes and may or may not have *ribosomes* attached to it. Its function is to form and convey *proteins* and *lipids* within the cell.

endorphins Chemical compounds derived from material in the *pituitary gland* and used by the brain as a natural *analgesic*. Their effects in this respect are similar to those of *opiates*, but they may also have further functions in regulating some of the endocrine glands. See also *enkephalins*.

endoscope Instrument for looking inside the body. Most now employ *fibre-optics* and consist of a long tube that can be inserted through a body orifice or small surgical incision, connected to a binocular eyepiece or a camera. Some endoscopes also carry attachments for carrying out a *biopsy* or *diathermy*. The use of an endoscope is called endoscopy.

endothelium Ultra-thin layer of cells that forms the outer surface of the membranous lining of the heart chambers, blood vessels and lymph vessels. Other body cavities are lined with *epithelium*, which also forms much of the outer surface strata.

end-plate Tiny area on a muscle cell membrane separated by a small gap (*synapse*) from the *motor end-plate* of a neurone (nerve cell). The nerve causes contraction of the muscle by emitting a *neurotransmitter* across the synapse to receptors on the end-plate.

enema Process in which fluid (also called the enema) is injected into the *rectum* through the *anus*. To soften and remove impacted faeces, an enema of soapy water or olive oil may be administered; to treat internal infection and inflammation, an enema containing *corticosteroids* could be used; and before X-raying the lower colon, a (radio-opaque) barium enema might be given.

energy Product in the body of the "combustion" of glucose and fats using oxygen (causing both the release of energy and the formation of the waste products, water and carbon dioxide). The result is the capacity for activity at both the cellular and organic levels. In the cells of the muscles, energy release is effected by the conversion of *adenosine triphosphate* (ATP) to either adenosine diphosphate (ADP) or adenosine monophosphate (AMP), a process that is reversible and can be constantly resupplied as long as the cell receives nutrients. At the organic level, the amount of energy used can be calculated from a measure of oxygen consumed: the unit of measure is the *calorie*. The number of calories of energy a person uses in a day depends on the individual (age, sex, body type and environmental factors) and on the exertion required. Without any exertion at all, however, a person is thought to use 1,700 to 1,900 calories a day, just in vital processes.

enkephalins Alternative spelling of *encephalins*.

enteric fever Fever – and other symptoms – of the type caused by *typhoid fever* and *paratyphoid*.

enteritis Inflammation of the small intestine. (If the stomach is also inflamed, the condition is *gastroenteritis*.) Causes include bacterial and viral infection, poisoning, and allergic reaction. Symptoms are abdominal pain, vomiting, and diarrhoea; with the form of enteritis known as *Crohn's disease*, symptoms may be more serious. Treatment depends on diagnosis of the cause.

enuresis See *bed-wetting*.

enzyme Protein product of a cell that acts as a catalyst for one specific chemical change. To effect all the chemical changes in the body required for digestion and the other processes of metabolism, there are several thousands of different enzymes in the body, the formulation of each regulated by a specific *gene* in the chromosomes. Because of this genetic connection, there are some disorders that result from a hereditary lack of specific enzymes (such as phenylketonuria). As catalysts, enzymes remain unaffected by the chemical reactions they promote; many of these reactions break down complex substances in food into simpler constituents.

eosinophil Type of *granulocyte* that occurs mostly in tissue surfaces of the body and is implicated in allergic reactions.

epicardium Membranous outer layer of the heart wall, which also forms the inner layer of the double *pericardium* membrane.

epidemic Outbreak of infection that arises suddenly and spreads rapidly to affect a significant proportion of the population of a community, either where the disease was not previously present or where the epidemic substantially increases the proportion of the population affected compared with normal levels. Usually the epidemic subsides after a period, either temporarily or permanently. The most common form is an *influenza* epidemic.

epidemiology The study of disease occurrence, distribution, incidence, prevalence and effects within populations, and of the means of their prevention or control. It may include infectious diseases; conditions related to a particular environment, such as nutritional deficiency or effects of pollutants; or links between disease and lifestyle, such as smoking and *cancer* or diet and heart disease.

epidermis Outer layer of the skin, itself divided into four layers. The innermost layer, the germinative or Malpighian layer, is composed of cells constantly replicating and rising through the next two layers (the stratum granulosum and the stratum lucidum, in which their *keratin* content increases by degrees) to become the outer layer, the cornified layer, which consists entirely of dead cells with keratin instead of *cytoplasm*.

epididymis Narrow, convoluted tube that surmounts each *testis* and draws from it, in a number of small vessels, the *sperm* to be mixed with fluids to form *semen*, which is ejaculated at *orgasm* via the *vas deferens* to which it is attached. The overall volume of the epididymis is very small, but in length it can amount to six or seven metres (20 to 23 feet).

epidural anaesthetic Form of *anaesthesia* that deadens sensation from a chosen area of the spine down. The anaesthetic is injected between two vertebrae into the space between the *dura mater* (the outermost of the three *meninges* membranes that surround the spinal cord) and the *arachnoid membrane* (the middle one). The technique is commonly used in *labour*, and thus does not interfere with the controlled breathing that many women find useful in these circumstances.

epiglottis Flap of cartilage covered with mucous membrane, situated at the base of the tongue in the throat. It closes off the top of the *larynx* and trachea (windpipe) during swallowing, so preventing food or drink from going down the air passages.

epilepsy General term for a type of disorder characterized by seizures that involve uncoordinated and vigorous electrical activity in the brain. Symptoms correspond both with the area or areas of the brain involved, and with the specific form of the disorder. The most serious form is grand mal epilepsy, in which a patient falls unconscious, perhaps simultaneously uttering a cry; the muscles stiffen and then jerk and twitch; there may be bladder incontinence and the tongue may be bitten. After a couple of minutes, the patient may drift peacefully into a deep sleep or enter a trance-like state. Seizures in Jacksonian epilepsy may also reach these extremes, but build progressively from localized twitching of the limbs. Focal epilepsy affects only those areas of the body that correspond to local areas of the brain undergoing the abnormal electrical activity. In petit mal epilepsy there may be no more than a brief period of unconsciousness. In all forms, there may or may not be an initial *aura*, a warning that a seizure is imminent. Causes may be unknown, a head injury, disease in the cerebral cortex (which may produce additional symptoms of hallucinations), a very high temperature, drug allergy, an electric shock or asphyxia – and anyone at all, at any time of life, can be subject to a seizure. Treatment is generally with drugs, and aimed to reduce frequency of seizures without causing inhibiting side-effects. Patients must not drive or operate dangerous machinery until the seizures are well-controlled.

epinephrine American term for *adrenaline*.

episiotomy Surgical cutting of one side of the entrance to the *vagina* during *childbirth*, so as to make more room for the emergence of the baby, and to prevent possibly extensive tearing of the tissues. It is performed usually at a stage when the area has already been anaesthetized, and is surgically repaired by stitching immediately after the birth.

epistaxis Medical term for *nosebleed.*

epithelium Tissue that in several cellular forms constitutes much of the outer surface strata of the body and the lining of body cavities. The chambers of the heart and the vessels that convey blood and lymph, however, are lined with a thin layer of *endothelium*.

Epstein-Barr virus (EBV) A type of *herpes* virus responsible for *glandular fever*, symptoms of which are due to the way in which the virus attacks the immune system. EBV is also the cause of Burkittís lymphoma (a specific form of *cancer* causing tumours of the jaw and elsewhere, largely among African children) and has been implicated in various other diseases.

equilibrium Condition achieved either by the sense of *balance* (centred in the *inner ear*) or by all the internal organs concertedly (*homeostasis*).

erection Enlarged and rigid state of the *penis*. A manís penis becomes erect when he is sexually excited – physically, mentally, or in both ways. By reflex, blood engorges the outer spongy tissues of the penis, and is prevented from leaving by the contraction of muscles around the veins. Following *orgasm*, or when the excitement fades, the muscles relax and the blood drains so that the penis again becomes flaccid. The term is sometimes also used for the similar engorgement of a womanís *clitoris* when she is sexually aroused.

ergonomics Study of human working environments and the effects they have on health and efficiency.

ergotism Dangerous form of poisoning caused by consumption of the rye fungus ergot. The immediate effect is contraction of all the blood vessels, resulting in tingling in the limbs, vomiting, severe headache and diarrhoea; there may also be convulsions, and death. Even if the patient lives, emergency treatment is necessary to prevent *gangrene* in the extremities and *cataracts* in the eyes. Ergot also provides some useful drugs – although overdosage can again cause ergotism.

Erikson, Erik (1902–1994) American psychoanalyst who published a textbook that became a classic in North America, on *Childhood and Society*. His particular interest was the influence of tradition and culture on the development of personal individuality.

erogenous zone Area on the body that is a focus for sexual arousal when physically stimulated.

eruption Either the appearance on the skin of a rash or bulbar lesion; or the cutting of a tooth through the gum.

erysipelas Contagious bacterial infection of the skin, particularly of the face and scalp, that sometimes causes severe symptoms. Affected areas of skin become inflamed and swollen, and the patient suffers a high temperature and vomiting. Untreated, there is a risk of complications of nephritis and pneumonia. Treatment is with antibiotics, but the condition may recur.

erythema Symptom of several conditions characterized by red patches on specific areas of the skin. Erythema nodosum, for example, appears as a complication of a number of infections, and produces red, oval swellings (nodules) on the skin (generally of the lower leg). Other symptoms include high temperature, fatigue and muscle pain; the nodules gradually turn brown and fade. Treatment is to alleviate the symptoms as much as possible.

erythroblastosis foetalis Alternative name for *Rh factor incompatibility*.

erythrocyte Red blood cell. It is a disc-shaped cell that has no nucleus but contains the pigment *haemoglobin*, which is the vehicle in the blood for the transport of oxygen from the lungs to the tissues. Erythrocytes are formed mostly in the *bone marrow*; throughout the process of formation (erythropoiesis, or erythrogenesis) all cell stages except the final one have a nucleus.

erythrocyte sedimentation rate (ESR) Measure of the rate at which, under standardized conditions, erythrocytes (red blood cells) settle out of suspension in a fixed quantity of blood plasma. Sedimentation more rapid than normal indicates the presence of a chronic infection, rheumatological disorder or, sometimes, a tumour.

erythropoietin Kidney hormone that increases the rate at which *erythrocytes* (red blood cells) are produced in the *bone marrow*, as a response to a reduction in the oxygen level of the bloodstream. It is a major component of the feedback mechanism for controlling the formation of red blood cells.

Escherichia coli Rod-shaped bacteria that normally inhabit the gut without causing problems but can sometimes lead to urinary or intestinal infection and food poisoning. Harmful species may be eaten in infected meat, giving abdominal pain and diarrhoea, sometimes with bleeding. Treatment is with antibiotics and fluid replacement.

esophagus American spelling of *oesophagus*.

ESP Abbreviation of *extrasensory perception*, a subject of research in *parapsychology*.

ESR Abbreviation of *erythrocyte sedimentation rate.*

estrogen American spelling of *oestrogen.*

ethanol Also called ethyl alcohol, the alcohol in intoxicating drinks, produced through the fermentation of sugar in fruit or cereals by yeast. Its effect on the body is to depress certain centres in the brain, although initially there may be symptoms of stimulation. In medicine, as rubbing alcohol or surgical spirit, alcohol is rubbed on to the skin of bed-ridden patients to prevent the formation of bedsores and is used as an antiseptic. See also *alcoholism*; *methanol.*

ether Volatile organic liquid formerly used as an *anaesthetic*. Because of the side-effects caused by its irritation of the respiratory passages and stomach lining, it has now generally been replaced by other, safer anaesthetics.

ethics of medical practice Moral undertaking by any medical practitioner to do his or her best in the care and cure of patients, no more (by way of experimentation, for example) and no less (through negligence or incompetence). Ethics do not necessarily coincide with legal restrictions – it is not illegal for a male doctor to commit adultery with a willing female patient, for instance, but it is unethical, and the doctor may be struck off the register. In many countries doctors on qualifying have to swear an oath much like the one devised some 2,400 years ago by *Hippocrates* (or his school), defining medical ethics.

ethmoid Bone in the skull that forms the base for the nose, cheeks and much of the sockets (orbits) of the eyes. As the roof of the *nasal cavity*, it is pierced by many holes through which the olfactory nerves pass.

ethnology Study of racial characteristics and differences, medical, cultural and social, and the effects of racial mixing. It is more a branch of anthropology than of medicine.

etiology American spelling of *aetiology.*

eugenics Until recently, eugenics referred only to a discredited programme for improving (human) racial stock by the deliberate breeding of select individuals chosen for their ideal characteristics. Now, however, it refers rather to the science of eliminating hereditary diseases and disorders through *genetic counselling.*

euphoria Feeling of great happiness and contentment, that all is unusually well with the world and likely to remain so. In unjustified circumstances, euphoria may indicate a mental disturbance. Alternatively, it is sometimes produced as a side-effect of certain drugs.

Eustachian tube Tube each side of the head that connects the *nasal cavity* and the back of the throat with the *middle ear*. Its major function is to equalize air pressure on each side of the *eardrum* – a function which it may not be able to fulfil when external pressure changes rapidly (as in a high-flying aircraft) or when there is infection in the nose or ear. The tube also drains secretions from the middle ear down the throat. It is named after the Renaissance Italian anatomist Bartolommeus Eustachius (*c.*1520–1574) of Rome.

euthanasia Deliberate taking of somebodyís life when continued existence would mean only further suffering. It is illegal, in any circumstances, even if the person specifically requests death. Ethical and legal questions arise, however, when a patient is allowed to die through the withholding of treatment, or when there is a question over the definition of "life" in relation to the person.

evolution Gradual development through a series of forms, usually taken to mean biological evolution of a species over time. As originally advanced by Charles Darwin in 1859, it embraces evolution by natural selection ("survival of the fittest"), the idea that pre-existing or spontaneous variations between individuals that confer survival advantages in a particular environment make it more likely that individuals possessing such characteristics will live to reproduce; such characteristics will therefore be preferentially inherited by succeeding generations and come to predominate within the group. Over prolonged periods, differing levels of adaptation between groups gives rise to different species, and to an evolutionary hierarchy from primitive to higher organisms. The discovery of *DNA* (the molecule that encodes genetic information) and the development of techniques of genetic analysis have enabled greater understanding of evolutionary links between species.

exanthem Medical name for any kind of *rash* that accompanies an infection; the term is sometimes given as exanthema.

excision Surgical cutting out of tissue or an entire organ.

excitability Either the capacity of a nerve or a muscle to fulfil its function; or the susceptibility of an individual to nervous agitation or arousal.

excretion Elimination from the body of waste products. It includes the passing of *faeces* through the process of *defecation*, of *urine* through urination (micturition), of carbon dioxide by exhalation, or of sweat and water through the skin.

exercise Activity that maintains the size and capacity of the muscles for work, generally undertaken voluntarily in order to keep fit. Without exercise, muscles waste away. There are many forms of exercises, some of them specifically remedial (physiotherapy). Regularity in exercising is essential, however; strenuous activity by a person unaccustomed to it may have dangerous results.

exhalation Breathing out – part of the process of *respiration*, by which the body takes in oxygen from the surrounding air and gets rid of carbon dioxide, the waste product of the bodyís metabolism. It is achieved by relaxing the muscles of the *diaphragm* (the muscular sheet partitioning the chest and abdominal cavities) as directed by the respiratory centre in the brain. As it relaxes, the diaphragm effectively rises, at the same time as the ribcage sags and contracts, and air in the lungs is forced out.

exhaustion Condition of extreme physical *fatigue*, often also accompanied by impairment of intellectual capacity. There may be a desperate desire to sleep or at least rest, "roaring" in the ears, and inability to focus the eyes; muscular co-ordination may be inhibited and speech badly slurred.

exhibitionism Exposure of the genitalia, suddenly and unexpectedly, to one or more people (especially people of the opposite sex) in a public place. Exhibitionists are virtually always men, and their act is a form of sexual deviation in seeking to gain sexual satisfaction from anotherís shock or humiliation.

exocrine gland Gland that uses a duct to convey its secretions to the requisite site – unlike *endocrine glands* which emit their secretions directly into the bloodstream. Exocrine glands include the *sweat glands* and *sebaceous glands*.

exophthalmos Protrusion of the eyeballs, giving a rather wild, staring appearance. Causes include injury and infection of the *orbit* in which the eyeball sits – but by far the most common cause is *hyperthyroidism*.

expectorant Drug that promotes the secretion of sputum (or the loosening of mucus) in the upper respiratory tract, so that it can be coughed up. Many cough medicines contain expectorants; some, in high dosages, may cause vomiting.

extension Process of straightening a limb or digit that has been bent (flexed), generally relying on the complementary actions of two sets of muscles. One set (the extensor muscles) contracts forcibly to bring one of the two bones of the joint in line with the other. The other set (*flexor* muscles) passively dilates in order to allow the maximum extension, or contracts slightly to control the extension to a desired angle. The term is sometimes alternatively used to mean the same as *traction*.

extensor Muscle that actively causes *extension*.

exteroreceptor Sensory nerve ending sited in the skin or an outer mucous membrane that responds to stimuli emanating from outside the body. All of what are called "the five senses" rely on exteroreceptors. Those sensory nerves that monitor internal stimuli include *proprio(re)captors* and chemoreceptors.

extracellular fluid All the fluid of the body that surrounds cells (as opposed to the fluid within the cells).

extradural In the tiny space between the *dura mater* – the outermost of the three *meninges* membranes that surround the brain and spinal cord – and the surrounding tissue (in the head, the skull).

extrasensory perception (ESP) One of the paranormal phenomena that is the subject of research in *parapsychology*.

extrasystole Fairly common – and usually harmless – form of *arrhythmia* of the heart: the effect is of a missed beat, or a series of half-beats. The reason, as the term implies, is actually an extra beat, emanating from an area of the heart other than the sinoatrial node (the natural *pacemaker*), that takes place before the normal beat and prevents the natural beat from occurring at all. Because the extra beat is generally very weak, it may not be felt – and the effect is of a beat missed altogether. An increased occurrence of an extrasystole should, however, be assessed by a doctor.

extra-uterine pregnancy Alternative term for *ectopic pregnancy*.

extrovert Personality of an individual who enjoys company, would not choose to be alone, and thus tends to socialize frequently. Extroverts commonly dominate conversations and events, and are statistically good leaders – but are apt to lose interest in long-term projects and routine.

exudate Liquid that "weeps" from a *weeping wound*, comprising *leukocytes* and proteins that constitute part of the bodyís normal inflammatory defence mechanism. It is not the same as *pus*.

eye Organ of sight, consisting basically of a *lens* that focuses light on a highly sensitive *retina* which sends neural messages to the brain for interpretation. To reach the lens, however, light has first to travel through a transparent outer layer – the *cornea* – and through the watery, non-refractive *aqueous humour*, at the discretion of muscles that control the size of the circular gap in the pigmented *iris* called the pupil. The other side of the lens, the light travels through the jelly-like *vitreous humour* (again non-refractive) before ideally being focused on the *rod* and cone *cells* of the retina. Nerves connected with the rods and cones in turn connect with the *optic nerve* from each eye and lead – via the optic chiasma – to the brain. The entire mechanism of the eye (the eyeball) is enclosed in a tough white fibrous layer (sclera) and located in a closely fitting socket of bone within the skull, the *orbit*. Common defects in vision are *myopia* (shortsightedness), *hypermetropia* (longsightedness), *presbyopia* (longsightedness of old age) and *colour blindness*. Other conditions that cause visual problems include *migraine*, high blood pressure (*hypertension*), *cataract* and *glaucoma*. Infections in and around the eye include *blepharitis, conjunctivitis, dacryocystitis* and *stye*.

eyelash One of the protective hairs (medical name: cilium) that fringe the *eyelids*.

eyelid Membrane-lined covering of skin, muscle and connective tissue over the front of each eye, fringed at the front with a protective row of hairs (eyelashes). The *lacrimal glands* keep the mucous membrane lining (*conjunctiva*) moist and clean. Disorders of the eyelids include *blepharitis, chalazion, conjunctivitis* and *stye*.

F

face lift Cosmetic surgery to rejuvenate the appearance of the face by the careful removal of specific areas of skin in order to tighten the areas that are left. Areas most commonly removed are around the eyes (bags around the eyes) and on the neck (double chin), but sometimes also above the eyebrows. Incisions follow *Langer's lines*, and *stitches* are kept as small as possible in order to minimize scarring.

facial nerve Seventh cranial nerve, which supplies motor and sensory functions to muscles of the face, scalp, cheeks and lips (the "muscles of expression"), the foremost part of the tongue, the *salivary glands* under the tongue, and the *lacrimal glands*; a branch also connects with the bones of the *middle ear*.

facies Facial expression used as a diagnostic aid. A number of disorders result in quite distinctive facies (such as the staring eyes of hyperthyroidism, or the vacancy of adenoidal infection).

faeces Excreta, passed out through the *anus*. The faeces represent a combined mass of the final waste products of digested food, bile pigments, watery mucus and other glandular secretions, and indigestible or foreign matter (especially bacteria). After temporary storage and accumulation in the *rectum*, faeces are ejected in the process of *defecation*. Consistency and colour – sometimes even chemical analysis – may be a significant diagnostic aid to a doctor. For example, black faeces (melaena) may be caused by the presence of partly digested blood from a haemorrhage in the digestive tract, whereas pale fatty faeces may indicate a disorder of the liver or gall bladder. *Impaction* of the faeces within the rectum or *colon*, for any reason, is experienced as *constipation*.

Fahrenheit Temperature scale devised by the German instrument-maker Gabriel Fahrenheit (1686–1736) who lived for many years in England. On it the freezing point of water is 32°F; the boiling point is 212°F; and normal blood temperature is 98.4°F (as distinct from 0°C, 100°C and 37°C on the now more customary *Celsius* scale).

fainting Medical name syncope, temporary semiconsciousness or unconsciousness, caused by sudden emotional shock, unaccustomed standing or kneeling, or injury which in turn causes a decrease in the blood supply to the brain. There may be an initial *aura*, comprising visual disturbance and a cold sweat. The effect is usually over in minutes or even seconds.

faith healing Cure apparently effected solely by a patientís faith in the power or mediation of the healer. Many faith healers work through "the laying-on of hands" by which the patients believe a form of spiritual energy is transmitted. A few healers disclaim any religious element to their work.

fallen arch Permanent failure of the ligaments to support the bones and muscles of the middle of the foot – the arch between the heel and the ball of the foot – so that the entire under-surface of the foot is flat on the ground. It is commonly caused by muscular weakness or overexertion, or obesity, during childhood; physiotherapy at that time may be remedial.

Fallopian tube Either of two tubular structures in a womanís abdomen extending from each side of the upper wall of the *uterus* (womb) to very close to an *ovary*. During the fertile period of each episode of the *menstrual cycle*, a single *ovum* leaves one of the ovaries and is caught in the frond-like *fimbriae* at the head of the nearby Fallopian tube. From there it travels down inside towards the uterus. On its way it may (if sexual intercourse has taken place recently) meet an oncoming *sperm* by which it is fertilized – for *conception* ordinarily occurs in the Fallopian tube – forming a *zygote* (a small ball of cells, the first stage in forming an embryo). The zygote then travels on down to the uterus for *implantation* (embedding in the wall of the womb to begin a pregnancy). Occasionally, it implants instead inside the Fallopian tube, causing an *ectopic pregnancy*, which may require emergency surgery. Blockage of the Fallopian tube, for example, by *pelvic inflammatory disease*, is a common cause of infertility; deliberately preventing passage of an ovum by occluding (blocking), cutting and/or tying the Fallopian tubes is a method of permanently sterilizing a woman.

Fallot's tetralogy Congenital malformation of the heart amounting to four separate but interconnected defects, first described by the French doctor Étienne Fallot (1850–1911). The defects are: constriction of the artery bringing blood from the lungs; a gap in the wall (septum) between the *ventricles*; location of the junction of the *aorta* so that it thus connects with both ventricles; and abnormal thickening of the wall of the right ventricle. Babies born with the tetralogy are *"blue babies"*. The condition can be surgically corrected.

false pregnancy Medical name pseudocyesis, the condition of a woman who undergoes most of the physical symptoms of *pregnancy* (including abdominal swelling and increase in weight, morning sickness and lack of menstrual periods) but who is in fact not pregnant. The cause is virtually always emotional – a form of wish fulfilment – and some of the effects are those of emotion on the *pituitary gland*. Treatment includes psychiatric care.

false teeth Common name for *dentures*.

familial disorders Disorders towards which some families seem to have a predisposing factor that may or may not be hereditary.

family doctor Local *general practitioner* responsible for primary care, the first contact a patient has with the health services. Patients may consult with any illness, and the family doctor is responsible for deciding whether referral to a specialist or for hospital admission (secondary care) is needed, or whether any necessary treatment can be provided without such assessment. Modern family doctors also provide a range of public health and preventive services, such as *immunization* or *screening* tests.

family planning Common expression for the use of any method of *contraception* in order to avoid repeated or inconvenient pregnancies. The term is used also in the Third World for some programmes for popular education on (and even provision of) various contraceptive methods.

famine Regional shortage of food, leading to widescale *malnutrition* and epidemic outbreaks of *deficiency disorders*.

farmer's lung Inflammation of the air-sacs (*alveoli*) in the lungs, caused by an *allergy* to fungal spores in badly dried hay; it is an occupational hazard of farmers who use hay to feed livestock. Treatment is by avoidance – recurrent bouts can lead to a chronic and progressive form of lung tissue degeneration.

fascia Layer of membranous *connective tissue* that sheathes most organs within the body. For example, fascia divides the dual surface stratum of the skin from deeper tissues; other fasciae cover the muscles.

fat A type of *lipid* (natural substances including fats, certain *steroid* hormones and various other complex molecules found in the body), one of the three main food groups, which, weight for weight, has twice the energy content of *protein* or *carbohydrate*, and thus represents the major form in which energy is stored in the body. Storage is mostly in *adipose* tissue (the fatty layer) under the skin, which provides efficient insulation but in excess leads to *obesity*. Dietary fats also provide *essential fatty acids* (those that cannot be made in the body) and are vital for absorption of certain *vitamins* in the intestines. Foods rich in fats include dairy products, eggs, oily fish and meat, and vegetable oils. When eaten in the diet, fats are converted in the body to *triglycerides* (a combination of *fatty acids* and glycerol), the form in which fat is stored. Dietary fats are classified as saturated, mainly from animal products and regarded as relatively unhealthy; or unsaturated (mono- or polyunsaturated), found in most vegetable oils and oily fish, which are vital to normal body functioning. High levels of certain forms of *cholesterol* (another dietary lipid mainly found in animal products, and also made in the body) in the bloodstream may contribute to the atheroma (fatty deposits in arteries) underlying *arteriosclerosis* (arterial damage).

fatigue Physical – and to some extent mental – tiredness, felt mostly as a lack of inner energy, muscular weariness, and a strong desire for rest or sleep. That fatigue has mental aspects is evident from the difference that mood makes: absorbing interest or success can both drive away fatigue. The physical effects in the muscles follow the using of available energy resources faster than the waste products can be carried away in the blood. Other causes of fatigue include inadequate diet, unaccustomed stress, disease and high environmental temperature. Treatment is to rest and remedy the cause.

fatty acid Major constituent of various *lipids* including *triglycerides* (see *fat*), supplied in food generally as oleic, palmitic or stearic acid, or synthesized in other forms within the body. Those fatty acids that cannot be made in the body and so are vital within the diet are called *essential fatty acids*.

fatty degeneration Degeneration of cells deprived of nutrients (generally through poor circulation, but sometimes instead because of dietary insufficiency or alcoholism) and consequent accumulation of *fat* they can no longer dispose of. Cells involved are commonly those of the heart or liver, and the effects may be life-threatening.

favism Inherited allergy of the red blood cells (erythrocytes) to substances ingested by eating the fava broad bean. Symptoms are *anaemia*, high temperature, diarrhoea and nausea, and may lead to coma as more red blood cells are destroyed. Treatment may include a blood transfusion. The condition occurs mostly in countries of the Near East.

feces American spelling of *faeces*.

feedback mechanism Self-regulating balancing system within the body by which levels of the constituents of the blood, lymphatic, hormonal or digestive systems are controlled and monitored. An example of positive feedback is the secretion by the pancreas of the hormones insulin and glucagon – one to lower blood sugar (glucose) level when it is too high, the other to raise the level when it is too low. In negative feedback, the increase in output of a hormone or enzyme acts as its own regulator, eventually shutting off output (an example is *adrenocorticotropic hormone*).

feminization Appearance in a man of the characteristics of an adult woman: enlargement of the breasts, disappearance of the hair on the face and body, and softness of the musculature. (The voice, once broken, remains the same, however.) The cause is hormonal imbalance, and the treatment therefore usually includes male *sex hormones*.

femoral triangle Anatomical name for a triangular area on the inside of the thigh, containing the femoral artery, vein and nerve. The area is also defined by the sartorius muscle, the adductor longus muscle and the inguinal ligament.

femur Thigh bone, the long bone in the upper leg; it is the largest bone in the body. At the hip, the ball-shaped head of the femur articulates with the *acetabulum*, a socket to which all three bones comprising each side of the pelvis contribute. At the knee, the femur articulates with the *tibia* (shin bone), and a groove in it accommodates the tendon-covered kneecap (patella).

fertility Ability of a man or woman to have children. The term is used also to refer to a statistical measure of the birth rate of a region or population.

fertility drug One of a number of drugs used to promote ovulation by stimulating the *ovaries* to produce and release mature *ova* (egg cells). These may be used in women with infertility stemming from ovulatory problems, with the aim of increasing the chance of conceiving following sexual intercourse. The method sometimes causes multiple births. Such drugs may also be used to boost ovulation ("super-ovulation") as part of assisted reproduction techniques such as *in vitro* fertilization (IVF) – "test tube baby" technology – when the aim is to cause multiple ova to be released, which are then collected for fertilization in the laboratory.

fertilization Fusion of a mature *ovum* and a *sperm*, an event that represents *conception* – the formation of a *zygote* (a small ball of cells, the first stage in forming an embryo). When this occurs after *sexual intercourse*, it usually takes place in a *Fallopian tube* (the tube that carries ova from the ovaries towards the womb). Although there may be many sperm in the tube, only one can penetrate and so fertilize the ovum – changes in the membrane surrounding the ovum prevent other sperm from entering afterwards. Dividing by cleavage (splitting), the zygote travels on down the Fallopian tube (becoming first a *morula* then a *blastocyst*) to the *uterus* (womb) for *implantation*. *Gestation* has begun. This is fertilization *in vivo* (within the body). Fertilization may also take place in the artificial environment of a laboratory; known as *in vitro fertilization* ("test tube baby" technology).

fetishism Sexual desire that focuses on something less than a complete person – thus on a part of a person (such as the hair, a foot), on a personís clothing or accoutrements (a shoe, a dress, underwear, and especially individual types of these) – or on a class of objects (rubber items, leather items). The object of desire is the fetish. Treatment is generally through psychiatric counselling and *behaviour therapy*.

fetus American (also alternative British) spelling of *foetus*.

fever Body temperature higher than normal (normal is 37 C or 98.4 F, measured in the mouth; 37.2 C or 99 F in the rectum), associated also with shivering and headache, thirst and muscular aches; in addition there may be nausea and either diarrhoea or constipation. The medical term is pyrexia and the cause is almost always an infection – although, rarely, fever results from a blood disorder or cancer. Medical diagnosis should be sought if fever lasts for more than a day, if vomiting occurs, or if the temperature rises as high as 39.4 C

(104 F). A temperature higher than 40.5 C (105 F) may cause delirium. Certain infections (such as malaria) are accompanied by specific cycles of temperature variation. Treatment depends on the cause, and may include antibiotics if it is a bacterial infection. Drugs such as aspirin and paracetamol can help to reduce fever.

fibre in the diet See *dietary fibre*.

fibre-optic Describing an instrument that makes use of *fibre-optics*.

fibre-optics Science and use of synthetic fibres that transmit light from one tip to the other. A long, thin bundle of fibres (endoscope), inserted through a body orifice or incision and taking its own light with it, can thus pick up an image from inside the body and relay it to the surface, no matter how convoluted the fibres become.

fibrillation Fast and irregular series of muscle contractions, particularly of the muscles that form the chambers of the heart. The cause in other body muscles is degeneration of the nerves supplying the muscles. In the heart the effect is to separate the beating of the *atria* from that of the *ventricles*. Atrial fibrillation most often results from *heart disease*, *arteriosclerosis* or *hyperthyroidism*, and can be treated with drugs. Ventricular fibrillation – caused by electric shock, coronary thrombosis (*myocardial infarction*) or drugs – prevents the pumping of blood around the body and requires emergency treatment as for *cardiac arrest*.

fibrin Strand-like product of the action of *thrombin* (the major blood *clotting* agent) on *fibrinogen* in the blood *plasma* at the site of a wound. In the form of a network, filaments of fibrin trap blood *platelets* and slow local blood flow, thus causing coagulation, clotting, and the beginning of the healing process.

fibrinogen Protein present in blood *plasma*, which reacts with the enzyme *thrombin* at the site of a wound to form filaments of insoluble *fibrin*. Fibrinogen ordinarily remains in solution in plasma because thrombin is formed only at the site of an injury.

fibroid Benign growth of fibrous muscle tissue in the uterus (womb) or sometimes the vagina. The presence of a fibroid (or fibroids) is a common condition, generally resulting in no symptoms at all. Rarely, however, they become so large as to press on other abdominal organs or to cause pain and heavy menstrual bleeding; in this state they might inhibit fertility or – in pregnancy – even cause a miscarriage. Treatment is unnecessary unless symptoms are troublesome. If they are, fibroids can sometimes be removed by surgery, although in severe cases hysterectomy (removal of the womb) may be necessary.

fibrositis Inflammation of fibrous tissue, particularly of that supporting or forming the muscles of the back. Symptoms are pain, especially in very localized areas of muscle, and stiffness. Heat or massage may be effective as treatment.

fibula Thinner of the two bones that frame the lower leg (the other is the shin bone – the *tibia*). It is also the outer of the two, and articulates at the top with the tibia, just below the knee, and at the bottom with the tibia and the *talus*, which part of it overhangs as the ankle bone. The fibula takes no body weight but acts as an anchorage for many leg and foot muscles.

filament Thin strand of tissue or chain of cells.

filariasis Infestation of the lymphatic system by any of several types of parasitic *roundworms* carried by mosquitoes. Symptoms are inflammation and blockage of lymph vessels, leading in some cases to massive swelling; one example is *elephantiasis*.

filling In dentistry, the stopping of a carefully prepared hole in a tooth, using any of several mediums, usually to treat *tooth decay* (caries).

filtration Straining of a liquid (through a membrane or other form of very thin tissue, through a fibrous surface such as paper, or through a mesh) in order to trap and extract particles or constituents too large to go through the pores of the filter.

fimbria One of the filaments or strands that make up a sort of fringe – particularly the frond-like fimbriae at the top end of each *Fallopian tube*, which receive an ovum from the nearby ovary.

finger Digit on the hand, usually differentiated from the thumb (from which it differs by having three bones – phalanges – rather than two). Movement at the joints between phalanges is effected by tendons along upper and lower surfaces, connected to muscles in the forearm. The skin of the fingertips is particularly well supplied with touch sensors, nerves and blood vessels. The pattern of lines and whorls – fingerprints – are unique to each person.

first aid Any form of emergency treatment designed to help a patient before the arrival of full medical services. In many cases it is a matter of *artificial respiration* (especially using *mouth-to-mouth resuscitation* or *cardiopulmonary resuscitation*) or of pressure on a wound to prevent blood loss (*haemorrhage*). Other common forms of emergency therapy include the *Heimlich manoeuvre* (for a patient who is choking), immobilizing a *fracture* (or dislocation), and assisting at a childbirth following the unexpected onset of *labour*. An important part of first aid consists simply of providing warmth, comfort and reassurance until professional help arrives.

fissure Abnormal split or crack in a tissue surface (skin or mucous membrane). A common type is an anal fissure, in which the skin of the anus splits, usually during the defecation of impacted faeces. Pain from a fissure is always acute. The term is used also for some normal clefts in tissue, such as between lobes of the brain or in the enamel of a tooth.

fistula Hole in tissue, generally discharging fluid. A fistula abnormally connects two body cavities or one body cavity and the exterior. Some result from ulceration; others from an abscess; and a few represent inadequate repair after surgery. Rarely, a fistula may occur spontaneously.

fit Either a sudden acute attack of one or more relatively violent symptoms, as with paroxysms of coughing or, more seriously, with convulsions in grand mal *epilepsy*; or the quality of *health* of a person in good overall condition (who is, therefore, fit).

fixation In *psychoanalysis*, the arrest of development in a personality at a stage before maturity, generally as a result of emotional trauma. Consequent behavioural abnormalities may eventually amount to *mental illness* or *personality disorders*. But in common usage, relating to psychology, the term is equivalent to *obsession*. In microscopy, the term is used for the process of fixing a specimen within a solid medium, or by freezing, for examination.

flat foot Condition of a foot with a *fallen arch*.

flatulence Presence of air and gas (*flatus*) in the stomach or the intestines, caused mostly either by hasty eating or drinking (and consequent swallowing of air) or by fermentation of food in the stomach and the small intestine. Flatulence results in discomfort and the symptoms of *indigestion*, and an urge to expel the flatus upwards or downwards. Treatments for indigestion often help.

flatus Air and other gas in the stomach or intestines, causing *flatulence*.

flea Small, wingless jumping insect that sucks blood through the skin of mammalian hosts as a parasite. In so doing, most fleas inject an anticoagulant fluid in order to increase blood flow locally – and may thus transmit disease (for example the rat flea carries the bacteria that cause bubonic plague).

Fleming, Alexander (1881–1955) Scottish bacteriologist who, when working to find ways of destroying bacteria in 1928, accidentally discovered *penicillin*. It was left to others to isolate the active principle, but by 1943 mass production was in hand as part of the war effort. He was awarded a Nobel Prize in 1945.

flexion Process of bending a limb or digit, generally relying on the complementary actions of two sets of muscles. One set (the flexor muscles) contracts forcibly to bend one of the two bones of the joint towards the other; the other set (extensor muscles) relaxes in order to allow the maximum flexion or contracts slightly to control the flexion to the desired angle. The extensors may then act to straighten the joint.

flexor Muscle that causes *flexion*.

floating ribs Lowest two pairs of *ribs*, attached at the back – as are all the ribs – to thoracic *vertebrae* of the spine, but at the front unattached to any bone or even cartilage, supported instead only by muscles in the chest wall (intercostal muscles).

flooding In psychiatry, obliging a patient repeatedly to confront a feared object, either in fact or in thought, in order to overcome a *phobia*. If motivation is high, the treatment may be rapidly effective – although emotionally wearing for the patient.

'flu Common abbreviation of *influenza*.

flukes Several species of flatworm that may infest the body as parasites. Adults have suckers with which they attach themselves, and cause serious symptoms. Major sites of infestation – specific to each species – are the liver, lungs, blood vessels, and intestines. Eggs released by the flukes pass out in the faeces and, in countries with poor sanitation, hatch into larvae that penetrate certain types of snail. After another stage of development the flukes leave their snail hosts and form cysts on vegetation or enter another host (where they may be consumed by humans), or directly penetrate the bare foot of a human.

fluoride Fluorine compound, ions of which (when absorbed by the enamel of the teeth) help to prevent *tooth decay* (caries). The process of adding fluoride to public water supplies is called fluoridation. Dietary deficiency of fluoride may have an adverse effect on tooth enamel and possibly some components of bone – but long-term excess may conversely cause brown mottling and weakening of the tooth enamel (fluorosis), although this is very rare.

fluoroscope Older machine for viewing "live" X-ray pictures by relaying images to a screen coated in a substance that fluoresces when X-rays are projected on it. More modern versions use special television monitors or image intensifiers.

flush Temporary reddening of the face, with or without a simultaneous wave of heat being felt. It may be a sign of some infections. A flush with a wave of heat is more generally known as a *hot flush*, as may occur during the *menopause* in women.

flutter Another term for *arrhythmia* of the heart.

flux Abnormal or excess flow from an organ or body cavity.

focus Point of convergence of rays of light that pass through a *lens*. In the eye that point is ideally on the *retina*, and vision is consequently sharp and clear. To achieve this, the lens is elastic and may be made more concave or convex – according to the distance from which the light is travelling – by being stretched or squeezed by tiny muscles and ligaments. But this elasticity (*accommodation*) is limited, especially as one gets older, and the point of focus may fall either in front of the retina (*myopia*, or shortsightedness) or at a theoretical point behind the retina (*hypermetropia*, or longsightedness), with consequent visual deficiencies. Such deficiencies can be corrected by using corrective *glasses* or *contact lenses*.

focusing *Accommodation* of the *lens* of the eye, in order to *focus* rays of light on the *retina*.

foetus Stage of *gestation* of an unborn child from the eighth week to the end of labour (childbirth); before that period it is called an *embryo*.

folic acid Vitamin of the B complex linked with the activity of vitamin B_{12} in facilitating cell division, and thus essential to the synthesis of nucleic acids, particularly during pregnancy. Main dietary sources of folic acid include liver, yeast, kidney and leafy green vegetables. A deficiency may lead to megaloblastic *anaemia*.

folk medicine Practices and customs originating in localized communities around the world that are aimed at treating and curing ill health. Some are mere superstition but many rely on medicines made from local plants and herbs, extracts from some of which are under increasing investigation to assess their healing properties. Many modern drugs began life as synthesized versions of the main chemical components of traditional plant remedies, for example, the heart drug digitalis (from foxgloves). In some areas of the world, folk medicine remains the only kind of therapy available.

follicle Small sac-like cavity that produces and secretes a cellular body or a glandular substance. Examples are *ovarian follicles* (producing ova), *hair follicles* (hair roots) and thyroid follicles (*thyroid hormone*). The term is used also for certain types of *cyst*.

follicle-stimulating hormone (FSH) Hormone produced and secreted by the anterior (front) of the *pituitary gland*. In women, during the first half of each episode of the menstrual cycle, FSH stimulates the maturing of one *ovarian follicle* to the stage at which the follicle finally releases its ovum (*ovulation*). In men, FSH stimulates the *testes* to produce sperm. In both men and women, injections of FSH may improve fertility; in women, however, it may do so to the point of producing multiple births.

fomentation Application of a *poultice*. (The term is sometimes used also to mean the application of *liniment* or similar lotion.)

fontanelle Either of two openings – the anterior (front) and posterior (back) fontanelles – on the top of a babyís *skull*, representing gaps where the sutures, or lines of fusion, between the eight bones that make up the skull meet. At birth these bones have not yet fully fused together, allowing the skull a degree of flexibility within the birth canal during childbirth. During the next year and a half, the edges of the bones gradually knit together and ossify (become incorporated into the normal bony structure of the skull), closing both fontanelles. Until this occurs, the gaps are protected by a tough membrane, easily resilient enough to withstand normal touching and washing. Despite this, the largest fontanelle – at the front of the skull – is often called the "soft spot", perhaps because it tends to bulge when the baby cries.

food Mixture of *carbohydrates, fats, proteins, trace elements, vitamins* and *fibre* that a person eats. Although a balance between these elements is advisable – and some evidence exists that such a balance comes naturally – relatively few people actively seek to create or maintain a balance that suits their age, weight, sex or lifestyle. Most people (for one reason or another) eat more, or less, than necessary to provide the energy required (measured in *calories*).

food additives Any ingredients not normally present in a particular food but added to make it less liable to decay, more palatable, nicer to look at or smell, or look like other food. Some are natural substances, such as salt, but many are chemicals, and the increase in the use of such food additives has been matched by a similar increase in the number of people who suffer from *food allergies*; so many people take care not to eat foods containing additives.

food allergy *Allergy* to a specific food or constituent in food. Some reactions may be severe, amounting even to anaphylactic shock, for which emergency treatment is necessary.

food chain Series of living organisms linked by the fact that each forms part or all of the staple diet of the next organism higher in the series. Humans are at the top of many food chains.

food poisoning Disorder of the digestive system caused by the consumption of food contaminated by bacteria (such as *Salmonella*) or their toxins (as with *botulism*), by chemical poisoning (as with insecticides not washed off), or by natural poisoning (as with poisonous berries or fungi). Food poisoning due to infections can be transmitted by contamination at source, as with vegetables contaminated with animal faeces or shellfish caught in sewage-polluted waters, by poor hygiene among food handlers, or by inadequate storage conditions or preparation of foods that allows bacteria to multiply. Inadequately cooked or cooked then reheated meals are particular culprits. Symptoms in most cases are restricted to vomiting, diarrhoea, abdominal pain and prostration; more serious forms may result in death. Treatment depends on the cause but may aim only at alleviating the symptoms until recovery; sometimes antibiotics may be necessary.

foot Extremity of the leg, from the ankle to the toes. It consists of five long metatarsal bones that frame the arch of the foot between the *calcaneus* (heel hone) and the toes, the seven tarsal bones of the ankle (equivalent to the bones in the palm of the hand), and the bones at the joint of each *toe* (phalanges). The big toe has two bones; the other toes have three each. Movement of the foot and toes is governed by muscles in the lower leg, and tendons in the foot. Sometimes the muscles and ligaments that support the arch of the foot suffer failure, resulting in a *fallen arch* and *flat foot*.

foramen Natural passage within an otherwise relatively solid structure of the body. The foramen magnum, for example, is the hole in the occiput of the skull through which the spinal cord and its surrounding membranes pass.

forceps Pair of pincers with a specialized pair of pincer-heads. There are various forms of medical forceps, all designed for specific purposes and having heads to suit. Some are designed to extract teeth; others to clamp arteries or hold dressings in place; yet others to hold bones or other tissues in place during surgery or the reduction of a fracture; and still others to gently draw a baby from the birth canal.

forebrain Large area of the brain comprising the tissues furthest to the front and top: the *thalamus* and the *hypothalamus* (together known as the diencephalon), and the *cerebral hemispheres*. Some authorities also include the nearby *pineal body*, and the *pituitary gland* which hangs beneath the hypothalamus. The forebrain represents the part of the brain that differs from the brain of any other creature, both in proportional size and in intellectual and emotional capacity.

forensic medicine Branch of medicine concerned with producing evidence for a court of law. Techniques are thus geared to investigation – of blood or other body fluids found at the scene of a crime, of the nature and cause of injuries or death, of drugs and poisons and their uses, and so on. Most practitioners are experts in *pathology* and may report to a *coroner*ís court following a *post mortem*.

foreskin Common name for the *prepuce*.

formula List detailing the exact composition of a compound substance. A formula may be used by a dispensing chemist (pharmacist) to fulfil a doctorís prescription for a drug. The term is sometimes also used for forms of milk prepared for bottle-feeding babies.

fossa Natural hollow or depression within an otherwise relatively solid structure of the body. The cubital fossa, for example, is the vaguely triangular depression in the bone at the elbow.

fostering Rearing and caring for. The term is used mostly of families who take in and look after children who are not related, with or without financial assistance from other parties. It is not uncommon for local welfare authorities to remove children from families with a particularly corrupting or violent background, and place them – temporarily or otherwise – in the care of authorized and experienced foster parents (although such a removal can independently cause emotional trauma to the children). Fostering by itself does not entitle a child so fostered to be regarded for legal purposes as one of the fostering family: that requires the legal formalities of adoption and, generally, the permission of at least one of the true parents.

fovea Natural hollow or depression in a body structure. The fovea retinae, for example, is the shallow depression at the centre of the *retina* of the eye, the area that is the optimum focus for the visual field. The fovea femoralis is a pit in the head of the femur (thigh bone).

fracture Break in a bone. Fractures are classified in various ways. A compound fracture is one in which the skin is broken, a simple fracture remains within the skin; a comminuted fracture involves a splintered bone, and is described as a complicated fracture if other organs and tissues are injured by the splinters; an impacted fracture occurs when one of the two new "ends" of the bone caused by the break is driven into the other. To these initial types may be added further descriptions relating to the form of the break. A transverse fracture is a break straight across a bone; an oblique fracture is a diagonal break; a spiral fracture is caused by twisting; and a greenstick fracture (which occurs only in children whose bones are still flexible) breaks only half through the bone. The most common sites of fracture are the collarbone, the wrist and the ankle. In every case, treatment is immobilization – preferably using a splint – until medical aid is available. A doctor may or may not immediately reduce the fracture (set the bone), but immobilization is necessary thereafter, usually in a plaster cast, while the bone mends. *Traction* (tension) may also be applied to keep it healing straight. If the skin is broken, too, the wound requires cleaning and the application of antiseptics.

fraternal twins Twins that are the result of the simultaneous fertilization of two *ova* by two *sperm*. They may or may not be of the same sex, have a *placenta* each in the uterus (womb), and after birth resemble each other only as much as any siblings. Identical twins, on the other hand, are the result of the fertilization of an ovum that in cleaving splits into two complete *zygotes*.

freckles Brown spots on fair skin, caused by the presence of the pigment *melanin* in unusual quantity – often following long-term exposure to strong sunlight.

Freud, Sigmund (1856–1939) Viennese psychologist who revolutionized the theory and practice of psychology. Much of his understanding of mental disturbance was based on his precept that some forms of sexual repression are necessary for ordinary *psychosexual development*, but that behavioural problems begin when those repressions are channelled in unusual ways. He called his method of approach and confrontational treatment *psychoanalysis*.

frigidity Lack of sexual desire in a woman, amounting in some cases to complete disinterest in sexual activity. The cause is most often emotional, and treatment may thus concentrate on sympathetic diagnosis of an underlying problem (which may involve fear or ignorance of sex).

frostbite Icing up of the tissues, caused by extreme cold. Initial symptoms involve numbness and pallor in the affected parts (often the extremities). At this stage, treatment should be warming in water of about blood temperature – rubbing is no good, for there is no circulation to assist – and precautions against bacterial infection (to which frostbitten skin is highly susceptible). Ice, once in the tissues, however, causes irreparable damage, and treatment may require amputation.

frozen shoulder Long-term pain and stiffness at the shoulder, resulting from inflammation of the *bursa* at the joint. The cause is commonly unknown, or may be injury; sometimes a frozen shoulder follows a stroke. Treatment is to relieve pain, and may also include *corticosteroid* injections and physiotherapy.

FSH Abbreviation of *follicle-stimulating hormone*.

fugue Abstracted mental state in which somebody acts either normally or abnormally (but not necessarily peculiarly), and thereafter "wakes" with no memory of the period or of the events involved. The fugue generally represents a state of *hysteria* resulting from repressed emotions, which may be released in some behavioural form during the fugue.

fulguration Destruction of tissue by a device that uses the principle of *diathermy* (heat through electricity). The method is employed to treat skin blemishes, especially warts and other growths, and – as an attachment to fibre-optic *endoscopes* – to treat growths in the bladder. See also *cauterization*.

fulminant Acute – sudden, severe and temporary. An alternative form of the term is "fulminating".

fumigation Ridding an environment of parasitic organisms through the use of gases and fumes that are poisonous to them.

functional disorder Type of disorder that produces symptoms for which there is no apparent organic or structural cause. The term thus generally refers to symptoms caused by the emotions – such as stress and anxiety – or by a disturbed mental state.

fundus Area inside a hollow organ farthest away from its opening. The fundus uteri, for example, is the inner end or uppermost part of the *uterus*, farthest away from the cervix.

fungus One of four types of simple organism: yeasts, moulds, rusts and toadstools (including mushrooms). Some forms of yeasts and moulds strongly resemble bacteria and can live as parasites on or in human beings. Despite that resemblance, many fungi are resistant to antibacterial drugs. Diseases and disorders caused by fungi include *actinomycosis, aspergillosis, athlete's foot* (tinea pedis), *blastomycosis, candidiasis, farmer's lung, histoplasmosis, ringworm* and other forms of *tinea*. At the same time, many yeasts and moulds are extremely beneficial as food sources of vitamin B and in the production of *antibiotics* such as *penicillin*.

"funny bone" Area on the back surface of the elbow where the ulnar nerve lies over the *humerus*. Although protected to a degree by the bony olecranon process of the *ulna*, the funny bone is subject to occasional knocks – causing a distinct jar of the nerve, felt as a sharp tingling and numbing sensation that may travel all the way to the little finger (which is where the nerve ends).

furuncle Another name for a boil. The occurrence or recurrence of several boils at a time is known as furunculosis.

fusion In surgery, the joining of two bones immovably, especially of two vertebrae in the spine. It is also called arthrodesis.

G

gait Mode of walking, which may be affected by any of many conditions.

Galen, Claudius (*c.*AD 125–200) Greek physician, biologist and medical writer in imperial Rome, whose descriptions of the workings of the body – many of them right, and some of them ludicrously wrong – were accepted throughout Europe as medical fact for about fourteen centuries after his death.

gall bladder Sac, in shape and size much like a pear, and located under the right lobe of the *liver*, and that acts as a reservoir for the concentration of *bile* produced in the liver. From the gall bladder, triggered by a specific hormone produced when partly digested food enters the *duodenum*, bile is released into the common *bile duct* and from there into the duodenum. There it aids the digestion of fats. Common disorders of the gall bladder include *gallstones* and inflammation (*cholecystitis*).

gallstone Calculus (stone) made up of *bile* pigments, *cholesterol* (derived mainly from animal fats in the diet) and calcium salts, and located in the *gall bladder* or, less commonly but with more severe results, in the common bile duct. Formation of gallstones (cholelithiasis) occurs when the chemical structure of bile changes to make cholesterol less soluble. Symptoms may be absent, or there may be acute pain (biliary colic), *jaundice* and inflammation of the gall bladder (*cholecystitis*) and the common bile duct. Treatment is only necessary if the stones cause symptoms, and may be by surgical removal of the stones (cholelithotomy) or of the entire gall bladder (*cholecystectomy*), by breaking up the stones using ultrasound therapy, or by drugs to dissolve the stones.

gamete Mature *ovum* or *sperm*, able to contribute half the factors necessary for *conception*. A gamete (produced by the type of cell division known as *meiosis*) contains only half the normal number of chromosomes, so that the *zygote* formed by the fusion of an ovum and a sperm has the full complement.

gamma globulin Form of *globulin* present in blood *serum* that is useful in conferring passive *immunity* to specific diseases and conditions resulting from blood incompatibility. Conversely, insufficiency of gamma globulin (as may occur following *chemotherapy*) tends to render a patient susceptible to infection.

gamma radiation Very penetrating form of electromagnetic radiation given off by some radioactive elements. Under very strict conditions, gamma rays may be used therapeutically in *radiotherapy*.

ganglion Collection or bundle of *neurones* (nerve cells) representing a "relay station" for the transmission of nerve impulses down the length of one or more nerves. The term is used also for a type of *cyst* that forms on the synovial sheath of a *tendon*, generally on the back of the hand or on the wrist.

gangrene Death and consequent decay of an area of tissue following the cutting off of its blood supply. Causes are thus conditions that interrupt the arterial blood flow, including injury (as might result from frostbite, burns, crushing or a wound), infected bedsores, arteriosclerosis, *Raynaud's disease*, a strangulated hernia, diabetes mellitus or thrombosis. Gangrene is classified as either "dry" (without bacterial invasion) or "moist" (with additional bacterial invasion). In both conditions the edges of tissue affected may be demarcated by a red line on the skin surface. Dry gangrene causes painful withering of the tissue, loss of sensation, and a change of colour in the skin surface gradually to black. Moist gangrene produces red blistering of the skin, with heat, before showing the same symptoms, accompanied also by a putrefactive smell. Another form of gangrene of this type (gas gangrene) is caused by direct bacterial invasion of a wound. In all cases treatment is surgical removal of the affected tissue, with ample doses of antibiotics.

gastric juices Digestive fluids produced by the lining of the stomach. Main constituents are *hydrochloric acid*, pepsinogen (which causes the further production of the enzyme *pepsin*), *rennin* and mucin (which in turn is the major constituent of *mucus*). Another constituent is the "intrinsic factor" that helps with the absorption of the essential vitamin B_{12}. All of these together compose an acid mixture that breaks down food and kills potentially harmful organisms (such as bacteria) ingested with it.

gastric ulcer Type of *peptic ulcer* (area of erosion in the lining of the gut wall) located in the stomach lining. It occurs when acid and other substances naturally present in the stomach become overconcentrated or attack a weak spot in the lining, and ulcer development is linked with the presence of a bacterium called *Helicobacter pylori*. Symptoms are pain and nausea, usually treatable with *antacid* drugs or combination therapy with antibiotics to eradicate the Helicobacter. Complications include perforation or bleeding, which may necessitate surgical treatment. Full diagnosis is essential in order to distinguish it from stomach *cancer*.

gastritis Inflammation of the stomach lining. Causes of *acute* (short-term) gastritis include infection, excessive alcohol consumption, food poisoning, drug poisoning or ingestion of corrosive or irritant substances. Symptoms are stomach pain, raised temperature, a "furred" tongue, and possibly vomiting. Chronic (long-term) gastritis is usually due to infection with a bacterium called *Helicobacter pylori* and may cause few symptoms, or may progress to *gastric ulcer*. The acute condition usually clears spontaneously; *antacid* drugs may help control symptoms. Treatment of chronic gastritis usually requires combination therapy with antibiotics to eradicate the Helicobacter.

gastroenteritis Inflammation of the stomach lining and part of the small intestine, causing diarrhoea and vomiting, which may be severe. Causes include bacterial or viral infection and toxins (*food poisoning*). Most cases resolve within a few days and all that is necessary is to maintain fluid intake. In severe cases and in infants, the patient may become dehydrated and fluid replacement through a drip may be needed.

gastroenterology Study of the functioning, diseases and disorders of the digestive system, including the *stomach* and *intestines, pancreas, liver* and the *bile* apparatus.

gene The basic unit of genetic material, controlling all cell functions. Formed of a specific sequence of *deoxyribonucleic acid* (DNA) or *ribonucleic acid* (RNA), genes are found paired in great numbers (all in a specific order) on strands – *chromosomes* – in cell nuclei. Each gene is responsible for a particular task in the cell; some control the production of proteins, others regulate the rate at which production proceeds, yet others regulate the intake of protein-building materials, and still others control the manner in which the genes operate. In the sex cells (*sperm* and *ova*), chromosomes are single rather than paired, so that when the cells fuse during *fertilization*, half of the genes of the new generation come from the mother and half from the father. Hereditary characteristics are thus passed from one generation to the next; which particular characteristics occur in the offspring depends on the way the genes are paired and whether individual genes of each parent are *dominant* or *recessive*.

general medicine Medical care provided by a general physician who treats most disorders not requiring the attentions of a surgeon or a specialized practitioner.

general paralysis of the insane Final and most serious symptom of tertiary *syphilis*, usually involving *dementia*, paralysis and convulsions.

general practitioner (GP) Doctor licensed by the countryís medical authority (in the UK, the General Medical Council) to provide primary care and treatment outside a hospital setting. In the UK, GPs also determine access to secondary care by hospital specialists. Most British GPs treat patients on the National Health Service (NHS) scheme, and are paid by the Government according to the total number of patients registered with them as well as by special payments for particular work such as childhood immunizations. Two or more GPs working in joint accommodation may form a partnership or a group practice; a group practice whose accommodation is owned and supported by the local municipal authority is a health centre.

generic drugs Drugs called by their approved, technical, names and not by proprietary names of a manufacturerís devising. For example, diazepam is the generic name of the tranquillizing drug whose proprietary name is Valium.

gene therapy Treatment that aims to cure or alleviate disease by manipulating a patientís *genes* through techniques of *genetic engineering*. Currently most research is conducted in genetic disorders caused by a single defective gene, so that introducing one normal *dominant* gene, or replacing the defective gene with a normal one, could be sufficient to alleviate the condition. Ultimately conditions caused by a combination of genes might be amendable to therapy. It is also possible that such treatment may be useful in introducing helpful genes into cells, for instance, tumour-suppressing genes for *cancer* treatment.

genetic code Information carried by *deoxyribonucleic acid* (DNA) and *messenger ribonucleic acid* (RNA) that determines the structure and function of proteins produced in each body cell. A sequence of chemicals called nucleotides make up the DNA strand codes for different amino acids (the building blocks of proteins); this "message" is taken up by messenger RNA and carried out of the cell nucleus, through the nuclear membrane to a *ribosome* (a specialized unit within the cell), and translated there by transfer RNA into instructions for linking chains of *amino acids* together to make specific proteins. Defects in this process may cause a mutation that alters the proteins produced and may lead to harmful changes for the organism as a whole.

genetic counselling Advice given by a *genetics* specialist to prospective parents on their chances of having children with hereditary congenital abnormalities. Such advice may be offered when the individual or other family members have such a condition or are found to be carrying it, or when the parents have had an affected child (to discuss the risk of a further pregnancy being affected). As well as assessing the risks to future generations, genetic counselling advises on methods of prevention, diagnosis and treatment.

genetic engineering Means of altering the characteristics of an organism by conferring on it a hereditary trait of another organism. This is achieved by a sort of *gene* "transplant", in which genes from the other organism are inserted into the host organismís *DNA*. This involves distinguishing the specific gene(s) coding for the characteristic(s) desired, "cutting" the relevant gene or genes from the *chromosomes*, usually using special enzymes, isolating them, then splicing these into a new "host" chromosome, often using some form of vector (transfer agent). The technique enables human gene coding for vital substances such as insulin, growth hormone or interferon to be inserted into bacteria, so that large quantities of the substance can be produced for medicinal use (recombinant DNA technology), avoiding the use of potentially contaminated material from corpses or of animal substitutes whose action may be slightly different. Other uses include the production of genetically modified cereal crops and vegetables, such as weedkiller-resistant soya; and techniques of *gene therapy*.

genetic "fingerprints" Every person is the result of the pairing of two unique sets of *genes* inherited one from each parent. Every other individual (except an identical twin) thus has another unique set of genes, but genes that may be partly traceable in certain sequences of genetic material in the *chromosomes* to the parents. This means that it is possible not only to identify definitively any person by examining his or her genetic material, but also to identify positively whether a person is the father or mother of a particular child.

genetics Study of heredity. Heredity depends on *genes*. A multitude of paired genes (all in a specific order) make up paired *chromosomes* present as strands of *deoxyribonucleic acid* (DNA) in the nuclei of cells. Through the sex cells of two parents, an individual inherits 23 pairs of chromosomes, the genes of which determine all hereditary characteristics and the development of the body itself, depending only on how specific genes or combinations of genes are paired with the corresponding genes from the other parent – whether one is *dominant* or *recessive*. Some *congenital disorders* both minor (such as colour blindness) and serious (such as haemophilia or Huntingtonís chorea) may be inherited through the presence or absence of specific genes (or even whole chromosomes). Prospective parents anxious about whether they stand a greater chance than most to have children with genetic abnormalities may seek *genetic counselling*. Throughout life, genes continue to produce proteins according to the *genetic code*.

genetic traits Characteristics inherited from parents. Whether a trait is inherited depends on whether the *gene* or genes for it are *dominant* over any *recessive* ones that it or they may be paired with. If the trait relies on a recessive gene, and that gene is paired with a dominant gene for a different trait, the recessive trait is not manifested. Brown eyes, for example, represent the presence of a gene that is dominant over the gene or genes for blue eyes: only if an individual inherits two, paired recessive genes or sets of genes does he or she have blue eyes. Other genetic traits may predispose somebody to certain disorders and diseases; a few are *X-linked disorders*.

genitalia External organs of the reproductive system – the penis and scrotum in a male and the vulva in a female.

genital phase In *psychoanalysis*, the final stage of *psychosexual development* in an individual, the state at which most sensations and emotions that lead to sexual gratification are associated with the *genitalia*. The stages that precede it are the oral, anal, phallic and latent stages.

genitourinary system Another term for the *urogenital system*.

genome The genetic material of an organism, contained in the *genes* on *chromosomes*, which codes for all its biological functions; the term is often used to refer to the genetic material passed on to the next generation by the unpaired *chromosomes* in a single sex cell (an *ovum* or a *sperm*, either containing 23 unpaired chromosomes). The completion of the *Human Genome Project* (a massive international research effort) means that the complete sequence of genes (though not all their functions) forming the human genome is now known.

genotype Either the composition of one or more pairs of genes that together determine a hereditary characteristic; or the genetic make-up of one or more people who have a specific characteristic.

geriatrics Study of the disabilities, disorders and diseases that occur in old age. As a branch of medicine it comprises also care for the elderly.

germ Pathogen, a disease-causing *micro-organism*, particularly an invasive or infective one. The term is used also to describe a form of matter that has the potential to develop into an organism or other collection of cells (such as a seed or spore).

German measles Common name for *rubella*.

gerontology Study of the physical and mental changes involved in *aging*, and of ways to maintain health and vitality after middle age.

Gestalt psychology Equivalent in *psychology* of holistic medicine, in that it is an approach that regards mental processes as parts of one great organization, all equally essential and interdependent contributors to a whole. Much of the experimental work done from its inception in the late 19th century, however, centred solely on the nature of *perception*, and the change in "quality" of a perceived object when perceived in different circumstances. By the 1950s, its insight into this aspect of mental processing had become part of most psychiatristsí background knowledge.

gestation Duration of time within which a *blastocyst* becomes an *embryo*, then a *foetus*, and is finally born as a baby. For humans, gestation lasts about 40 weeks. Gestation thus represents the time spent in the womb, but may refer also to the physical development undertaken during that time. The equivalent, on the motherís part, is *pregnancy*.

gigantism Relatively rare condition in which somebody grows to an abnormal height because of the oversecretion of *growth hormone* (somatotropin) by the *pituitary gland* during adolescence. Later in life, if there is oversecretion of growth hormone (because of a pituitary tumour) the result is *acromegaly*.

gingivitis Inflammation of the *gums*, especially where the teeth meet the gums. The cause is almost always *plaque* (bacteria-containing deposits on the teeth), but is occasionally ill-fitting or dirty dentures, diabetes, pregnancy or gum overgrowth due to certain drugs. Symptoms are pain, swelling of the gums, and a tendency for them to bleed. *Periodontitis* may develop and the teeth may become loose in their sockets. Early stages are easily treated by an improvement (under a dentistís supervision if need be) in teeth-cleaning technique. Periodontitis may require more intensive dental treatment.

gland Body organ that produces a secretion, often a *hormone*, either directly into a system in which it is to take immediate effect (endocrine glands) or via ducts (exocrine glands). Endocrine glands include the *adrenal glands, ovary, pancreas, parathyroid glands, pituitary gland, prostate gland, testes* and *thyroid gland*. Exocrine glands include the *salivary glands* and *sweat glands*.

glandular fever An infectious disease (previously called infectious mononucleosis) caused by a virus, the Epstein-Barr virus. It produces swelling of the *lymph nodes* in the neck, armpits and groin, with lethargy, high temperature, headache and sore throat; there may also be weight loss. The condition mostly affects adolescents and young adults. Possible complications include enlargement of the spleen and kidney malfunction. Symptoms may persist for some weeks and some of those affected develop *chronic fatigue syndrome*, which may last for many months afterwards. Treatment is to alleviate the symptoms and to rest when necessary.

glasses Pair of *lenses*, in frames, of specific shape and measurement to correct visual defects of the eyes (such as *myopia* and *hypermetropia*). In glasses with convex lenses, light is refracted to a nearer focus, thus assisting the eyes to focus on the *retina* an object that would otherwise be focused behind it; such glasses correct hypermetropia (longsightedness). In glasses with concave lenses, light is refracted to a more distant focus, thus assisting the eyes to focus on the retina an object that would otherwise be focused in front of it; such glasses correct myopia (shortsightedness). The lenses of some glasses are divided into two areas of different refractive power (bifocal lenses). The purchase of suitable glasses (also called spectacles) usually follows an eye examination and vision test by an ophthalmic optician.

glaucoma Condition in which increasing intraocular pressure within the eyeball causes visual disturbances such as blurring, auras around light sources and tunnel vision and, if left untreated, leads to eventual blindness. It may occur secondary to other eye diseases that impair the flow of fluid (aqueous humour) within the front part of the eye, but most cases occur without other forms of eye disease. Acute glaucoma results from sudden blockage of drainage of aqueous humour from the angle of the eye and results in pain and marked blurring. It requires urgent treatment. In chronic simple glaucoma the build-up of pressure is gradual and usually occurs without pain. Symptoms become apparent only gradually. Glaucoma becomes increasingly frequent after middle age. What causes the build-up of pressure is usually unknown – although it is more common in longsighted people, and there may be hereditary factors; occasionally glaucoma arises as a complication of *diabetes* mellitus or eye infection. Early treatment with eyedrops to improve fluid outflow from the eye, and tablets to reduce production of fluid, is essential. Surgical drainage may, however, be necessary.

glia Abbreviated form of the term *neuroglia*.

globulin Form of *protein* that has any of several specific functions in the bloodstream. Some serum globulins – such as *gamma globulin* – are part of the *immune system*, operating as *antibodies*. Others act as vehicles for the transport of fats (lipids) or metallic elements.

glomerulonephritis Inflammation of the *glomeruli* (filtering units) in one or both *kidneys*, occurring most commonly as a complication after a bacterial infection of the upper respiratory tract. Symptoms are headache and backache, puffiness of the face, and discoloration of the urine. Because these symptoms result mostly from temporary damage to the glomeruli, causing salt and water retention, treatment is generally no more than dietary restriction of salt and liquids until the condition clears. In chronic, progressive glomerulonephritis, however, additional symptoms are vomiting and, possibly, kidney failure, for which treatment may include drugs and *dialysis*.

glomerulus Network of tiny blood vessels at the concave tip of a *nephron*, the primary filtration unit within a *kidney*. Through the glomeruli, each nephron discriminates between blood (and useful products for reabsorption) and waste fluid; the waste fluid is channelled down a *renal tubule* and along a ureter to the bladder, to be disposed of as *urine*.

glossitis Inflammation of the tongue. Causes include general infection of the mouth and throat through poor oral hygiene, cigarette smoking, alcohol consumption, anaemia, malnutrition, and the use of certain antibiotics. Symptoms are pain, roughness and darkness of the tongue surface, and difficulty in swallowing; the saliva may also be thicker than normal. Treatment depends on the cause and usually requires correction of the underlying problem. Symptom relief may be obtained with mouthwashes in very mild cases of glossitis.

glossopharyngeal nerve Ninth cranial nerve, which is the motor nerve for the *parotid glands* and some of the *pharynx*, and the sensory nerve for the back of the tongue and soft *palate*.

glottis Very short part of the main air passage from the *pharynx* (the back of the throat) to the *trachea* (windpipe) which includes the space between the *vocal cords*. By extension, the term may also mean the vocal cords or the *larynx*.

glucagon Hormone produced and secreted by the *pancreas* to raise the level of glucose (sugar) in the blood. It promotes the reabsorption of glucose from the tissue cells. Too little glucagon in the blood may result in dangerously low blood sugar levels (*hypoglycaemia*). Its effect is the opposite of that of *insulin*.

glucocorticoid hormone Any of the *corticosteroids* secreted by the *adrenal glands* that are essential to the metabolism of food ingested (as opposed to those corticosteroids which regulate the bodyís balance of salt and water). Glucocorticoids include *cortisone* and *hydrocortisone*.

glucose Essential form of sugar that supplies energy to the body through its "combustion" with oxygen (so forming water and carbon dioxide). Produced by the breakdown of carbohydrates taken in as food, it is stored in the form of glycogen in the liver and, to a lesser extent, in the muscles. Its presence and balance in the bloodstream is regulated by several hormones, particularly *insulin* and *glucagon*; too much glucose (*hyperglycaemia*) or too little (*hypoglycaemia*) leads to potentially dangerous symptoms.

glucose tolerance test Test of the bodyís capacity for metabolizing *glucose* (blood sugar), used in the diagnosis of *diabetes* mellitus. Having had no food or drink for some time, a patient swallows a measured amount of glucose. Blood and urine samples are taken at regular intervals for a few hours and analysed to reveal the level of glucose, which is a measure of the bodyís utilization of glucose and an indirect test of *insulin* secretion from the *pancreas* (the gland in the abdomen that produces insulin).

glue ear Accumulation of fluid in the middle ear cavity, due to repeated or persistent infection of the middle ear (*otitis* media), usually itself a sequel of respiratory infections. It most commonly occurs during childhood, due to failure of the Eustachian tube, which connects the middle ear with the back of the nose, to drain the fluid that accumulates during chronic inflammation. Symptoms are pain and temporarily impaired hearing. Sometimes the eardrum ruptures, releasing pus. Many cases improve spontaneously, and most children grow out of the problem. Where symptoms are severe, the fluid may be drained during surgery, and grommets – small tubes – inserted into the eardrum to allow the fluid to drain.

glue sniffing Common form of *solvent abuse.*

gluten Dual form of protein found in cereals. Abnormal sensitivity to (one of the two constituents of) gluten results in *coeliac disease.*

glyceryl trinitrate Drug absorbed sublingually (that is, by being dissolved under the tongue) or through the skin; it reduces blood pressure by dilating blood vessels (a vasodilator). One of its most common uses is to treat *angina pectoris*. Patients with this condition may take the drug before physical exertion. It is also known as nitroglycerine.

glycogen Form of carbohydrate – made up of chains of *glucose* molecules – in which glucose is stored in the body (mostly in the liver, but also in the muscles). When energy is required, glycogen readily and rapidly breaks down into glucose.

goitre Swelling of the *thyroid gland* in the neck. Formerly some goitres became large and unsightly; modern treatment generally prevents this stage from being reached. Causes include a diet containing insufficient iodine (necessary for the production of the *thyroid hormone* thyroxine), a lack of which causes the gland to swell to try to compensate; spontaneous *hyperplasia* (overgrowth) or overactivity of the gland (*hyperthyroidism*, leading to thyrotoxicosis); a tumour either on the thyroid or on the *pituitary gland*; and an autoimmune disorder in which the body produces antibodies to its own tissues. Treatment depends on the cause, but may include iodine or hormonal supplements, or surgery.

Golgi apparatus Type of organelle within a *cell*, consisting of membranes and vesicles in an overall tubular shape. Its purpose is to store and transport *proteins* manufactured in the cell.

gonad Reproductive organ that produces *gametes*: the *ovary* or *testes.*

gonadotrophin Also spelled gonadotropin, any of several hormones produced and secreted by the *pituitary gland* that cause the gonads (*ovary* or *testes*) to produce *sex hormones* or sex cells (*ova* or *sperm*). They include *follicle-stimulating hormone* (FSH) and *luteinizing hormone*, and may be used in injections to treat infertility. The pituitary gland of a pregnant woman does not produce gonadotrophins, however, and to compensate the *placenta* produces (human) *chorionic gonadotrophin* (HCG), a very similar hormone, some of which is excreted in the urine (forming the basis of most pregnancy tests).

gonorrhoea Contagious bacterial infection of the mucous membranes of the genitalia (and occasionally the anus, mouth or eyes); it is a *sexually transmitted disease*. Symptoms in men are a thick yellowish discharge from the infected site (generally the penis), and inflammation of the *urethra* (the tube conducting urine and semen through the penis) leading to pain and difficulty in urination. Rarely in a man, there are no symptoms although he is infectious – and there are seldom symptoms in a woman. Women who do have symptoms experience a discharge from the infected site (generally the vagina), and pain. Women may pass the infection on to their babies during birth, causing eye infection (ophthalmia neonatorum). Diagnosis may require examination of the bacteria in a culture medium. If untreated, the condition may spread throughout the reproductive organs, resulting in sterility, and may cause complications in the eyes, heart and joints. Treatment – which must be of both sexual partners – is with penicillin or other antibiotics.

gout Condition of painful inflammation in specific joints and in the skin, caused by the presence of crystals of uric acid and its salts in the blood. Uric acid is normally excreted in the urine; gout occurs when there is excess acid or when excretion is impaired, as may be the case after abnormal quantities of food and drink, following certain injuries, or during a course of diuretic drugs. There is also a hereditary factor. Usually, one joint is most affected (often that of the big toe), which swells and the skin surface becomes red and shiny. Untreated or recurrent gout may lead to permanent joint and kidney damage. Treatment is with drugs that increase uric acid excretion, and bed rest.

GPI Abbreviation of *general paralysis of the insane*.

Graafian follicle Another name for a mature *ovarian follicle*, named after the Dutch doctor Regnier de Graaf (1641–1673), who first described it.

graft Organ or area of tissue taken from one part of a personís body and surgically transposed to another part of the same or some other personís body; a form of transplant. The term is used with particular reference to skin grafts (generally grafts of skin from one area of tissue to another within the same person), corneal grafts (grafts of whole corneas from recently dead donors), and kidney grafts (transplants of one or both kidneys from a donor). In every case, tissue must be as closely matched as possible in order that the possibility of tissue rejection is minimized.

grand mal A serious form of *epilepsy* or of an epileptic seizure.

granulation tissue Tissue formed as the first stage in the healing of a wound, structured mostly of tiny blood vessels and fibres of connective tissue. It tends to develop in hemispherical outgrowths. Occasionally, with certain diseases (such as tuberculosis, leprosy and syphilis) or as a reaction to certain substances (such as starch or zirconium), great masses of granulation tissue (granulomas) may form.

granulocyte Any *leukocyte* (white blood cell) that not only ingests "foreign" particles but has granules in its *cytoplasm*. Granulocytes include *basophils, eosinophils* and *neutrophils*.

Graves' disease Another name for thyrotoxicosis, resulting from *hyperthyroidism*. It was first described by the Irish physician RJ Graves (1797–1853).

greenstick fracture Type of bone *fracture* particularly common in children and adolescents, in which the bone does not break right through.

grey matter Grey-coloured nerve tissue of the brain and spinal cord, forming the cortex (outer layer) of the *cerebral hemispheres* and *cerebellum* in the brain, and the medulla (inner layer) of the spinal cord. It differs from *white matter* in having much less *myelin* sheathing around the constituent *neurones* (nerve cells).

grief Persistent sorrow following bereavement or loss. An effect individual to each sufferer, it may be difficult for anyone else to give genuine comfort. "Symptoms" are apathy, disinterest and introspection. Treatment, when possible, may include emotive distractions, practical help around the home, companionable meditation or recollections – and possibly tranquillizers (as prescribed by a doctor).

gripe Fierce contraction of the stomach or intestines, either through hunger or indigestion.

groin Area of the abdomen where the legs join it. Technically, therefore, everyone has two groins – but the term is generally used to mean the area mostly covered by pubic hair in adults, stretching across the lower abdomen between the creases where the thighs fold.

grommet Short, flanged tube inserted into and through the eardrum to allow drainage of mucus from the *middle ear* in cases of *otitis* media. The grommet usually comes away of its own accord as the eardrum heals.

group therapy Form of psychotherapy in which two or more patients talk freely to each other in the presence of a therapist. The participants may thus come to understand each otherís problems and comprehend them as their own (or like their own), and the therapist may thus gain new insights from the patientsí discussion. In this way, there is also less likelihood that the therapist may become the dominant influence in a patientís life that single therapy often promotes. The term is used also for regular discussion groups participated in by people suffering from the same condition, such as drug addiction or alcoholism, without the presence of a therapist.

growth Increase in the total number or size of cells in the body. In normal development, growth is controlled by *growth hormone* (somatotropin), produced and secreted by the *pituitary gland* from before birth, but is subject also to hereditary factors, environmental factors, diet, any disease, and the effects of certain other hormones. Abnormal growth generally stems from a defect of the pituitary gland, and may result in *gigantism* in an adolescent or *acromegaly* in an adult. Cells are continually replicating to replace dead or worn-out cells – and much of the time they are dying at an equal or near-equal rate, and being shed. However, when cells multiply unnecessarily, a *tumour* is formed, and may be *benign* or *malignant* (cancer). Some organs swell under specific circumstances (*hyperplasia* and *hypertrophy*).

growth hormone Somatotropin, a hormone produced and secreted by the *pituitary gland* that promotes cell replication in the long bones of the limbs, promotes the synthesis of proteins, and thus promotes overall growth. Oversecretion of the hormone causes *gigantism* (in children) and *acromegaly* (in adults); undersecretion in childhood results in (properly proportioned) *dwarfism*.

Guillain-Barré syndrome A neurological disorder due to an abnormal reaction in the peripheral nervous system. Typically it follows two to three weeks after a minor infection of the respiratory tract or intestine. Symptoms include weakness in the limbs and sometimes paralysis, which may spread to include the muscles controlling respiration. Recovery may take many months and a few patients are left with permanent disability. Treatment of early symptoms with immunoglobulins can hasten recovery. In cases where respiratory muscles are affected, artificial respiration on a ventilator may be needed.

guilt Conscious or unconscious feeling or remorse about an event or emotion. A powerful force in psychology, guilt may result in repression of memories or emotions and cause behavioural anomalies associated with *neurosis*.

gullet Common name for the *oesophagus*.

gums Medical name gingiva, the raised pads of dense connective tissue covered with mucous membrane that surround the lower portions of the teeth. In close contact with material that enters the mouth, the gums are especially subject to the effects of poor oral hygiene, which often causes inflammation (*gingivitis*).

gut Another name for the *alimentary canal*.

gynaecological disorders Disorders that affect the reproductive organs of women and girls.

Such disorders include the menstrual disorders *amenorrhoea, dysmenorrhoea, oligomenorrhoea* and *premenstrual syndrome, cancer* of the *cervix* or *uterus, endometriosis, fibroids*, local infections (such as cervicitis, endometritis, *salpingitis* and *vaginitis*), the effects of *menarche* or *menopause*, difficulties and abnormalities during *pregnancy*, and the effects of *sexually transmitted disease*.

gynaecology Branch of medicine that relates exclusively to women and girls and to *gynaecological disorders*. One special branch of gynaecology is *obstetrics* (concerned with pregnancy and childbirth).

gynaecomastia Enlargement of the breasts of a boy or a man. The cause is the presence in the bloodstream of female *sex hormones*, either as a comparatively minor, normal and temporary feature during puberty, or as a result of hormone therapy.

gyrus Small, raised area on the convoluted surface of a *cerebral hemisphere* of the brain between the indentations (sulci).

H

habituation Process in the body, and perhaps to an equal extent the mind, by which somebody becomes dependent on a drug. Addiction is gradual but relentless. Finally, the person cannot do without the drug, and craves for it when it is not available. See *dependence*.

haem Iron compound that is one of the two constituents of *haemoglobin*, part of the red blood cells (*erythrocytes*) vital for the transport of oxygen from the lungs to the tissues. It is haem that gives the red blood cells their colour.

haematemesis Vomiting blood. Causes may be relatively minor (such as swallowing blood from a nosebleed or tooth extraction) but tend more often to be more serious – such as *ulceration* of the oesophagus, stomach or duodenum, or severe gastritis. Occasionally a blood transfusion is necessary to replace lost blood, before the cause is diagnosed and treated.

haematocolpos Condition found in adolescent girls, in which menstrual blood accumulates inside the vagina because the *hymen* is not perforated. (The treatment is minor surgery to perforate the hymen.)

haematology Study of the composition and disorders of the *blood*.

haematoma Leakage of blood into the tissues, generally as a result of injury, which results in swelling and often a *bruise*. Usually the blood is gradually reabsorbed into the bloodstream and thus vanishes with no further effects. But when the haematoma is caused by disease, or is located in the head or lungs, symptoms may be more serious and require surgical treatment – occasionally as an emergency measure.

haematuria Presence of blood in the urine, sometimes making it pink or dark in colour. Causes are injury or disease in the urethra, bladder, ureters or kidneys – and diagnosis should be sought immediately.

haemodialysis Filtering of waste products out of the blood, as in a kidney machine. See *dialysis*.

haemoglobin Major constituent of the red blood cells (*erythrocytes*) and, through the presence of *haem*, responsible for their colour. Haemoglobin is a combination of the porphyrin haem and the protein globin, and is the agent for the transport of oxygen from the lungs to the tissues (as oxyhaemoglobin). Abnormal types of haemoglobin cause several serious disorders, such as *thalassaemia* and *sickle-cell anaemia*. Carbon monoxide is poisonous when inhaled because it preferentially combines with haemoglobin instead of oxygen.

haemolysis Abnormal degeneration of red blood cells (*erythrocytes*) into their component parts, which releases *haemoglobin* into the blood plasma. Causes include abnormal types of haemoglobin, malaria, blood group incompatibility (through perhaps mis-matching in a blood transfusion), and certain poisons. Common symptoms are anaemia, jaundice, high temperature with chills, and enlargement of the spleen. Treatment depends on the cause.

haemolytic disease of the newborn Destruction of red blood cells (*haemolysis*) in a *foetus* due to antibodies to the foetal *blood group* manufactured in the mother and passed through the placenta. The condition is also known as *Rhesus factor incompatibility* and is usually provoked when the pregnant woman is *Rhesus factor* negative but the baby is Rhesus positive (from the fatherís side). Effects in the foetus may include jaundice, severe anaemia, oedema, premature birth or stillbirth. Antibodies to foetal cells are formed in the mother during the birth of a first child (or occasionally after blood transfusion with Rhesus positive blood), so a second (or later) pregnancy is at risk; hence Rhesus negative women carrying Rhesus positive babies are given an injection after they have given birth (or have had an abortion) to destroy any foetal cells remaining in the motherís circulation, to avoid antibody production in her next pregnancy.

haemophilia Inherited disorder that results in an insufficiency in one of the *clotting* factors in the blood, most often Factor VIII (antihaemophiliac factor) and sometimes Factor IX (Christmas factor). In general, women are genetic carriers of the disorder, and men and boys actually suffer from it (it is an *X-linked disorder*; that is, one carried on the X-chromosome). Symptoms are prolonged bleeding from even a slight injury, and sometimes spontaneous internal haemorrhages, most often affecting muscles or joints. Treatment is with transfusions of plasma (the fluid component of blood, with the blood cells removed), which contains the missing factor, or of extracts containing the factor itself.

haemorrhage Bleeding. Large-scale haemorrhage from a wound may cause shock and, if from an artery or a major vein, death. Blood from an artery is bright red and emerges in spurts; blood from a vein is darker and emerges in a steady flow. The best first aid treatment for a haemorrhage is to apply firm pressure to or above the wound; a *tourniquet* should not be used. Slow but continuous haemorrhage may result in *anaemia*. Vomiting blood is *haematemesis*; blood in the urine is *haematuria*.

haemorrhoids Piles, painfully distended veins in the walls of the *anus*. First-degree haemorrhoids remain inside the anus and may bleed at the end of defecation, but have no other symptoms. Second-degree haemorrhoids may appear at the entrance of the anus or outside and may cause discomfort but return spontaneously, whereas third-degree haemorrhoids require manual pressure to return them inside. The cause is usually prolonged constipation. Treatment is generally through increasing the level of fibre in the diet to defeat constipation, sometimes with drugs to soften the faeces and reduce discomfort. Severe or persistent haemorrhoids may be treated by injections with sclerosing (hardening) agents, infrared coagulation or ligation (tying off). Third-degree haemorrhoids may require surgical removal.

hair Strands of *keratin* representing a specialized form of the outer surface of the skin (*epidermis*). Hair appears on much of the skin surface and (through the influence of both genetic and hormonal factors) particularly on the head and in the armpits and groin of both men and women, but also on the face, neck and torso in men. There is no hair on the lips, palms of the hands and soles of the feet. Each hair develops within a bulb-like hair follicle. Cells within the follicle continually produce new cells, forcing older ones, after hardening (keratinizing), upwards and out of the follicle to form both the root (within the skin) and the shaft (above). Each hair consists of three concentric layers: the outer layer is made up of scales, the middle one contains the pigment (colour), and the inner layer is usually hollow. The pigments, produced by cells at the base of the follicle, are black, brown or yellow which in combination produce all hair colours. An absence of pigment, through disease or hormonal changes of aging, results in white hair. Hormonal changes are also responsible for *baldness*.

hair follicle Tubular sheath of *epidermis* and connective tissue that surrounds the bulb of a *hair* root beneath the skin surface.

Haldane, J.B.S. (1892–1964) British mathematician, biometrist and science popularizer who was the author of an influential study of the effects of heredity on entire populations, and who first related conditions such as *colour blindness* and *haemophilia* to those same effects.

Hales, Stephen (1677–1761) English physiologist, chemist and divine who pioneered research into the structure of animals and plants. Following *Harvey*ís work on the circulation of the blood, it was Hales who first described and quantified *blood pressure*, and who examined the causative factors in a *stroke*.

halitosis Bad breath. Causes include poor dental hygiene and tooth decay, infection of the mouth, nose or throat, stomach or lung disorders, and breathing through the mouth instead of the nose. More serious causes include liver disease and *diabetes* mellitus. Treatment depends on the cause – but unless that is medically diagnosed, is generally by disguising the symptom.

hallucination Seeing or hearing something that is simply not there. A hallucination thus differs from an *illusion* (which is a mistaken interpretation of something that is there) and a *delusion* (an insistently incorrect interpretation of something that is there). The effect may be of dreaming while awake. Causes range from extreme fatigue, fever or cold, to drug abuse (as with alcohol), hysteria, and some forms of serious mental illness.

hallucinogen Any drug that causes *hallucinations*. Hallucinogens include cannabis, lysergic acid diethylamide (LSD) and mescaline.

hallux valgus Deformity in which the big toe (hallux) is crooked (valgus) – generally so crooked as to bend into or across the next toe. The cause is usually badly fitting shoes. Treatment in severe and inflamed cases may include surgery.

hammer toe Toe – commonly the one next to the big toe – in which through deformity the first joint cannot straighten and remains permanently flexed at a right-angle. Treatment involves a corrective shoe or, if necessary, surgery.

hamstring Any of several *tendons* attached at the back of the knee to muscles in the thigh. The muscles – which are sometimes also called hamstrings – bend the leg at the knee.

hand Extremity of the arm, from *wrist* to fingertips. Five long *metacarpal* bones frame the base and palm, articulating with bones at the joint of each finger. The *thumb* has two bones; the other fingers have three each. Hand movement, particularly grasping, is controlled by long *tendons* connected to muscles in the forearm and sheathed in *synovial* membrane, and also employs the many muscles of the hand.

handicap Specific mental or physical disability that causes somebody to be unable to do all the things that most other people can do.

hangnail Extraneous strand of skin tissue that has become partly detached from between the fold of skin at the side of a nail and the nail itself. Treatment is to cut it as short as possible.

hangover State of agitated dehydration that may follow a session of heavy drinking. Additional symptoms include headache, sensitivity to noise and light, vertigo, nausea and vomiting. There is no sure cure except time, although long (non-alcoholic) drinks and an *antacid* may help.

Hansen's disease Another name for *leprosy*.

hardening of the arteries Common name for *arteriosclerosis*.

hare lip Malformation of the upper lip in which the skin beneath one or both nostrils fails to develop, leaving a cleft. The cleft may or may not also be carried through the upper jaw and produce a *cleft palate*. Modern techniques of plastic surgery are capable of a virtually perfect mouth repair; the operation is generally carried out in the early years of life.

Harrison, Ross (1870–1959) American biologist and pioneer of tissue culturing. His technique, established in 1907, finally made it possible to study the development of cells outside their natural environments, and facilitated further research.

Harvey, William (1578–1657) English anatomist and pathologist who proved that the blood continually circulates around the body, thus undermining the precepts of centuries and virtually founding the modern age of scientific medicine. An able surgeon, he was also physician to the king (Charles I).

Hashimoto's disease Condition in which a disturbance of the *immune system* causes a great increase in white blood cells (*leukocytes*) and *antibodies*, all directed against the normal tissue of the *thyroid gland*. The thyroid gland consequently suffers long-term inflammation, swelling, and failure to produce its hormones. Symptoms include gradually increasing lethargy, dry skin, weight loss, and eventual *myxoedema*.

Haversian system Cylindrical system of honeycombed channels that form the structural units in hard *bone*, and centring on a Haversian canal – a hollow core in which a blood vessel is located. Within each system, in hollows called lacunae, are many osteocytes (cells that maintain bone as living tissue). It is named after the English anatomist C Havers (1650–1702).

hay fever Allergic response to the presence of pollen, grass dust, spores or similar airborne plant particles, known medically as allergic rhinitis. Symptoms consist of runny nose, sneezing and watering eyes due to inflammation of the nasal lining and conjunctivae (the membrane covering the eye), which is caused mostly by the release of *histamine* in the tissues. Treatment with *antihistamines* is often effective. If a specific allergen (a substance provoking the allergy) is identified, possibly by a *patch test*, *desensitization* (a method for reducing allergic responses by gradually building up tolerance to the allergen) may be possible.

head Topmost part of the body, structured round the skull and lower jaw (mandible) and containing the brain – the vital director and controller of the rest of the body, as well as the seat of awareness and memory – and thereby virtually all of the sensory organs. It is also the centre – through the nose and mouth – for taking in both air and food (and drink). The term is used also of the rounded topmost part of certain bones that form joints, such as the head of the femur (thigh bone).

headache Pain felt to be inside the head. Causes range from fatigue and anxiety, alcohol or other drug abuse, ear and eye disorders, *migraine* and referred toothache, to serious infections such as *otitis* media (or interna) and *meningitis, concussion* and other forms of injury, and disease of the brain itself. In general, however, most headaches are not serious. Treatment with a pain-killer such as aspirin or paracetamol is usually effective. Any headache that is not relieved by pain-killers, or is unusually severe, should be medically diagnosed.

health General overall well-being of somebody whose metabolic functions are all working competently, and who is neither underweight nor overweight. A peak form of health is fitness (or "being fit").

health food Food that actively promotes health – or at least is not known in any way to be detrimental to health. Such food is mostly based on natural ingredients, naturally obtained or grown (without the use of artificial fertilizers or pesticides), and consumed only in quantities that foster health. Properly, therefore, health foods demand a lifestyle consistent with them. Health food shops tend to stock grain and fruit products, eggs and dairy produce, and herbs and spices (including herbal medicines, lotions and infusions); there may also be sugarless confectionery.

health visitor Nurse with training in public health and preventive medicine whose main task it is to educate parents and relatives in how to care for their children, and especially for those children who are handicapped in any way. The main routine centres on visiting selected pre-school children in order to ensure that health considerations are being properly met, and to inform parents of any help they may be able to receive from the local health authority. Each health visitor is notified of all births in his or her area. Health visitors also regularly visit the elderly and those who are chronically ill.

hearing Sense that involves the reception and interpretation by the brain of sound. Sound travels through the outer ear to the *eardrum* (tympanic membrane). From there, the beginning of the *middle ear*, vibrations are transmitted through three tiny bones (the *malleus, incus* and *stapes*, in that order, together known as the ossicles) to the *inner ear* (also called the labyrinth). The inner ear contains the main sensory organ of hearing, the coiled *cochlea*, inside which are the basilar membrane and the *organ of Corti*, both receivers of vibrations which transmit sensory information via the auditory nerve to the brain for interpretation. See also *deafness*.

hearing aid Electronic device intended to assist *hearing* in people who are deaf, comprising a miniature sound receiver and an amplifier. The sound is then either relayed into the ear at a greater volume than normal, through an earpiece (for people with perceptive *deafness*), or relayed as vibrations through the bone behind the ear directly to the *inner ear* (for people with conductive deafness) using a vibrator.

heart Central focus and pumping station for the two almost entirely separate circulations of the blood – one circulation around the body, supplying the tissues with oxygen and returning with waste products such as carbon dioxide; the other to the *lungs* to effect the exchange of the carbon dioxide for more oxygen, returning with it to the heart for pumping around the body again. To do this the heart has four chambers: two for receiving blood (the left and right *atria*) and two for pumping out (the left and right *ventricles*). Chambers on the left side deal with blood coming from the lungs and going to the body; those on the right with blood coming from the body and going to the lungs. Between the two sides there is a strong partition or *septum*. About the size of a closed fist, the heart is made up of a special type of *muscle*, enclosed in membranous layers. The *heartbeat*, regulated and monitored by centres in the brain, is actuated by a tiny area in the upper inside surface of the right atrium (the *pacemaker*, or sinoatrial node) and causes simultaneous rhythmic contractions first in both atria; coinciding with ventricular dilation (*diastole*) and then in the *ventricles* (*systole*). *Valves* in the heart prevent the backflow of blood.

heart attack See *myocardial infarction.*

heartbeat Rhythmic double contractions of the heart muscle corresponding to the simultaneous contraction of the *atria* and relaxation of the *ventricles* (*diastole*) followed by the contraction of both ventricles (*systole*), effectively pumping blood around the body. The beat is actuated by a tiny area in the upper right atrium – the *pacemaker*, or sinoatrial node – and is regulated and monitored by centres in the brain in a way that corresponds to the changing activities and emotions of the individual. In certain areas of the skin where arteries are close to the surface, the beat may be detected as a *pulse*.

heart block Partial or total failure in the transmission of the electrical impulses of the heart *pacemaker* (sinoatrial node) from the *atria* to the *ventricles*. The result may be delay or complete lack of synchronization between contractions of the two chambers (between *diastole* and *systole*). Causes range from congenital heart disease to *coronary thrombosis*, rheumatic fever and myocarditis (inflammation of the heart muscle). Symptoms are breathlessness and faintness, vertigo and bouts of unconsciousness. The condition may be temporary and clear up of its own accord; treatment otherwise may include drugs or the implantation of an artificial heart pacemaker.

heartburn Symptom of *indigestion* characterized by a burning sensation at the bottom of the *oesophagus* (gullet). It is caused by the rising of partly digested acidic contents of the stomach, which may result in inflammation of the lower part of the oesophagus (oesophagitis). Various over-the-counter remedies are available to counter acidity and settle the stomach, but persistent heartburn should be medically assessed.

heart disease Vague term for any of the many disorders of the heart, including *angina pectoris, bacterial endocarditis, bradycardia, coronary artery disease, coronary thrombosis, heart block, heart failure*, high blood pressure (*hypertension*), *hypertrophy* of the heart, *tachycardia* and *valvular disease of the heart.* Treatment depends on the cause and may include drugs or surgery.

heart disease, congenital See *congenital heart disease.*

heart failure Failure of the *ventricles* (the larger chambers) of the heart to pump blood properly, so that circulation is impaired, and some organs – notably the lungs and the liver – become congested with blood. Additional effects are the accumulation of fluid in the tissues (oedema), the swelling of veins in the neck, and breathlessness. Causes include *coronary heart disease, valvular disease of the heart* and high blood pressure (*hypertension*). Treatment is mostly through diet and bed rest. *Diuretics* (drugs that promote urination) may be prescribed and surgery may be required, depending on the cause of the failure.

heart-lung machine Machine that takes over the functions of respiration and blood circulation for a patient who is temporarily unable to manage either. Tubes inserted into the patientís *venae cavae* (the main vein leading to the heart) draw venous blood out of the body, as the machine simultaneously feeds a constant supply of oxygenated blood into a major artery. Such machines are used mostly during surgery on the heart or greater arteries.

heart murmur Sound of the blood as it flows turbulently (instead of smoothly) through the heart, as may be heard by a doctor through a stethoscope. Most murmurs are harmless, but require full diagnosis when present.

heart pacemaker Natural or artificial *pacemaker* in the heart.

heart rate Measure of the speed of the heartbeat, in beats per minute. The rate depends on the activity or emotion of a person, or on the presence of disease. But a normal heart rate for a person at rest is between 70 and 80 beats a minute.

heart transplant Complex form of *transplant surgery* undertaken to replace a patientís diseased *heart* either with a healthy one from a donor (with or without the lungs as well); the term is sometimes used to refer to replacement with a mechanical version of a heart (*artificial heart*). A heart from a donor has to be closely matched in tissue type to the patientís tissues, in order to minimize the possibility of tissue *rejection*.

heart valve Any of the four major *valves* of the heart – two preventing backflow between the upper and lower chambers of the heart (the *tricuspid valve* and the *mitral valve*), and two preventing backflow into the heart once blood has left it (the pulmonary and the aortic valves).

heat exhaustion Extreme fatigue, caused by severe dehydration and desalination of the body following continuous exposure to unaccustomed heat. A common complaint of travellers to tropical countries, it is treated with long drinks and salt tablets.

heatstroke Failure of the bodyís mechanism of regulating internal temperature, following continuous exposure to unaccustomed heat. Symptoms include very high temperature without perspiration, headache, nausea, weakness and eventual unconsciousness; the condition (also called sunstroke) may cause convulsions or be fatal if left untreated. The patientís body should be kept cool by covering with damp cloths; drinks, especially drinks containing salt, should be administered to compensate for fluid loss. In severe cases fluid replacement through a drip into a vein may be required.

heavy metals Certain metallic elements of which even tiny quantities may produce serious symptoms of poisoning: some may even be absorbed through the skin. They include cadmium, mercury and lead.

heel Main weight-bearing portion of the *foot*, directly beneath the ankle. Inside is the heel bone (calcaneus) which is supported by a thick pad of tissue.

height Measure of how tall a person is. Height depends on age, sex, diet, hereditary factors, hormonal factors, environmental factors, and exercise. Every person is tallest at about 20 years of age; thereafter he or she tends imperceptibly to shrink. On a different time-scale, every person is taller in the early mornings than in the evenings because of the gradual daily loss of muscle *tone* later restored during sleep.

Heimlich manoeuvre Emergency method for saving a person from choking to death. It consists of standing behind the choking person, putting the arms round the front of the person, and clasping one wrist in the other hand just about over the personís diaphragm. A sudden and sharp pull on both arms, thrusting backwards and upwards on the patientís upper abdomen, may well cause sufficient pressure up the *oesophagus* to loosen an obstruction.

heliotherapy Use of sunlight (natural or artificial) as treatment, especially for skin disorders.

helminthiasis Infestation with *worms*.

hemat-, hemo- American spellings of words beginning haemat- or haemo-.

heme American spelling of *haem*.

hemiplegia Total *paralysis* of the muscles of one side of the body, usually also involving loss of sensation as well as of movement. The cause is disease or disorder in the opposite side of the brain, particularly following a *stroke*.

Henle's loop See *loop of Henle*.

heparin Natural *anticoagulant* produced and secreted by the liver and some *leukocytes* (white blood cells). Its effect is to prevent the blood-clotting enzyme *thrombin* from causing *fibrinogen* to become *fibrin*. Purified heparin may be injected as a drug into patients suffering from *thrombosis*.

hepatic portal vein Fuller version of the term *portal vein*, the main vein that carries blood containing the products of digestion from the intestines to the liver.

hepatitis Inflammation of the liver, caused usually by infection with one (or more) of a variety of hepatitis viruses, and also occurring as an *autoimmune disease* (in which the immune system attacks the bodyís own tissues) or through alcoholism or exposure to other toxins. Acute viral hepatitis may be transmitted through food and drink in areas of poor hygiene and sanitation, and is caused by hepatitis A or hepatitis E viruses. Symptoms are high temperature, nausea, vomiting, and loss of appetite; all these are followed by *jaundice*, which may last for three weeks. At this stage the hepatitis is over but may in turn be followed by mental depression. Thereafter recovery is usually complete. Hepatitis B virus infection, formerly called serum hepatitis, is transmitted in blood or blood products, contaminated hypodermic or tattooing needles, sexual contact or contact with other body fluids such as breast milk. Drug addicts and male homosexuals are particularly at risk. Symptoms, which may take many months to develop, include headache, fever, malaise and *jaundice*. Sometimes the hepatitis D virus is found along with hepatitis B, making the infection more severe. A similar form of hepatitis is caused by the hepatitis C virus. All forms of viral hepatitis, but particularly those caused by hepatitis viruses B, C and D, may progress to a chronic condition with long-term liver damage including *cirrhosis* and tumours of the liver; such complications may be fatal. A chronic condition of hepatitis also results from alcoholism, in which the alcohol causes liver cells to fill with fats, burst and die. The dead cells then inflame adjacent cells, and *cirrhosis* may follow. Treatment of acute viral hepatitis is generally with bed rest, and then only initially. Alcohol must usually be avoided for a prolonged period to prevent further liver damage. Those in close contact with the patient may be injected with *gamma globulin* as a precaution. Chronic hepatitis can now be treated with interferon, and autoimmune hepatitis may respond to corticosteroid or immunosuppressive drugs. Vaccines are available against hepatitis A (often given to travellers) and hepatitis B (given to medical staff and others at high risk).

herbalism Study and use of plants either for consumption or for medical purposes. Elizabethan herbalists were the dispensing chemists of their time.

heredity Combination of the genes of two parents to produce offspring with characteristics of both. The study of heredity is *genetics*.

hermaphrodite Individual whose body has a complete set of both male and female reproductive organs, or tissues derived from both. It is a very rare condition; *intersex* occurs slightly more commonly.

hernia Rupture, an abnormal protrusion of part of the alimentary canal – especially the intestines – through a gap in adjacent tissues. Most commonly, part of the intestine works its way through a weakened spot in the lower part of the abdominal wall (inguinal hernia), causing a swelling in the groin and some pain. A hiatus hernia occurs when part of the stomach rides up through the gap in the diaphragm meant for the *oesophagus* (gullet); symptoms may be no more than regurgitation. In babies or after abdominal surgery in adults, a hernia may appear at the navel (umbilicus). Rarely, other tissues – such as the peritoneum or part of the bladder – may be the protruding tissue. Most types of hernia can be reduced (replaced) fairly simply by manipulation, and kept in place if necessary by using a truss. Those that cannot may have to be dealt with surgically before they become strangulated (before the blood supply to the protruding portion is cut off by pressure and the tissue dies).

heroin Powerful narcotic analgesic drug derived from morphine (its technical name is diamorphine), generally in the form of a white crystalline powder. In most countries unauthorized possession of heroin is illegal. Its use is addictive (see *dependence*).

herpes Localized infection of the skin or mucous membranes by herpes viruses, resulting in clusters of small blisters. The herpes simplex virus has two forms, type I typically causing *cold sores* around the lips and nose; and type II usually causing genital herpes, a *sexually transmitted disease*. Occasionally either type may cause blisters in their nonpreferred area. The blisters are painful and, when they burst, highly contagious. Another herpes virus, called the varicella-zoster virus, causes *chickenpox* and, if the virus reactivates in later life, *shingles*. All forms of herpes virus infection may be treated with antiviral drugs. In herpes simplex infections these can speed healing but do not affect the tendency to recur. Treatment is only necessary in chickenpox among patients at risk of complications. In shingles, strong pain-killers may also be required.

Hess, Walter R. (1881–1973) Swiss physiologist and ophthalmologist whose researches into blood pressure finally enabled him to identify the centre in the brain that regulates it. He was awarded a Nobel Prize in 1949.

heterosexuality Preference and desire for sexual activity with somebody of the opposite sex.

Hewson, William (1834–1869) English anatomist who first discovered and described the relationship between *fibrinogen* and other contributory factors in the bodyís mechanism for blood *coagulation*.

hiatus hernia Fairly common type of *hernia* in which part or all of the stomach works its way upwards through the gap in the *diaphragm* (the muscular sheet dividing the chest from the abdominal cavity) meant solely for the *oesophagus* (gullet). Symptoms are generally minor, consisting of *indigestion* and a tendency towards regurgitation of acid stomach contents at least as far as the throat. Treatment may be no more than a change of diet and sleeping with the head higher than the feet; drugs may also help. However, if inflammation of the oesophagus (oesophagitis) occurs, surgery may be recommended.

hiccup Sudden single convulsive spasm of the diaphragm during inhalation, forcing an equally sudden closing of the vocal cords, resulting in a characteristic "hic". Causes include eating too fast, and the consequent indigestion, stomach irritants (including carbonated drinks and food that is too hot, too cold or too spicy) and more serious disorders (such as alcoholism).

high blood pressure Common name for *hypertension*.

Hill, Archibald V. (1886–1977) British physiologist whose work provided an explanation for the generation of heat in muscles during contraction, and in nerves during stimulation. His researches led to a new scientific capacity for thermometry and to a Nobel Prize in 1922.

hindbrain Rear lower part of the *brain*. It consists of the "bulbar area" of the *brainstem* – the *medulla oblongata* and *pons* – and the *cerebellum*. (The *midbrain* runs from where they join forwards to the *forebrain*.) Many of the cranial nerves, which nearly all serve the head and face, stem from the bulbar area.

hip Joint of the thigh bone (femur) with the pelvis, but commonly thought of as the bony extrusion of the *ileum*, the pelvic bone that provides the basis for the waist. As a joint, it provides the articulation of the femur with the *acetabulum*, a socket to which all the bones of the pelvis contribute. If *osteoarthritis* of the hip joint leads to crippling disability, it may be replaced with a man-made substitute.

hip replacement Surgical operation to replace the head of a diseased thigh bone (femur) so that articulation in the socket (*acetabulum*) is restored. This generally means severing the femur head and firmly attaching a metal prosthesis to the reduced bone. Patients can usually walk – with considerably greater freedom – within hours of the operation.

hippocampus Part of the cortex of each cerebral hemisphere that forms a swelling in the lateral ventricle of the brain. It is bathed by cerebrospinal fluid common to both hemispheres. Both hippocampi form a unit of the *limbic system*.

Hippocrates (*c*.460–370 BC) Physician, surgeon and medical writer, often called the "father of medicine" who lived on the Greek island of Cos. His humanity and empathy caused him (or his disciples) to formulate the famous Hippocratic oath which was the origin of medical ethics.

hirsutism Hairiness, involving either more closely growing hair than most people, or hair on more surface area than most people. The condition is generally caused by a hormonal imbalance (and is more common and more obvious in women than in men).

histamine Product of the breakdown of proteins in any tissue subject to injury or invasion, resulting in the process and symptoms of *inflammation*. A major constituent of the defence and repair mechanism of the body, histamine causes blood vessels to dilate and smooth muscle to contract. It may also be released in the body as a response to an *allergen*, and contributes greatly to the symptoms of *hay fever* and *asthma*. Drugs that counter the effects of histamine are called *antihistamines*.

histiocyte Form of *macrophage* (scavenger cell) that is not mobile but set within connective tissue.

histocompatibility Degree of matching between tissue types (generally of a patient undergoing transplant surgery and the donor whose organ is being transplanted). There are about twenty potentially different antigenic substances in most tissues. For a transplant not to incur *rejection* problems there must be the least number of differences between *antigens*, the greatest degree of histocompatibility.

histology Study of the tissues of plants and animals, using microscopes and staining techniques.

histoplasmosis Fungal infection of the lungs that often produces no symptoms and is most common in areas where there are many chickens or bats (it is from their excreta that spores may be breathed in). Rarely, a progressive form of the disease causes symptoms of a hoarse cough with blood in the sputum, chest pains, high temperature with chills and fatigue. Drug treatment is rapidly effective.

HIV Human immunodeficiency virus, the cause of *AIDS*, a condition in which the bodyís normal immune defences are severely impaired. HIV occurs in several forms and may be transmitted through contaminated blood, unsterile needles (including needles shared by drug addicts, those used in tattooing and contaminated medical instruments), sexual activity (so causing a *sexually transmitted disease*) or passed from mother to infant either at birth or during breast-feeding. Symptoms of AIDS may take many years to develop. Treatment with antiviral drugs may delay the development or progression of AIDS. Considerable research is being expended to find an effective vaccine against HIV.

hives Common name for *urticaria*.

HLA system Abbreviation of *human leucocyte antigen system*.

Hodgkin, Alan (1914–1998) English biologist who, with Andrew Huxley, carried out important research into the transmission of nerve impulses. Together they investigated the "sodium pump" mechanism, by which neural excitation causes a transfer of sodium and potassium ions between the inside and outside of a nerve fibre. Together they were awarded a 1963 Nobel Prize.

Hodgkin's disease Cancer of the lymphatic tissue, generally originating in one or more *lymph nodes*, but then spreading to the spleen and the liver, and possibly to the bones and bone marrow. Symptoms are enlargement of lymph nodes ("glands") in the neck, armpits or abdomen, fatigue and malaise; there may also be high temperature and sweating at nights, and itching. The condition is named after the English pathologist Thomas Hodgkin (1798–1866), who first described it in 1832. In early stages of the disease, cytotoxic (anticancer) drugs are very effective, although treatment has to be continued over many months. Later, however, surgery or radiotherapy – or both – may be required.

holistic medicine Approach to medical therapy that regards all disorders as conditions of the whole body (including the mind and certain social aspects), not just of a localized area or organ. Treatments therefore tend to involve many different facets of medical care, some from *complementary medicine*.

homeostasis Equilibrium in the internal environment of the body, maintained despite changes in the external environment. To maintain such an equilibrium is the purpose of all internal body systems.

homoeopathy System of therapy based on the idea that a disorder can be treated by tiny doses of a drug which in large doses itself produces symptoms of the disorder – that "like (at least in small doses) remedies like". Homoeopathic medicines consist largely of herbal preparations enormously diluted with water and milk sugar. The discipline is one of those commonly classified as belonging to *alternative medicine*.

homosexuality Preference and desire for sexual activity with an individual of the same sex, most often applied to males (female homosexuality is also known as lesbianism). It is no longer viewed as a psychological problem, but may impart certain health risks, especially exposure to *hepatitis* or *AIDS*. The causes of homosexuality remain disputed but both genetic factors and environmental influences during upbringing have been suggested. Many adolescents pass through a phase of homosexuality to become adult heterosexuals. Homosexuals who are unhappy with their preferences are unlikely to benefit from trying to change their sexual orientation and gain more from counselling to increase their acceptance of and comfort with their homosexuality.

hormone Glandular secretion that stimulates one or more specific organs in the body to fulfil their functions or to change their structure. Especially important hormones are *growth hormone* (somatotropin), *sex hormones*, gonadrotropins (*luteinizing hormone* and *follicle-stimulating hormone*), *thyroid-stimulating hormone* and the hormones produced by the *thyroid gland*, many of which are under the control of other hormones from the *pituitary gland*.

hormone replacement therapy (HRT) Hormones given to women around the time of the *menopause* (or after surgical removal of the ovaries, which produces an artificial menopause) to alleviate symptoms due to declining natural oestrogen levels – particularly hot flushes and vaginal dryness. HRT also prevents certain health risks such as osteoporosis and possibly heart disease, which are otherwise increased in postmenopausal women, but carries a small increased risk of cancer of the womb lining (endometrium). Treatment consists of the "female" hormone *oestrogen*, with or without a progestogen (another female hormone), and may be given as tablets, skin patches, gels or implants.

hospice Type of sanatorium in which care is given to patients who are dying. Each hospice ordinarily treats only patients with the condition in which the hospice specializes: one hospice may specialize in AIDS care, another in care for cancer patients, and a third in care for those dying of old age, for example. Such specialization allows modern, morale-raising and total care during a potentially problematical period for patients and their families. Many such hospices are run as charities.

hospital Complex of buildings designed for the diagnosis and treatment of patients of all ages and with all types of condition, either as in-patients (who stay at the hospital for their treatment) or as out-patients (as day visitors). Hospitals thus not only care for patients, they may have also to make provision for accommodating and feeding them, taking care of their laundry, and providing some form of entertainment. Most include operating theatres, X-ray facilities and a radiotherapy centre, an accident unit, burns unit, physiotherapy centres (with or without swimming pool), research and engineering laboratories, administration and records office, and even a mortuary. Many also have accommodation and canteen facilities for doctors, nursing staff and ancillary workers (and sometimes also for security staff), and car parks. In a large hospital the wards may be allocated to specific types of patients, such as geriatric (elderly patients), medical (non-surgical), obstetric and maternity, orthopaedic (bones and joints), paediatric (children), surgical, and so on. There are also usually clinics in various specialties for out-patients.

host Somebody who is infested with one or more *parasites*.

hot flashes American term for *hot flushes*.

hot flushes Series of waves of heat over the face, or over the whole body; with each wave, the face tends to flush red. They occur particularly in women at the time of the *menopause*, but also in women or men with emotional upsets or more serious forms of mental disturbance.

housemaid's knee Common name for *prepatellar bursitis*.

house physician Type of hospital doctor known also in the United States as an intern.

HPV Abbreviation of human papilloma virus.

Hubel, David (1926–) American neurobiologist who, with Torsten Wiesel, was awarded a Nobel Prize in 1981 for their work on how the brain interprets the sensory messages relayed to it by the *rods* and *cones* of the *retina* of the eye.

Huggins, Charles B. (1901–1997) American physician who in 1941 first pioneered *chemotherapy* as a treatment for *cancer*. In particular he treated patients with cancer of the prostate gland using female sex hormones, for many cases an effective method.

human chorionic gonadotrophin (HCG) Hormone produced and secreted in women by the *placenta* during pregnancy. It takes over the function of the *gonadotrophin* hormones normally secreted each *menstrual cycle* by the *pituitary gland* (the gland in the brain controlling the hormone secretion of other glands) to stimulate the production of *progesterone* by the *corpus luteum* in one *ovary* (the effects of the pituitary gland are not felt during pregnancy). The excess produced is excreted in the urine – the presence of which is the basis of most pregnancy tests. Tests of the amount of HCG in the blood are also used as one component of the triple marker test to screen for *Down's syndrome*. As a drug, HCG may be used in women to treat *premenstrual syndrome* or infrequency of *ovulation*; or in men to treat delayed puberty or undescended testes.

human leucocyte antigen (HLA) system A group of *gene* families and the *proteins* they code for, which act as *antigens* and are important to *histocompatibility* (tissue type compatibility between donor and recipient in *transplant surgery*). The proteins were first found on the surface of white blood cells (leucocytes) but are now known to occur on all cells with a *nucleus* (the part of each cell, within its own membrane, containing the *chromosomes* and their *DNA*). The gene families are described as A, B, C or D, and individual antigens within each family are given a number, such as HLA-B27. The presence of particular antigens – inherited from parents – is statistically associated with various diseases, and the degree of HLA matching between a donor and recipient is crucial to the risk of *rejection* after a transplant.

human papillomavirus (HPV) One of a group of over 50 viruses that may cause *warts* or *verrucas*, types of benign (harmless) skin tumours, including genital warts (on the penis or around the vagina or anus), which are a *sexually transmitted disease*. Certain strains of HPV that are sexually transmitted are linked with the development of cervical *cancer* (although additional factors are also involved); they may be detected by specialized tests performed with a *cervical smear test* before cancer develops, indicating the need for minor treatment and/or more frequent smear tests.

humerus Long bone of the upper arm, jointed at the shoulder with the scapula (*shoulder blade*) and at the elbow with both the *radius* and the *ulna*. In line with its name it represents the *"funny bone"* of the elbow where it lies directly beneath the ulnar nerve.

humours In modern medical terminology there are only two humours: the water fluid (*aqueous humour*) and the jelly-like substance (*vitreous humour*) each side of the lens of the eye. Formerly, and for many centuries, it was believed that there were four humours – earth, air, fire and water – of which the entire body was composed, the balance of which controlled the health and mental disposition of an individual. The humours were: black bile (earth), associated with a melancholic temperament; blood (air), with a sanguine temperament; yellow bile (fire), with a choleric temperament; and phlegm (water), with a phlegmatic temperament.

hunchback Common but offensive name for somebody who suffers from severe and irreparable *kyphosis* (outward curvature of the spine) as a result of congenital abnormality or, now rarely, following spinal *tuberculosis*.

hunger Physical symptoms following a lack of nourishment, caused to a great extent by a corresponding lack of blood sugar (glucose). In particular, the stomach begins a series of rhythmic contractions (which may be felt as "pangs" or "gripes").

Hunter, John (1728–1793) Scottish surgeon and lecturer in anatomy whose energy in the pursuit of medical knowledge of all disciplines was legendary in his time. Surgeon to the king (George III), member of the Royal Society, and keeper of his own menagerie for experiments, he deliberately infected himself with syphilis to prove one of his theories.

Huntington's disease Hereditary neurological disorder passed on as a dominant characteristic, meaning that any child who inherits the defective gene will develop the disorder – children of an affected parent have a 50% risk of getting the gene. The disease, which affects the *basal ganglia* of the brain (the parts involved with voluntary movement), was formerly called Huntingtonís *chorea* because it features involuntary jerks of the limbs and the muscles of the hips, shoulders and the face. Symptoms develop in middle age or later and also include behaviour changes, gradual dulling of the intellect and personality change, due to progressive degeneration of the nerve cells of the brain. Progressive *dementia* is likely. There is as yet no treatment, and affected patients often need institutional care. The gene responsible has now been identified, enabling screening tests to detect affected (adult) children of those with the disease, so that they can plan ahead before symptoms develop and receive genetic counselling about the risk to offspring.

Huxley, Andrew (1917–) English biologist, colleague and co-receiver of a 1963 Nobel Prize with Alan *Hodgkin*. He was also responsible for the discovery that *myofibrils* within a muscle do not contract when the muscle contracts but slide across each other – a discovery that was announced simultaneously by Hugh Huxley (1924– ; no relation).

hydatid cyst Large fluid-filled *cyst* surrounding the larva of a *tapeworm* (the smallest tapeworm of medical importance); some tapeworm larvae form multiple cysts. Each cyst may have its own fibrous capsule and – especially in the alveoli of the lungs – may cause tissue damage. If cysts form in the brain, blindness or convulsions may result. The most common site in humans, however, is the liver (where 75% of hydatid cysts occur) and symptoms are mild or non-existent. Rupture of a cyst may produce an allergic response. All such disorders resulting from the presence of one or more hydatid cysts are collectively called hydatid disease. Treatment is by surgical removal of the cyst, if possible.

hydrocele Swelling caused by the accumulation of watery fluid in a body sac, especially around the testes in the scrotum. Treatment is usually surgical drainage.

hydrocephalus Presence of excessive amounts of *cerebrospinal fluid* within the interlinked chambers (ventricles) of the brain. As a congenital or early childhood disorder, the whole head may enlarge because of pressure within the still flexible skull. In adults, whose skulls are rigid, the pressure on the brain is increased, causing lethargy and nausea. In either case, if levels of the fluid are not restored to normal fairly quickly (through surgery to remove a blockage or to effect drainage), brain damage may result. In children, the usual technique is to implant a *shunt* (tube) to drain fluid into a vein.

hydrochloric acid Powerful acid secreted in dilute form by the mucous lining of the stomach as a major component of *digestive juice*. Over-secretion is commonly associated with a *peptic ulcer* in the *duodenum* (duodenal ulcer).

hydrocortisone Drug form of the *corticosteroid* hormone cortisol, naturally produced and secreted by the *adrenal glands*. One of the *glucocorticoid hormones*, cortisol assists in the metabolism of carbohydrates, fats and proteins, and in the bodyís reaction to stress. Hydrocortisone is used to treat adrenal failure, some rheumatic conditions including rheumatoid arthritis, severe *allergy, asthma, eczema, dermatitis* and other forms of inflammation. It can be given as tablets, injections or skin creams. Side-effects include the development of *Cushing's syndrome*, muscle weakness, bone thinning and *peptic ulcer* formation; these may be serious in some people.

hydrogen peroxide Colourless astringent disinfectant, sometimes used in dilute solution as a disinfectant mouthwash or to syringe the ears. Stronger solutions may be used to bleach hair.

hydrophobia Another name for *rabies*.

hydrotherapy Treatment involving washing, bathing or swimming in water, especially as a means of comparatively weightless exercise in physiotherapy.

hygiene General term for the study and practice of personal cleanliness together with everyday precautions against disease, to promote and maintain health.

hymen Membrane that in young girls closes off the *vagina*. Partial rupture (perforation) of the membrane generally occurs before puberty; the first experience of sexual intercourse may also tear the membrane and cause slight bleeding. Menstruation when the hymen is still complete is rare, but if it occurs results in *haematocolpos*.

hyoid bone Small U-shaped bone at the front of the neck – above the Adamís apple and supporting the back of the tongue – which protects the epiglottis. Not directly attached to any other bone, it is held in position by muscles and ligaments.

hyperactivity Extreme overactivity, also called hyperkinesia, with alertness, restlessness, fidgeting, inability to sit still and less than average need for sleep. It may occur temporarily as a consequence of disease or drugs (including excess caffeine ingestion), but is usually applied to the form occurring naturally and persistently in children. This may be accompanied by symptoms of *attention deficit disorder* (ADD), the combination of both sometimes being called attention deficit hyperactivity disorder (ADHD).

hyperemesis Prolonged and severe vomiting. It occurs mostly in pregnant women, when it is known as hyperemesis gravidarum, and may be associated with *toxaemia of pregnancy*. It can lead to severe dehydration and sometimes liver damage, and if it persists into later pregnancy, despite ordinary countermeasures (see *morning sickness*), in severe cases it may be necessary to deliver the baby early.

hyperglycaemia Condition in which the glucose (sugar) level in the blood is too high. A symptom of several disorders, it appears particularly with *diabetes* mellitus as a result of the lack of *insulin*, and may lead to coma if untreated. Treatment is to reduce the blood sugar levels, in diabetics by the administration of insulin or other drugs.

hyperkinesia Another term for *hyperactivity*.

hypermetropia Longsightedness, an inability to focus the eyes on objects that are nearby. Rays of light from such objects are focused by the eyesí *lenses* – but at a point behind the eyeball and not on the *retina*. This is either because the lenses do not become convex enough or because the distance between the lens and the retina is unusually short (which may be the result of heredity). *Contact lenses* or *glasses* can correct the defect, which is more common after middle age.

hyperopia American term for *hypermetropia*.

hyperparathyroidism Excessive production and secretion of *parathormone* (parathyroid hormone) by the *parathyroid glands*, resulting in the loss of calcium from the bones to the blood. The effects (collectively known as von Recklinghausenís disease) are susceptibility to fractures and the formation of kidney stones.

hyperplasia Abnormal or special growth of an entire organ by an increase in the rate of normal multiplication by its cells. It occurs mostly through the action of *hormones* – as with the expansion of the womb and breasts during pregnancy, or of the thyroid gland (goitre) following oversecretion of thyroid-stimulating hormone by the pituitary gland.

hypersensitivity Extreme sensitivity of the body to the presence of a specific antigen, resulting in an allergic response or even anaphylactic shock.

hypertension High blood pressure, above the levels expected at any particular age – blood pressure generally increases with age. The cause may be unknown (essential hypertension), or it may result from kidney disease, hormonal disorders, heart or arterial disease, or any condition or drug that constricts (narrows) the blood vessels. People who are obese or under long-term psychological stress may be at increased risk, and there is often a family history of hypertension, *obesity*, or *heart disease*. Most of those affected have no symptoms, although occasionally there may be headaches and audiovisual disturbances, until resultant complications arise, such as *heart failure*, a *stroke*, kidney failure, *arteriosclerosis* or *cerebral haemorrhage*. Treatment of hypertension, if diagnosed before complications develop, can often avoid permanent damage. In cases where there is a specific cause, treatment of this may resolve the high blood pressure. In other cases, and in cases of essential hypertension, treatment generally consists of long-term drug therapy with *diuretics* (drugs that promote urination) and other drugs to keep the pressure down. Lifestyle changes, particularly weight-reduction, may also be advised.

hyperthyroidism Excessive production and secretion of thyroid hormones by the *thyroid gland* in the neck, leading to symptoms of thyrotoxicosis, including rapid heartbeat, sweating, anxiety, sensitivity to heat, hunger, weight loss and tremors. The cause may be overactivity or overgrowth of the gland, a tumour of the thyroid, a corresponding excess of *thyroid-stimulating hormone* (TSH) from the pituitary gland, or Graves disease, in which there are also protruding eyes and neck swelling (*goitre*). Treatment may be with drugs or radioactive iodine to decrease hormone production, but often involves the surgical removal of part of the thyroid gland.

hypertrophy Abnormal or special growth of an entire organ through an increase in the size of its component cells – the actual number of cells does not increase. (In this way it differs from *hyperplasia*.) It is through hypertrophy that muscles increase in size following long-term exercise.

hyperventilation Breathing abnormally rapidly without at the same time undergoing any exertion, and thus taking in an abnormally large amount of oxygen. The corresponding reduction of carbon dioxide in the blood may cause pins and needles, dizziness and muscle cramps and may eventually lead to unconsciousness. If persistent attacks occur, the condition is known as hyperventilation syndrome; it can be a feature of panic attacks occurring in *panic disorder* (attacks of acute distress, with fast heart rate, hyperventilation and sweating). Treatment of an acute attack is to rebreathe into a paper (NOT plastic) bag to increase carbon dioxide levels; persistent attacks may need psychiatric evaluation.

hypnosis State of extreme suggestibility induced by one person on another. In effect it resembles a form of sleep or trance under which, at the suggestion of the hypnotist, the patient may recount or even relive experiences which in normal consciousness would not be within recall, may feel or not feel pain, and may be given instructions to carry out after waking. The latter faculty may be used medically to relieve pain or to discourage the use of alcohol or cigarettes.

hypnotic drug Drug that by depressing certain centres in the brain induces sleep. Such drugs include *benzodiazepines* and some *antihistamines*. They should not be taken before driving or operating dangerous machinery.

hypochrondria Condition of constant anxiety over oneís own state of health, often involving belief in the existence of non-existent symptoms and the seeking of remedies for supposed ills. Severe forms amount to a *neurosis*.

hypodermic Syringe with a fine needle used to inject fluids (drugs or vaccines) through the skin into the body, or to extract body fluids.

hypoglycaemia Condition in which the glucose (sugar) level in the blood is too low. It occurs particularly as a result of an overdose of *insulin* (taken to combat the effects of *diabetes* mellitus) in combination with an insufficient intake of carbohydrates. Symptoms are high temperature, muscular weakness, faintness and confusion; coma may follow. Treatment is with glucose.

hypophysis Another name for the *pituitary gland*.

hypopituitarism Result of undersecretion of hormones by the *pituitary gland* (a gland in the brain that controls the secretions of other glands in the body). The effects depend on which other glands are secondarily affected, and may include low blood pressure, fatigue, weight loss, *diabetes* insipidus, reduced libido, headaches, visual problems, faintness and hair loss. In women, menstruation may cease and infertility may ensue; in children, the lack of *growth hormone* (somatotropin) stunts growth (although the proportions of the body remain normal) and sexual development. Causes include a pituitary tumour and haemorrhage (bleeding) after childbirth. Treatment may include hormone supplements or surgical removal of (or radiotherapy for) any tumour.

hypotension Abnormally low blood pressure, due to some other disorder. Causes include blood or fluid loss, as in haemorrhage, burns or severe diarrhoea or vomiting; severe allergic reactions, infections or abdominal emergencies; *myocardial infarction* (heart attack); hormonal imbalance, fainting and certain drugs. There may be no symptoms. In some cases blood pressure falls rapidly on standing up quickly (orthostatic hypotension), leading to dizziness, sweating and a feeling of lightheadedness. Very rarely, a patient may become semiconscious or undergo a state of extreme shock with circulatory failure. Treatment depends on the cause. In temporary blood pressure falls, as in simple fainting, lying flat with the legs elevated usually produces relief. Severe cases associated with major medical problems may require oxygen treatment and fluid replacement through a drip.

hypotensive drug Drug administered to reduce blood pressure.

hypothalamus Part of the *forebrain* that lies beneath the *thalamus* in each *cerebral hemisphere*, and beneath which lie the optic chiasma and the stalk of the *pituitary gland*. As the connection between the nervous system (represented by the thalamus) and the hormonal system (represented by the pituitary gland), it contains the nerve centres for such body functions as the libido, hunger and thirst, and body temperature.

hypothermia Dangerously low body temperature that results when, for whatever reason, the usual body mechanism for creating heat – shivering – is ineffective. It occurs most commonly in the elderly and the very young during weather that is exceptionally cold for an exceptionally long time. The term is used also for a therapeutic reduction in a patientís temperature as part of surgical procedure. Treatment is by gradual rewarming.

hypothyroidism Insufficient production and secretion of thyroid hormones by the *thyroid gland* in the neck, due to disease within the thyroid itself, overtreatment of *hyperthyroidism*, or a corresponding lack of *thyroid-stimulating hormone* (TSH) from the *pituitary gland*. Symptoms in adults, collectively called myxoedema, include lethargy, weight gain, thickening of the skin and coarsening of facial features, constipation and general mental and physical slowness. If untreated, complications may include heart failure, arterial disease, mental confusion and even coma. Undetected failure of thyroid development in newborn babies may lead to *cretinism* (failure of mental development with a characteristic expression and cry). Treatment is usually with thyroid hormone supplements. Early treatment in babies can avoid the effects of cretinism.

hysterectomy Surgical removal of a womanís *uterus* (womb); the neck of the womb (*cervix*), the *Fallopian tubes* and the *ovaries* may or may not also be removed. Reasons for the operation include *cancer, fibroids*, inflammation of the womb or Fallopian tubes, *menorrhagia* and an *ovarian cyst*. Removal is normally through an abdominal incision (although the womb by itself may be removed through the vagina). Afterwards, *menstruation* ceases. Hormones secreted by the ovaries if they remain, or prescribed by a doctor if not, should ensure that the patientís sexual desire and ability is unaffected, however.

hysteria Older term for a form of *neurosis* characterized by physical and behavioural symptoms, shallow emotional relationships, suggestibility, a facility for splitting aspects of life or thought into separate "compartments" (dissociation), and *repression*. In one form, conversion hysteria (now known as conversion disorder), the mental aspects of repression are converted into physical (behavioural) symptoms, such as paralysis or inability to speak, particularly when such symptoms may be useful to the patient. In the other form, dissociative hysteria (a group of related conditions now known as dissociative disorders), patients may have multiple personalities (some apparently ignorant of the others) or suffer from selective or total *amnesia*. Psychiatric treatment may help in either case. In common parlance, the term "hysteria" is used also for a state of high emotion caused by acute stress.

I

iatrogenic disorder Disorder that occurs as a result of treatment (by a medical therapist). It may arise unexpectedly or be an inevitable side-effect of the treatment.

icterus Medical term for *jaundice*.

id In *psychoanalysis*, part of the *unconscious* that comprises the primitive, instinctual urges for survival and reproduction. Its effects on behaviour are constrained by the self-awareness of the *ego* and by the knowledge of right and wrong superimposed by the *superego*.

ideation Process of imagining or having ideas.

identical twins *Twins* that result from a fertilized ovum that at its first cleavage splits into two complete *zygotes*, which then develop into separate foetuses. They are always of the same sex, share a single placenta, and their genetic "fingerprints" are virtually the same. Twins that result from the simultaneous fertilization of two separate ova by two sperm are *fraternal twins*.

idiopathic Describing a disorder that seems to appear for no reason.

idiosyncrasy In medicine, an unusual reaction in somebody to a specific form of treatment (or even to a particular food) – by way of either an extreme response or a minimal response. The term is less generally used in relation to allergic reactions (see *allergy*).

ileostomy Surgical operation to diver the *ileum* (the final part of the small intestine) and its contents to an artificial opening in the surface of the abdomen. It may be performed as a temporary measure to allow ulceration or other serious disorder of the colon (the large intestine) to heal before being reconnected. Or it may be a permanent necessity following intestinal cancer or surgical removal of the colon. Faeces are collected at the new opening in a replaceable hermetic bag.

ileum Final and longest part of the small *intestine*, which connects the *jejunum* with the short first part of the large intestine, the *caecum*. The ileum is responsible for the final absorption of the digestive products of fats and carbohydrates.

ileus Intestinal obstruction, usually of the ileum (small intestine). It may be due to a blockage, for instance, with a *hernia*, *adhesion*, *tumour*, *calculus* (stone), or infestation with *worms*; or to failure in *peristalsis* (the normal wave-like gut movements that propel the intestinal contents along), as may occur after surgery, trauma or peritonitis. Treatment depends on the diagnosis and may include removing any source of obstruction, or supportive treatment until peristalsis returns.

ilium Large bone at each side of the pelvis, forming what is commonly called the hip bone. (The other bones of the pelvis are the ischium and, at the front, the pubis.)

illusion Error in perception that involves misinterpretation by the mind of evidence provided by the senses. A mistaken impression about the environment or about the people around one is a common illusion in everyday life, and is usually corrected quickly. Factors such as drugs, fever or any of many forms of mental disturbance may promote longer-lasting illusions. A *delusion*, on the other hand, is a deliberate insistence on a belief in spite of sensory evidence to the contrary; and in a *hallucination*, a purely mental phenomenon, there is no sensory evidence at all.

immersion foot Alternative name for *trench foot.*

immune response Response of the *immune system* of the body to the internal presence of *antigens* (foreign bodies that are capable of causing a disorder). The response results mainly in the formation of *leukocytes* and *antibodies*, which act to neutralize the antigens.

immune system Body system that is its chief defence against invading organisms (pathogens) or foreign material identified as potentially harmful. The skin is one of the first barriers that such bodies have to cross, or they have to penetrate the defences of the airways to the lungs, such as hairs in the nose and lymphatic tissue (tonsils) in the throat. Once such *antigens* are inside the body, *leukocytes* in the bloodstream and in the *lymphatic system* – which can reach almost all areas of tissue – quickly find, surround and neutralize them. If necessary, the number of leukocytes is increased; some of them (*lymphocytes*) form specific *antibodies*. Most infections can be successfully dealt with in this way, although some may take a long time. Moreover, once specific antibodies have been formed, they remain in the body and may confer *immunity* to the same invader at a later occasion.

immunity Resistance of the body to specific diseases, either through the normal function of the *immune system* (in successful resistance to the presence of potentially harmful organisms or material, or by already having *antibodies* formed on a previous encounter) or through *immunization*. Antibodies formed by previous contact with a disease, and antibodies formed as a result of immunization with a harmless version of the antigen, are said to confer active immunity. Antibodies formed in another person (or animal) and introduced into the bloodstream are said to confer passive immunity. For example, antibodies in motherís milk confer some passive immunity to a baby in the first months of life.

immunization Conferring of *immunity* to specific diseases by medical means. It may be effected by inoculation (in which the body is obliged to form its own *antibodies* to a harmless version of an *antigen*) or by the injection of an *antiserum* (containing antibodies formed in another person or in an animal). During the first fifteen months of life, most babies in Western countries undergo an extensive immunization programme.

immunodeficiency A defect in the bodyís normal immune response, increasing the liability to infections, including infection by micro-organisms that would not cause disease in healthy individuals (opportunistic infection). Immunodeficiency can be present at birth or may be acquired, in *AIDS* or due to various drugs. Treatment depends on the cause but generally involves a combination of avoidance of infections and treatment of those that do arise, where possible.

immunoglobulin Any of certain proteins, found normally in the blood, that can act as an *antibody*.

immunology Study of the body processes and the scientific methods involved in conferring *immunity*.

immunosuppressive drugs Drugs that suppress the *immune system*, so that material in the body which would ordinarily be identified by the *leukocytes* as "foreign" is temporarily or permanently accepted. Such drugs allow surgical transplants of tissue that is closely matched, but not identical, to be grafted without *rejection*, but may also permit infections virtually free access to the body.

impacted Affected by being forced up against an obstruction. For example, impacted *wisdom teeth* are obstructed by others and cannot erupt in a normal position. An impacted *fracture* is one in which the two ends of a broken bone are driven hard into each other. Impacted *faeces* are obstructed in the intestine, and harden.

impetigo Highly contagious bacterial infection that mostly attacks children, sometimes in epidemics, and causes a skin rash which then forms yellow crusts, generally on the face and limbs. Treatment is with antibiotic creams and antiseptic baths. In adults, a chronic form of impetigo is known as ecthyma.

implantation Embedding of material of any kind in the tissues. The term applies to the attachment in and on the lining of the uterus (endometrium) of the *blastocyst* – the developed form of the fertilized ovum (*zygote*) after *conception* – at the point where the placenta then forms. Implantation also applies to the embedding of an artificial heart *pacemaker* within the tissues.

impotence Inability of a man to obtain, or to sustain, an *erection* of the penis, or failure to achieve ejaculation or orgasm during *sexual intercourse*. It may be due to physical problems, such as arterial disease or *diabetes* mellitus, or to psychological causes. Treatment with the drug sildenafil (Viagra) can give a viable erection provided there is normal sexual desire. Older treatments include injections into the base of the penis, and prostheses that maintain hardness.

inbreeding Bearing of children by parents who are closely related, particularly if their grandparents were also closely related. When this happens, the *genes* contributed to the children by each parent are significantly more alike than those contributed to most children, whose parents are not related. Consequently, if there are any *recessive* genes involving abnormal or undesirable traits, the recessive effect is less likely than with non-related parents to be cancelled out by a different *dominant* gene. For this reason, in most countries marriage between close relations is prohibited by law. See also *incest*.

incest Sexual intercourse between close relations, especially first-degree relatives, irrespective of whether the genetic relationship embraces a marital one or not. In most countries these are full or half-brothers and sisters, parents and their children, and grandparents and grandchildren, regardless of age, and these categories may also include a "child of the family", one brought up within a family even if there is no genetic relationship (such as an adopted child, stepchild, or the child of one of the parents by a former relationship). Reasons for the prohibition include natural distaste, the greater risk of genetic disorders among offspring of close relations (see also *inbreeding*) and protection of children from *sexual abuse* – incest can cause lasting psychological harm to children.

incidence Statistical measure of the number of new cases or episodes of a condition over a specified time period, usually one year; for instance, the number of heart attacks per 1,000 of the population (or population at risk, such as adults, or males) per year. See also *prevalence*.

incisors Eight chisel-shaped cutting teeth at the front of the mouth (four in each jaw), between the *canines* each side. Their purpose is to bite into or through food, as opposed to "stabbing" it (canines) or chewing it (*premolars* and *molars*).

incompatibility Antagonistic effect between certain pairs of similar forms (blood groups, tissue types, temperaments, and so on) when brought into close contact. See also *Rh factor incompatibility*.

incompetence Inability to fulfil an appropriate function. In medicine, the term is used mostly of *valves* (of the heart or of the veins) which "leak" and therefore fail to prevent backflow.

incontinence Lack of control over the sphincters (valve-like rings of muscle) and other muscles that hold back urine in the bladder or faeces in the rectum (or both). Causes range from muscular weakness (perhaps through giving birth), disease and *drug abuse* (including *alcoholism*), to injury, stress and excitement. Treatment depends on the cause and may include drugs, exercises to strengthen the muscles of the pelvic floor or, in some cases, surgery.

incubation period Interval between the time somebody is exposed to an infection, and the time symptoms first appear. Such an interval is specific to many infections, and may thus form the basis for calculating an appropriate duration of *quarantine*. For example, the incubation period for measles is 8 to 15 days. The term is used also for the length of time taken by a bacterial culture to become visible in a culture medium.

incubator Small, enclosed chamber in which atmosphere and temperature can be controlled and monitored. Incubators are used to maintain premature babies until they are strong enough to live independently, and to accommodate bacterial cultures under cultivation.

incus Tiny anvil-shaped bone in the *middle ear*. With the malleus (hammer) and the stapes (stirrup), which it lies between, it conveys sound vibrations from the *eardrum* to the *inner ear* and the sensory organs of hearing.

indigestion Any form of disordered digestion causing pain or discomfort in the lower chest or upper abdomen related to eating. The medical name is dyspepsia. Other symptoms may include a bloated feeling around the diaphragm, belching and sometimes regurgitation of the liquid contents of the stomach up at least as far as the throat (causing *heartburn*), flatulence, nausea or even vomiting. The cause is usually overeating, eating too quickly, or eating food that is too rich or that the stomach has difficulty in dealing with. Overindulgence in alcoholic drinks can also cause indigestion. Temporary indigestion is extremely common, and may be promoted by *stress*, *obesity* or a *hiatus hernia*. However, symptoms that do not settle or that persist for a long period should be medically assessed, as occasionally they may suggest a more serious disorder, such as *peptic ulcer*, hiatus *hernia*, *cholecystitis* (inflammation of the gall bladder), or, rarely, cancer of the stomach or oesophagus. Treatment of occasional indigestion is with *antacids* and lifestyle changes, such as weight loss, dietary modification and avoidance of stress. Prescribed treatment for persistent indigestion depends on a doctorís diagnosis.

induction In obstetrics, the bringing on of *labour* and *childbirth* by artificial methods in a woman whose *pregnancy* has continued beyond term (the date at which the baby was expected to be born) or is liable to be injurious to the mother or baby if continued. It is effected either medically, by insertion in the vagina of a *pessary* containing *prostaglandins*, or by gradual injection of a hormone (*oxytocin*) that stimulates uterine contraction; or surgically, by rupturing the membranes (amniotomy) and releasing some of the amniotic fluid that surrounds the foetus (breaking the waters), or both. In anaesthetics, induction is used to mean initiating anaesthesia of a patient.

industrial diseases Diseases associated with working in a particular industry; they are forms of *occupational diseases and disorders*.

infant mortality rate Statistical measure of the number of deaths of infants aged less than one year as a proportion (usually per thousand) of the total number of live births within a population over a specified time period, usually one year. It includes the neonatal mortality rate (deaths within the first four weeks after a live birth) and the post-neonatal mortality rate (deaths between four weeks and one year of age).

infantilism Persistence of the characteristics – physical and particularly mental – of infancy long past the appropriate age, and even into adulthood. Causes range from drug abuse (perhaps in the mother during pregnancy) to *mental retardation* accompanied by abnormally slow physical development.

infarction Death of part of the tissue that makes up an organ, after its blood supply has somehow been cut off (usually by a blockage in the artery or arteries that supply it with blood). Infection is not a factor (as with gangrene), but scarring at the site of the dead tissue (the infarct) takes place. The effects of infarction depend on where in the body it occurs. The most serious consequences follow infarction in the brain, heart or lungs, where death or long-term incapacity may result.

infection Invasion of the body by pathogenic micro-organisms – such as *bacteria, viruses, protozoans* or tiny *fungi* – that then temporarily multiply faster than the bodyís *immune system* (defence mechanisms) can deal with. The result is the appearance, after an *incubation period*, of local or general symptoms, some of which may be serious. Drug treatment is usually effective against virtually all except viral infections – some viruses are susceptible to antiviral drugs but for most, treatment is generally aimed at alleviating the symptoms as far as possible. Infections can be transmitted through inhalation of saliva or mucous secretions (such as air-borne droplets from a sneeze); through contact with the skin (contagion); through ingestion (organisms taken in with food or drink); through sexual intercourse (*sexually transmitted diseases*); from mother to child during pregnancy, childbirth or breastfeeding; or through blood, such as transfusions, contaminated medical equipment or insect bites. Sources may thus include other human beings, animals, insects or soil. The method of transmission is usually specific to each infection, although a few can be transmitted in more than one way. Methods of preventing infection range from good hygiene and *antisepsis* to *vaccination*.

infectious disease Disorder that results from *infection*.

infectious mononucleosis Older term for *glandular fever*.

inferiority complex Set of strongly emotive feelings and ideas repressed into the *unconscious*, causing a somewhat obsessive lack of confidence. The result is either exaggerated avowals of inadequacy and inferiority, or behaviour that unconsciously compensates for that – such as aggressiveness. In *psychoanalysis*, the term represents the state of mind of a child who has natural feelings of sexual desire for the parent of the opposite sex, but also realizes that it cannot be fulfilled.

infertility Inability to have children. In a woman, physical causes may be failure of the *ovaries* to produce ova, obstruction of the *Fallopian tubes*, or disease or injury in the *uterus* (womb) or *vagina*; there may also be psychological causes. In a man, causes usually centre on the quantity or quality of the *sperm* he produces, or on problems in actually completing *sexual intercourse* successfully. Treatment for some of these causes, in women and men, is possible. Drug treatment may be used to stimulate ovulation, or surgery to repair physical defects. In other cases, modern reproductive technology such as *in vitro* fertilization (to produce "test tube babies") may be used.

infestation Presence on or in the body of parasites – such as *fleas, lice, mites, ticks* or *worms*.

infirmary Old name for a hospital, clinic or sanatorium at which patients are treated and medicines dispensed.

inflammation Local reaction of body tissues to injury (including bites and stings), irritation (including an allergic response) or infection. It occurs as a defensive mechanism, and results in redness and swelling – possibly with the formation of *pus* – heat and pain. Body fluids and an increased blood supply are diverted to the area, partly under the influence of *histamine* (an inflammatory chemical), to assist in healing. White blood cells (*leucocytes*) congregate in order to entrap and neutralize infective organisms or material. Despite all this, inflammation may sometimes become chronic. Treatment depends on the cause and may include various drugs to suppress inflammation or relieve pain.

influenza Highly infectious viral disease that attacks the air passages of the throat and lungs. Symptoms are headache, muscle weakness, shivering with chills, high temperature – which may at times reach 40 C (104 F) – a sore throat, and a cough; all may last for about a week. The usual treatment is with bed rest and aspirin. Secondary infections may occur as complications, especially infections of the ear, nose and throat. Treatment is usually to alleviate symptoms while the patient recovers. Complications due to bacterial infection may be treated with antibiotics. A vaccine is available for vulnerable people at high risk of complications, and such patients may be prescribed a new drug called zanamivir (Relenza) to speed recovery and reduce the risk of complications.

infra-red radiation Electromagnetic radiation of wavelength longer than the red of the visible spectrum: the invisible radiation of heat. As heat treatment, infra-red radiation may be used by therapists to soothe muscular disorders and rheumatic aches. In *thermography*, infra-red radiation emitted by the body is recorded on specially sensitive film or processed by a computer for the diagnosis of certain conditions that produce internally localized heat.

infusion Either the gradual injection of fluid into a vessel (such as dextrose or saline solution into a vein); or the steeping of plant material in boiling water so that the active principles dissolve out.

ingrowing toenail Painful growth of the side edge of a toenail down into the soft skin of the toe. Causes include uneven cutting of the toenail, and tight shoes. Treatment includes daily cleaning and lifting of the nail. But if infection occurs, and persists, surgery (to remove the nail) is the final resort. The likelihood of ingrowing toenail is lessened by cutting the nails straight across, and not in a curve.

inguinal hernia *Hernia* in the groin, the crease where the thigh meets the abdomen.

inhalant Gaseous or atomized form of drug that can be inhaled to soothe respiratory problems (such as those caused by asthma).

inhalation Breathing in – part of the process of *respiration*. It is effected by the lowering of the diaphragm (under the unconscious control of the respiratory centre in the brain) at the same time as the ribcage is drawn upwards and outwards. This causes a partial vacuum in the suddenly extended *lungs*; air then floods in under atmospheric pressure.

inheritance In medicine, sum of the effects of the *genes* in the *chromosomes* of an individualís cell nuclei, half contributed by one parent, half by the other.

inhibition In psychology, conscious or unconscious wish to avoid taking a specific action because something unpleasant or immoral might happen or because something unpleasant or immoral happened last time. A person with no inhibitions is thus free of all constraints about possible unpleasant or immoral consequences. In neurology, the term describes the braking effect of certain nerve impulses on the functioning of specific muscles or organs.

injection Introduction into the body of fluid, using a syringe (hypodermic needle). Fluids injected are usually drugs or vaccines, and usually those which would have either no effect or an unwanted effect if they were taken orally. Drugs may be injected into a vein, into a muscle, into the skin or below the skin. Certain forms of *enema* are also considered to be injections.

injury Physical wound and associated damage. A wound that is either physical or mental, or both, is a *trauma*.

inkblot test Psychological test of visual associations, involving meaningless but suggestive shapes – like inkblots – on a plain background. By analysing a patientís verbal associations on seeing each of the standardized inkblots, a psychologist may gain insight into the patientís personality and state of mind. The tests are sometimes called Rorschach tests after their founder, Hermann Rorschach (1884–1922).

inner ear Innermost part of the ear, responsible for both *hearing* and *balance*, and sometimes alternatively called the labyrinth. The organ is embedded in the temporal bone of the skull, and surrounded by friction-reducing fluid (perilymph). The part of the organ responsible for hearing is the coiled *cochlea*, from which the auditory nerve relays sensory messages to the brain. Attached to the cochlea are the *saccule* and the *utricle*, and attached to them are the *semicircular canals* – all components of the organ of balance (sometimes called the membranous labyrinth) and containing their own fluid (endolymph). Inflammation and infection of the inner ear, *otitis* interna (or labyrinthitis), affects both hearing and balance – typically causing partial deafness and dizziness – and may be difficult to treat.

inoculation Alternative term for *vaccination*.

inquest Form of court hearing presided over by a *coroner* – with or without a jury – and convened to discover and declare publicly the exact cause of death of somebody who dies suddenly or in circumstances suggesting that age or natural causes were not wholly responsible. Medical and legal evidence may be heard.

insanity Legal term for a condition of such mental illness or instability in a person that he or she cannot be held legally responsible for his or her actions.

insemination The ejaculation by a man of *semen* into a womanís *vagina* during *sexual intercourse*, for the purpose of having a child. Where this natural form of insemination cannot, for one medical reason or another, be carried out, semen may be introduced into the vagina or *uterus* through various techniques of *artificial insemination*.

insomnia Inability to fall – or to remain – asleep. The most usual cause is stress, anxiety or excitement. Other causes include constant pain or noise, indigestion, physical discomfort, and disease. The result is perpetual tiredness. Treatment depends on the cause. Sleeping pills may be prescribed, but should be taken only as directed by a doctor.

instinct Basic drive (or "primitive urge") within humans towards specific goals – survival or reproduction – leading to equally specific patterns of behaviour in particular circumstances.

insulin Hormone secreted by the *islets of Langerhans* in the *pancreas* to control the level of glucose (sugar) in the blood. It promotes the absorption of glucose into tissue cells, and also affects *lipid* balance. Too little insulin in the body (as with *diabetes* mellitus) may result in dangerously high blood sugar levels (*hyperglycaemia*); too much may result in dangerously low levels (*hypoglycaemia*).

integument Medical name for the *skin*.

intellect Part of the mind that can draw on both *memory* and *intelligence* in order to reason creatively, and by so doing manifest itself as cleverness.

intelligence Practical ability to make use of both *memory* and knowledge to arrive quickly at workable solutions to problems. (It is therefore not the same as simply having a quick memory for knowledge.) See also *instinct*.

intelligence quotient (IQ) A measure of intelligence based on scores in an *intelligence test*, usually abbreviated to *IQ*.

intelligence test Any of many forms of test intended to grade an individualís *intelligence*, related to a scale on which the average intelligence of a population is generally measured at 100. The score may then be called an *IQ*. Most tests comprise a series of sets of problems that may be based, for example, on visual discrimination, mathematical perception, progressive reasoning or verbal comprehension, and the time taken to complete the tests is also relevant. For medical diagnosis, the tests may be used to assess mental subnormality (*mental retardation*) or progressive loss of intellectual function in disorders that affect the brain.

intensive care Round-the-clock fully monitored care of a patient who is seriously ill, usually in a special hospital ward where emergency equipment and facilities are always to hand.

interferon Substance produced in minute quantities by body cells under the influence of an occupying *virus*; it inhibits the growth of many different types of virus within the species that produced it. There are three types, made by different types of cell: alpha-, beta- and gamma-interferon (derived from white blood cells, fibroblasts and lymphocytes respectively). Human interferons have now been commercially produced as a drug in bacterial cells, using techniques of *genetic engineering*, but large-scale synthesis is too expensive for widespread use, and interferons have not proved as effective against the full range of human viral infections as was originally hoped. It has, however, become useful – if expensive – therapy in the treatment of viral *hepatitis*, *multiple sclerosis* and certain forms of *cancer*.

intermittent claudication Cramp in the calf muscle of the leg during exercise but not at other times. The cause is an inadequate supply of blood to the muscle, generally as a result of fatty deposits (*atheroma*) in the supplying blood vessels, but sometimes because of a blood clot or other form of blockage. The condition often becomes progressively worse. Treatment is with drugs – *vasodilators* may be useful if the arteries are not diseased – and, as a last resort, surgery.

intertrigo Inflammation of the skin in areas where two surfaces rub together, such as underneath the breasts or in the groin, especially in obese people. Friction plus sweating cause the surface of the skin to chafe, leading to irritation and soreness. Sometimes infection occurs, especially with Candida yeasts, making the symptoms worse. Treatment is with skin creams to soothe the area and treat any infection. Scrupulous hygiene and drying of the area, and attempts at weight loss, may help to prevent recurrence.

intersex Individual whose body has characteristics intermediate between – or combining – those of ordinary men and ordinary women. (A *hermaphrodite* is different in having two complete sets of reproductive organs.)

intervertebral disc Tough disc of fibrous cartilage that separates the vertebrae of the spine (except those at the lower end which are fused together). Such discs give the whole of the spinal column its flexibility, also acting to reduce impact and friction in movement, and in fact constitute a total of one quarter of its length. Displacement of the pulpy middle part of a disc (*prolapsed intervertebral disc*) can lead to long-term pain in the back or in the leg served by a nerve that is pressed on by the displaced disc (*sciatica*).

intestines Length of the *alimentary canal* between the *stomach* and the *anus*, in which the major stages of *digestion* take place, nutrients are absorbed, and waste products are left to be propelled (by *villi* and by *peristalsis*) along its mucous lining for eventual *defecation*. The small intestine – small only in diameter, but four times longer than the large intestine – begins at the *pylorus*, the narrow exit from the stomach, and continues as the *duodenum, jejunum* and *ileum*. By the time food has reached its end, all fats and carbohydrates have been absorbed. The large intestine begins at the pouch-like *caecum*, to which the blind-ended *appendix* is attached; thereafter, the three sections of the *colon* (ascending, transverse and descending) lead to the *rectum* and the anus. Veins surrounding the intestine carry blood and the products of absorption through the portal vein to the liver; the intestines are also well supplied by the lymphatic system. Nerves that regulate the flow of intestinal contents are part of the *autonomic nervous system*.

intoxication Altered brain activity, caused by poisoning. Intellectual capacity is impaired and there may be confusion, impaired consciousness or hallucinations. If the poisoning is by alcohol, the effects are likely to be temporary (as long as alcohol consumption ceases), although there may be acute dehydration and headache afterwards (*hangover*). Poisoning by other drugs, gases or by heavy metals may produce progressively worse symptoms.

intramuscular Into or inside a muscle.

intrauterine contraceptive device (IUCD) Form of *contraception* fitted within a womanís womb (uterus) and believed to act at least partly by preventing implantation of a fertilized *ovum* in the wall of the womb. It consists of a thin, coiled metal or plastic device in a range of shapes (it is also known as the "coil" or "loop"). Often covered with copper or hormones that are slowly released to enhance the contraceptive effect (so the device needs periodic renewal), it must be fitted by a doctor, using a syringe-like applicator. Although an effective means of contraception, it may cause heavy or painful periods; it is also linked with an increased risk of *pelvic inflammatory disease* and *ectopic pregnancy* (pregnancy outside the womb, often in a *Fallopian tube*), and occasionally the device may be naturally expelled from the womb. Insertion of an IUCD is also effective as a means of emergency postcoital contraception up to five days after unprotected intercourse.

intravenous Into or inside a vein.

intravenous pyelogram, (IVP) X-ray pictures of a kidney (pyelogram) following the injection of radio-opaque material into a vein, making visible the functioning of the kidney as it collects and excretes the material through to the ureter and bladder. It is particularly useful for detecting the presence of an obstruction such as a stone (calculus).

introvert Somebody who is self-reliant, more interested in his or her own thoughts and activities than in those of others, and thus likely not to socialize or seek companionable entertainment. Many introverts are dependent on routines and tenacious in striving for goals.

intussusception Telescoping of a weakened part of the intestinal wall, during which the inner layer of intestinal wall is sucked along as though it was part of the intestinal contents, thus increasing the overlap as it goes. Complete intestinal obstruction generally results. The condition particularly affects young children, but may be caused in adults by a polyp or tumour. Symptoms are severe pain, pallor, and vomiting; a red jelly-like material may be visible in the faeces. Emergency hospitalization is necessary, where a barium or gastrografin enema occasionally restores both shape and function to the intestine. Surgery may be required, however.

invalid Somebody who is ill, and particularly one who – temporarily or permanently – has difficulty with independent mobility.

in vitro fertilization Fertilization of an *ovum* by a *sperm* under medical supervision in a laboratory. Zygotes produced in this way may develop into a *blastocyst*, be surgically implanted in a womanís womb, and duly form an embryo, a foetus, and be brought to birth in the normal fashion (commonly known as a test-tube baby).

iodine Non-metallic *trace element* essential to the functioning of the *thyroid gland* – an iodine deficiency leads to *goitre*. It occurs in sea foods, most forms of household salt, and some vegetables. Medically, it can be used in an alcohol solution (tincture) as an antiseptic, and a radioactive form may be used in the diagnosis of thyroid, lung, liver or kidney disorders.

ion Atom of molecule that is electrically charged following the gaining or losing of one or more electrons; the charge may thus be negative (anion) or positive (cation). Most salts form ions when they dissolve in water.

ionizing radiation Any form of radiation – such as X-rays and gamma radiation – that causes substances to be converted to *ions*. See *radiation*.

IQ Measure of *intelligence*, arrived at by means of any of the many forms of *intelligence test*, and related to an average intelligence standard of a population numerically set at 100. In some children, and especially in those who are mentally handicapped, an IQ score may be used to define degrees of intellectual progress or subnormality (*mental retardation*). In others, a high score may be used to suggest a need for special forms of education. Geniuses are ordinarily reckoned to have IQs of more than 150.

iris Pigmented (coloured) part of the eye round the dark pupil, representing a small ring of finely muscled tissue between the cornea and the lens, surrounded by the watery aqueous humour. Under the direction of the autonomic nervous system, the tiny muscles in the iris regulate the amount of light that reaches the lens and retina by dilating or constricting the pupil. Iris pigmentation is the same in all eyes; but in brown eyes it is closer to the surface; in blue it is deeper.

iron Metallic element present in some quantity in the body, and essential to the composition of the blood. More than half of the iron in the body is as the major constituent of *haemoglobin* – the red colouring matter in blood that carries oxygen from the lungs to the tissues; the rest is used to supply oxygen to the muscles or stored. Meat, particularly liver, is a good dietary source, as are eggs. Iron deficiency may lead to *anaemia*.

irradiation Process of subjecting part of a patientís body to any form of *electromagnetic radiation* or *radioactivity*, for the purpose of diagnosis or treatment.

irrigation Washing out of a body cavity – particularly of the ears or the colon – usually by means of a syringe and water or an antiseptic fluid.

irritability Sensitivity and response to specific stimuli. Muscles, for example, display irritability by contracting under the stimuli provided by the associated nerves.

irritable bowel syndrome Bouts of abdominal pain occurring in spasms, sometimes with *diarrhoea* or *constipation*, or both alternating. Sometimes also called mucous colitis or spastic colon, it may be due to abnormal contractions of the muscles of the intestinal wall, or to abnormal sensitivity to the presence of food in the intestines, but is not linked with any physical changes in the guts. The cause is unknown but it may follow intestinal infections and is sometimes precipitated by *stress*. It may seriously interfere with a personís lifestyle, but does not lead to serious disease, although medical diagnosis is essential to rule out other conditions. Treatment may include drugs to reduce pain or spasm, or to soften the faeces. Dietary changes and relaxation techniques may also help.

irritant Chemical or substance that irritates a tissue, especially the skin or the eyes, causing *inflammation* or other responses representing defensive mechanisms.

ischaemia Reduction in the supply of blood to an area of tissue, caused most often by disease of the blood vessels, such as *atherosclerosis*. Effects vary according to the blood vessels involved: *angina pectoris* results if the vessels are in or near the heart; *intermittent claudication* if in the legs, a mild *stroke* if within the skull. Long-term damage is minimal if treatment – which depends on diagnosis of the cause – is prompt. Delayed treatment may cause the affected area of tissue to die (*infarction*).

ischium Almost semicircular bone forming the lower part of each side of the pelvis. (The other bones of the pelvis are the ilium and the pubis.)

Ishihara tests Method for detecting *colour blindness*. It involves looking at a series of cards on which there are dots of many sizes and colours, the colours of similar tonal value. Within the dotted design, and clearly visible to people with normal vision, is a recognizable image – usually a large numeral. Colour-blind people may not be able to distinguish the image – or may see the image on some cards only. The tests thus indicate also the type of colour blindness that may be present.

islets of Langerhans Clusters of specialized cells scattered throughout the *pancreas*, which produce and secrete the hormones *insulin* and *glucagon*. (Alpha cells produce insulin, and beta cells glucagon.)

isolation Medically, either keeping a patient with an infectious or contagious disease separate from uninfected people, or keeping a patient with a disorder that lowers resistance to infection separate from other potentially infectious patients. The term is used also in surgery to mean separating one tissue structure from another, and in psychology to mean an individualís awareness of solitude.

isotope Form of a chemical element in which the atomic nuclei have the same number of protons as other forms but a different number of neutrons. Radioactive isotopes emit alpha, beta or gamma particles (or radiation) and so over time decay inhto other isotopes or even other elements. Some radioactive isotopes may be artificially created by bombarding elements with neutrons, and are extensively used in *radiotherapy*.

itching Medical name pruritis, irritation of the nerve endings just under the skin. Causes are many, and mostly minor, but include various skin disorders, liver disorder and stress. Many local infections – with or without a rash – cause itching. Soothing creams and lotions may help, but a persistent itch should be medically diagnosed.

IUCD Abbreviation of *intrauterine contraceptive device*.

J

Jacksonian epilepsy Form of *epilepsy* that focuses on the cerebral cortex (the outer portions of one or both hemispheres of the brain), with the result that convulsive movements usually spread ("march") from one extremity (such as the thumb) inwards up towards the face and from there proceed over one side (or possibly the whole) of the body.

Jarvik, Robert K. (1946-V) American cardiologist and engineer, inventor of the first artificial heart to be successfully attached to a patient (Barney Clark, who remained alive for a further 112 days in 1982). "Attached" it had to be, for it was too complex to be implanted. Later versions have become smaller and implantable.

jaundice Medical name icterus, a yellow coloration of the skin, mucous membranes and "whites" of the eyes, caused by an excess of the bile pigment *bilirubin* in the blood. The excess may result from obstruction of the bile ducts, as with *gallstones* (obstructive jaundice); from liver disorder (such as *hepatitis* or *cirrhosis*), which causes failure to dispose of bile normally (hepatocellular jaundice), or from the formation of proportionately too much bilirubin, due to increased destruction of red cells in the blood in various conditions (haemolytic jaundice). Jaundice is often accompanied by itching and the passing of dark urine. Treatment depends on diagnosis of the cause.

jaw Either the *mandible* (lower jaw) or the *maxilla* (upper jaw).

jejunum Almost half the total length of the small intestine, between the *duodenum* and the *ileum*, in which the processes of digestion begun in the stomach continue. (A major disorder of the jejunum is *coeliac disease*.)

Jenner, Edward (1749–1823) English pioneer immunologist whose understanding and adoption of *vaccination* founded the science of immunology. He was the first to deliberately inoculate a person with cowpox in order to render him immune to smallpox.

jet lag Physical disorientation of the body when its *circadian rhythms* (daily variations driven by the "body clock") are not parallelled by the environmental time of day. It happens after travelling by air through several time zones, and causes disruption not only of the sleep and alertness patterns but also of body temperature mechanisms and some glandular functions. Over wide time differences, the body may take up to a week to adapt fully to the new time zone. Planning of flight times and activities, and avoiding alcohol in-flight, can reduce the effects. A doctor could prescribe a short-acting sleeping tablet to enable sleep during the flight. In the USA, *melatonin*, a hormone that regulates body cycles, is available as a supplement and may help to combat jet lag.

joint Connection between two bones, often – but by no means always – to provide movement (*articulation*). Articulatory (synovial or "mobile") joints may be hinge joints, which allow movement in one plane only (as at the knee); rotating joints, which allow a turning movement of a limb (as with the forearm at the wrist); or ball-and-socket joints, which allow a wide range of movements (as at the shoulder). Movement is effected by the muscles, tendons and ligaments under the control of the nervous system, and the bones themselves are kept slightly separated by a layer of *synovial* membrane to decrease friction. Some joints are only just mobile, articulating merely because of the compressibility of cartilage between the bones (as in the spine). Other joints are rigidly fixed, some with thick cartilaginous bands (as in the pelvis), and others directly fused together (as in the adult skull).

jugular vein Any of six veins in the neck, draining blood from the brain, scalp, face and neck. The two large internal jugular veins run down each side of the neck; the two external jugular veins run similarly but much closer to the skin surface. From the latter run the two anterior jugular veins, down the front of the neck.

Jung, Carl Gustav (1875–1961) Swiss psychologist, one-time disciple of Sigmund *Freud*, who founded his own school of psychology – analytical psychology – because he disagreed with Freudś insistence on the dominant effects of sexuality on personality and behaviour, as proposed by *psychoanalysis*. He also derived the notion of a collective unconscious that waś the evolutionary force behind human development.

K

kala-azar Severe form of *leishmaniasis*.

kaolin China clay (aluminium silicate). In purified, powdered form it is an effective absorbent material that may be administered orally to treat digestive disorders and types of food poisoning that lead to diarrhoea and vomiting. Kaolin may also be used in *poultices*.

Kaposi's sarcoma A form of malignant skin tumour arising from blood vessels close to the skin surface, and causing dark patches or nodules. It is common in Africa and among patients with *AIDS*. Treatment may be with radiotherapy or, in advanced disease, chemotherapy (anticancer drugs).

keloid Fibrous scar tissue that has overgrown its site of healing, and remains rough and misshapen. It is formed particularly in areas of skin under continual tension, and particularly in black people.

keratin Fibrous protein that constitutes the basic substance of the nails and the hair; it is found also in the top layer of the skin, and is a specialized development of it.

keratitis Inflammation of the *cornea* of the eye (the membrane covering the front surface of the eye), causing pain, blurred vision and watery eyes. It may be due to bacterial or viral infection, injury to the eye or exposure to irritants such as dust or chemicals. Treatment depends on the cause, but may include removal of irritants and covering the eye until the cornea heals, sometimes with the use of drugs (given as eyedrops) to treat any infection.

keratoplasty The transplantation of part or all of the layers of the *cornea* from a donor to replace diseased parts of the eyes of a patient, also known as a corneal graft. Often, the patientís own deepest corneal stratum is left in place as a foundation or base on to which the donorís complementary corneal strata can be grafted.

ketosis Condition in which there is an abnormal quantity of ketones – products of the normal metabolic breakdown of fats – in the tissues of the body. Ketones are normally further broken down for use or disposal, but that mechanism may fail if fats are used to provide energy (instead of sugars), as in cases of starvation or *diabetes* mellitus.

kidney Either of two large glandular organs that are fundamental to the balance and purification of water in the body. The kidneys are located at the back of the abdomen, at about waist level; on top of them lie the *adrenal glands*. Blood containing impurities flows into the kidneys from the renal arteries; it is processed by the tiny filtering units (nephrons) in the cortex and the medulla of each organ. Useful products are returned to the blood for reabsorption; waste fluids are collected in renal tubules and ducted to the renal pelvis, a central reservoir from which the *ureter* conveys the fluids (as *urine*) to the bladder for eventual passing through the *urethra*.

kidney disease Any disorder that affects the tissues or the operation of the *kidneys* (urine-producing organs). Symptoms commonly include an increase or decrease in the passing of *urine*, abdominal pain, *oedema* (accumulation of fluid in the tissues), and the appearance of blood or other substances in the urine. Diseases that directly affect the kidney include *nephritis* (inflammation), *nephrolithiasis* (kidney stone) and *cancer*; many other diseases affect the kidneys indirectly. Treatment depends on the cause. Failure of both kidneys to function requires immediate emergency treatment.

kidney failure Complete breakdown in the function of one or both *kidneys* (the urine-producing organs). One kidney, provided that it is in good condition, can usually carry out the work of two if necessary. Failure of both, however, demands emergency treatment before poisonous wastes begin to accumulate catastrophically in the body. A *dialysis* machine (kidney machine) can perform the same filtration processes as the natural kidney, but requires time in training and in psychological adjustment. If available, a *kidney transplant* is generally the best option.

kidney stone Hard mass of mineral salts (calculus) responsible for *nephrolithiasis*.

kidney transplant Grafting one or two healthy kidneys from a donor into a patient who has *kidney failure*. There may be problems of tissue *rejection*, and the use of *immunosuppressive drugs* may have to be extensive. The alternative, however, is the regular use of a *dialysis* machine.

kiss of life Very successful form of *artificial respiration*, provided that there is no obstruction to the air passages.

kleptomania Irresistible desire to steal. Objects stolen may have no value nor even be desired for themselves. It represents an aberration from mental normality, and is particularly associated with depression or stress.

knee Joint half-way down the leg, in which the lower end of the thighbone (*femur*) articulates with the upper end of the shinbone (*tibia*), protected by the kneecap (*patella*). The ends of the bones are both covered first by cartilage and then by the lubricated *synovial membrane* of a *bursa*, attached to the patella. The patella itself is enclosed within a strong tendon linked to the muscles that straighten the leg. Ligaments around the joint prevent dislocation.

knee-jerk Reflex kick of a leg (on which no weight is being put) when the *tendon* just below the kneecap (patella) is tapped sharply. How fast and how hard the kick takes place may be of diagnostic use to a neurologist. The reflex action does not involve the brain but is the result of an "emergency" message delivered to the spinal cord by the nerve endings that register the degree of stretch in the tendon.

knock-knee Curving of the lower legs (medical name: genu valgum) so that when the knees are together the feet are apart. Common as a temporary phase in very young children, in adulthood the condition may cause considerable stress on (and arthritis in) the leg joints.

Koch, Robert (1843–1910) German bacteriologist whose major discoveries came about as a result of his lifelong study of *tuberculosis*. His initial discovery was that tuberculosis was caused by a bacillus, and in 1882 he identified the actual bacterium. In 1905 he received a Nobel Prize for his work.

Korsakoff's psychosis Mental disorder that results from brain damage (most commonly caused by alcoholism leading to serious vitamin B_1 deficiency). The patient cannot learn anything new, cannot impress anything occurring in the present on the memory, although events and skills from the distant past may be remembered clearly. In order to compensate for having no memory of recent events, the patient may frequently invent a completely fictitious history. There may also be poor muscular co-ordination. Treatment depends on the actual cause, but often includes vitamin B_1 supplements.

kwashiorkor A type of *malnutrition* resulting from severe dietary deficiency, especially of protein; it is common among children in tropical Africa. Symptoms include malaise and apathy, diarrhoea, a protuberant abdomen, pallor of the skin and discoloration (reddening) of the hair. There may also be *oedema* or deformity in the legs and feet. Treatment is to remedy the deficiency, where possible.

kyphosis Abnormal curvature of the spine outwards, arching (or hunching) the back. Apart from congenital disorder, it may be caused by disorders of the spine (such as *ankylosing spondylitis* or *osteoporosis*) or by long-term muscle weakness or bad posture. The abnormal curvature outwards in one part of the spine may be balanced by an abnormal inward curvature (*lordosis*), generally lower down. Treatment, where possible, may include physiotherapy and a spinal support.

L

Laban Rudolf (1879–1958) German choreographer whose notation system for recording simultaneous movements of the arms and legs in dancing became very useful in anatomical studies. His system included the means of rapidly noting a movementís speed, vigour and direction.

labia Lips of the *vulva*. The larger, outer pair are the labia majora, and the inner, smaller pair are the labia minora. Both pairs contain lubricating glands. In the singular – labium – the term may refer to the lip-like edge of a bone, a lip of the mouth, or the cervix of the uterus (neck of the womb).

labour Sequential process of *childbirth*, usually said to comprise three stages. The first stage begins – either naturally or by *induction* – when uterine contractions can be felt, gradually increasing in frequency over a total of between five and ten hours. The effect of the contractions is to dilate the *cervix* (neck) of the *uterus* (womb). Some of the *amnion*, the membranous sac that has surrounded the foetus till now, is forced through the cervix and bursts, releasing amniotic fluid (the "breaking of the waters"). The second stage of labour begins when the cervix is fully dilated and the contractions have increased in frequency and intensity. The babyís head enters the *birth canal* and the mother feels an urge to "bear down" and push the baby out. This is the stage at which physical effort is made, and generally lasts for less than an hour. Positional and breathing exercises may help, and the doctor may offer a painkiller to the mother. The baby gradually comes out into the world, usually head first. The third stage of labour comprises the delivery of the *afterbirth* – mostly the *placenta* and membranes of the amniotic sac – and may take a further half-hour.

labyrinth Medical term for the *inner ear*. Inflammation of the inner ear is called labyrinthitis or *otitis* interna.

lacrimal gland Gland in the upper, outer corner of the eye (behind the upper eyelid) that stores and secretes tears, which wash the eye and are produced copiously in crying (lacrimation).

lacrimation Production and secretion of the fluid that washes the eye and that in times of stress becomes more copious as tears. From the *lacrimal gland*, the fluid is conveyed through twelve tiny ducts to the eyeball, where blinking spreads the fluid evenly. The fluid is collected again at the inner corner of each eye by two larger ducts which connect with a vertical reservoir – the lacrimal sac – which in turn drains into the nose.

lactation Production and secretion of milk by the *mammary glands* in a motherís breasts. Controlled by the *hormones* prolactin (for production) and oxytocin (for secretion), both under the direction of the *pituitary gland*, the process is stimulated mostly through the action of a newborn baby sucking on the *nipple* – no true milk is produced until after the baby is born.

lactic acid Chemical produced in the muscles during exertion after all the available oxygen has been used up in converting blood sugar (glucose) into energy. Accumulating in the muscles, it is lactic acid that causes *cramp*. It is also produced in milk as it turns sour, through the bacterial fermentation of milk sugar (lactose).

lactose intolerance Inability to absorb lactose, or milk sugar. This is due to absence or low activity of an enzyme (lactase) required by the intestines to break down lactose into simpler sugars. Drinking milk then produces diarrhoea because the unabsorbed lactose acts as a laxative. The condition is common among Oriental and African peoples. Treatment is to avoid milk and milk products.

Lamarck, Jean-Baptiste de (1744–1829) French naturalist whose views on evolution were influential throughout Europe. He suggested that traits and skills acquired by one individual of a species could be passed on, by heredity, to the offspring. This theory remained popular until Charles *Darwin*ís work was published. Lamarck also wrote an authoritative work on invertebrate zoology.

Landsteiner, Karl (1868–1943) American researcher into the constituents of blood, who first distinguished the *blood groups*, A, B, AB and O, and showed that some were incompatible with others. Thereafter he contributed towards discovering the *Rhesus* (RH) *factor*. For his work he was awarded a Nobel Prize in 1930.

Langer's lines Lines visible in the skin representing the aligned formation of connective tissue beneath. The best examples are the creases of the palms of the hands. Surgery using incisions parallel to Langerís lines reduces surface scarring.

Langerhans, islets of See *islets of Langerhans*.

lanolin Fat obtained from sheepís wool. Very greasy, it is used as a skin softener or, mixed with certain oils, as a medium for drugs in ointments that penetrate the skin surface.

lanugo Fine down of hair that covers most of a foetus between the fifth and ninth months of pregnancy, but is usually shed before birth.

laparoscopy Examination of the abdominal cavity and its contents by means of a laparoscope – a fine, lighted tube that is inserted into the abdomen through a small surgical incision, and that has an eye-lens at the top end. Various attachments may be fitted, such as blades, laser and *diathermy* (heat coagulation) equipment, so that as well as its use in diagnosis, a variety of procedures which formerly required major surgery to open up the abdomen can now be performed laparoscopically. These include taking small tissue samples (*biopsy*), aspirating (sucking out the contents of) cysts, blocking the *Fallopian tubes* for *sterilization* in a woman, collecting ova for *in vitro* fertilization ("test tube baby" techniques) and some operations such as removing the *gall bladder* or parts of the *colon*.

laparotomy Surgical incision made in the abdominal wall in order to perform an operation on tissues or organs inside the abdomen, or to make an investigatory examination.

laryngectomy Surgical operation to remove part or all of the *larynx*. It is usually carried out to prevent the spread of *cancer*, and associated lymph glands may also be removed for that reason. Breathing is unimpaired afterwards but, because the voice-box and vocal cords are removed, special techniques and equipment are needed to enable production of speech sounds; adaptation may therefore take time.

laryngitis Inflammation of the *larynx* (the part of the throat containing the vocal cords), particularly on the *vocal cords*. It is usually the result of the spread of a respiratory infection, such as a cold, or of tonsillitis, or may be due to irritation by fumes or chemicals, or to overuse of the voice. It is commonest in heavy smokers and heavy drinkers. Symptoms are extreme hoarseness or the inability to talk at all, with pain on trying to do so. Breathing may also be difficult, and there may be a painful cough. In extreme cases, especially in children (when it is known as *croup*), the air passage may become obstructed. Treatment depends on the cause, but normally includes resting the voice for at least a couple of days, humidifying the environment and steam inhalations. If bacterial infection is suspected, antibiotics may be administered, especially in treating young children who sometimes develop complications. Very rarely, obstruction of the airways may necessitate surgery to restore proper breathing. The condition may become chronic.

larynx Voice-box, a cartilaginous, cylindrical unit at the front of the neck, just below the throat, that surmounts the *trachea* (windpipe) and contains the *vocal cords*. At the top of the larynx, the *epiglottis* acts as a valve to stop food from entering this primary air passage. One of its structural cartilages (the thyroid cartilage) forms the *Adam's apple*. The larynx of a man at puberty grows to be much larger than that of a woman, which accounts both for his more prominent Adamís apple and for the lower voice.

laser Device that amplifies light into a very concentrated beam, producing high energy. This can be utilized in medicine to target a very specific area without damaging surrounding tissue – a laser can be used like a scalpel, its heat acting to cauterize and seal minor blood vessels even as it "cuts". Different types of lasers, including the argon laser, excimer laser, YAG laser and diode laser, are used for different operations, including removal of some types of *birthmark* from the skin, destroying areas of precancerous tissue on the *cervix* (neck of the womb), unblocking coronary arteries (those supplying the heart muscle) and various forms of eye surgery, including operations on the *retina* and (as a treatment for *myopia*, or shortsightedness) the *cornea* (the membrane covering the front of the eye).

Lassa fever Serious virus disease, most common in West Africa, whose symptoms include very high temperature, muscle pains, headache, slow heartbeat and loss of appetite. There may also be pain on swallowing, and tests may show a low white blood cell count. About half of all patients recover, slowly; others deteriorate into confusion and coma, leading to death. Treatment is to isolate the patient and to alleviate the symptoms as far as possible; injections of *gamma globulin* from a recently recovered patient may help. The drug ribavirin may help combat the causative virus.

lassitude Vague term for apathetic lethargy or weariness.

laudanum Alcoholic extract of *opium* formerly used as a *narcotic* painkiller.

laugh Spontaneous sound that expresses amusement. Occasionally, however, it represents apprehension or even mild hysteria, and it is probably in this sense that a laugh is instinctive.

laughing gas Common name for the anaesthetic gas *nitrous oxide*.

laxative Drug or other substance taken orally in order to promote *defecation*. A laxative may be prescribed to treat *constipation*, but should not be taken on a regular basis in any other circumstance. Laxatives work in various ways. Some irritate the intestinal wall of the *colon* and *rectum* (as do senna and castor oil) or lubricate it (as does liquid paraffin). Others increase volume of the faeces so that the urge to defecate is also increased. The volume may be increase the by raising the amount of water in the intestines (which is what magnesium and sodium salts do), or by bulking out the faecal contents of the intestine with roughage such as bran.

laxity Slackness or looseness, as opposed to rigidity or tension.

lead poisoning Form of poisoning caused by swallowing or inhaling lead. Acute and chronic forms seriously affect the normal functioning of parts of the body, although the symptoms may be different. Acute or sudden lead poisoning, often through inhalation, causes severe abdominal pain with cramps, vomiting, delirium, convulsions and coma; tests show *anaemia* and the presence of lead in the blood and urine. Chronic or long-term poisoning is indicated by a characteristic blue coloration of the gums ("lead line"), fatigue, headache, irritability and breathlessness. There may also be abdominal pain and digestive disorders, with gradual signs of nerve damage (including loss of intellectual capacity). Treatment in both cases is with *chelating agents* (drugs that bind to metals, enabling their excretion). Any nerve damage must be diagnosed and treated, if possible, by a specialist.

learning disabilities Special difficulties experienced by certain children in the process of learning, caused by some natural (or perhaps only habitual) failure in concentration, memory or physical co-ordination. Undiagnosed *deafness*, on the other hand, may lead to a childs being incorrectly said to have learning disabilities.

lecithin One of a number of *lipids* that contain phosphoric acid (phospholipids) and feature in the *liver* as part of the fat metabolism process.

leech Bloodsucking parasitic worm that has suckers at each end by which to attach itself externally to its host. Bites cause irritation but are hardly ever dangerous. It is extremely difficult to prise a leech off until it is gorged with blood; the best method to detach one is to attack it with a lighted cigarette or with salt. Leeches were formerly used for medicinal bloodletting.

Leeuwenhoek, Anton van (1632–1723) Dutch cloth merchant and amateur scientist. Using a combination of magnifying lenses he made himself, he constructed a primitive microscope and observed and described for the first time the true nature of muscle fibres, red blood cells, spermatozoa, and even a bacterium.

left-handedness Use of the left hand (and probably foot) as the dominant one of the pair. The tendency is shared by only about 1 in 11 people, and potentially reflects a dominance of the right hemisphere of the brain.

legionnaires' disease Bacterial infection of the lungs that caught the attention of the world when 29 of 182 people known to have contracted the disease (then unidentified) at or near the 1976 American Legion convention in Philadelphia, Pennsylvania, died from it. The bacterium tends to reside in moist places, especially in ventilation systems that have humidifiers. Symptoms are lethargy and muscle pain, followed by high temperature and respiratory distress; *kidney failure* may also occur, as may the extreme symptoms of *pneumonia*. Treatment is with antibiotics, especially erythromycin.

leishmaniasis Group of infections caused by a protozoan parasite that is carried by sandflies. There are two forms: kala-azar and cutaneous leishmaniasis. With kala-azar, a serious disorder, the parasite attacks the cells of the bone marrow, spleen and lymphatic system. Symptoms include enlargement of and damage to the *spleen* and *liver*, recurrent high temperature, *anaemia* and weight loss; tests may show a low white blood cell count. Cutaneous leishmaniasis involves local ulcerative sores. Treatment of either form of the disease is with drugs containing antimony.

lens Small discoid unit of refraction in each eye, that helps to focus light on the *retina*. The amount of light passing through the lens if regulated by the muscles in the *iris* which control the size of the *pupil*, and the focusing is carried out by muscles attached to the lens which change the shape of the lens itself. Opacity of the lens, caused by a *cataract*, causes blurred vision. Artificial lenses, of plastic or glass, are the basic elements of both *contact lenses* (worn on the surface of the eyeball) and *glasses* (worn in a frame over the nose).

leprosy Also called Hansenís disease, a slow and progressively destructive bacterial infection that may be transmitted by direct contact; children seem to contract it more readily than adults. The infection centres on the skin, mucous membranes and nerves. There may be small areas of pale, disfigured skin that lose sensation (tuberculoid leprosy). Or there may be reddened nodules on the skin, loss of sensation over wide areas, eye inflammation and recurrent bouts of fever (lepromatous leprosy), which can lead to deformity and paralysis. Some people contract a combination of both types. th a combination of drugs (multidrug therapy). In some cases surgery may be able to repair some of the damage. A potential vaccine is under development.

lesbianism Womenís form of *homosexuality*.

lesion Localized area of tissue damage, caused by injury or disease, and inhibiting function.

lethargy Feeling that to do anything at all would be too much of a physical and mental effort. A continuous state of lethargy may indicate a mental disorder – although it is relatively normal in convalescence or under hypnosis.

leuc-/leuk- Both these forms of the same Greek word, used as a prefix in medical terms, mean "white". Different authorities may use either form in their terminology.

leucocyte White blood cell. Unlike red blood cells (*erythrocytes*), white blood cells have a nucleus. There are three main types: *granulocytes*, which include *basophils, eosinophils* and *neutrophils*; *lymphocytes*; and *monocytes*. All together represent a major element of the *immune system*, engulfing, destroying or neutralizing invading micro-organisms and other foreign bodies, producing *antibodies*, and increasing in number as necessary to do so. At the site of a wound they congregate to protect against infective invasion (and on their own death form *pus*).

leucopenia Reduced number of white blood cells (*leukocytes*) in the blood.

leucotomy Surgical operation in which areas of the white nerve fibres of the brain are severed. Originally this was done to separate the connections between the frontal lobe of one *cerebral hemisphere* and the corresponding *thalamus* (prefrontal leucotomy, also called lobotomy), as a treatment for severe "emotional tension", but this has now been abandoned since side-effects were so severe. A modified form of operation that uses intensive diagnostic *scanning* accurately to locate a much smaller area of fibres to destroy is occasionally still undertaken for various psychological symptoms such as anxiety, depression or obsession, or for severe pain, if other treatments have failed. Selective lesions of brain fibres are made by cutting or using an electric current, heat or freezing.

leukaemia Form of *cancer* that affects the organs which produce blood (mostly the bone marrow) and causes the production of far too many, and misshapen, white blood cells (*leucocytes*), thus also inhibiting the formation of other blood cells. The result is *anaemia*, bleeding (through lack of the clotting factors) and extreme susceptibility to infections (through lack of much of the normal immune system in the bloodstream). Treatment depends on the type of white cell being overproduced and on the rate at which the disease advances, but usually includes *cytotoxic* (cancer-killing) drugs and *radiotherapy*; treatment is also necessary for any infections contracted.

leukocyte Alternative spelling of *leucocyte*.

LH Abbreviation of *luteinizing hormone*.

libido Personís level of sexual drive, attained through *psychosexual development*, and varying – depending on both internal and external influences – even within one person at different times. In *psychoanalysis*, which attributes considerable mental and behavioural significance to sexuality, libido is correspondingly fundamental.

life Plane of existence. The concept is clouded by moral and legal obscurity, not to mention problems of simple definition. (When does a human life begin? Is a seed alive? What is the difference between "brain death" and death – is it life?)

life expectancy Number of years somebody might be expected to live, calculated on averaged statistics relating to age, sex, location of birth or residence, and any other relevant factors, assuming also that current conditions remain in force.

life-support machine In fact a collection of medical machinery that takes over the functions of respiration and of blood circulation for a patient who can no longer manage either. The machinery may also infuse nutrients and remove waste products.

ligament Band of tough, flexible (but inelastic) *connective tissue* fibres that holds together, supports and protects two bones at a *joint*, or organs within a body cavity. Ligaments at hinge joints define the limits of movement.

ligature Length of nylon, catgut, silk or wire used to tie round a vessel to stop the flow of its contents.

lightening Noticeable relief (at any time from about the thirty-sixth week of *pregnancy*) of the sensation that the abdomen is heavily distended, and consequent feeling of restored comfort. It follows the descent of the foetus into the lower part of the *uterus* (womb) and its settling into the *pelvis*.

limbic system Neural network in the brain that connects the outer cortex of the *cerebral hemispheres* with the *hypothalamus*, and is directly related to survival and reproductive instincts, basic emotions and short-term memory.

linctus Cough syrup or other syrupy medication.

Lind, James (1716–1794) Scottish naval doctor whose recommendation that British sailors take a daily ration of lime juice virtually eliminated the age-old occupational hazard of sailors, *scurvy*. He also tried to improve other aspects of nautical health.

liniment Lotion for topical application on the skin surface, usually to treat muscular sprains or strains. Many liniments contain alcohol. An alternative name is embrocation.

lipid Any of certain carbon compounds that are insoluble in water and in the diet are invaluable for their energy. The main type comprises *fats*, which are associated with *fatty* acids. *Steroids* and sterols (such as *cholesterol*) are also lipids.

lipoma Benign (non-cancerous) *tumour* consisting of fatty cells.

lipoprotein Any of a group of *proteins* that combine with *lipids* and thus convey them in the bloodstream or lymphatic system. They contain various proportions of *triglycerides*, *cholesterol* and other components. The various types include high-density lipoprotein (HDL), which is believed to be beneficial as it "mops up" lipids in the bloodstream that might otherwise clog the arteries, and low-density lipoprotein (LDL), which acts as the major form of transport for blood *cholesterol*; high levels of LDL are linked with an increased risk of *arteriosclerosis*.

lips Two outer surfaces of the mouth, where mucous membrane meets ordinary skin surface, and where there is a concentration of tiny muscles and nerve endings that assist not only in eating and sensing with the mouth but also in speech. A medical term for the lips is labia, a word used also (and more commonly) for the lips of the vulva.

listeriosis Condition caused by eating foods contaminated with a bacterium (listeria) common in many animals. Infection may cause few symptoms, or a íflu-like syndrome, but sometimes leads to serious complications including *septicaemia* and *encephalitis*. It can also cause foetal death, miscarriage or serious infection of the newborn, so pregnant women are advised to avoid high-risk foods – soft cheeses (such as Brie) and p té. Treatment is with antibiotics.

Lister, Joseph (1827–1912) English pioneer of *asepsis* in surgery. His introduction of carbolic acid (phenol) for spraying in the air of operating rooms and later for sterilizing surgical instruments and dressings, transformed methods that had not changed for centuries (when more patients died of post-operative infection than from the direct results of the surgery itself).

litholapaxy Breaking up of a calculus (stone) in the urethra or bladder, using either a flexible instrument passed up the urethra (a lithotrite) which crushes the stone, or carefully focused bursts of *ultrasound* which smash it into fragments. Both methods render a surgical incision unnecessary; the fragments pass out with the urine.

lithotomy Surgical operation to remove a calculus (stone) from the urethra, bladder, ureter or kidney. It is undertaken usually only when *litholapaxy* has for one reason or another been ruled out.

liver Large organ located under the right side of the *diaphragm* (to which it is attached by ligaments) and partly overhanging the stomach. Made up of four major lobes and thousands of interconnected lobules within them, it is the site of the metabolism of virtually all the nutrients taken in with the diet – fats, proteins and carbohydrates – which are conveyed in the blood as products of digestion to the liver by the *hepatic portal vein*. There, glucose is converted to glycogen (so that it can be stored), thus regulating blood sugar levels; vitamin A and *fatty acids* are formed; *amino acids* are broken down so that poisonous waste products (such as ammonia and urea) can be excreted; *fibrinogen* and other blood clotting factors are secreted, as is *heparin*, a blood thinning factor; *bile* is formed and released into the *gall bladder*; and worn out red blood cells, excess hormones and certain toxins (such as alcohol or drugs) are processed for disposal. Major disorders of the liver include *cirrhosis, hepatitis* and *cancer*.

lobe Major segment of certain organs, such as the lungs and liver. In general lobes are round in shape or distinguished by surrounding bands of connective tissue or by linear fissures.

The lower part of the ear flap (pinna) is also known as a lobe, prominent in some people and almost non-existent in others.

lobotomy Old term for prefrontal *leucotomy*.

lobule Lesser unit of a *lobe*, contributing both to its structure and to its function. In form it is generally a tiny sac, tube or area of tissue.

local anaesthetic Type of anaesthetic that deadens sensation in only a part of the body. See *anaesthetics*.

lochia Normal discharge of uterine material through the vagina following *childbirth*. Lasting perhaps three weeks in all, there are usually three stages. The first is a discharge mostly of blood; the second is of blood and mucus together, and is brown; and the third is yellowish-white, comprising cellular debris.

lockjaw Common name for *tetanus*.

locomotion Walking movement that is both voluntary and independent of artificial means or assistance.

locomotor ataxia Also called tabes dorsalis, a condition corresponding to tertiary *syphilis* that has affected the sensory and motor nerves. Symptoms, in the absence of treatment, are sharp pains anywhere from the waist down and gradual loss of voluntary co-ordination in the limbs. There may also be bladder incontinence and blurring of eyesight. To reach this stage in the disease is now rare: penicillin treatment ordinarily halts its progress earlier.

locum tenens Often abbreviated to locum, a doctor or surgeon standing in for another who is away.

Loewi, Otto (1873–1961) Austrian physiologist who discovered the chemical nature of the communication between nerve cells (*neurones*). Until his work, it had been thought that impulses were transmitted electrically.

longevity Comparatively long duration of a lifespan. Social, environmental and hereditary factors may all be involved.

longsightedness Common term for *hypermetropia* or *presbyopia*.

loop of Henle Loop in a *renal tubule* of the kidney that corresponds to a tiny filtration unit. It creates pressure and forms a surface area within the tubule through which the blood capillaries surrounding it can reabsorb water and useful fluids back into the bloodstream.

lordosis Abnormal curvature of the spine inwards (often causing a personís buttocks to stick out). Apart from congenital disorder, it may be caused by disorders of the spine or hip, or by long-term muscle weakness or bad posture (as perhaps with *obesity*). The abnormal curvature inwards may be balanced by an abnormal outward curvature (*kyphosis*), generally further up. Treatment, where possible, may include physiotherapy and a spinal support.

lotion Liquid medication for applying externally to the skin, generally as a soothing wash or a disinfecting bath.

louse Any of three types of small, wingless insects that can inhabit the hair and skin surface of humans as a parasite. Infestation with lice is called *pediculosis*.

lumbago General term for pain in the lumbar region – the lower back. Causes include muscular strain (from lifting or carrying), a *prolapsed intervertebral disc* (more commonly known as a slipped disc), which may be accompanied by *sciatica*, curvature of the spine through disorder or long-term bad posture, or kidney or gynaecological disorders. Treatment, where possible, depends on the cause, but may include drugs to relieve pain or sometimes surgery.

lumbar puncture Diagnostic surgical procedure in which cerebrospinal fluid is drawn off in a syringe from the space between two of three membranes surrounding the *spinal cord* (the *subarachnoid* space) in the lumbar region (the lower back). The specimen drawn off may then be examined for evidence of disorders such as *meningitis*. A virtually identical procedure may be used to inject fluids into the subarachnoid space: *epidural anaesthetics* or antibiotics, for example.

lumen Space surrounded by the walls of a vessel or sac in the body, as within a blood vessel or the intestine, or a circular gap in the centre of a doughnut-shaped organ (such as the *prostate gland*).

lung Either of two large, spongy organs located on each side of the chest cavity, and covered in layers of membrane called the *pleura*, the outer of which is attached to the rib cage. The lungs constitute the main centres for the exchange of gases involved in *respiration*. Air breathed into the *trachea* (windpipe) is diverted into either of the two *bronchi*, at which point it reaches a lung. Inside the lung, the air continues down the bronchus, which branches into smaller *bronchioles*, which again branch into a multitude of tiny *alveoli*. It is through the thin walls of capillaries surrounding the alveoli that oxygen in the inhaled air is exchanged for carbon dioxide in the blood, to be exhaled at the next breath. The right lung, with three lobes, is slightly larger than the left, with two, because the left has to make room for the heart immediately beneath. The short circulation of blood between the heart and the lungs is quite separate from the much longer circulation around the rest of the body.

lung cancer Cancer in a bronchial passage or in a *lung*. A dangerous disorder, it may not be diagnosed until the cancer has already spread (by *metastasis*) elsewhere in the body. Symptoms are at first only a mild cough, becoming progressively worse, with blood in the sputum and increasing breathlessness. There may then be the collapse of a lung, or pneumonia, and weight loss and lethargy are common. Most people who contract lung cancer are or have been heavy cigarette smokers. Treatment is usually too late for removal of the lung to be totally successful; *radiotherapy* and *cytotoxic* (cancer-killing) drugs may be used.

lung function tests Tests to check on the operation of one or both *lungs*. The complexity of each test and the devices involved correspond to what the therapist is trying to find out. Some tests merely measure the volume of air inhaled or exhaled; others actually analyse the contents of exhaled air and compare the results with venous and arterial blood composition.

lupus Group of disorders that may or may not be interrelated, but all of which produce scaly or disfiguring lesions on the skin. Lupus erythematosus, of which there are two forms, is thought to be an *autoimmune disease* (in which the immune system attacks the bodyís own tissues). The lesser form, discoid lupus erythematosus, produces symptoms of reddened scaly areas of skin made worse by sunlight but fading over time; treatment generally involves antimalarial drugs. Systemic lupus erythematosus has the additional symptoms of rheumatoid arthritis, and may also affect the kidney and other functions. Lupus vulgaris is a rare condition corresponding to *tuberculosis* (bacillary invasion) of the skin, which, untreated, may cause severe scarring. Treatment of lupus erythematosus is with *corticosteroids* or immunosuppressant drugs, which may prevent further attacks for long periods. Lupus vulgaris treatment is as for tuberculosis.

luteinizing hormone (LH) *Gonadotropin* produced and secreted by the pituitary gland. In women it promotes *ovulation* and the formation of a *corpus luteum*, and thereafter stimulates the synthesis of *progesterone*. In men it promotes the formation of *androgens* (male sex hormones) in the *testes*.

Lyme disease Infectious disease transmitted by tick bites, which, in most of those affected, causes a characteristic expanding, red skin rash up to a month after the bite. Other symptoms include fever, headache and joint pains, and there may be later complications including *arthritis* and heart and nerve damage. Treatment is with antibiotics.

lymph Clear fluid derived from blood but with its own complex circulatory system in the body (the *lymphatic system*), from which it is returned to the blood in the thoracic duct or right lymphatic duct. Its purpose is to wash and cleanse the tissues, particularly of cellular debris and bacteria, and combat infection, for which it contains *antibodies* and *lymphocytes*.

lymphadenitis Inflammation of groups of *lymph nodes* in an area of tissue. It is a usual reaction where the tissue itself is subject to infection. For example, infection in the pharynx generally results in swollen lymph nodes in the tonsils and neck. Treatment is of the causative infection.

lymphatic system Circulatory network of vessels in the body that convey *lymph* to and from the tissues; as with the blood vessels, valves prevent backflow. The system has its own glandular filtration units (*lymph nodes*) and in producing *lymphocytes* and *antibodies* is part of the bodyís *immune system*.

lymph node Small rounded bodies in the *lymphatic system*. They represent junctions in the *lymph* circulatory network, and correspond both to glands (in producing and secreting *lymphocytes* and *antibodies*) and to filtration units (in filtering out waste products and bacteria before the lymph rejoins the blood). Cells that are detached from cancerous tumours on internal tissues are commonly conveyed first to local lymph nodes, where they may begin to cause secondary growths; it is for this reason that in surgery to remove cancers, the local lymph nodes are usually also removed.

lymphocyte Form of *leukocyte* (white blood cell) that is produced and released by the *lymph nodes*, and found also in the bone marrow, thymus, spleen and intestinal wall. Part of the *immune system*, there are two main types of lymphocyte: B-lymphocytes which produce antibodies, and T-lymphocytes which identify "foreign" tissue and move to destroy or engulf it (and are thus prominent in the process of tissue rejection).

lymphoma One of several types of malignant lymph node tumour that includes *Hodgkin's disease* and non-Hodgkinís lymphomas. Progressive lymph node enlargement, widespread or confined to a particular area, may be accompanied by symptoms such as fever, weight loss, lethargy and sweating. The progress of the disease may be rapid or slow, with the prognosis varying accordingly. Treatment with anticancer drugs (*chemotherapy*) can be very successful, particularly if started early in the course of the disease. In some cases radiotherapy is given as well. Surgery may also be used in Hodgkinís disease, and bone marrow transplants in non-Hodgkinís lymphomas.

M

Macleod, John J. Rickard (1876–1935) Scottish physiologist whose research into the metabolism of carbohydrates in the body led to his contributing (with Sir Frederick Banting and C. H. Best) to the discovery of the existence and effect of *insulin*, for which he and Banting were awarded a Nobel Prize in 1923.

macrophage Particularly large type of *phagocyte* present in most tissues of the body. Part of the immune system, macrophages engulf and so neutralize invading infective organisms. Many are free to move (within the bloodstream or lymphatic system, for example); others are fixed within connective tissue (*histiocytes*).

macula Small area within a much larger area that is distinguishably different in colour but not in texture or composition. The term thus applies to a spot or birthmark (*naevus*) that is not raised on the skin surface, to the small yellowish area on the retina of the eye surrounding the *fovea*, and to certain areas on the bones of the inner ear.

Magendie, François (1783–1855) French physiologist who first proved the distinction between the motor and sensory functions of the *peripheral nervous system*, and explained the mechanism of a *reflex*. A dietician, he also assessed the protein values of many foods and described the effect of many herbal remedies.

maggot Fly larva in the shape of a small caterpillar. A very few may parasitize humans.

magnesium Metallic *trace element* essential to the proper functioning of the nervous system. Magnesium sulphate (Epsom salt) is used as a *laxative*, and magnesium hydroxide (Milk of Magnesia) as an *antacid*.

magnetic resonance imaging (MRI) Method of *scanning* that employs the known differences in the rate of absorption of specific radio frequencies by the nuclei of the water molecules within the body when placed in a strong magnetic field. Analysis of these signals is used to produce a computer-enhanced, three-dimensional picture of a part of the body on a screen and in permanent films. MRI scanning has great advantages over *X-rays* for diagnosis as it does not involve any radiation exposure; it is painless and believed to be totally safe. It is used especially to map the brain and central nervous system, and also for diagnosis of conditions in the chest and abdomen, as well as to enhance surgical accuracy in complex operations by enabling real-time viewing of the area being operated upon.

maintenance therapy Careful monitoring of dosages during a course of treatment with drugs, in order to maintain a patientís overall condition at a specific optimum level in cases where too small a dose may cause serious symptoms to reappear.

malabsorption syndrome Set of symptoms caused by the failure of part of the small intestine or one or more of its enzymes to fulfil its role in the process of digestion. Often the failure is in respect of a specific substance – commonly fats, but also perhaps certain *vitamins* or *trace elements*. The syndrome may be caused by any of several conditions affecting digestion – such as *coeliac disease, cystic fibrosis* and *pancreatitis* – and results in diarrhoea, anaemia, oedema, weight loss and other signs of deficiency and *malnutrition*. Treatment depends on the cause and may include drugs or surgery.

malaise General feeling of tension with lethargy, of being ill with no definitive symptoms. Malaise may precede or indicate the onset of a disorder, particularly an infection.

malaria Serious infection caused by a protozoan parasite transmitted through the bites of mosquitoes, and relatively common in tropical and subtropical regions. Symptoms may develop from a few days up to a year after a mosquito bite. Once in a patientís bloodstream, the young protozoans congregate in the internal organs (especially the liver) before taking again to the bloodstream and invading the red blood cells. The resulting destruction of red blood cells in sufficient quantity causes *anaemia* and a fever that peaks and vanishes – only to recur regularly as waves of protozoans mature and invade the bloodstream. One rarer form of malaria, also called malignant malaria or blackwater fever, causes red blood cell destruction and kidney damage and is sometimes fatal; in other, benign, forms fever may recur after intervals of three days (tertian fever) or four (quartan fever), each bout preceded by shivering and accompanied by headache, vomiting and, often, delirium. Treatment is with antimalarial drugs, which should also be taken as a preventive measure by people travelling to areas where malaria is endemic (widespread). Medical advice is needed to determine the drug most effective at the time for a particular area, and drugs do not provide complete protection: precautions against being bitten by mosquitoes are also vital. Medical research is attempting to find a vaccine effective against malaria.

male Pill Form of *contraception* not yet available to the general public but designed to be the equivalent for men of the progesterone-based Pill that confers (temporary) infertility on women.

malformation Failure of an organ or area of tissue to form properly before birth, during the years of growth and development, or after healing. Causes include hereditary factors. Abnormality resulting from disease or injury is more often termed *deformity*.

malignant Likely to become quickly worse if left untreated, and potentially dangerous even if treated. In reference to tumours, the term indicates a *cancer* that may be not only destructive and inhibitive where it is, but also likely to spread by *metastasis*. The opposite is *benign*.

malingering Pretending to be ill, usually to avoid work or to seek unnecessary medical treatment. In the latter form it may be a cry for help, a bid for attention and a semblance of sympathy. It may also be a means of avoiding responsibility or a feared event; it may even represent a mental disorder – but it is generally extremely difficult to diagnose or prove.

malleus Tiny hammer-shaped bone in the *middle ear*. With the *incus* (anvil) and the *stapes* (stirrup), it conveys sound vibrations from the *eardrum* through to the *inner ear* and the sensory organs of hearing.

malnutrition Results in the body of a diet that is either altogether inadequate or is deficient in nutrients (even if overall intake is large). The main symptoms are gradual physical deterioration accompanied by apathy and susceptibility to infections. These are symptoms too of *malabsorption syndrome* – which may also cause malnutrition. Treatment is to make up the deficiency.

Malpighi, Marcello (1628–1694) Italian anatomist and physiologist who was the first to use a microscope to investigate the structures of the body. In particular he discovered the tiny blood vessels of the alveolar sacs in the lung (making possible an understanding of respiration) and confirmed Harveyís theory about the circulation of the blood, but he also wrote important descriptions of the structures of the skin, various glands and the brain.

malpractice Treatment that involves negligence or incompetence on the part of a doctor or other member of medical staff.

mamillary body Either of two small lobes that hang underneath the brain below each *thalamus* and behind the top of the *pituitary gland.* (An alternative spelling is mammillary.)

mammary gland Gland that secretes milk in a motherís breast, during *lactation*. Each gland is in fact a linked collection of glandular lobules surrounded by fat, all secreting milk that is then ducted into reservoirs, or ampullae, before discharge through the nipple.

mammography Investigation of a womanís breast tissues using X-rays or, sometimes, infra-red rays, projected on to photographic films or fluorescent screens.

mammoplasty Surgery to alter the size or shape of one or both of a womanís breasts.

mandible Lower jaw, containing a maximum of sixteen teeth in an adult (and ten in a child). It is hinged with the skull in front of each ear (at the temporomandibular joints). The force with which the muscles can clench the jaw tightly is immense, although the hinge joints are relatively insecure.

mania Mental condition of urgent and emotional excitement or obsessional desire, leading to a breakdown in self-restraint. There may be *euphoria*, feverish activity, rapid and uncontrolled speech, apparently illogical trains of thought, extravagant and domineering behaviour, all of which may lead further to irritability and violence, and *delusions*. Treatment is usually with drugs; hospitalization or institutionalization may be necessary in severe cases.

manic-depressive illness *Psychosis* (severe mental illness in which the patient loses contact with reality) in which a patient is subject to extreme *depression* that alternates with bouts either of relative normality or of *mania*. It may also be called bipolar disorder. During manic phases the person may appear elated or frenetic, with euphoria or irritability, incoherent speech, impulsiveness, extravagance and poor judgement, sometimes becoming violent if grandiose plans are thwarted. Changes between moods may or may not be triggered by external factors, but the extremes of apathy reached in depressive phases and the extremes of activity and violence reached in manic phases (if they occur) mean that hospitalization is often necessary. There may be a hereditary predisposition to manic-depressive illness. Treatment is with psychiatric intervention and drugs, either *antidepressants* or antipsychotic agents.

manipulation Form of therapy used in disciplines such as *osteopathy*, comprising treatment by *massage* and by manual friction and *traction*.

MAO inhibitor Type of *antidepressant* drug (in full a monoamine oxidase inhibitor) which works by inhibiting the action of the enzyme monoamine oxidase in the brain. Because serious side-effects may be experienced by patients given the drug who eat certain ordinary foods, who have high blood pressure, or who are simultaneously taking certain other drugs, MAO inhibitors are now not commonly prescribed.

marasmus *Wasting* and emaciation in an infant, caused by *malnutrition, malabsorption syndrome*, a serious disorder of the heart, kidneys or lungs, or by long-term bacterial or parasitic infection. It may also be a symptom of *maternal deprivation*. Treatment depends on diagnosis but in all cases will include supportive nursing care and gradual building up of food and fluid intake.

marrow Tissue central in long bones. See *bone marrow*.

masculinization Appearance in a woman of the characteristics of an adult man: a growth of hair on the face and body, a deepening of the voice, and an increase in musculature. The cause is hormonal imbalance, and the treatment therefore usually includes female *sex hormones*.

masochism Desire and practice of obtaining sexual pleasure from sensations of physical (or mental) pain, inflicted on oneself either by oneself or by others. Psychiatric counselling may help.

massage Practical form of therapy in which the muscles (or joints) of the limbs and torso are subjected to external manual friction and traction by a trained operative, primarily to improve muscle tone and local blood circulation, but also sometimes to reduce *oedema* or to soothe muscular spasm.

masseter Main muscle each side of the jaw, attached to the *mandible* (lower jaw) and the *zygomatic arch*, which contracts to close the jaws. Proportionately very powerful, the muscle confers great strength to the bite.

mast cell Type of cell in connective tissue that contains especially large quantities of *histamine, heparin* and *serotonin*, all substances secreted when inflammation or an allergic reaction occurs.

mastectomy Surgical removal of a womanís breast, usually to treat breast *cancer* that has progressed too far to be treated by *lumpectomy* (removal of the tumour alone, conserving the breast). Simple mastectomy removes breast tissue alone, sometimes enabling the skin and nipple to be retained so that an artificial prosthesis (implant) can be inserted to preserve the appearance of the breast. Lymph nodes in the armpit may be removed at the same time in case *metastasis* (spread) of the cancer has already begun. A cancer that has already spread further may require a radical or modified radical mastectomy, which removes the whole breast and the skin, the surrounding lymph nodes and sometimes the underlying muscle. After the operation *radiotherapy* and/or *chemotherapy* may also be given. *Plastic surgery* to reconstruct the breast may be possible at the time of the mastectomy or later, or a prosthetic (false) breast may be worn. Psychological adaptation both to the loss of the breast and to the possibility of recurrence (return of the cancer) may require counselling, and regular follow-up is needed to check for recurrence.

mastication Chewing. Use of the *masseter* (and temporalis) muscles to rhythmically bring the *mandible* (lower jaw) forcefully up to the upper, to grind food between the teeth and mix it with saliva for swallowing.

mastitis Inflammation of a womanís breast, generally caused by bacterial infection, especially some weeks after childbirth when the nipples may have become slightly damaged through suckling. Unless there are signs that an abscess is forming, the condition should not interrupt breast-feeding. Cystic (or chronic) mastitis, however, is not inflammation but the presence of small cysts in the breast tissues. Resulting from hormonal imbalance, it occurs particularly just before *menstruation*, and particularly again just before the *menopause*. Treatment of infection is with antibiotics, which generally produce rapid relief.

mastoid Describing the flattened, roundish, bony process of the skull behind each ear. From it are attached the major neck muscles, and within it is a mucous-membrane-lined cavity (antrum) connected with the *Eustachian tube* and middle ear. Infection can spread from the middle ear to cause mastoiditis, which generally responds to treatment with antibiotics but in severe cases may require surgical removal of part of the mastoid bone (mastoidectomy).

masturbation Stimulation of oneís own genitals for the purpose of achieving a sexual climax (*orgasm*).

materia medica Study of substances used in medical treatments, in diagnostic methods, and in the synthesis of medications. The term refers particularly to drugs.

maternal deprivation Effect on an infant of having no available mother (or mother-figure). There is considerable distress and "failure to thrive", generally because the infant does not consume any food. The symptoms in severe cases may eventually be those of *marasmus*.

maternity services All the medical services centring on *pregnancy* and *childbirth*. These include services provided by obstetricians, physiotherapists and *midwives*, and care that may continue for some months after childbirth.

maxilla Upper jaw (and, strictly, the whole of the bone at the front of the face that also forms part of the eye socket), in which the upper teeth are set (sixteen in an adult, ten in a child). It is against the fixed maxilla that the hinged *mandible* (lower jaw) provides the bite.

measles Highly infectious viral disease, with alternative medical names rubeola and morbilli, occurring most commonly in children. Initial symptoms, after an incubation period of 8 to 15 days, are a very high temperature and a catarrhal sore throat with a cough; the condition is infectious from this point on. Two days later, small spots, red with a white centre, appear inside the cheeks (Koplikís spots), tending to fade a further two days later when a rash develops. The blotchy orange-pink rash typically originates behind the ears, spreads to the face, and then travels down the neck to the whole body. The rash lasts for five or six days, during which time the disease remains infectious. The cough may persist for ten days or so afterwards, and complications may include *pneumonia*, middle ear infections and *encephalitis*. Treatment is to alleviate the symptoms and prevent complications. A vaccine is available and is usually given in infancy along with mumps and rubella vaccine (MMR vaccine); contracting the disease usually confers lifelong immunity.

meconium Greenish-brown greasy *faeces* produced for the first one or two days of life by a newborn baby, consisting mostly of cellular material swallowed in the womb, mucus and bile pigments.

Medawar, Peter B. (1915–1987) British immunologist whose experiments on the toleration or *rejection* of tissue grafts in embryos, although they did not lead to the advances expected, did clarify the nature of the problem of tissue rejection. He was awarded a Nobel Prize in 1960.

median nerve Nerve responsible for flexing the muscles of the forearm and the thumb, and for sensation on the thumb side of the hand. It is close to the skin surface at the wrist. In *carpal tunnel syndrome*, it becomes trapped by a band of ligament round the wrist.

medical Physical examination that represents an all-over check-up on the condition of the body and its systems. It may be a requirement in occupations subject to occupational diseases, or in taking up any active post. It may also be a requirement for certain insurance policies.

medical record Non-statutory record kept (and owned) by a doctor, a health centre, community clinic or local hospital authority, detailing what that doctor/clinic/hospital authority knows about the medical, social and family history of a patient, any disorders or diseases experienced and the treatment given, and additional information such as a log of blood pressure measurements, cervical smear results or immunizations. Such a record is likely to be incomplete and quite possibly inaccurate, especially for patients who have moved around or changed doctors frequently. Nevertheless, the record may be extremely useful to a doctor (or surgeon) treating the patient for the first time, and in the UK there are plans for a nationally accessible computerized record of all NHS patients. Patients are now entitled to ask to see their medical record (details may only be withheld if they are judged potentially harmful or overly distressing to the patient) and, subject to a fee, to obtain copies of relevant parts.

medicine Either the science and practice of maintaining health and curing illness (and some authorities would add "by non-surgical means"); or any medication.

meditation Disciplined concentration of thought on a single theme. Based on – or as part of – a religious practice, breathing exercises may be carried out simultaneously. Included in therapies associated with the principle of *holistic medicine*, it is believed by some people to have some medical benefit.

medium Specific environment or agent that promotes the occurrence of an event. Thus any substance used for the *culture* (growth) of micro-organisms is a culture medium; and any radio-opaque substance swallowed or injected so that internal organs can be X-rayed is a contrast medium.

medulla Inner part of any tissue or organ that has an inner and an outer (cortex) part that are distinguishably different (such as the brain, adrenal gland and kidney).

medulla oblongata Topmost part of the spinal cord, within the skull, comprising the lowest part of the *brainstem.* Most nerve impulses entering or leaving the brain do so through the medulla oblongata, and it is also the control centre for the regulation of the heartbeat, breathing, blood pressure, salivation and swallowing.

meiosis Method of cell division by which the sex cells are formed, resulting in cells that contain only half the number of chromosomes that other types of cell contain. Such cells become either *sperm* or *ova*, and the full number of chromosomes is again made up when one fertilizes the other (at *conception*), and the combination forms a *zygote*. Unlike *mitosis*, the ordinary form of cell division which results in two daughter cells, meiosis (through eight stages) creates four daughter cells at a time.

melaena Black and tarry *faeces*, resulting from the action of digestive enzymes on iron compounds in blood that has somehow escaped into the intestines. It may be associated with vomiting blood (*haematemesis*), and requires medical advice.

melancholia An alternative term for *depression*.

melanin Dark *pigment* that occurs in the surface tissues – in the second layer (dermis) of the skin, in the hair, and in the iris and *choroid* of the eyes. It is the active production of more melanin in the skin than usual, through the effect of sunlight on melanocytes (special cells that produce melanin), that causes freckles and a suntan.

melanoma Form of *cancer* that centres on an area of melanocytes – the cells that produce the dark pigment *melanin*. They thus occur mostly in the skin (especially where the skin is pigmented with a *mole*), but also occasionally in the surface of the eye, and even in the mucous membranes of the mouth. Indications that a melanoma is forming include a change in colour or size, bleeding or itching of a *birthmark* or mole. Treatment is usually with surgery and, if necessary, chemotherapy.

melasma Outbreak of brown patches in the skin of the face, caused by the presence of larger than normal quantities of the dark pigment *melanin*. Strong sunlight makes the condition worse. When caused by hormonal factors – as in pregnant women, or in women who use oral contraception – it is called *chloasma*.

melatonin Hormone produced by the *pineal gland* in the brain, which regulates *circadian rhythms* (daily variations driven by the internal "body clock"), including sleep cycles. Secretion occurs during periods of darkness and is switched off by bright light: it thus responds to external day-night cycles and synchronizes internal rhythms to them. Fluctuations in melatonin levels are believed to contribute to *seasonal affective disorder* and *jet lag*; melatonin supplements taken at appropriate times may help to combat jet lag.

membrane Smooth surface-layer of tissue that covers other tissue surfaces, in particular to surround an organ (such as the heart and lungs) or to line a cavity (such as most of the external orifices of the body, including the mouth, nose and vagina). Many such membranes secrete *mucus* or *synovial* fluid; others are lubricated with *serum* (such as those that surround the heart and lungs). The *hymen* is a unique form of membrane. The term is used also for the two-layer *lipoprotein* "skin" that surrounds a cell.

memory Mental store of knowledge and ideas, impressions and events previously experienced, and the capacity for re-presenting them to the consciousness on demand. The faculty depends on several areas of the brain, relating in particular to the length of time the information has been stored and to the importance it was given on the occasion. Loss of memory (*amnesia*) may be selective in the same fashion.

menarche Onset of *menstruation* in a girl who has reached puberty. The exact age at which it occurs depends on hormonal changes in the body, and is also associated with overall weight. Failure of the menarche to occur at the due time is known as primary *amenorrhoea*.

Mendel, Gregor J. (1822–1884) Austrian abbot and scientific gardener whose discovery that plants bred true – but with "dominant" and "recessive" traits in a fixed ratio – paved the way for the modern study of *genetics*.

Ménière's disease Disorder of the inner ear, affecting the functions of hearing and balance. It is believed to be caused by fluid build-up in the inner ear, leading to increased pressure in the fluid within the *semicircular canals* (which control sensations of balance). Symptoms are recurrent bouts of *tinnitus* (ringing in the ears) and *vertigo* (dizziness), with nausea and temporary deafness. With repeated attacks, hearing may be impaired. Treatment is to alleviate the symptoms as far as possible, including drugs to reduce dizziness during attacks. In persistent cases, drugs may be given as a preventive measure. Sometimes injections into the inner ear or surgery are used for uncontrollable symptoms.

meninges Three layers of membranes that surround the brain and the spinal cord. They comprise the *dura mater*, the *arachnoid membrane*, and the *pia mater*. Between the two latter, in the subarachnoid space, there is *cerebrospinal fluid*. Inflammation of the meninges is called *meningitis*.

meningitis Inflammation of the *meninges* (the membranes surrounding the brain), as a result of infection by various bacteria or viruses. Symptoms are those of a heavy cold, followed by severe headache, very high temperature, vomiting, sensitivity to light and sound, and muscular spasm (especially involving a stiff neck). There may be confusion and, in extreme cases, convulsions. In meningococcal meningitis there is a characteristic rash with bleeding under the skin. Meningitis is a medical emergency as without treatment it may cause permanent brain damage or death. Treatment depends on diagnosis of the infective organism. Most forms of viral meningitis do not respond to antiviral drugs, although these are occasionally used. Otherwise the only treatment is bed rest, but fortunately viral meningitis rarely causes serious damage. Bacterial meningitis requires urgent antibiotic treatment. Immunization against certain – but not all – forms of meningitis is now possible.

meningocele Protrusion of the *meninges* through an abnormal gap in an incompletely formed spinal column (*spina bifida*), remaining covered only by a stretched layer of skin. Usually, the spinal cord itself is not misplaced, but the surrounding meninges bulge out on one side. It is one of the congenital *neural tube defects*.

menopause Cessation of ovulation and thus of child-bearing capacity in a woman, also accompanied by cessation of *menstruation* (periods). The exact age at which it occurs (any time between the mid-30s and the later 50s, average age 51) depends on hormonal changes in the body, and generally follows a pattern in which menstrual periods gradually become either irregular and more widely spaced or gradually diminish in volume. The menopause is popularly known as the "change of life"; the medical term is the climacteric, and it is only diagnosed when a woman has had no menstrual periods for a year. Rarely, periods may stop abruptly. The hormonal changes involved may also lead to *hot flushes*, minor disturbances of the heartbeat (palpitations), and dryness of the vagina, which may cause discomfort during intercourse. Many symptoms can be alleviated by hormone supplements (hormone replacement therapy, HRT), which also reduce the increased risk of osteoporosis to which postmenopausal women are liable.

menorrhagia Unusually heavy *menstruation*, sometimes also with prolonged duration of menstrual periods. Causes are many, but include inflammation of the lining of the womb (endometritis), the presence of *fibroids*, pelvic inflammatory disease and *endometriosis*. Some cases are linked with hormonal imbalances, when the condition is known as dysfunctional uterine bleeding. Heavy periods may also occur when an intrauterine contraceptive device (IUCD) is in place. If menorrhagia is severe and prolonged, *anaemia* may result. Treatment depends on the cause but may include drugs or surgery.

menstrual cycle Relatively regular reproductive cycle in women between the *menarche* and *menopause*. Statistically, it averages 3–6 days *menstruation*, about 8–11 days infertile period, 1–4 days fertile period, and 8–11 days infertile period before menstruation again. Not all menstrual cycles are regular, however. The cycle is controlled and monitored by the *pituitary gland* and *sex hormones*, and represents complex physical changes in the tissues of a womanís sexual organs. During the first infertile period, one *ovum* matures in an *ovarian follicle*. At *ovulation* the mature ovum leaves the ovary and begins to travel down the nearby Fallopian tube – and this is the fertile stage at which a sperm might fertilize the ovum following *sexual intercourse*. Meanwhile, the follicle the ovum has left develops a *corpus luteum*, which secretes *progesterone*. This hormone causes the endometrium (lining of the womb) over the following days to thicken and take on an extra blood supply in case *fertilization* occurs and the fertilized ovum becomes implanted in the endometrium. If fertilization does not occur, the thickened, bloody lining of the womb is finally shed, days later, as the menstrual flow at the end of the cycle.

menstruation Relatively regular bleeding through the vagina, representing each time the end of one episode of the *menstrual cycle* that has not resulted in the *fertilization* of an *ovum* (*conception*). Onset of menstruation at puberty is the *menarche*. Thereafter, lack of a menstruation when expected may indicate *pregnancy*, hormonal imbalance or severe undernourishment. The *menopause*, the end of menstruation, represents the end of a womanís child-bearing capacity.

mental deficiency Obsolescent alternative term for *mental retardation*.

mental disorders Conditions that affect the mind and, consequently, behaviour or the ability to learn. Congenital conditions involving incomplete or faulty development of the "thinking" part of the brain result in *mental retardation*. Effects may be noticed only months or even years after birth. In the first few months of life, several organic conditions may affect mental development in a similar way. These include *hypothyroidism* (leading to *cretinism*) and *phenylketonuria* (PKU). Different from these is *mental illness*, in which the normal functions of the mind (generally of an adult) are disturbed. Causes may include injury to the brain, long-term stress, acute emotion, or be unknown.

mental illness Condition in which the normal functions of the mind (generally of an adult) are disturbed, affecting thinking, emotions, memory or perception. Causes may include injury to the brain (as by trauma, disease or poisoning with drugs – including alcohol – or with certain heavy metals), long-term stress, acute emotion, or may be unknown. Mental illness may be categorized in three types: *personality disorders, neuroses* and *psychoses*. Of these, personality disorders, featuring maladaptive behaviours, generally most approach (and overlap with) normality. Patients with neuroses are aware of – and distressed by – their behavioural oddities, which may take the form of extreme anxiety, depression or exaggerated behaviour; whereas those with psychoses are unaware of them, having lost contact with reality and insight into their condition. Treatment depends on the diagnosis but may include counselling, various forms of therapy or drugs. Patients with severe psychoses may require hospitalization to protect themselves or others.

mental retardation Subnormality of mental function, caused by incomplete or arrested development of the "thinking" part of the brain, to the extent that special education and care are required. It may also be termed mental deficiency or mental handicap, and is classified according to severity of IQ (intelligence quotient) deficit (the average IQ is 100) – mild (IQ 50 to 70), moderate to severe (IQ 20 to 50) and profound (IQ less than 20). The condition may be congenital (present at or caused by birth), for instance, *Down's syndrome*; result from unknown causes, from hereditary factors, or from contraction by the mother while pregnant of any of several diseases (such as *rubella* – German measles). Or mental retardation may affect a child while growing up, and be caused either by organic disease (such as *hypothyroidism* or *phenylketonuria*), by extreme psychological cruelty, or by injury. People with mild mental retardation may live a relatively normal life in the community, while those with profound retardation usually require life-long, often institutional care.

mercury poisoning A collection of symptoms, known as *Minamata disease*, due to inhaling mercury vapours or ingestion or absorption of mercury through the skin. Acute poisoning causes abdominal pain, vomiting and diarrhoea, sometimes with bleeding. It may lead to kidney failure. Chronic poisoning with smaller doses over a prolonged period causes digestive and urinary disturbances, mouth ulcers and dental problems. Late effects include anaemia and nerve damage. Treatment is first to remove the source of exposure, which may require extensive decontamination procedures. Thereafter it involves supportive measures to alleviate the symptoms as far as possible, and sometimes treatment to counteract kidney damage and anaemia. Severe acute poisoning is sometimes treated with a *chelating agent* (which removes the toxic metal from the bloodstream).

mesentery Folded sheet of *peritoneum*, attached to and supporting many of the abdominal organs – especially the intestines – and slung from the rear top of the abdominal wall. Between its two layers are many blood vessels and lymph nodes supplying the tissues enclosed.

mesmerism Form of *hypnosis* practised therapeutically by the Austrian astrological physician FA Mesmer (1734–1815), who called it "animal magnetism", thought of it as a natural power that anyone could use, but set himself up on it as a sort of scientific faith healer.

mesoderm One of the three distinct types of tissue that make up the very early form of *embryo* (the others are the *ectoderm* and the *endoderm*). It is from the mesoderm that the bones, muscles, cartilages, sex organs, kidneys and, above all, the blood, are formed after it has divided into two layers. The space between the layers becomes the body cavity of the thorax and abdomen.

mesomorph Individual whose body shape is neither unduly tall nor unduly short, neither unduly fat nor unduly thin – and who is therefore neither an *ectomorph* nor an *endomorph*. Such individuals generally have a sturdy, well-muscled frame.

messenger RNA Form of *ribonucleic acid* (RNA) that conveys the "instructions" of *deoxyribonucleic acid* (DNA) in the nucleus of a cell out of the nucleus to a *ribosome*, in the cytoplasm. There, another form of RNA (transfer RNA) translates the instructions into specifications for the amino acids to be synthesized in protein chains.

metabolic rate Measure of the processes of *metabolism*, generally described as the *basal metabolic rate* (BMR).

metabolism Complex process in the body that converts all the substances taken in as food and drink to useful products and to energy, and that at the same time filters out and disposes of waste products. The entire process relies on a capacity to break down molecules into smaller constituents (*catabolism*) and to reform other molecules from smaller constituents (*anabolism*).

metacarpus Palm and base of the hand, and the five bones that form it.

metaphase Second stage in the form of cell division known as *mitosis*; or fourth and seventh stages in the alternative form of cell division, *meiosis*.

metastasis Process by which a *cancer* spreads around the body. Cells that detach from a malignant tumour may travel through the bloodstream, in the *lymphatic system*, or across a body cavity, depending upon the location of the primary tumour, and lodge in secondary tissues. Replication of the cells then results in the formation of a new cancer. Cancers of the lung and the breast, for example, most commonly metastasize via the lymphatic system; of muscle or of bone, via the bloodstream; of one area of the peritoneum in the abdominal cavity, to another similar area.

metatarsus Main part of the foot, between heel and toes, including the five bones inside the arch.

methadone Narcotic drug that may be used to wean addicts off heroin; alternatively it is sometimes prescribed as a powerful analgesic or as a cough remedy. Long-term use may result in addiction.

methanol Methyl alcohol, or wood spirit. A form of alcohol different from ethyl alcohol (*ethanol*, the alcohol in alcoholic drinks and that has some medical applications), methyl alcohol is highly toxic and if swallowed in any quantity can cause blindness. It is a constituent of methylated spirits and of some liquors that have been poorly made and distilled.

microbe Alternative term for a *micro-organism* (such as a bacterium or virus), but with the added implication that it may cause disease, thus equivalent to a germ or pathogen.

microbiology Study of living organisms of microscopic scale – *micro-organisms* – especially those that cause disease.

microcephaly Congenital condition in which the head has not grown to a size that corresponds with the body, and the brain remains incompletely formed. If the child lives, there is inevitable severe *mental retardation.*

micro-organism Living organism of microscopic scale (also called a microbe). A minority of the vast total number cause infection, including *bacteria, viruses, protozoans*, and some *fungi*. Of these extremely basic creatures, protozoans have properties of animals and fungi have properties of plants; bacteria have properties of both; and there is debate about whether viruses should be described as "living" at all. And apart from micro-organisms that fall between those defined in these groups – anomalies such as the infective agents of *actinomycosis* and *typhus* – there are others that appear to be unique in type.

microscope Device or machine with which to examine objects at great enlargement. In an optical microscope, magnification is achieved by combinations of lenses, using light as a viewing medium. It can resolve objects as small as a bacterium. In an *electron microscope*, a beam of electrons travelling in a vacuum is focused by electrostatic "lenses", to resolve objects as small as viruses.

microsurgery *Surgery* that requires such minute delicacy that it is carried out using a binocular microscope (an operating microscope) and special precision instruments. Such techniques are used particularly for reconnecting tiny nerves and blood vessels while restoring accidentally amputated limbs and digits, and for certain operations in eye and brain surgery.

microtome Device or machine that cuts material such as tissue samples into very thin slices, for examination with a microscope. Objects are usually embedded in wax or a synthetic resin before being sliced.

microtubule Tube or vessel in the body so small as to be visible only through a microscope.

microvilli Types of *villus* in the body so small as to be visible only through a microscope.

micturition Medical term for urination, the passing of *urine*.

midbrain Central portion of the *brain*, representing not only the final connection of the end of the spinal cord (the *brainstem*) with the *cerebral hemispheres*, but the connection also between the *cerebellum* (of the *hindbrain*) and the *forebrain*. The midbrain is the site of the *reticular activating system* (which is responsible for the degree of consciousness) and for movement of and in the eyes.

middle ear Part of the ear that transmits the vibrations of sound from the *eardrum*, by means of three tiny interconnected bones (the malleus, incus and stapes, in that order) to the *inner ear*. The bones are located in an air-filled cavity within the temporal bone that is connected also with the *Eustachian tube* (that leads to the pharynx) and is lined with mucous membrane. Infection of the middle ear is called *otitis* media.

midwife Skilled obstetric nurse or therapist responsible for the care and assistance of mothers during *pregnancy, labour* and *childbirth*, and perhaps for some time afterwards.

migraine Severe one-sided *headache*, with a characteristic throbbing character, usually accompanied by nausea and vomiting and sometimes by photophobia (intense dislike of light). Some people have an aura warning that the migraine is about to start, which may consist of visual disturbances such as tunnel vision or zig-zag light patterns, or limb symptoms such as tingling, numbness or weakness. These symptoms usually resolve before the headache starts. The cause is an abnormality in the blood flow within the brain, with arterial spasm followed by dilation. Various factors such as certain foods, or stress, may trigger attacks. The migraine may last for hours or even days and makes normal activities impossible. In an acute attack an injection may be given to relieve pain. Drugs are also available that can be taken long-term to prevent frequent attacks.

milk Fluid secreted by the *mammary glands* of a motherís breasts following childbirth, containing fats, sugars and protein, trace minerals and some antibodies. For the first few days of *lactation* the breasts secrete *colostrum*, which is yellowish, and contains far more protein and far less sugar than the later, true milk. Cowsí milk contains less sugar and more protein than motherís milk; comparatively deficient in vitamins, it should not be fed to very young children.

milk teeth First set of teeth (baby teeth), known medically as the *deciduous teeth*.

Minamata disease Effects of *mercury poisoning* following the consumption of contaminated food. Symptoms (representing progressive and irreversible brain damage) are muscle weakness, loss of sensation, loss of muscular co-ordination affecting vision, speech and hearing, and eventual paralysis; coma and death may follow. The disease is named after a community in Kyushu, Japan, which suffered a catastrophic outbreak in 1953 after eating shellfish from water polluted by mercury compounds.

miscarriage Spontaneous expulsion of a foetus from the uterus before the 24th week of *pregnancy* (the time when it is judged capable of independent survival; loss after this time is a stillbirth), known medically as a spontaneous *abortion*. It is extremely common, occurring in as many as one in five established pregnancies. Causes include any of many developmental abnormalities in the foetus, a structural abnormality of the *uterus* (womb) or infection or injury in the mother. The initial symptom of an impending miscarriage is bleeding from the vagina, which requires immediate medical diagnosis. This may represent a threatened abortion, with the foetus still alive, and treatment may be possible; once the foetus has died it is termed inevitable abortion. Sometimes an incomplete abortion occurs, and parts retained in the uterus need to be removed by a minor operation (*dilatation and curettage*, or D and C) to prevent complications in the mother. Repeated miscarriages are termed recurrent abortion.

mite Small external parasite that lives on the surface of the skin and feeds on cellular debris. Related to *ticks*, mites are comparatively harmless; a very few cause infestations of the skin (such as *scabies*) or more general disorders.

mitochondrion Organelle within a cellís cytoplasm responsible for producing energy, especially for muscle contraction. Within a dual membrane, each mitochondrion contains *adenosine triphosphate* (ATP), the breakdown of which (into adenosine monophosphate or adenosine diphosphate) releases energy.

mitosis More usual kind of *cell* division that through four stages results in the formation of two daughter cells identical to the original cell, each with a nucleus that contains a full complement of 23 pairs of *chromosomes*. This is quite different from the kind of cell division that forms sex cells (*meiosis*), which over eight stages forms four daughter cells each containing a nucleus with only half that number of chromosomes.

mitral valve Valve between the left atrium and the left ventricle of the *heart*. Blood is allowed to flow from the upper chamber (atrium) to the lower (ventricle), but prevented from returning by the valveís two flaps (cusps).

molars Back teeth – three in each side of each jaw – which have a generally flattish occlusal (biting) surface, although it may be crinkly, suitable for the chewing and grinding of food. Other teeth are chisel-shaped (incisors) or have points (canines); between the canines and the molars are the premolars. *Wisdom teeth*, which erupt only at adolescence or later (or sometimes never at all), are the rearmost molars.

mole Area of skin pigmented with an unusual amount of *melanin*. Moles come in all sizes and shapes, are generally any shade of brown to black, may be flat or raised, and may or may not have hair growing on them. A flat mole that is present at birth is often called a *birthmark* – but many moles appear as the body grows. Rarely, a mole turns malignant (*melanoma*).

mongolism Obsolete term for *Down's syndrome*.

moniliasis Former name for *candidiasis*.

monoamine oxidase inhibitor Full name of an *MAO inhibitor*.

monoclonal antibody *Antibody* formed by the artificial cloning of a cell, and comprising just a single type of *immunoglobulin*. Such antibodies are produced by fusing together antibody-forming *lymphocytes* (B-lymphocytes) and cancerous cells, both from mice. The resultant hybrid cells multiply fast and produce the same antibodies as the original lymphocytes.

monocyte White blood cell (*leukocyte*) that engulfs and thus neutralizes bacteria and cellular debris in the bloodstream. It has a larger nucleus and more cytoplasm than other luekocytes, and is three times the size of an *erythrocyte* (red blood cell).

Monod, Jacques L. (1910–1976) French biochemist who with a compatriot first suggested that *genes* might be responsible not only for growth and development within cells, but also for metabolism.

mononucleosis Condition in which the blood contains far more than usual of the type of white blood cells called *monocytes*. When this results from a viral infection that produces symptoms affecting the whole body, the condition is called *glandular fever* or infectious mononucleosis. Treatment depends on the cause. In glandular fever the main treatment is rest.

Montessori, Maria (1870–1952) Italian educationist and child expert who, by working out how to teach mentally handicapped children, discovered a method of teaching all children that was more successful, and less restrictive and discouraging, than the contemporary educational system. Her method – later widely adopted – was to encourage children to find their own pace at which to learn, by providing the equipment and the environment.

morbidity Condition of being ill. By extension the term refers to the proportion of a population that is suffering from any specified disease.

Morgan, Thomas Hunt (1866–1945) American biologist and pioneer geneticist who used fruit-flies to demonstrate that hereditary traits are carried by *chromosomes*, and that the *genes* which constitute the chromosomes are individually or in combination responsible for single traits. He went on to suggest that these traits might eventually be mapped to their respective gene or genes (which has subsequently been done for many traits).

moribund In a state of dying.

morning sickness Nausea, and possibly vomiting, experienced by as many as half of all women during the early months of *pregnancy*, often, but not always, on rising in the mornings. It usually stops by the fourth month, and is believed to help protect the foetus against possibly harmful ingredients in food – women who get morning sickness are slightly less likely than others to miscarry. Severe sickness during pregnancy (*hyperemesis* gravidarum) is uncommon but can indicate toxaemia of pregnancy, a serious condition, and may lead to dehydration and sometimes to liver damage. Severe or persistent morning sickness should be reported to a doctor. For many women, a simple countermeasure is to eat a biscuit or a slice of bread before getting out of bed. Avoiding rich or greasy foods and ensuring adequate rest can reduce nausea, and some women find supplements of vitamin B complex helpful.

morphine Alkaloid drug derived from *opium*, which is a powerful *analgesic* (and cough suppressant) – and a potentially addictive *narcotic*, for which reason its use is legally restricted to the relief of severe and persistent pain. Side-effects are euphoria, nausea, constipation, weight loss and confusion; it also has a depressant effect on breathing. Forms and derivatives of morphine (such as the non-addictive codeine) are widely used in medicine.

mortality Being subject to death. By extension the term is used for the proportion of a population (or a specified section of a population) that dies within a specified time and/or of a specified cause.

Morton, William T. G. (1819–1868) American dentist who in 1846 first demonstrated publicly how *ether* might be used as an anaesthetic for dental – and therefore general – surgery. Following a series of bitterly contested litigations instigated by rivals, however, he was almost entirely forgotten.

mortuary Department in a hospital or other medical institution to which dead bodies are taken and temporarily kept. There, each body is examined and, if required, a *post mortem* (autopsy) carried out to find out the cause of death, before a death certificate is issued.

morula Initial solid round mass of cells that develops from the combined *ovum*-and-*sperm* (zygote) just after *conception*. Later, the ball of cells becomes hollow in the middle, forming the *blastocyst*, which then implants in the uterine wall (endometrium).

mosquito Small flying insect found mostly in the tropics, with a long proboscis specially adapted to penetrate the skin of mammals and draw out blood. It is the females that carry the infective organisms transmitted by mosquitoes to humans, resulting in such diseases as *malaria*, viral *encephalitis* and *yellow fever*.

motion sickness Nausea, and possibly vomiting, caused by the movements of the vehicle in which the sufferer is travelling; also called travel sickness, car sickness, air sickness and seasickness. The effect results from the abnormally constant demands such movements make both on the organs of balance in the inner ear, and on the eyes in adjusting to a persistently moving objective. An *aura* (one of various sensations that act as a warning) may precede an attack, consisting of yawning or a slight rise in temperature. Treatment may include *antiemetics* (antisickness drugs) or *antihistamines*; the same drugs may also be taken before a journey to prevent motion sickness.

motor cortex Area in the grey matter of the *cerebral cortex* of the brain that generates the neural impulses which produce voluntary movements. The motor cortex of the right cerebral hemisphere controls voluntary muscle contractions on the left side of the body; specific areas within the motor cortex control specific voluntary movements.

motor end-plate Slightly flattened end of the *axon* of a *neurone* (nerve cell) that is attached to a muscle. When a nerve impulse passes along an axon, it is transmitted through the end-plate to the muscle – and the muscle contracts or relaxes.

motor neurone disease Any of three forms of a disorder that produces progressive degeneration of nerve cells in the brainstem or spinal cord. The cause is unknown, but some forms are inherited; onset is usually in middle age or later. Symptoms include increasing muscle weakness and wasting, from the extremities inwards. Progressive muscular atrophy may take up to twenty years to develop fully and cause death; amyotrophic lateral sclerosis (Lou Gehrigís disease) up to three years; and progressive bulbar palsy (which attacks the throat) usually two. Treatment is to alleviate the symptoms as far as possible; physiotherapy may help. The drug riluzole may reduce symptoms in some forms of motor neurone disease, but does not represent a cure.

mountain sickness Alternative name for *altitude sickness*.

mourning Evident sign of *grief* after the death of a loved one, of which there are many other behavioural manifestations.

mouth ulcer Common term for an *aphtha* or aphthous ulcer.

mouth-to-mouth resuscitation Also called the kiss of life, an excellent form of *artificial respiration* once it has been established that there is no blockage in the air passages.

MS Abbreviation of *multiple sclerosis*.

mucous colitis Alternative term for *irritable bowel syndrome*.

mucous membrane Surface layer of *membrane* upon other tissue, that produces and secretes the lubricating and slippery fluid, *mucus*. It is made up of *epithelium* containing a multitude of tiny glands, and has a base of connective tissue founded on a very thin muscular stratum. Many vessels and cavities within the body, and orifices that reach the outer skin surface, are lined with mucous membrane (the medical term for which is mucosa).

mucus Lubricating and slippery fluid produced and secreted by *mucous membranes*. It protects underlying surfaces, aids the passage of various vesselsí contents, and is also the vehicle for some enzymes. Its major constituents are compounds of protein and carbohydrate (glycoproteins).

Muller, Hermann J. (1890–1967) American geneticist and radiologist, whose research into genetic *mutation* – during which he succeeded in effecting the experimental mutation of *genes* using X-rays – won him a 1946 Nobel Prize.

multiple sclerosis Serious disorder caused by damage and hardening (sclerosis) in the *myelin* sheaths around the nerves in scattered areas of the brain and spinal cord; this affects the function of the nerves involved. The onset is usually in young adults. Initial symptoms are muscular weakness and tingling or numbness in one or two limbs; there may also be blurred vision, bladder incontinence or vertigo. Later symptoms may include all of these and other more serious effects of neural damage, depending on the actual nerves affected, which may include spastic paralysis (weakness accompanied by increased tone and spasm of the muscles), shaking, speech disorders and visual loss. In the most common form of the disorder, there are periods of relapse and remission, when some or all of the symptoms resolve. In time, more deficits may remain after each relapse, leading to progressive disability. Some cases show a steady deterioration from the outset. The advance of the disease may be slow or rapid. A few patients recover spontaneously; many endure decades of problems and remissions before stabilizing; those who do not stabilize are at risk of pulmonary or urinary complications. Treatment is to relieve the symptoms as far as possible, and may include physiotherapy and drug treatment of spasticity and incontinence. *Corticosteroids* may be used during relapses. Treatment with beta interferon can reduce the relapse rate and may lessen eventual disability.

mumps Medical name infectious parotitis, a virus infection of the *salivary glands*, most common in children. Initial symptoms are malaise and nausea, with a headache and high temperature. The patient is already infectious at this stage. Then the temperature soars even higher – probably to somewhere around 40ºC (104 F) – and the salivary glands on one or both sides of the cheeks (the parotid glands) and under the jaw (the submandibular glands) swell painfully, remaining sensitive to the touch. There may be difficulty in opening the mouth. After three to six days the symptoms fade, but the child remains infectious until the swelling has completely gone. In adults, mumps may cause further infections of the pancreas, brain, testes or the ovaries, and in males after puberty testicular involvement can cause infertility. Treatment is isolation of the patient and alleviation of the symptoms as far as possible, and may include analgesic drugs. A vaccine is available, and is usually given in childhood along with measles and rubella immunization (MMR vaccine).

murmur In medicine, term referring to a *heart murmur*.

muscle Fibrous tissue in which the cells are able to contract or relax, so producing movement (or ensuring stability). Muscle cells are contained within a matrix of connective tissue in which the nerves (that direct the functions of the muscle) and the blood vessels (that supply the nutrients which make contraction or relaxation possible) also lie. There are three types of muscles. Striated, or skeletal, muscles are those which are attached to the bones of the skeleton and by which voluntary movements are effected. They are made up of bundles of fibres, each themselves made up of even tinier fibres (*myofibrils*) in a sort of striped (striated) pattern: contraction causes the *actin* and *myosin* "stripes" to pull to each other. Smooth muscle represents a type of muscle over which an individual has no voluntary control, and which effects the operations of such organs as the stomach and intestines, the bladder and even the blood vessels; its myofibrils are not striated. Cardiac muscle is the strong, specialized form of muscle of which the heart is comprised; myofibrils overlap at the end-plates known as intercalated discs. Within, and part of, the cardiac muscle is the small sinoatrial node, the natural *pacemaker* for the heartbeat. Contraction of all of these types of muscles relies on actin and myosin, and the presence of *glycogen* as fuel, phosphates for the transfer of energy, and oxygen (in the form of myoglobin).

muscle relaxant Type of drug that relaxes the muscles and may therefore be used as a *premedication* before surgery. Other uses include the relief of muscular *spasm* (as for example caused by tetanus or a stroke).

muscular dystrophy Any of a group of potentially severe disorders in which muscles progressively waste away although the nerves supplying them remain functional. The affected muscle fibres degenerate and are gradually replaced by fatty tissue. Almost all of the disorders in the group have hereditary factors – which may aid diagnosis. Other pointers towards diagnosis include age of onset and the progress of the disease; a muscle *biopsy* (tissue sample taken for testing) or electromyographic testing of muscle function may be useful. The most common form is Duchenne dystrophy, in which the muscles of the pelvis and back in boys aged less than four waste away. Treatment is to alleviate the symptoms and the difficulties associated with them as far as possible, and may include physiotherapy. The gene for Duchenneís muscular dystrophy has now been identified, so screening and gene therapy may be possible in future.

mutation A change in the genetic structure of a cell or individual not resulting from the normal genetic processes. This may be an alteration in a single *gene* (called a point mutation) or a change in the structure of a *chromosome* or in the number of chromosomes. A mutation may occur spontaneously or be caused by outside agents (called mutagens) such as radiation; it can also be induced (deliberately or accidentally) by *genetic engineering*. A mutation in the *DNA* of an ordinary body cell (a somatic mutation) affects only the individual; if it occurs in one of the sex cells (*ova* or *sperm*) it may be passed on to the next generation. The effects range from no noticeable change to lethal consequences, depending on the gene(s) affected.

mutism Inability to speak. Such an inability may result from total deafness since birth, from congenital malformation of (or later injury to) the vocal apparatus, from the effects of a *stroke*, or from brain damage. The term is used also for a refusal to speak (elective mutism) as may be caused by psychological trauma or depression.

myasthenia gravis Disorder caused by a reduction in the power of the *neurotransmitter acetylcholine* (one of the chemicals that enable nerve transmission) to effect muscle contractions in certain muscles of the body. It is an *autoimmune disease* (caused by the immune system attacking the bodyís own tissues) affecting women more often than men, in which muscles become fatigued very easily, sometimes to the extent that they are effectively paralysed. The muscles affected most commonly are those of the face and neck, giving symptoms of drooping of one or both upper eyelids (ptosis), blurred or double vision, and mispronounced speech. Treatment is with rest and perhaps anticholinesterase drugs, which can alleviate symptoms temporarily; surgical removal of the *thymus* gland (a gland in the neck that is part of the immune system) may be beneficial and in extreme cases *corticosteroid* drugs or plasma exchange treatment are used.

mycosis Infection by a *fungus*. Common mycoses include *ringworm* and *candidiasis*.

myelin White compound of protein and fats that is produced by certain cells (Schwann cells) and entwined around the *axons* of specific *neurones* (nerve cells). Gaps in this myelin sheath between the Schwann cells – called the nodes of Ranvier – somehow enable a nerve impulse to travel much faster than along a non-myelinated (or "non-medullated") nerve cell, perhaps by "skipping" from gap to gap. The white matter of the brain and spinal cord appears white because of the amount of myelin surrounding the nerve fibres.

myelitis Inflammation of the *spinal cord*, generally as a symptom of a major neural disorder (such as *multiple sclerosis*). It produces paralysis below its own level in the body. The term is also sometimes used for *osteomyelitis* (inflammation of the bone marrow). See also *poliomyelitis*.

myelocele Severe form of *neural tube defect* in which the spinal cord and one or more pairs of spinal nerve roots protrude through an abnormal gap in an incompletely formed spinal column, and are exposed to the outside through a corresponding gap in the skin. Paralysis and total lack of sensation from the waist down (including inevitable urinary incontinence) accompany an ever-present susceptibility to dangerous infection. The condition may be complicated by *hydrocephalus*.

myelography A type of X-ray examination of the spinal cord following the injection of a special dye (contrast medium), which shows up on the resulting X-ray photograph (called a myelogram).

myeloma Cancer of the bone marrow, also called multiple myeloma or myelomatosis because of its tendency to spread rapidly; it may affect any bone. Symptoms are fatigue and anaemia, followed by pain in the bones and susceptibility to fractures and to respiratory and urinary infections. Diagnosis may follow detection of X-ray changes within the bones, an abnormal *immunoglobulin* (a protein that acts as an *antibody*) released into the bloodstream, or a characteristic protein (called Bence-Jones protein) in the urine. Treatment is with chemotherapy, and often local radiotherapy to relieve pain; sometimes radiotherapy of the whole skeleton is used.

myocardial infarction Death of part of the heart muscle following the cessation of its blood supply. The usual cause is *coronary thrombosis* (a blood clot in one of the arteries supplying the heart muscle) due to *arteriosclerosis* in the coronary arteries (*coronary* *artery disease*). It is popularly known as a heart attack. The left ventricle is usually the centre of infarction, causing sudden severe pain in the chest that may spread to the jaw or left arm and is often accompanied by sweating and nausea or vomiting. The heartbeat may become ragged, and even stop. Emergency hospitalization is required to avoid complications, which can include shock, rupture of the heart muscle, *heart failure*, pulmonary embolism (a clot that travels to the lung blood vessels, see *thromboembolism*) or damage to the heart valves. However, in many cases recovery, although slow, is complete. Early treatment with thrombolytic ("clot-busting") drugs lessens the risk of fatal complications. Patients require intensive nursing and monitoring, sometimes with resuscitation in cases of cardiac arrest. Later drug treatment or surgery may be required depending on the extent of the damage and the risk of further attacks.

myocardium Heart muscle, the middle layer of the three that make up the heart wall. (The outer layer is the epicardium; the inner the endocardium.) Myocarditis is inflammation of heart muscle, which may lead to *heart failure*.

myofibril Tiny filament that with a multitude of others makes up just one fibre in the mass of fibres that comprises a *muscle*. It represents a filament within the *cytoplasm* of a muscle cell. Each myofibril is itself made up of two types of protein in strands, *actin* and *myosin* (visible under the microscope as distinct bands in striated muscle). When muscle contraction takes place, the myosin "pulls" the actin past itself and "holds on" in the new position.

myopathy Any disorder in which there is muscle weakness and wasting with or without neural damage.

myopia Shortsightedness, the inability to focus the eyes on distant objects. In fact, light from such objects is focussed by the eyesí lenses – but within each eyeball and not on the *retina*. This is either because the lenses become too convex or because the distance between the lens and retina is unusually long (which may be the result of heredity). *Contact lenses* or *glasses* can usually correct the focus, and surgical or *laser* treatment may permanently rectify the defect.

myosin Form of protein in the *myofibrils* of a *muscle* and one or two active units in muscle contraction (the other is *actin*).

myxoedema Set of symptoms resulting from underactivity of the thyroid glands (*hypothyroidism*). They include coarsening of the skin surface, sensitivity to cold, constipation, weight gain, fatigue and lethargy; there may also be huskiness of the voice. It is treated with the thyroid hormone thyroxine.

myxovirus One of a group of RNA-containing viruses, including the one that causes *influenza*, and related to those that cause *measles* and *mumps*.

N

naevus Medical name for a *birthmark.*

nail Layer of *keratin* on the top surface of the tips of the fingers and toes. Each nail grows from a root hidden under the fold of skin from which the nail appears (the cuticle), the keratin continually sliding forward over the nail bed towards the end of the digit. The white crescent at the base of each nail is called a lunula.

narcissism Very high regard of oneself and extreme prejudice towards oneís own interests. When exhibited to an abnormal degree, narcissism may be an indication of a *personality disorder.* In *Freudian* terms, it occurs where the *ego* becomes the lòve object.

narcolepsy Tendency to fall asleep suddenly at any time during the day, whether convenient or not – while eating, driving or having sex, for example. Narcolepsy produces bouts of shallow sleep that do not contribute to established circadian fatigue or sleep patterns. Sleep bouts are sometimes preceded by an extraordinarily vivid dream in which the sufferer feels awake but, often, paralysed (called a hypnagogic hallucination). Narcolepsy is occasionally associated with another condition (cataplexy) that causes patients to collapse as if fainting, but with no loss of consciousness. There is no cure, but stimulant drugs may be given once the diagnosis – which is often missed – is made, and may counteract some of the symptoms. New drugs that act more specifically are being tested.

narcotic *Analgesic* drug that also causes loss of sensation or of consciousness (narcosis) by depressing brain function. Many are *opiates*, and addictive, and are subject to illegal abuse. Authorities are divided over whether the term should also include anaesthetics and sedatives.

nasal cavity Area behind the nostrils, and like them divided by a septum, connecting (via two more nostril-like openings) with the *nasopharynx.* In the walls of each side are the sensory nerve endings that represent the source of the sense of smell, connecting with the *olfactory bulb.*

nasal septum Dividing partition (septum) formed of bone and cartilage that separates the nostrils and nasal cavity.

nasopharynx Mucous-membrane-lined air passage between the nasal cavity and the soft palate at the top of the throat; the "back of the nose".

Nathans, Daniel (1928–1999) American microbiologist who investigated the possibility of "mapping" genes by working on the genetic material of viruses. He was awarded a Nobel Prize in 1978.

natural childbirth Delivery of a child without the use of any medication for the mother. Most methods make use of special breathing exercises that may assist at specific stages of *labour.* Some also require a darkened environment, some a braced standing posture, and some that the mother give birth in a bath of warm water. In all methods, the purpose is that the mother should truly experience everything that happens. The fact remains that during some childbirths *analgesics* are necessary, and other medical equipment may be vital in an emergency.

naturopathy Form of mainly dietary therapy, usually regarded as a form of *complementary medicine*, based on the principle that substances (and environments) found in nature must be better for the body than any synthesized substances or those with chemical additives. Medications recommended are therefore generally herbal preparations; careful exercise – especially swimming – also features prominently.

nausea Feeling that one is about to vomit. Depending on the strength of the stimulus, and its interpretation by the brain, vomiting may or may not actually follow. Nausea may be caused by a disgusting sight or smell, or may be a symptom of various disorders. It is most commonly experienced as a result of severe *indigestion*, of travelling in an unsteady vehicle (*motion sickness*), or of pregnancy (*morning sickness*). Treatment is with antiemetic (antisickness) drugs.

navel Another name for the *umbilicus*.

nearsightedness Common name for *myopia*.

necrosis Death of an area of tissue, possibly of a whole organ. Necrosis generally follows a failure of the blood supply, through injury (particularly frostbite damage), disease or blockage, possibly due to a blood clot. In the brain, necrosis may follow a *stroke*, and in the heart, a *myocardial infarction*.

nematode worm Another name for a *roundworm*.

neonate Baby in the first month of life.

neoplasm Growth of new tissue. The term is applied most often to the appearance of a benign or malignant *tumour*.

nephritis Inflammation of one or both kidneys, centring usually either on the part of a kidney that filters the blood (the glomeruli, thus *glomerulonephritis*), on the part that differentiates between reusable water and urine (the tubules, thus interstitial nephritis), or on the part that collects the urine for disposal via the ureter (the renal pelvis, thus *pyelonephritis*). The cause is often obscure, and in some cases may be an allergic reaction to a streptococcal throat infection. Symptoms can include blood or protein in the urine and often *oedema* (fluid accumulation in the tissues). Treatment depends on diagnosis, but if the kidney is seriously incapacitated, *dialysis* (artificial filtration of the blood, taking over the functions of the kidney) or kidney transplant may be necessary.

nephrolithiasis Presence of one or more *calculi* (stones) in a kidney, caused by an excess of calcium, uric acid, or magnesium and other salts in the bloodstream. Symptoms are generally caused only when the stone moves from where it was lodged, or when it obstructs the flow within the kidney. There may then be severe pain (renal colic) and vomiting; sometimes blood appears in the urine. Treatment is with analgesics and large volumes of liquids. Ultrasound may be used to shatter the stone so that the pieces pass out naturally; surgical intervention may be necessary to crush or remove large calculi.

nephrology Study of the functioning and disorders of the *kidneys*.

nephrosis Degeneration of the tubules of the kidneys – those parts of the organ that filter off reusable water for reabsorption, and channel waste products (urine) towards the renal pelvis. It is most often caused by poisoning – by drugs, chemicals, or by bacterial toxoids – or by injury. In many cases, if external *dialysis* (kidney machine) is available for a period the tubules heal and function perfectly well again.

nephrotic syndrome Disorder of the kidneys that results in severe retention of water in the tissues (*oedema*). It may be a symptom of various kidney disorders, such as *glomerulonephritis* (see *nephritis*). The immediate cause is the filtering off by the kidney of too much protein, channelling it to the urine instead of into the bloodstream. Diagnosis may be complicated by the fact that some symptoms – such as high blood pressure – are themselves potential root causes. Other symptoms include general malaise and fatigue. The outlook is variable. Treatment depends on the cause, but includes *corticosteroid* drugs.

nerve Strand of fibres, made up of nerve cells (or *neurones*), that transmit neural impulses to and from the brain and spinal cord. Sensory nerves convey information from the sense organs towards the brain; motor nerves convey information away from the brain (to the muscles); most major nerves contain both sensory and motor fibres. There are several *nervous systems*, which overlap and together are responsible for controlling nearly all aspects of living and being. The central nervous system (CNS) consists of the brain, cranial nerves and spinal cord. The peripheral nervous system consists of the 31 pairs of spinal nerves, branching from the spinal cord, and their extensions to the sensorimotor (voluntary) peripheral nerves and the autonomic (involuntary) sympathetic and parasympathetic systems. Most of the larger peripheral nerve fibres are covered in a protective sheath of *myelin*. Disorders directly affecting nerves include *neuritis* (inflammation of the nerve), *multiple sclerosis* (degeneration of the myelin sheath), *poliomyelitis* (degeneration of the nerve), *spina bifida* (protrusion of the membranes covering the spinal cord) and pressure on a nerve (perhaps caused by a *prolapsed intervertebral disc*). Areas of the brain are affected by *cerebral palsy*, leading to spasticity, and *stroke*, leading to paralysis.

nerve block Blocking – for therapeutic reasons or by disease – of a nerve supplying part of the body, which prevents the transmission of pain impulses to the brain, and so makes the whole area feel completely numb.

nerve cell Another name for a *neurone*.

nerve fibre In common usage, much the same as a *nerve*; but technically, the same as an *axon*.

nervous breakdown Common term for a mental condition generally caused by stress and resulting in a personís inability to cope with prevailing situations. It may precede or be part of any mental illness.

nervous system Any of several systems in the body involving collections of associated *nerves*. Each system has its own specific function, and some nerves are incorporated in more than one system. The most important system is the *central nervous system*, comprising the brain and spinal cord; this system controls and monitors the entire working of the body (and mind). Nerves branching from this system across and around the rest of the body make up the *peripheral nervous system*, of which all the sensory and motor nerves are a part. The nerves responsible for controlling and regulating internal and involuntary body functions (such as heartbeat, monitoring of glandular secretions, regulation of the process of digestion, and so on) are those of the *autonomic nervous system*, which is itself divided into two subsystems – the *sympathetic nervous system* and the *parasympathetic nervous system*.

nettle rash Common name for *urticaria*.

neuralgia Pain originating from a *nerve* of the *peripheral nervous system* (those outside the brain and spinal cord), most commonly the trigeminal nerve in the face. All pain is felt by means of the nerves, but some pains result from disorders of the nerves themselves, as when a nerve is pinched or is damaged through disease or injury; sometimes the cause may simply not be known. Such pain may be severe and result in distress over long periods. Treatment depends on the nerve affected but may include drugs or, as a last resort, surgery.

neural tube defect Any of a group of congenital disorders caused when for some reason the brain and the spinal cord, and/or parts of the surrounding structures, fail to develop properly before birth. In *spina bifida* – perhaps the best-known form – only certain parts of the spine may be lacking. Other forms include *meningocele* and *myelocele*. Surgery can sometimes correct, or partially remedy, the defect; however paralysis, incontinence and other physical and mental handicaps are common sequels. Various tests during *pregnancy* aim to detect neural tube defects so that the woman can be offered an *abortion* if affected. The risk of these disorders is reduced if the intending mother takes folic acid supplements from before the time of conception.

neurasthenia Neurotic symptoms that resemble those of *depression*, and may include listlessness, weariness, irritability, insomnia and loss of self-confidence. They may precede or be part of a *neurosis*, or the cause may be an infection or an injury affecting the brain. The term is obsolete.

neuritis Inflammation of a *nerve* of the peripheral nervous system (those outside the brain and spinal cord). Many conditions that are called neuritis (or, if more than one nerve is involved, polyneuritis) do not in fact involve inflammation (as denoted by the suffix -itis), and would be better termed *neuropathy* (nerve damage or disease). However, inflammation can occur, through bacterial or viral infection. Treatment depends on the diagnosis and may include rest or drugs.

neuroglia Cellular structure that forms the connective tissue between the nerve cells (neurones) of the brain and spinal cord. Cells that make up the neuroglia (or just glia) include astrocytes, microglia and *oligodendrocytes*, all of which have specific functions. There are ten times as many glia as neurones.

neurology Study of the functions and disorders of the *nervous system*.

neuromuscular disorders Disorders affecting the muscles (often involving *paralysis*), caused by damage or disease in the *nerves* that supply them.

neuron Alternative spelling of *neurone*.

neurone Nerve *cell*, made up of a nucleus located inside a cell body, several branching *dendrites* which act as receptors for nerve impulses from other neurones (or from nerve endings in the skin or mucous membranes), and one branching *axon* which passes on the neural impulses to an adjacent neurone across a *synapse* (or to a muscle). Together, neurones make up the "fibres" of a *nerve*. A nerve impulse represents the electrochemical transmission of a weak electric current along a neurone.

neurophysiology Study of the processes involved in the transmission of nerve impulses between *neurones* (and between neurones and muscles).

neurosis Disturbance of mental function that may have effects on behaviour or reason. Unlike sufferers from the more serious *psychoses*, patients with neuroses retain insight and so are often unhappy about their mental state. Neuroses range from states of *anxiety, depression* and *hypochrondria*, to *obsessions, phobias* and forms of *hysteria*.

neurosurgery Surgery to treat diseases and disorders of the *nervous system*, particularly of the brain and spinal cord.

neurotransmitter Chemical substance released from the tips of the *axons* of *neurones* (nerve cells) in order to pass nerve impulses on to the *dendrites* of adjacent neurones across an intervening *synapse*. Different parts of the nervous system use different neurotransmitters. The most common is *acetylcholine*; others include dopamine, *noradrenaline* and *serotonin*.

neutrophil White blood cell – a *leukocyte* of the type called a *granulocyte* – that ingests bacteria and is an important part of the immune system.

niacin Vitamin of the B complex, also called nicotinic acid. It is synthesized in the body to a small extent, but is required also in the diet. Useful sources of the vitamin are meat, certain cereals, peas and beans, and yeast extract. It is not much affected by cooking. Deficiency of niacin leads to *pellagra*.

nicotine Alkaloid drug inhaled through the burning of tobacco in cigarettes. Poisonous and potentially addictive, in small doses it has a slight stimulant effect on the autonomic nervous system but in time leads to a dangerous suppression of various internal reflexes, causing raised blood pressure, an accelerated heartbeat, deterioration in digestion, and other symptoms.

night blindness Medical name nyctalopia, a defect in the *rods* of the retina of the eye, caused by a lack of *rhodopsin*, that leads to particular difficulties in vision outside any lighting but full daylight or good artificial light. The lack of rhodopsin may correspond to a dietary deficiency of vitamin A (retinol), or to an eye disorder. Treatment is to increase the input of vitamin A.

night terrors Phenomenon occurring in young children, who scream in their sleep and appear terrified, but have no memory of any causative dream. There is no evidence of a relation between night terrors and stress or unhappiness in the daytime environment.

nipple Small raised area at the centre of the *areola* of the *breast*. In women it represents the site of the openings of the milk ducts following lactation, for the suckling of a baby. Babies suck by reflex when a nipple is placed in their mouth. Bleeding from the nipple may be a serious symptom, for instance of breast cancer.

nit Tiny egg laid by a *louse*, sometimes found adhering to hair or clothing.

nitroglycerine See *glyceryl trinitrate*.

nitrous oxide Commonly called "laughing gas", an *anaesthetic* now used only in combination with oxygen, halothane or other gases, so that the symptoms of agitation and excitement in patients (which gave it its common name) no longer occur.

nocturia Having to wake up from sleep at night in order to urinate. It is a fairly common feature of later middle age and old age, and of pregnancy. It is commonly a symptom of *prostate* disorders in men, but may also occur in other conditions, such as diabetes.

node Junction of a system or network, especially one from which operations within the system radiate. Types of node in the body include the sinoatrial node (the pacemaker of the heart, a junction of special muscle fibres from which the electrical impulse of the heartbeat radiates), lymph nodes (junctions of the lymphatic canal system, at which lymph glands are located), and the nodes of Ranvier (gaps in the myelin sheath surrounding the axon of a nerve cell, which accelerate the passage of a nerve impulse).

nodes of Ranvier Minute gaps between the Schwann cells which make up the *myelin* sheath that surrounds the *axon* of a *neurone* (nerve cell). The gaps, occurring at regular intervals along the length of the axon, allow a nerve impulse to "skip" from gap to gap without having to travel the full length of the axon, and thus increase the speed of a nerve impulse.

nodule Small and discrete lump or swelling.

noise Unintelligible sound that may be unpleasant or downright intolerable. At high enough intensities, noise can permanently damage hearing. It has also been discovered that noise pollution may lead to medical symptoms in much the same way as any other kind of environmental pollution, and presents a particularly strong case for attention as an occupational hazard.

non-accidental injury Form of child abuse that results in repeated physical injury to a child, often from a very early age – it is most common in babies under six months old. It is usually perpetrated by parents or step-parents, and occasionally by other carers, who are often young and have disturbed relationships and social problems, such as unemployment, debts or ill-health, and often suffered similar maltreatment themselves while young. Injured children more often result from an unwanted pregnancy or are handicapped. Signs suspicious of non-accidental injury include multiple bruises made at different times, cigarette burns, bites and badly healed fractures: the children are commonly in a distressed or withdrawn state and underweight for their age. Treatment includes urgent intervention from health and social services and support for the whole family. Children at high risk of injury may have to be removed to a safer environment; possibly affected children may be placed on an at-risk register, with increased family surveillance.

non-specific urethritis (NSU) Relatively mild *venereal disease* centring on inflammation of the urethra (the tube that ducts urine from the bladder to the outside). The cause is infection by one of many micro-organisms – hence it is "non-specific" (although *Chlamydia* is often identified) – contracted through sexual intercourse with someone who already has the disease. Symptoms in men are pain and a discharge from the penis. In women, symptoms may be absent, or there may be pain and a discharge from the *vagina*, and infection may spread to the *cervix* of the womb. Treatment is usually with *antibiotics*. The condition may recur or cause further infectious complications.

noradrenaline Hormone that is the main agent of the *sympathetic nervous system*. It is used as a *neurotransmitter* by the *neurones* of the system, and in the bloodstream has much the same effect as does *adrenaline* – to which it is chemically related: it prepares the body to meet emergency circumstances, and so constricts the blood vessels (thus raising blood pressure and slightly reducing blood flow to the digestive organs), dilates the pupils of the eyes, and stimulates the release of energy-giving glucose from the liver.

norepinephrine American term for *noradrenaline*.

nose Organ on the front of the face that houses the receptors of the sense of smell (which is why it projects from the face) and is a means of filtering, warming and moistening air on its way to the lungs. Behind the nostrils – which are separated by a septum of bone and cartilage – is the *nasal cavity*, in whose walls are the olfactory nerve endings. And behind the cavity are two further nostril-like openings into the *nasopharynx*. The nostrils and nasal cavity are lined with mucous membrane, which produces copious watery mucus in response to irritation, infections such as the common cold, or allergies such as hay fever.

nosebleed Medical name epistaxis; bleeding from the nose, most commonly caused by injury or by continuous sneezing, and generally the result of the breaking of a minor blood vessel. However, nosebleed can happen spontaneously, especially in children and the elderly (whose blood vessels may be subject to some deterioration), in boys at puberty, and in people with high blood pressure or anaemia. Pinching the nostrils together, packing them with gauze, or applying an ice-pack to the bridge of the nose may help to stem the flow. *Cauterizing* (destroying by heat) the bleeding vessel is a quick and effective treatment in severe cases.

nostrils External openings of the *nose*, known medically as the nares.

notifiable disease Any of the few infectious diseases whose appearance a doctor is required by law to notify to the local government health authorities, so that general health measures (such as mass immunization) may be taken if necessary, or that its statistical incidence may be recorded.

NSU Abbreviation of *non-specific urethritis*.

nuclear medicine Any form of diagnostic test using radioactive isotopes as tracers to assess metabolic processes in the body. Substances that can be transported ordinarily within the body are labelled with a radioactive isotope (the most common is technetium-99) and injected, inhaled or swallowed; their progress around the body can be detected with special cameras or imaging equipment, or their appearance in blood or urine may be monitored.

nucleic acid Either *deoxyribonucleic acid* (DNA) or *ribonucleic acid* (RNA), the genetic material of almost all living organisms, consisting of chains of *nucleotides*, in the case of DNA wound round each other in the famous double helix structure. They are the basis of inheritance and also the keys to cellular protein synthesis and replication, and so are essential to the existence, maintenance and reproduction of cells.

nucleolus Part of a cell nucleus that is essential to the synthesis of *ribonucleic acid* and *ribosomes*, and thus in turn of proteins. It is a dense spherical structure that disappears during cell division.

nucleotide One of the compound molecular links in the chains that make up *nucleic acids* (DNA and RNA), comprising a purine (adenine or guanine) or a pyrimidine (thymine or cytosine in DNA, uracil or cytosine in RNA) base linked to a sugar, plus a phosphate group. Nucleotides thus comprise the units from which *genes* are formed.

nucleus Part of a cell that contains the *nucleic acids deoxyribonucleic acid* (in the form of chromosomal strands of *genes*) and *ribonucleic acid* (mostly in the form of the *nucleolus*). These elements determine the function, maintenance and reproduction of the cell. All are held inside a nuclear "envelope", a dual membrane; outside are cytoplasm and the organelles. The term is used also for a specific group of cells within the brain.

nurse Person trained to look after those who need medical care, either in a hospital or similar institution, or in the patientís home. There are various grades, reached by taking and passing qualifying examinations. Some nurses specialize in particular forms of nursing (obstetric, dental, psychiatric or geriatric care, for example); others concentrate on management and administration skills (nursing officers); yet others are concerned more with community health and social welfare.

nutrition Beneficial effect on the body of the proper absorption of healthy forms of food and drink. Nutrition provides for growth and development (including healing when necessary), and for energy, and depends to a major degree on diet. Too much or too little food, or food that is too rich or too low in nutrients – all hinder nutrition in its proper sense. Much of the study of nutrition, however, centres on malnutrition and deficiency disorders, particularly those that are prevalent in the Third World.

nyctalopia Medical name for *night blindness*.

nymphomania Abnormal and excessive desire by a woman for frequent sexual intercourse.

nystagmus Rapid involuntary movements of the eyes, usually from side to side, sometimes up and down or round and round. It may be the result of a congenital disorder associated with poor eyesight, a disorder in the balance mechanism of the inner-ear, including motion sickness, or various brain disorders. Similar jerking movements of the eyes occasionally occur without underlying disorders when the individual is tired or when a succession of objects flash past the eyes. Treatment depends on the cause.

O

obesity General condition of somebody who is very overweight. People are considered medically obese if their weight is more than 120 per cent of the ideal for their height, build, age and sex. Such an accumulation of fat in the body usually results simply from eating more food than the body needs to supply its daily energy requirements. Obesity runs in families, and there may be a genetic element, although poor eating habits often begin in childhood. Untreated, obesity may lead to cardiovascular problems, joint disorders and other serious medical conditions. Reduction of *calorie* input through carefully controlled dieting is usually the best treatment. In extreme cases, drug treatment or even surgery may be considered.

obsession *Neurosis* with a dominant idea or purpose that has an unreasonably strong influence upon a personís behaviour – although other aspects of life may not be neglected. The obsession may centre on an activity or on an environment (including specific people), and may itself cause anxiety by its persistence. For example, somebody may be obsessed by a fear of germs and, as a result, always wear gloves for fear of touching a contaminated object (or person). Treatment, when necessary, is most often through psychiatric counselling.

obstetrics Branch of medicine specially concerned with pregnancy and childbirth. It involves medical care for women during pregnancy and for about six weeks after childbirth. A practitioner is known as an obstetrician.

obstructive airways disease Condition in which breathing is hampered due to *bronchospasm*. It may become chronic (long-term) and permanent, as in chronic *bronchitis*.

occipital Pertaining to the occiput – the back of the skull.

occlusal Biting surface of a tooth.

occlusion Closing together. The alignment of the teeth of the upper and lower jaws when clenched together is thus one form of occlusion, known more simply as the bite. The term also refers to blockage of a blood vessel by either a clot or disease.

occupational diseases and disorders Conditions to which people are particularly at risk by virtue of their work; any occupation that involves exposure to dust, extreme heat or cold, constant damp, infectious organisms, chemicals or radiation is theoretically liable. They include traditional industrial disorders that were accepted hazards of workers in certain industries, particularly those dealing in toxic substances or infective micro-organisms. Examples include *pneumoconiosis* and other lung disorders in coal miners and others continually inhaling various kinds of dust; *farmer's lung, anthrax* or *brucellosis* in agricultural workers; *mercury poisoning* in various industrial and medical manufacturing workers; and *asbestosis* in construction workers. In most industries, safety precautions are now laid down by law and there are now far fewer patients with such conditions than previously. However, other occupations may present their own hazards, such as *decompression sickness* in professional divers; *dermatitis* in many occupations involving exposure to chemicals, vegetation or prolonged water immersion, such as greengrocers and hairdressers; vibration white finger (see *Raynaud's disease*) in people using vibrating tools;

repetitive strain injury in word-processor operators; and *stress* in almost any pressurized work environment.

occupational therapy Activity of a long-term or convalescent patient to occupy the mind, perhaps to teach a new skill or reinvigorate a weakened part of the body – for example after a *stroke* – and generally to encourage an attitude of creative independence from medical care. It may represent part of *rehabilitation*.

Ochoa, Severo (1905– 1993) American biochemist who was awarded a Nobel Prize in 1956 for his research into how phosphate compounds are used in the body to store the energy derived from metabolism (a function of *adenosine triphosphate*, ATP). He also carried out significant research into understanding how enzymes work.

oculomotor nerve Nerve supplying some of the muscles that move the eye. Also known as the third cranial nerve, it controls the muscles that move the eyeballs, the muscles that regulate the size of the pupils and the shape of the lenses, and some muscles in the eyelids.

oedema Accumulation of body fluids in the tissues, generally causing swelling of a part of the body. There are many possible causes, including vascular disorders, disorders of the lymphatic system, heart or kidney disorders, injury, or local infection. An old name for oedema is dropsy. Treatment depends on the cause but may include diuretic drugs (to increase the amount of urine passed).

Oedipus complex In *psychoanalysis*, the repressed desire of a son for sexual love from and with his mother (or mother-figure), and the repressed jealousy therefore of his father (or father-figure). The complex, according to *Freud*, represents a stage in normal development during childhood; retained after that time, it may give rise to abnormal sexual behaviour. The equivalent complex in girls and women is the Electra complex.

oesophagus Muscular tube that passes swallowed food and drink from the *pharynx* to the stomach, commonly known as the gullet. Gravity provides the main motive force, but there is also some muscular movement (*peristalsis*) which squeezes swallowed material down towards the stomach, and a strong *sphincter* at the end of the oesophagus to prevent food from being regurgitated. The oesophagus lies behind the trachea (windpipe) in the neck. Inflammation of the oesophagus (oesophagitis) may be caused by an infection (such as *candidiasis*), by swallowing a corrosive substance or be a complication of *hiatus hernia* that causes partly digested food to be regurgitated.

oestrogen Any of several female *sex hormones* that at puberty instigate the appearance in women of *secondary sexual characteristics* and thereafter regulate the *menstrual cycle*. Most oestrogens are produced and secreted by the *ovaries*; the adrenal glands also have a minor role. Oestrogens, natural or synthetic, are used medically as supplements to make up for hormonal deficiencies and as a major constituent in oral *contraception* preparations. They may also be used to treat men with cancer of the *prostate gland* (although there are inevitable side-effects of *feminization*).

ointment Medication in the form of a thick cream or grease that is to be smoothed on the skin or applied to a mucous membrane.

olecranon Projection of the *ulna* that forms the sharp point of the elbow, commonly called the "funny bone".

olfactory Pertaining to the sense of *smell*.

olfactory bulb Area of nerve fibres above and behind the nasal cavity that sends sensory messages concerning odours direct via the *olfactory nerve* to the brain, where they provide the sense of smell. The messages originate in the sensory receptors within the nasal cavity.

olfactory nerve Nerve that carries impulses concerning the sense of smell from the *olfactory bulb* (in the nasal cavity) to the brain. Also known as the first cranial nerve, it does not connect with the *thalamus* as do all other nerves responsible for sensory messages.

oligodendrocyte Type of cell that with other *neuroglia* forms the connective tissue between the *neurones* (nerve cells) of the brain and spinal cord. Oligodendrocytes make up the *myelin* sheath surrounding these neurones (as the Schwann cells do for the neurones of the peripheral nervous system).

oligomenorrhoea Infrequent or sparse menstruation. It is common at the *menarche* and for a time thereafter, and again approaching the *menopause*. At other times medical diagnosis should be sought. Hormonal treatment may be recommended.

oliguria Minimal or infrequent urination, a symptom of fluid loss or fluid retention. When it occurs for no obvious reason, medical diagnosis should be sought.

omentum Part of the *peritoneum* comprising a large flap of membranous tissue hanging from the stomach over the front of other abdominal organs, representing a second protective and insulating layer of the abdominal wall.

onanism Alternative term for either *coitus interruptus* or *masturbation*.

oncology Study of the effects and treatment of *tumours*.

oophorectomy Surgical operation to remove one or both *ovaries*, performed to remove a tumour, cyst or, rarely, an implanted fertilized ovum (*ectopic pregnancy*); it may also be carried out during a *hysterectomy* for various reasons. If both ovaries are removed the woman will undergo a surgical *menopause*, and *hormone replacement therapy* may be prescribed.

open-heart surgery Complex surgical procedure that involves laying open the heart in order to reach the muscular ducts and valves within. During such surgery, the normal functions of the heart are usually taken over by a *heart-lung machine*, and the heart itself is stopped; a large team of expert staff is required.

operation Any form of surgical procedure major enough to require *anaesthesia*. For most patients an operation begins with the administering of *premedication* (a "pre-med") about an hour before being wheeled on a trolley to the operating theatre. If the patient is to have a general anaesthetic, primary anaesthesia (which produces rapid unconsciousness) is administered by injection in an anteroom to the theatre. The anaesthetist then connects the patient to a machine that provides anaesthetic gas, oxygen and so on to keep the patient in a state of unconsciousness. Alternatively a local anaesthetic is administered to deaden sensation in the part of the body to be operated upon. The operation itself is carried out in conditions of complete *asepsis*, and controlled and monitored in all aspects by specialized expert staff. One or more surgeons perform the surgery, but the anaesthetist is responsible for the well-being of the patient. The effects of the anaesthetic are allowed to wear off either in a recovery room (under the care of senior nursing staff) or back in the hospital ward.

ophthalmia Old term for any inflammation in and around the eye. The most common form is *conjunctivitis*.

ophthalmology Study of the functioning, diseases and disorders of the eyes. Medically qualified practitioners are ophthalmologists.

ophthalmoscope Either of two types of special instrument that enables an ophthalmic optician or ophthalmologist to examine the *retina* of the eye. One type directs a thin beam of light into the eye in such a way that the specialist can look down the beam; the other creates an image of the retinal surface between the specialist and the patient. Because retinal blood vessels are so easily visible, information from inside the eye can also help in diagnosing many more general disorders, such as high blood pressure and diabetes.

opiate Addictive narcotic drug derived from *opium*. Opiates include *morphine* (from which *heroin* is synthesized) and codeine, and they are highly effective painkillers. But because of their other properties, most are strictly controlled by law.

opisthotonos Arching of the entire body backwards in a rigid spasm, a symptom of certain kinds of poisoning (such as by strychnine) or of tetanus.

opium Dried preparation of the juice from the seed pods of one kind of poppy (not the ordinary red type seen on the roadsides). From it, many addictive and narcotic drugs (*opiates*) can be made; for this reason, its preparation and sale is strictly controlled by law.

opportunistic infection Infection caused by an infective organism that attacks the body only when the normal metabolic processes have undergone some change. Some micro-organisms, for example, become harmful only after a patient has undergone a long-term course of antibiotics. Opportunistic infections are characteristic of the immunosuppression that occurs in *AIDS*.

optic chiasma Crossing-over of portions of the two *optic nerves* that relay sensory messages from each eye back to the visual cortex in the occipital lobes of the brain. It is located close to the pituitary gland.

optic nerve Either of the two nerves that relay the sensory information from the eyes to the visual cortex of the brain, where they are interpreted as the sense of *vision*. The information originates in the nerve endings of the rod and cone cells in the *retina* of each eye, and travels up the two optic nerves; fibres from one side of each of the optic nerves cross over within the brain (at the optic *chiasma*), so that part of the vision in each eye is interpreted by the opposite side of the brain.

optician Qualified practitioner trained in fitting and dispensing *glasses* and *contact lenses* (dispensing optician) and often also in testing vision (ophthalmic optician or optometrist).

oral Pertaining to (or taken by) the mouth.

oral contraceptive Means of *contraception* taken orally, such as the *Pill*.

oral phase In *psychoanalysis*, the first stage of somebodyís *psychosexual development*, the stage at which most sensations and emotions that lead to a form of sexual gratification are associated with the mouth. The stages that follow are the anal, phallic, latent and genital phases.

orbit The eye socket. Each orbit is made up of parts of no fewer than seven bones of the skull.

orchitis Inflammation of one or both *testes* (the male sex organs inside the testicles that produce sperm), often caused by general viral illness (as, for example, with *mumps*). Symptoms are local swelling and pain; there may also be nausea. Orchitis affecting both testes and caused by mumps may lead to sterility. Treatment is with pain-killers and sometimes antibiotics or corticosteroids and by support of the scrotum, together with treatment of any other contributory infection.

organ Any separable part of the body that has a specific function. The constituent element or elements that give the organ its function are collectively its *parenchyma*.

organ of Corti Part of the inner ear comprising a fold of membrane that runs the length of the spiral *cochlea* and which contains many tiny hair cells. Sound entering the ear causes movements in the middle ear that produce vibrations in the fluid filling the cochlea, which in turn causes vibrations of the hair cells. The vibrations result in nerve impulses which travel along the auditory nerve to the brain, where they are interpreted as sounds. The organ of Corti is thus central to the sense of hearing. They are named after the Italian anatomist A Corti (1822–1888).

organ transplant *Transplant surgery* involving one or more whole *organs* supplied by a donor (who may be alive or recently dead).

organelle Microscopic structure that, like the *nucleus*, floats within the *cytoplasm* of a *cell* but has a different specialized function. Organelles include *mitochondria* and the *endoplasmic reticulum*.

organism Living creature capable of independent life and, singly or in combination, of reproduction. A few organisms comprise only a single cell; most are multicellular and made up of different types of cells. The definition includes all plant and animal life and almost all micro-organisms – although viruses are an anomaly because they can exist only in host cells and may not "live" otherwise.

orgasm Sexual climax. In men it involves the involuntary and ecstatic *ejaculation* of *semen* from the urethra of the *penis* through several waves of muscular contraction. In women it comprises involuntary and ecstatic contractions of the muscular walls of the *vagina*. Continued failure to achieve orgasm may usually be ascribed to psychological difficulties.

ornithosis Alternative term for *psittacosis*.

orthodontics Branch of dentistry specializing in correcting and improving the alignment of the teeth, generally during childhood. Orthodontists may, for example, prescribe and fit dental *braces* to straighten teeth. Less commonly, they may fit expanding denture-like "plates" to widen or straighten the jaw-line.

orthopaedics Study of the effects and treatment of the diseases and disorders that cause damage to the bones and joints. Orthopaedic surgery thus commonly involves operations to remedy conditions in which bones have been broken, dislocated or become deformed, and the specialty is closely concerned with the study of rheumatic and arthritic complaints.

Osler, William (1849–1919) Canadian doctor who first identified the infective organism responsible for endocarditis as a bacterium. A prolific writer, in the 1890s he wrote a textbook on medicine that became a standard reference work.

osmosis Mechanism by which a weak solution passes through a semi-permeable membrane into a stronger solution, but not vice versa. The membrane in this case acts as a sort of one-way filter, although it is the difference between the concentrations that brings about the filtration. It is of crucial significance to the process of *dialysis*, as occurs both naturally in the kidneys, and in dialysis machines that are sometimes used to take over their function.

ossicle Tiny bone – particularly any one of the three auditory ossicles in the *middle ear* (the incus, malleus and stapes).

ossification Hardening into bone. The final stage of bone formation (osteogenesis), it represents the enclosing of special cells (osteoblasts) within a matrix of connective tissue fibres and calcium salts in crystalline form. The whole structure then becomes rigid – but remains permeated by blood vessels and nerves so that if a fracture occurs, healing can take place. Before birth, and for some years afterwards, bone gradually replaces some areas of cartilage and even (in the skull) membrane. Abnormal growth of bone tissue may occur in *acromegaly, osteoarthritis* and disorders involving excess calcium in the blood.

osteitis Inflammation of the whole thickness of a bone, usually also including the marrow and the layer of membranous tissue that surrounds the bone. Symptoms and treatment are as for *osteomyelitis*.

osteoarthritis Degeneration of the cartilaginous layer over the bones at a joint, leading to friction and deformity of the actual bone surfaces. The hip, knee and finger joints are the most commonly affected. There are several disorders that may cause such degeneration – including rheumatism or obesity – but injury and long-term stress at the joint may have the same effect. In addition, old age may retard the normal processes of healing. Main symptoms are local pain and loss of mobility; the joint may become visibly deformed. See also *arthritis*. Treatment is with analgesic and anti-inflammatory drugs (such as aspirin or ibuprofen) and rest. Reducing the load on the joint by weight loss or a walking stick may help in the long-term. Surgery may be necessary if simple measures do not succeed, and may include replacement of the affected joint with an artificial substitute.

osteology Study of the composition, diseases and disorders of the bones.

osteomalacia Softening of the bones in an adult because of a lack of calcium, in turn caused by a deficiency in the body of vitamin D (which helps to extract calcium from food ingested); in children a similar condition is called *rickets*. Symptoms are bone pain and a tendency towards fractures. Diagnosis is sometimes difficult. Treatment is to make up the deficiency and if possible correct any deformities.

osteomyelitis Inflammation of bone, caused by infection either spread from elsewhere in the bloodstream, or directly through contamination at a fracture. Symptoms are severe pain, redness and swelling. Treatment is with large doses of antibiotics (and, if necessary, surgical draining); the infection must be completely eliminated or the condition may recur and cause bone deformity or fracture.

osteopathy Manipulative system of therapy based on the precept that disorders stem mostly from bone displacement (causing compression of nerves, habitual misuse of the muscles – for example through bad posture, irritation, or any other potentially undiagnosed source of pain, muscular spasm or even a behavioural problem). Treatment is generally with carefully applied local massage, and may be particularly effective with rheumatic disorders of the back and shoulders.

osteoporosis Degeneration of the bones caused by the loss of both calcium salts and other structural elements, sometimes referred to as "brittle bones". To some extent part of the normal aging process, the condition may also result from injury, infection, hormonal imbalance or prolonged treatment with *corticosteroids*. Women become much more liable to osteoporosis after the *menopause*. Symptoms are pain, a tendency towards fractures, and shrinking of the body stature (through shortening of the spine). Treatment depends on the cause but may include drugs to reduce further bone loss. Preventive measures include a diet with sufficient calcium and vitamin D, or supplements, and exercise from an early age to build up bone mass. In women, hormone replacement therapy (HRT) taken to alleviate menopausal symptoms also reduces the risk of osteoporosis.

otitis Inflammation of the ear (otitis externa/media/interna is inflammation of the outer/ middle/inner ear; inflammation of the inner ear is also called labyrinthitis). Symptoms of the three forms differ, although the cause in every case is a bacterial, viral or fungal infection. Otitis externa usually takes the form of a local infection of the skin surface, and there may be itching and earache, with a possible discharge. Otitis media is often spread from infection of the mouth, throat, sinuses or bronchial tubes, and causes severe pain, high temperature and temporary deafness; occasionally the eardrum ruptures, releasing pus. Repeated infections in children can lead to *glue ear*. Otitis interna (or labyrinthitis) is a serious condition with symptoms including pain, vomiting, deafness and constant *vertigo*, which may undermine the patientís sense of reality. In otitis externa, dressings and antibiotic drops generally eliminate the problem. Treatment of otitis media is aimed at alleviating the symptoms but may include antibiotics or surgical drainage of accumulated fluid. Otitis interna (or labyrinthitis) requires specialist treatment that may last for several months.

oto(rhino)laryngology Study of the functions, diseases and disorders of the ear, (nose) and throat, often abbreviated to ENT.

otosclerosis Hereditary malformation of bone in the middle ear that may lead eventually to deafness by the time of adolescence unless treated surgically. The malformation centres on the *stapes* (stirrup), a tiny bone that transfers sound vibrations between the middle and inner ear. Surgical replacement of this bone with a synthetic substitute is now more common than the surgical creation of a false "window" between the parts of the ear (fenestration). There may be some residual deafness.

otoscope Instrument for examining the outer ear, comprising a means of looking down a beam of light that can be directed along the ear canal to the *eardrum*.

ovarian cyst *Cyst* on an *ovary*. Ovarian cysts can be painful and may cause bleeding. Although most are not malignant, some are, and these can be extremely dangerous. Treatment may involve *oophorectomy*. They may also become large enough to inhibit other abdominal organs, or become twisted on a stalk and so painfully stretch the containing tissue.

ovarian follicle One of the multitude of niches within an *ovary* in which a single *ovum* develops. As long as its ovum remains unreleased, each follicle secretes the sex hormone *oestrogen* (together with a small quantity of *androgen*). Relatively few ova actually mature and are released from the ovary at ovulation (in the middle of the menstrual cycle), rupturing their follicles to do so. A ruptured follicle, however, becomes an outlet (corpus luteum) for the sex hormone *progesterone*. Ovarian follicles are also called Graafian follicles, after the Dutch physician Regnier de Graaf (1641–1673).

ovary Either of two identical sex organs in a womanís abdomen, located above and to each side of the uterus (womb) and connected to the uterus – for all but a very short initial length – by the Fallopian tubes. Each ovary retains a multitude of immature ova (eggs) in tiny niches (follicles), and alternately releases one mature *ovum* per menstrual cycle (at ovulation). The ovaries also secrete *sex hormones* under the direction of the *pituitary gland*: *oestrogen* from follicles containing immature ova, and *progesterone* from follicles containing a *corpus luteum* after an ovum has been released.

ovulation Release of a mature *ovum* by one of the *ovaries* at the middle of the regular *menstrual cycle*. From its *ovarian follicle*, the ovum travels down a Fallopian tube towards the uterus (womb); if it comes into contact with a *sperm* on the way, *conception* may occur. On the follicle left by the ovum, a *corpus luteum* is formed.

ovum Female sex cell produced by an *ovary* in an *ovarian follicle*. Each ovary has a multitude of follicles containing immature ova, only one of which reaches maturation during every menstrual cycle. The mature ovum is released by its ovary (ovulation) to travel down a nearby Fallopian tube towards the uterus (womb). Fertilization of the ovum by a sperm (following sexual intercourse), if it occurs, generally takes place in the Fallopian tube; the fertilized combination of ovum and sperm is called a zygote. Very occasionally, more than one ovum is released at ovulation and may, if fertilized simultaneously, result in fraternal twins or other multiple births.

oxygen therapy Treatment by administering oxygen gas. It may be used as an emergency measure in patients with heart failure, shock or respiratory problems, or routinely as for example with premature babies and during general anaesthesia. One well-known form in which oxygen therapy is applied in intensive care units is with an oxygen tent.

oxygenation Recharging of blood low in oxygen with a new supply taken from the air inhaled into the lungs. It is effected through the exchange of carbon dioxide for oxygen in the *alveoli*, through the thin alveolar walls. See *respiration*.

oxyhaemoglobin Combination of oxygen with the red pigment *haemoglobin* that is formed in red blood cells when *oxygenation* occurs in the lungs as a normal part of breathing. It is in the form of oxyhaemoglobin that oxygen is carried by the blood to the bodyís tissues. The presence of oxyhaemoglobin turns the blood a much brighter red colour.

oxytocin *Hormone* secreted by the *pituitary gland* that stimulates the uterine contractions of *labour* and childbirth, and that promotes *lactation* in the breasts thereafter. A preparation of synthetic oxytocin may be used to induce labour, under the direction of an obstetrician (see *induction*).

ozone Gas made up of three oxygen atoms to each molecule – as opposed to ordinary oxygenís two per molecule. A poisonous gas, its concentration in the upper atmosphere round the earth is nevertheless vital to shield the world below from much of the sunís ultraviolet radiation.

P

pacemaker Either the *sinoatrial node*, a bundle of nerve tissue in the heart that regulates the rhythm of the *heartbeat* by emitting electrical impulses, or a surgically implanted device that fulfils the same function if the natural mechanism malfunctions, as in heart block. Such devices consist of an insulated wire electrode attached to the surface or to the lining of the heart, leading to a battery-powered circuit.

paediatrics Branch of medicine that deals with the care and health of children from birth to maturity – physically, mentally and socially.

paedophilia Desire of an adult for sexual activity with a child. More commonly experienced by men than women, the condition is often caused by psychological and social factors that affect sexuality at adolescence. Recent increases in statistics of child sexual abuse would seem to indicate that paedophilia is far more widespread than hitherto suspected. Treatment may include *behaviour therapy* or drugs to reduce *libido*.

Paget, James (1814–1899) Celebrated British physiologist and surgeon who specialized in diseases of the bones and joints, and in *cancers*. Several disorders that he was the first to describe in detail are now called after him, including Pagetís disease of (the) bone, also known as *osteitis* deformans.

Paget's disease (bone) A disorder of bone in old age involving thickening and disorganization of bone structure, especially in the skull, long bones of the limbs, spine and pelvis. The medical name is osteitis deformans. There may be no symptoms, or the changes may cause pain or deformity; where the skull is affected the senses of sight and hearing may be impaired. Treatment is with drugs to halt bone damage.

Paget's disease (nipple) Ulceration and irritation around the nipple, representing the outward sign of an underlying form of breast cancer. Treatment is usually by surgery, sometimes radiotherapy and, in extensive cases, chemotherapy.

pain Acute sensation of anguish that may be regarded as the bodyís reaction to (and warning of) injury or internal disorder. Pain from most external injuries is focused at the site of the injury, although processed by means of the sensory nerve pathways to the brain. The identical sensation caused by some internal disorders, however, may be *referred pain*, felt as if located elsewhere. Common forms of pain are *headaches* (including *migraine*), *toothache, backache, rheumatism* and the malaise experienced sometimes in association with *premenstrual syndrome*. Most pain can be relieved by painkilling drugs (*analgesics*) or other forms of therapy.

painkilling drugs Proprietary and prescribed drugs known medically as *analgesics*.

palate Roof of the mouth. The hard palate, at the front of the mouth, consists of mucous membrane backed by bone. The soft palate, at the back, is muscle tissue covered by mucous membrane which forms the roof of the mouth from the back teeth to throat; the *uvula* hangs down from the back of it.

palliative Relieving symptoms, but not curing the root cause of them; also, a medicine that is effective in this way.

palpation Examination and diagnosis by careful feeling with the fingertips. Often employed by doctors to probe for internal swellings, palpation is also recommended to women as an easy way for them to detect any lumps in the breasts.

palpitation Abnormally fast or strong (and possibly irregular) *heartbeat* that may be an indication of *heart disease* or other disorders. Palpitations also commonly occur in healthy people, however, usually after exercise, overeating or unwise drinking. Palpitations may also result from serious anxiety or stress (in which case the symptoms may be self-replicating because the patient is constantly alarmed by them).

palsy Old word for *paralysis*.

pancreas Large, rather conical *endocrine gland* ion the upper abdomen, which lies horizontally between the *duodenum* and the spleen. One of its functions is to produce various enzymes (particularly those concerned with the digestion of fats), which drain through the pancreatic duct to the common bile duct and then to the duodenum. In addition, it contains clusters of cells that form the *islets of Langerhans*, which secrete the hormones *insulin* and *glucagon* into the blood circulation to control the levels of blood sugar (glucose). A defect in this latter function causes *diabetes* mellitus.

pancreatitis Acute or chronic inflammation of the *pancreas* (the enzyme- and insulin-producing gland lying at the back of the abdominal cavity). Symptoms of the acute condition are severe pain in the upper abdomen and shock, vomiting and high temperature. The cause may be an injury but often remains unknown, although it is associated with alcoholism and *gallstones*. Complications include cyst formation, and it may recur. Chronic pancreatitis may be symptomless or may cause similar but less severe symptoms; however, it leads on to pancreatic failure, which causes *diabetes* due to lack of insulin and *malabsorption* of foods. Diagnosis and treatment of acute pancreatitis demand urgent hospitalization. The patient must have no food or drink by mouth and requires intravenous feeding; anticholinergic drugs are given. The diabetes following from chronic pancreatitis requires treatment with insulin, and enzyme supplements are given to correct the malabsorption; a low-fat diet will have to be followed as well.

pandemic Disease more widely spread than an *epidemic*, and thus affecting large numbers of people in many countries.

pannus New tissue, with many blood vessels, that grows over existing tissue and causes damage. One site for it is on the synovial membrane or cartilage of a joint, and pannus may thus be a precursor of *rheumatoid arthritis*, because the new tissue eventually ossifies and the joint loses flexibility. Another site for pannus is on the cornea of the eye, generally following inflammation (conjunctivitis).

pantothenic acid Vitamin of the B complex, which occurs in many foods. It has an essential role in the process that converts carbohydrates to energy, and contributes to the metabolism of *fatty acids*.

Papanicolaou, George (1883–1962) Greek-born American anatomist and physician, deviser of the *Pap test* for the early detection of cervical cancer.

papilla Nipple- or mushroom-like projection from a tissue surface. There are several different kinds of papillae in the body, almost all of them tiny. The most abundant are those on the tongue that contain the *taste* buds.

papilloma Benign (non-cancerous) growth on a mucous membrane, on the skin, or in a glandular duct. Most are small and nipple-like in shape; a few are mushroom-shaped.

Pap test Test for pre-cancerous cells in the cervix (neck) of the *uterus* (womb), now more commonly called a *cervical smear test*. Its name is an abbreviation of that of its originator, George Papanicolaou.

Paracelsus, Phillipus Aureolus (1493–1541) Swiss chemist and doctor whose real name was Theophrastus Bombastus von Hohenheim. A quack in many respects, Paracelsus nevertheless considerably enlarged the contemporary medical knowledge and use of many minerals in therapy, and is thus often regarded as the father of chemistry in medicine.

paracetamol Non-prescription *analgesic* (pain-killer) used to treat minor aches and pains. It has a less irritant effect on the stomach than *aspirin*, but overdose may cause liver damage.

paraesthesia Spontaneous tingling sensations in the skin, often described as "pins and needles". It most often occurs as a temporary phenomenon due to pressure on a peripheral nerve (as in falling asleep lying on an arm) but may also follow various forms of nerve damage such as *neuritis*, or pressure on or disease in the spinal cord.

paralysis Partial or total loss of function in a muscle or a group of muscles, especially those normally under voluntary control. Such loss is generally caused by damage either to the relevant peripheral nerve or to areas of the *central nervous system* (brain and spinal cord). If a peripheral nerve is damaged, the associated muscles lose all function and gradually waste away (called flaccid paralysis). If the central nervous system alone is damaged, paralysis is restricted – some capacity may be retained (such as reflexes), and there is no wasting away. Treatment depends on diagnosis of the cause, but commonly includes *physiotherapy* or *arthrodesis* (fixing of a joint) or nerve transplants (for flaccid paralysis). Paralysis of one side of the body is called *hemiplegia*; of the lower half of the body is called *paraplegia*.

paramedical services Personnel who work in conjunction with doctors and other qualified medical staff but who themselves have no medical degree – although they may have had considerable training and experience. They include nursing staff, ambulance crews, trained first aid personnel and physiotherapists, radiographers, porters and technicians in hospitals.

paranasal sinus Type of *sinus* located in the bones of the face.

paranoia Relatively rare mental disorder that may perhaps be regarded as a precursor or symptom of other, more serious, ones. It is usually regarded as a *psychosis* characterized by an attitude towards reality that includes *delusions*, particularly ones that involve a mistaken belief of persecution.

paranormal phenomena Usually taken to mean visible, physical manifestations of some power that either emanates from a disparate (supernatural) entity or is related through some psychic link to a person present. In the latter sense, such phenomena may also include examples of the powers of the mind studied in *parapsychology*, such as *extrasensory perception* (ESP). Technically, *faith healing* and other non-medical "miracle cures" (of conditions both physical and psychological) are also paranormal phenomena.

paraplegia *Paralysis* of the body below the waist, specifically of both legs. Partial or total loss of sensation may also be involved, and the normal excretory functions may be impaired. The cause is generally damage to the spinal cord; the effects are generally irreversible.

parapsychology Study of the abilities of the mind to generate manifestations of *paranormal phenomena* or to be aware of information for which there is no immediate source (*extrasensory perception*, ESP).

parasite Organism that uses the body of another as its ordinary environment and its source of nourishment (its host). Human ectoparasites (which live on the surface of the body) include fleas, *mites* and *fungi*; endoparasites (which live inside the body) include *bacteria, viruses* and *worms*. Many cause no problems to the host; some disrupt body functions and destroy tissue; others carry or cause diseases. The study of parasites is called parasitology.

parasympathetic nervous system System of nerves which, with the *sympathetic nervous system*, comprises the *autonomic nervous system*. Distributed throughout the body from the centres in the cranial nerves of the brain and the sacral nerves leading from the spinal cord, the system effectively "calms down" the body after stress through anxiety or exertion. Among other functions it slows down the heartbeat and rate of breathing, and permits the full resumption of the normal digestive processes. It is also responsible for regulating the reduced level of neural activity during sleep and some sexual functions.

parathormone Alternative name for *parathyroid hormone*.

parathyroid glands Four *endocrine glands* located in pairs each side of the *thyroid gland* in the neck. They monitor the calcium level in the blood – if the level falls, they release *parathormone*. Malfunctioning of the glands so as to produce too little parathormone (hypoparathyroidism) is relatively rare; excessive secretion of the hormone (*hyperparathyroidism*), however, may occur for no evident reason.

parathyroid hormone A hormone secreted by the *parathyroid glands*, located within or close to the *thyroid* gland in the front of the neck. Its release or retention regulates the level of calcium in the blood, so maintaining the calcium-phosphate balance between the blood and the tissues (especially the bones). Too much parathyroid hormone causes calcium to be withdrawn from the bones into the blood; too little leads to lowered blood calcium levels, which may cause *tetany* (muscle spasms) – pharmaceutical preparations of the hormone are available to treat this condition.

paratyphoid Form of *typhoid fever* caused by infection with *Salmonella paratyphi A, B* or *C*. It is generally contracted in areas of poor sanitation by consuming contaminated food or drink. Symptoms include a rash, high fever, slow heartbeat and abdominal pain; pneumonia is a possible complication. Treatment is generally with the drug chloramphenicol unless test cultures prove bacterial resistance to it. Vaccines are available against paratyphoid A and B.

Paré, Ambroise (1510–1590) French military surgeon whose experience in caring for the wounded in battle led to notable improvements in contemporary medical practice. Because of his surgical skill, he was made court physician to the kings of France, and is now considered father of modern surgery.

parenchyma Active part of an organ, as opposed to structural tissue (stroma).

paresis Muscle weakness caused by nerve damage, a lesser form of *paralysis*.

paresthesia American spelling of *paraesthesia*.

parietal Forming the containing surface of a body cavity. The parietal bones thus form the dome and sides of the skull, and the parietal pleura is the outer membranous structure that surrounds each lung.

parkinsonism Symptoms of *Parkinson's disease* when caused by some other disorder, such as *encephalitis* or a brain tumour, or by poisoning with certain drugs or chemicals.

Parkinson's disease Disorder that affects the *basal ganglia* of the brain (involved with controlling movements), producing distressing physical symptoms but rarely interfering with mental processes. There is a deficiency in the *neurotransmitter* dopamine (one of the chemicals that enables nerve transmission). Symptoms include tremors in the limbs (particularly when at rest), lack of facial expression, a monotonous voice, increasingly stooped posture and a shuffling gait. The disease most commonly affects middle-aged or elderly people. The cause of the degeneration in parts of the brain in Parkinsonís disease is not known, although similar symptoms (parkinsonism) may be provoked by certain drugs or diseases. There is no cure, although symptoms may be relieved to some extent by various antiparkinsonian drugs (such as levodopa).

parotid glands Two triangular *salivary glands*, each located behind the upper back corner of the mouth, in front of the ear.

parotitis Inflammation of the *parotid glands*. Most commonly the result of the viral infection *mumps* (infectious parotitis), although it may also be caused by other viral or bacterial infections in the salivary apparatus or the mouth in general.

paroxysm Common term for a spasm or convulsion, but medically also an attack or sudden increase in severity of the symptoms of a disorder.

parturition Medical name for *childbirth*.

Pasteur, Louis (1822–1895) French chemist and microbiologist whose work was of inestimable value to both science and industry. Having demonstrated once and for all that micro-organisms could cause fermentation or disease, Pasteur was responsible for the discovery and general use of several important vaccines and for the sterilization process now known as *pasteurization*.

pasteurization Sterilization process applied to a liquid food, especially milk and wine, that involves heating it to a particular temperature for a specific length of time (to destroy bacteria), followed by rapid cooling.

patch test Test for *allergens* in which small amounts of potentially allergenic substances are applied to the skin (or to minor scratches in the skin surface) to see if an allergic reaction takes place. Such reactions, generally of swelling and redness, may take up to three days to occur.

patella Medical name for the kneecap, a disc of bone that protects and supports the front of the knee joint, held in position by the tendon of the quadriceps femoris muscle in the upper leg.

paternity test Test to determine who is the father of a child, by which the "genetic fingerprints" of groups of genes in cells taken from both child and presumed father are compared. Combinations in the composition of genetic material are unique in every individual, whose genes are naturally derived half from one parent, half from the other. Even a small percentage of matching genetic material thus discloses relationship. Until recently, paternity tests relied on a similar comparison of *blood groups*, and were competent to determine only who might, and who could not, be the father of the child in dispute – not who was.

pathogen Micro-organism (commonly called a germ) or substance that by its presence in the body causes disease.

pathology Study of the effects on the body of diseases and disorders, in order to understand how they arise and how they may be treated. A specialist in this discipline is a pathologist, who may investigate samples of the tissues and body fluids of living people or dead ones (in a *post mortem* examination or autopsy).

patient Anyone receiving any form of medical care.

Pavlov, Ivan (1849–1936) Russian physiologist and researcher into the circulation of the blood and the digestive processes. It was for the latter that he was awarded a Nobel Prize in 1904, and through his continued investigations into the subject later devised and published his influential ideas concerning *conditioned reflexes*.

pectoral Pertaining to the chest. The term is also used to refer to any of the chest muscles.

pediatrics American spelling of paediatrics.

pediculosis Infestation with lice – medically only lice of the genus *Pediculus*, but by extension also with the crab louse, *Phthirus pubis* – which cause intense itching and skin lesions through scratching. There are two types of *Pediculus* louse: one attacks the scalp, the other the body; *Phthirus pubis* infests pubic hair. All may be eliminated by means of various powders or chemicals.

pedophilia American spelling of paedophilia.

peduncle Any of several fibrous bands connecting two parts of the brain, or any thin, stem-like connecting process.

pellagra Deficiency disease caused by lack of the vitamin B *niacin* (nicotinic acid) or the amino acid *tryptophan*, from which niacin is normally synthesized. The condition may occur with cirrhosis of the liver (perhaps through alcoholism), with a severe gastric disorder, or where maize (corn) forms the staple diet. Symptoms are serious: nausea, vomiting, a sore mouth and red tongue, scaly discoloration of the skin on the neck, chest and hands, and depression. Treatment is with vitamin supplements.

pelvic inflammatory disease (PID) Inflammation of the reproductive organs – the *uterus* (womb), *ovaries* and *Fallopian tubes* (the tubes that connect the ovaries with the womb) – in a woman. It follows from infection spreading from elsewhere in the pelvis, such as *Chlamydia* infection of the vagina, other *sexually transmitted diseases* and even *appendicitis*; it may also occasionally spread via the blood, such as from *tuberculosis*. In the *acute* form it may cause abdominal pain, although there may be no symptoms. If not treated with antibiotics it can become *chronic* (long-term) and lead to blockage of the Fallopian tubes and subsequent *infertility* or *ectopic pregnancy*; surgery may then be needed.

pelvis Funnel-shaped structure. In the body the best known pelvis is the strong, wide combination of six bones that takes the weight of the spinal column and head, and transfers it to the legs. This pelvis is in two halves: each comprises a pubis, an ischium and an ilium; the halves join at the front (pubic symphysis) and back (at the sacrum), and the whole contains and protects the contents of the lower abdomen (viscera and internal sex organs). A womanís pelvis is comparatively wider than a manís, to provide a wide enough canal for childbirth. Another pelvis is the funnel-shaped structure in the kidneys, which collects urine and ducts it into the ureter to be passed to the bladder.

pemphigus Name for any of a number of skin diseases characterized by a blistery rash; the blisters are large and filled with clear fluid. There are several types of pemphigus: some are caused by infection, others may be disorders of the *immune response*. No cure is known, although the symptoms may be relieved by drugs.

Penfield, Wilder Graves (1891–1976) American neurologist and surgeon who made significant discoveries about the way in which memory is stored in the brain. Searching for the location and make-up of permanent memory, and experimenting with epileptic patients, he learned that the brainís "card-index file" of memories is situated in the temporal region.

penicillin Antibiotic drug originally derived from a *Penicillium* mould but now made synthetically. The first of the *antibiotics*, it remains valuable, effective against many bacteria and some other kinds of infection – although not against viruses. The effect of the drug is to prevent the rebuilding of the cellular wall of the bacterium while it is multiplying. In modified form, "semi-synthetic" penicillin is effective against a wider range of organisms, and against most of those that have developed resistance against the basic form (penicillin G). All penicillins can produce allergic reactions; moreover, patients allergic to one type are allergic to all.

penis External tubular organ in the lower abdomen of a male that has two functions: to discharge *urine* from the *bladder* via the urethra and, when erect (when its internal sponge-like tissue is engorged with blood) through sexual excitement, to ejaculate *semen* at *orgasm*. Erection facilitates *sexual intercourse*; inability to gain or maintain an erection is known as *impotence*; and the medical condition in which erection is persistent is *priapism*. The skin covering the penis is extremely flexible, expanding as the penis erects, and contracting at other times. The foreskin (*prepuce*) covering the sensitive tip of the organ – the glans penis – is sometimes removed for traditional or medical reasons (*circumcision*).

pepsin Enzyme secreted in the stomach that initiates protein digestion by breaking down protein molecules into smaller nitrogenous compounds called peptones, which are soluble in water. Pepsin itself is formed by the action of hydrochloric acid (in digestive juice) on another stomach secretion called pepsinogen.

peptic ulcer Area of erosion in the lining (mucosa) of the stomach (gastric ulcer), in the first part of the *duodenum* (duodenal ulcer), the *jejunum* (jejunal ulcer) or, rarely, in the *oesophagus* (oesophageal ulcer). The immediate cause is the action of the combination of *pepsin* and hydrochloric acid, which are naturally present, either in concentration or upon a particularly weak spot in the lining. What might cause such concentration or weakness – and the observed relationship with anxiety or other forms of stress – is not fully understood, although aspirin, anti-inflammatory drugs and corticosteroids may predispose to the erosion. Duodenal and gastric ulcers have also been linked with the presence of a bacterium called *Helicobacter pylori*. The main symptom is pain, sometimes linked to eating, especially after consuming alcohol, aspirin, and certain foods, or sometimes provoked by hunger. There may also be nausea and sometimes vomiting. Complications include bleeding, obstruction and perforation, the latter being a medical emergency. Symptoms may be relieved by antacids. Various drugs are used to promote ulcer-healing and, where helicobacter infection is suspected, combination therapy with antibiotics is used to eradicate it as well. Occasionally surgery may be required, and is vital to treat severe complications such as haemorrhaging or *perforation* (rupture).

peptide Compound made up of two or more amino acids linked by special chemical bonds (peptic bonds). Molecules comprising chains of amino acids linked by such bonds – such as protein molecules – are known as polypeptides.

perception Subjective awareness: what the mind makes of the information given it by the senses.

percussion Method of external examination by which an experienced doctor can determine the size, location and consistency of some of the patientís internal structures. The method is simply to tap a finger placed on the suspect site (generally on the chest) with the fingers of the other hand, and to interpret the resultant sound (*auscultation*) and vibration.

perforation Hole or gap created in a normally continuous tissue. Occasionally made for medical reasons, as in the fenestration operation to make a hole in the eardrum to drain fluid from the inner ear in patients with *otitis* media, its unexpected occurrence is generally more serious. It is potentially dangerous if the perforation allows the contents of an organ to leak elsewhere (as with perforated ulcers in the intestine). Treatment, often urgent, is usually by surgery.

perfusion Passing of a specific fluid through one or more blood vessels to specific body tissues. For example, blood perfuses through the tissues to the lungs; *cytotoxic drugs* may be perfused through a catheter to an artery near the site of a cancer so that treatment is concentrated locally.

pericarditis Inflammation of the sac of membranous material that surrounds the heart (the *pericardium*). Acute or chronic, it may be caused by various disorders – such as rheumatoid arthritis, uraemia, certain infections, and cancer – or occur on its own. Symptoms are pain, fever, breathlessness and fast heartbeat; treatment depends on the cause, but often includes pain-killing drugs (*analgesics*).

pericardium Double-layered membranous sac that surrounds the heart. Between the outer, fibrous layer and the softer inner one (which is attached to the outer wall of the heart) is a small space filled with friction-reducing fluid.

perinatal Of the period from the sixth month of pregnancy to one month after childbirth.

perineum Surface area of the body between what is commonly called the groin – fibrous tissue covering the lower edge of the pubis bone of the pelvis – and the *anus*. In women this includes the external *genitalia*; in men it comprises the area from behind the *scrotum* to the anus.

period Common term for the time at which a woman undergoes *menstruation*.

periodontitis Inflammation of the tissues that attach the teeth to the jaw – not just of the gums (*gingivitis*), but also of the membranous ligament around the roots and the hard material that cements the roots in their sockets. It stems from plaque deposits on teeth due to imperfect cleaning, but some people are predisposed to it. Chronic periodontitis causes gaps between gums and teeth, and loss of some fibrous and bony material that would otherwise support the teeth; often there is tooth loss. The condition is common in older people. Cleaning of the teeth by a dentist may help prevent progression in the early stages. Later, more complicated dental procedures may be needed.

periosteum Thin but strong double-layer of connective tissue that covers the bones, except at joints. The outer layer is well supplied with nerves and blood vessels; the inner one is more cellular. The periosteum provides attachment points for ligaments, tendons and muscles, and is essential to healing after fractures.

peripheral nervous system Every part of the bodyís nervous system that is not part of the brain or spinal cord (*central nervous system*). Whereas the central nervous system might be said to act to control and interpret, the peripheral nervous system may be said to provide most of the information (through the senses and sensory nerves) and direct (through the motor nerves) the bodyís ordinary physical functions.

peristalsis Involuntary contractions of the rings of muscles forming the outside of the intestines (and some other tubes in the body such as the oesophagus), which squeeze the contents along in waves. The effect is achieved by the action of a longitudinal muscle link with the latitudinal rings.

peritoneal dialysis Method of internal renal *dialysis* (taking over the normal functions of the kidney) for patients with kidney failure, using the *peritoneum* (the membrane lining the abdominal cavity) as the membrane through which blood is filtered. It is only when, for whatever reason, the use of an *artificial kidney* (kidney machine) is not suitable, since there is a relatively high risk of complications. Treatment may, however, offer greater patient mobility (see *continuous ambulatory peritoneal dialysis*).

peritoneum Membrane that lines the interior abdominal wall and encloses, protects and (as the *mesentery*) supports the organs of the abdomen, leaving in between the peritoneal cavity. Glands in the membrane secrete fluid that lubricates the abdominal organs.

peritonitis Inflammation of the *peritoneum* (the membranes lining the abdominal cavity), which may be due to infection spread from elsewhere in the body via the bloodstream (primary peritonitis) or to *perforation* (rupture) of an abdominal organ, such as may occur in *peptic ulcer* or with an inflamed *appendix* (secondary peritonitis). In both cases symptoms are abdominal pain and fever with, in the case of primary peritonitis, weight loss and fluid accumulation in the abdomen. In the case of secondary peritonitis, contamination by digestive juices or bacteria causes sudden, severe pain and shock. In primary peritonitis treatment is sometimes possible with antibiotics and intravenous fluids, along with treatment of the cause. In secondary peritonitis surgery to repair the perforation is usually urgently required.

pernicious anaemia Deficiency disorder caused by the bodyís failure to absorb vitamin B_{12} (cyanobalamin) or, rarely, through lack of the vitamin in the diet. Normally an "intrinsic factor" secreted by the stomach catalyses the absorption of vitamin B_{12}; if the factor is absent, however, the result is the onset of *anaemia*, with further symptoms of lassitude, difficulties in the sense of balance, and a sore tongue. In severe cases neurological symptoms may also occur. Treatment is by vitamin B_{12} injections, which may need to be continued for life in the case of intrinsic factor deficiency.

persona Somebodyís *personality* as perceived by others. It may be genuine, or false and adopted and projected as a means of dealing with the world.

personality Character of a person, including any particularly good or bad traits, as perceived by others; it may be very different from the *persona* projected by the person, and different again from his or her true (but unapparent) nature.

personality disorders A group of psychological conditions in which there is long-standing behavioural maladjustment, characterized particularly by total self-involvement and indifference to the reactions of others. It is distressing to the individual and/or to others associated with him or her, and generally persists over time, although some characters improve with maturity. Types of disordered personalities include the obsessive (meticulous, concerned with small details, continually checking, stubborn and insecure), the avoidant (anxious, self-conscious, oversensitive to real or imagined criticism or rejection), borderline (easily bored, unable to find fulfilment, unstable, exploitive and manipulative, indulging in intense but disordered relationships), dyssocial (callous, uncaring and irresponsible, unable to form relationships, disregarding authority, aggressive and often violent), hysterical (requiring constant emotional attention, shallow, unstable, superficial and manipulative), paranoid (suspicious, distrustful, hostile and self-important) and schizoid (solitary, introspective and emotionally withdrawn, unable to respond to others or to derive pleasure from experiences, sometimes living in a fantasy world and prone to eccentric behaviour – may progress to *schizophrenia*). Treatment may involve psychotherapy, although personality disorders are often claimed to be untreatable.

perspiration Another word for sweat and sweating. Part of the bodyís mechanism for controlling body temperature (under the direction of the *autonomic nervous system*), the sweat glands deep in the skin secrete their mixture of salty water, lactic acid, urea and potassium salts through ducts to the surface at the *pores*, in order to cool the body by its evaporation. Heat is of course the main triggering factor, but another is acceleration of the heartbeat, as occurs with fear – hence a "cold sweat". If perspiration is not removed by washing the skin (and clothes), it may be broken down into unpleasant smelling products by bacteria, causing the condition called bromhidrosis. Excessive sweating is termed hyperhidrosis, and may be a symptom of a disorder (such as *hyperthyroidism*).

pertussis Medical name for *whooping cough*.

Perutz, Max (1914–) British biochemist who specialized in the structural analysis of proteins through X-ray diffraction crystallography. It was for his work in elucidating the structure of *haemoglobin* and other globular proteins that he received a Nobel Prize in 1962.

perversion Deviation from what is normal. The term is most commonly used of an adultís desire for sexual activity and sexual pleasure in a way that is regarded as abnormal. What is considered normal of course differs between societies (and from time to time in history) – although such deviations as *bestiality, exhibitionism, fetishism, masochism*, and *sadism*, all for sexual pleasure, are fairly universally regarded as perversions. Counselling, psychotherapy and psychiatry (aversion therapy) may help some people control their perversion; society may require others to undergo drug treatment to reduce sexual drive.

pessary Drug-containing soluble capsule which, when inserted into the vagina, dissolves allowing the drug to act both concentratedly and locally. The term is also used for a metal or plastic device fitted into the vagina to support the womb (uterus) after a *prolapse*. See also *suppository*.

PET Abbreviation of *positron emission tomography*.

petit mal Lesser form of *epilepsy*. The term refers specifically to a brief loss of consciousness, without collapse.

pH Scale that indicates acidity or alkalinity. A pH of 7 represents neutral; below 7 is acid, above is alkaline. The term refers to the concentration of hydrogen ions in a solution.

phagocyte Cell in the body that is able to engulf and so destroy smaller, potentially harmful organisms and cells identified as "foreign". Part of the bodyís defence mechanism against infection or poisoning, phagocytes include several types of *leukocytes* (such as *histiocytes* and *neutrophils*) and *macrophages*. The engulfing process is called phagocytosis.

phalanges Bones of the toes and fingers; the big toes and thumbs have two phalanges, all other digits have three. The singular is phalanx.

phallus Another word for *penis*, especially (non-medically) as a symbol of masculinity or potency; also, technically, the incompletely formed penis of a male embryo.

phantom limb Limb, or part of a limb, that has been amputated but still feels as if it is there, possibly because of neural stimulation in the remaining portions of the nerves that used to transmit information from the amputated part. Such sensations usually fade after a few months, although some may persist for ever.

pharmaceutical Of or for a pharmacy (made to be dispensed by a *pharmacist*), or to do with drugs and other medicines.

pharmacist Somebody who is qualified and, in most countries, legally authorized to stock and dispense medicines. Pharmacists work at pharmacies either within dispensing chemistsí shops or hospital departments, health clinics or other medical institutions.

pharmacology Study of drugs and their properties, and of how they may best be used in medical practice.

pharmacopoeia Authorized book listing drugs, their properties, variants and alternatives, and detailing dosages, legal requirements and other information of use to somebody who prescribes or deals with medicinal drugs.

pharyngitis Inflammation of the *pharynx* (the part of the throat connecting the mouth and nose with the gullet and airway), involving a sore throat and difficulty or pain in swallowing. A common disorder, often associated with *tonsillitis*, the common *cold* or other infections of the throat, mouth or nose, it may also follow heavy cigarette smoking or alcohol consumption. Those affected should drink plenty of fluids and avoid cold or smoky atmospheres. Other treatment depends on the cause, if determined, and may include antibiotics if bacterial infection is suspected.

pharynx What is normally thought of as the throat and the "back of the nose", the passage for food from the mouth to the oesophagus (oropharynx), and for air from the nasal passages (nasopharynx) to the larynx (laryngopharynx) and windpipe (trachea). Connected with it are the organs of the mouth, the external organs of the nose, the Eustachian tubes (leading to the inner ear), the larynx and the oesophagus.

phenol Chemical name for carbolic acid, a disinfectant used from very early after the discovery (by Joseph *Lister*) of the importance of *asepsis*. Although poisonous if swallowed, phenol and its compounds are still used in lotions and ointments to clean and disinfect wounds and infections.

phenotype Perceived combination of characteristics in an individual that derive from the effects of his or her genes together with, and in reaction to, the effects of environment.

phenylketonuria (PKU) Inherited congenital inability of the body to metabolize phenylalanine, a substance present in many foods. The result is a gradual build-up in the body of phenylalanine which, if undetected, leads to mental retardation, convulsions and other severe symptoms. However, in most countries all newborn babies are blood-tested for PKU, and those found to have the disorder are put on a phenylalanine-free diet at least until physical maturity.

phimosis Tightness of the *prepuce* (foreskin) over the glans penis so that it cannot be pulled back over it. The condition tends to promote infection and so is usually resolved by *circumcision*.

phlebitis Inflammation of the tubular wall of a *vein*, most often in the legs in association with *varicose veins*. Other causes include damage to the vein wall, infection, *autoimmune disease* (in which the immune system attacks the bodyís own tissues), or even cancer elsewhere in the body. Symptoms are pain, tenderness and local redness in the skin. Clotting of the blood at the site (thrombophlebitis) may follow. Treatment is with elasticated support of the area, and anti-inflammatory and analgesic drugs. (Anticoagulants are not used when inflammation is present.)

phlegm Non-medical term for mucus formed and secreted in the nose, throat, bronchi or lungs. It originally represented one of the four *humours*.

phobia Form of *neurosis* in which there is an unreasonable but overpowering terror of a specific event, thing or environment. Avoidance of the subject of the phobia may cause considerable difficulties to the patientís way of life. Treatment is through psychiatric counselling and *desensitization* techniques; drugs may also sometimes be used.

phonation Use of the voice to produce recognizable consonants and vowels.

phonetics Study, in linguistics, of *phonation* and its relation to the learning of language (or languages).

photomicrograph Photograph of an object subject taken using a microscope.

photophobia Inability to tolerate bright light. The condition may be a symptom of eye infection, migraine, measles, rubella or, more seriously, of meningitis. It may occasionally be natural (as with some albinos) or induced (through certain drugs that dilate the pupils of the eye, or as one of the withdrawal symptoms following excessive alcohol consumption).

photosensitivity Abnormal sensitivity of the skin to sunlight, sometimes producing a severe reaction in which the skin "bubbles" and blisters. Barrier creams are generally ineffective as protection, and for many people the best solution is to avoid sunlight as much as possible.

phrenic nerve Nerve that originates in three centres of the spinal cord, travels between the heart and lungs, and (under the direction of the brain) supplies and controls the diaphragm, causing it regularly to contract and so facilitating *respiration* (breathing).

phrenology Discredited Victorian method of determining a personís character by "reading" the conformation of undulations on his or her skull. Behind it was the notion that the habitual use of specific areas of the brain inside the skull was somehow also represented externally.

physician Medical practitioner authorized, after qualifying, to diagnose and treat patients. In Britain the term excludes surgeons; elsewhere the description is all-encompassing.

physiology Study of how living organisms, and organs within them, function. The work of a physiologist may thus be regarded as an extension of that of an anatomist (who is concerned with the structures of organisms and their organs).

physiotherapy Use of external, physical methods to treat disorders of internal mechanisms. Many such treatments include activity performed by the patient under the direction of the physiotherapist (such as remedial exercises and training). Others are directly manipulative (such as massage) or involve the use of heat, infra-red or ultraviolet radiation, electricity or ultrasound.

pia mater Membrane containing nerve tissue and many tiny blood vessels that completely surrounds and is attached to the outside of the brain and the spinal cord. The innermost of the three *meninges*, it is lubricated by *cerebrospinal fluid* between it and the *arachnoid membrane*.

Piaget, Jean (1896–1980) Swiss psychologist and biologist who specialized in research into the cognitive development of children. He identified three main stages in the way children learn to think. At first they merely collect information; then logical use is made of the information collected; finally, around adolescence, formal reasoning based on that process of logic is possible.

pica Urge to eat something that is not food and that even may be harmful – such as soil, coal, grass or fabric. Relatively common in very young children, it occurs occasionally in patients with mineral deficiencies (including some pregnant women) and in those who are mentally disturbed.

pigmentation Presence in the body – particularly in or visible through the skin – of substances conferring colour (pigments). Skin pigments include *melanin*, the protective dark pigment found also in the iris of the eyes; pigments in the blood, commonly visible through the skin, include *haemoglobin* and sometimes *bile* pigments (as in *jaundice*). Some types of poisoning also produce characteristic changes in pigmentation.

piles Common term for *haemorrhoids*.

pill Solid, compacted form of a drug in the shape of a disc or spheroid, sometimes also coated to make it easier to swallow. Except for some pills intended to be sucked in the mouth or dissolved under the tongue, most pills achieve their effect as the drug is absorbed through the stomach or intestines. Some, which would be destroyed by digestive juices, have an enteric coating which protects them until they enter the intestines.

Pill, the (contraceptive) Common name for an oral contraceptive. See *contraception*.

pimple Small site of inflammation on the skin, containing *pus*. Pimples can occur anywhere on the skin surface, and the most common cause is local infection of blocked *pores*. A rash of them on the face, back or chest is generally known as *acne*.

pineal gland Small, round gland on a stalk of tissue at the back of the brain, between the two cerebral hemispheres, also known as the epiphysis. It produces the hormone *melatonin*, secretion of which responds to light-dark cycles and regulates *circadian rhythms* (daily variations driven by the internal "body clock"). The gland calcifies (takes up calcium) with increasing age, providing a useful marker on skull X-rays.

pink eye Form of *conjunctivitis* caused by bacterial or viral infection (as opposed to irritants, allergy or parasitic infestation).

pinna Ear flap (also called an auricle), the external structure of the *ear* consisting of a lining of cartilage covered by skin.

pituitary gland Also called the hypophysis, a small round structure on a stalk of tissue attached to the hypothalamus at the base of the brain between the two cerebral hemispheres. Protected by a cavity in the bone at the centre of the skull, the pituitary gland has two lobes, both of which produce vital *hormones*. The anterior (front) lobe produces hormones that stimulate other endocrine glands into secreting their own respective hormones: *thyroid-stimulating hormone* (TSH); *adrenocorticotropic hormone* (ACTH), which regulates secretion of corticosteroids from the adrenal glands; *luteinizing hormone* (LH) and *follicle-stimulating hormone* (FSH); *prolactin*, which promotes lactation; and *growth hormone* (somatotropin). The posterior (rear) lobe produces *vasopressin*, which controls water excretion, and *oxytocin*, which stimulates contractions of the uterus in childbirth. The production and secretion of all these hormones is monitored and regulated by areas of the *hypothalamus*.

PKU Abbreviation of *phenylketonuria*.

placebo Pharmacologically inert substance prepared in the form of a drug (as a *pill*, lotion or medicine). It is used either as a control by which to monitor the effect among a number of patients of a particular (real) drug, or is prescribed to satisfy the demands of a more-or-less hypochondriacal patient. Often, the mental reassurance of being given medication is in itself beneficial to a patient; this is known as the placebo effect.

placenta Disc-shaped organ attached to the lining of the *uterus* (womb) during pregnancy, to which the *amnion* surrounding the embryo or foetus is linked via the *umbilical cord*. It represents the interface between mother and child. The motherís blood circulation in the uterine wall exchanges its nutrients for the waste products in the childís circulation just the other side of a thin film of cells in the placenta; no direct contact between circulations takes place. From early in the pregnancy the placenta acts as a gland, secreting *hormones* that sustain the pregnancy: *chorionic gonadotropin, oestrogens* and *progesterone*. The placenta reaches peak efficiency in the 34th week of pregnancy, after which it gradually degenerates. Once the baby is born (the second stage of labour), the final or third stage is the expulsion of the placenta, which forms a major part of the *afterbirth*.

plague Rare but dangerous bacterial infection transmitted by rat fleas. Bubonic plague causes headache and very high temperature, followed by acute swelling of the lymph nodes (into *buboes*). Bleeding under the skin, causing black patches (hence the name "black death"), may then ulcerate. Bacteria entering the lungs cause pneumonic plague, in which sputum coughed up is directly infectious. If untreated, both of these conditions are fatal. Modern treatment – with streptomycin, chloramphenicol or tetracyclines – is highly successful.

plantar reflex *Reflex* movement to arch the foot when a finger or a blunt object is drawn along the outside of the sole from heel towards little toe. This reflex is unusual in that it is not present until the age of 1 to 2 years; before that time, the reflex movement to the same stimulus is to stretch the foot, extending the big toe upwards (the *Babinski reflex*) – a sign in later life of damage to the central nervous system.

plantar wart Another name for *verruca*.

plaque Hard, rough surface consisting of bacteria and organic debris that accumulates on *teeth* that are not cleaned regularly or vigorously enough. Where dental hygiene is particularly poor, *gingivitis* (inflammation of the gums) and *tooth decay* (dental caries) may result. The term is used also for a raised area of *scar tissue*.

plasma Clear, slightly yellowish fluid that is the solution in which *erythrocytes* (red cells) and *leuklocytes* (white cells) of the *blood* are in suspension. Consisting mostly of water, and containing proteins, sugars, various mineral salts, carbon dioxide and nitrogenous wastes, plasma may be used in transfusion to treat shock or protein loss. Unlike *serum*, it retains the constituents essential to the blood clotting mechanism.

plasmapheresis Method of increasing the number of blood cells in the *blood count*. A quantity of blood is drawn from a patient and given time for the cells to gravitate and settle. The *plasma* is then skimmed off, and the remaining concentrate reinfused into the patient. Used to enhance the performance of athletes, the process is known as blood doping.

plaster Type of small bandage consisting of a strip of medicated gauze (that covers a wound) surrounded by adhesive material (to stick the dressing to the skin around the wound). Plasters are made in many shapes and sizes.

plaster of Paris Quick-drying calcium sulphate (gypsum) cement fine enough for making detailed models of *dentition* from wax impressions (plaster models), and strong enough to use in bandages to form a rigid casing to protect and immobilize a fractured limb (plaster cast).

plastic surgery Surgery performed to repair damage or deformity in the skin and other surface tissues. It includes such operations as to replace or conceal scar tissue, or to reconstruct a hare lip or cleft palate. Closely associated is *cosmetic surgery*.

platelet Part of the *clotting* mechanism of the blood. Also called thrombocytes, platelets are tiny discs that aggregate together in the presence of a wound, so causing *coagulation*.

pleura Double-layered membranous sac that covers each lung. The inner layer (visceral pleura) is attached to the outside of the lung; the outer (parietal pleura) is partly attached to the chest wall. In the small space between them is a lubricating fluid.

pleurisy Inflammation of the *pleura* (the membranes around the lungs), usually caused by infection (such as pneumonia) but sometimes by structural damage (such as injury or cancer). Symptoms are pain and shallow breathing. The fluid between the pleural layers loses consistency, and the resultant friction between the layers causes a characteristic "pleural rub" heard through a stethoscope. Treatment corresponds to the cause, but commonly includes painkilling drugs (analgesics) and antibiotics.

pleurodynia Pain in the muscles of the chest wall, but not related to the lungs (although a patient may not be able to distinguish this). It may be a symptom of local rheumatism.

plexus Local network of blood vessels, lymph vessels or nerve fibres.

PMS Abbreviation of *premenstrual syndrome*.

PMT Abbreviation of premenstrual tension. See *premenstrual syndrome*.

pneumoconiosis Any lung disorder caused by the inhalation of fine dust over a period of time. Such disorders are now becoming rarer as a result of great improvements in working conditions; formerly, diseases such as *asbestosis* and *silicosis* were the scourge of the industrial labour forces.

pneumonia Inflammation of one or more lobes of the *lung*. The most common cause is bacterial infection – although both viral and fungal forms occur – and the primary effect is to clog the *alveoli* (air sacs) with *pus* so that no exchange of gases takes place and the lung becomes solid. Symptoms depend on how far the infection spreads. Lobar pneumonia affects one or more lobes of a lung; bronchopneumonia affects also the *bronchioles* (smaller airways) and the *bronchi* (major airways). The patient suffers chest pain, high temperature and rapid heartbeat and coughs up thick (often reddish) *sputum*. *Pleurisy* may occur, and the patient may become confused. Treatment depends on identification of the infective organism, but generally includes *antibiotics* and therapies to assist breathing.

pneumothorax Presence of air between the membranes of the *pleura*. Usually caused by a penetrating injury – although sometimes occurring spontaneously – the condition is potentially dangerous in that at best breathing is seriously impaired, at worst the lung may collapse. If the injury is such as to allow air in but not out (tension pneumothorax), both lungs may collapse and the patient die. In any case, emergency treatment and hospitalization are required to evacuate the air and restore lung function.

podiatry American term for *chiropody*.

poison Substance that when taken into the body (by swallowing and ingesting, by inhaling or absorption, or by injection) damages or destroys tissue, or hinders or prevents the functioning of body mechanisms. Poison injected into the body by reptiles or arachnids (including scorpions) is called *venom*. Specific types of poison have specific *antidotes*: in cases of poisoning it is therefore essential to know what poison has been taken.

poliomyelitis Infectious disease of the central nervous system caused by any of three polio viruses. Most common in hot climates, it particularly affects residents in areas of poor sanitation. Initial symptoms are high temperature, sore throat and headaches, with gastric upset. Most patients recover with no further problems; others, however, go on to experience muscle stiffness, and some then proceed to weakness and *paralysis* of one or more muscles that may be permanent (hence the alternative name of the disease: infantile paralysis). There is no treatment other than drugs to relieve the symptoms; modern oral or injected vaccines provide good protection.

pollen Powdery organic material produced by male plants that for humans is a common *allergen*, especially in respect of *hay fever* and *asthma*.

pollen count Number of grains of *pollen* recorded in one cubic metre of atmosphere at ground level, used as a measure for warning local *hay fever* and *asthma* sufferers of when atmospheric conditions may be particularly problematic for them.

pollution Soiling or destruction by fouling of potentially useful resources, such as air, or water in rivers and oceans. By extension it is also the effects of one individualís carelessness or activity (for example, noise) on others.

polyarteritis Simultaneous inflammation of a number of arteries, usually giving symptoms only of a moderately high temperature. Polyarteritis nodosa is an autoimmune disease involving arterial inflammation. Its symptoms include abdominal pain, asthmatic attacks, muscular aches and internal swelling. Polyarteritis nodosa may be fatal. Treatment is by suppressing the inflammation with steroids.

polycythaemia Condition of increased concentration of red blood cells in the *blood*, either through a corresponding decrease in the normal quantity of the suspension medium (*plasma*), or through an increase in the volume of the red cells themselves. The latter may occur spontaneously, as a disorder of the bone marrow, or as a side-effect of some respiratory and circulatory disorders or certain cancers. Treatment is by drawing off blood or, in some forms, by *radiotherapy*.

polygraph Machine that records on a chart several pulses simultaneously, as perhaps of a vein, an artery, and the heart, and possibly the conductivity of the skin (to detect sweating). Linked with a tape-recorder, the apparatus has been used as a lie-detector.

polyp Growth on a mucous membrane, particularly in the nose, ear, uterus (womb) or lower bowel. Generally benign (noncancerous) and with a short stalk, polyps in the colon and large intestine (especially if multiple) may however become cancerous. Polyps that cause obstruction or are malignant may be removed by surgery or cauterization.

polypeptide Type of *peptide* molecule.

polysaccharide Form of *carbohydrate* that is the main source of energy in almost all human diets. It is a complex sugar (consisting of many molecules of simple sugars) which in the body is used either as a means of storing energy (as *glycogen*) or to form connective tissue. *Starch* is a polysaccharide.

polyunsaturated fats Fats, occurring in vegetable oils, that consist of molecules that have many carbon atoms linked by double or triple bonds. They are "unsaturated" because theoretically they could absorb additional hydrogen atoms, and are considered to be dietetically more healthy than "saturated" fats (such as those in animal products).

polyuria Frequent and copious urination, caused either by continuous drinking or by disorders such as (either form of) *diabetes* or *nephritis*.

pompholyx Form of recurrent *eczema* that affects the hands and feet. Irritating blisters form under the skin surface and remain until the skin over them eventually peels. Creams containing *corticosteroids* help to reduce the itching and thus the likelihood of secondary infection through scratching.

pons Link between two parts of an organ – particularly the band of nerve fibres across the front of the *brainstem* (the pons Varolii) that connects the *medulla oblongata* and the *thalamus*.

population People of an area, considered statistically in *demography*.

pore Tiny aperture in the skin representing the top of a sweat duct. See *perspiration*.

pornography Material in the form of literature, pictures, taped sound or film that is intended to stimulate erotically but that may have a corrupting influence on its audience. The definition relies on a consensus of opinion, but most people would find portrayals of *perversion* or of children as participants of sexual activity pornographic.

porphyria Hereditary condition in which the nitrogenous compounds (porphyrins) that normally combine with iron and the protein globin to produce the red blood pigment *haemoglobin* are formed in excess. It affects either the liver or the composition of the blood as formed in the blood marrow. Symptoms include discoloration of the urine (to pink or purple) when it is left to stand, skin blistering with sensitivity to sunlight, *neuritis*, abdominal pain – and, usually, mental disturbance. It is possible to prevent attacks to some degree by avoiding conditions or substances known to be triggering factors – such as sunlight or certain drugs. Treatment otherwise is to relieve symptoms.

portal vein Also called the hepatic portal vein, a short but important *vein* into which blood containing the products of digestion drains from the stomach, the large and small intestines, and the rectum, together with blood from the pancreas and the spleen. It is channelled to the *liver*, from where metabolic products proceed to where they are most useful and the remaining blood goes on to the heart for reoxygenation via the lungs.

portwine stain Reddish-purple *birthmark* (naevus) that is the result of an extra-large network of blood vessels below the skin formed before birth. In some areas of the body it constitutes an increased risk of injury. Cosmetic surgery to conceal a portwine stain is seldom successful.

positron emission tomography (PET) Scanning technique that detects low-level radioactive emissions from a mildly radioactive sugar, previously injected into the body, as it is metabolized. Used to scan for brain damage or to obtain an image of the chest or abdominal cavity, PET is completely harmless to the patient and provides a full cross-sectional picture on a screen.

post mortem Full-scale examination of a dead body to determine the cause of death and the presence of any contributory factor; also called an autopsy.

postnasal drip Continuous flow of mucus from the back of the nose down the *pharynx*. Medical diagnosis of the cause is advisable.

posture Bearing of the body, with particular reference to the straightness of the back when standing or sitting, or to the positioning of limbs. A patientís posture may convey diagnostic information to a doctor. Poor posture may give rise to various muscular and skeletal disorders.

potency In medicine, the ability of a man to gain an *erection* and so have *sexual intercourse*; or the strength and effectiveness of a drug or treatment.

potentiation Increase in *potency*. Alcohol, for example, potentiates the effects of some drugs, notably *hypnotics* and *tranquillizers*.

Pott, Percivall (1713–1788) English surgeon who was the first to identify a *carcinogen* (soot, leading to cancer of the scrotum in chimney sweeps), and is thus regarded as the father of cancer research.

Pott's disease Spinal *tuberculosis* that causes degeneration and disintegration of a *vertebra*, resulting in a hunchback-like curvature and, possibly, compression of the spinal cord. It may be contracted by drinking infected milk. Treatment includes antitubercular drugs and physiotherapy.

Pott's fracture Serious *fracture* and *dislocation* at the ankle, involving a break in one or both of the bones of the lower leg (tibia and fibula), a tearing of the ankle ligaments, and an outward displacement of the foot. Treatment is to set the broken bones and immobilize the joint for six weeks or longer.

poultice Dressing that holds hot, wet material to the skin surface to soften the skin (as to get a boil to come to a head), promote improved circulation, reduce inflammation or relieve pain. Also called fomentation, the process is generally not very successful.

pox Any infectious disease causing pus-filled skin eruptions which, before modern treatment methods, left pock(mark)s – hence the name. Such diseases include *chickenpox* or *smallpox* and also *syphilis*.

precocity Evidence of a stage of (usually intellectual or sexual) development being reached at an age much earlier than average.

pre-eclampsia Potentially dangerous condition in which high blood pressure develops during *pregnancy*, often with oedema of the ankles and sometimes the hands, and sometimes protein in the urine. It is also known as pregnancy-induced hypertension. Treatment with rest and drugs to reduce blood pressure is important to halt the development of *toxaemia of pregnancy* and *eclampsia* (fits and possibly coma, which can be fatal to the mother or baby).

pregnancy Period lasting on average 40 weeks (266 days from conception or 280 days from the first day of the last menstrual period) during which a woman has a developing baby in her *uterus* (womb). Pregnancy begins with *conception*, when an *ovum* is fertilized by a *sperm*. From that tiny beginning an embryo develops within the womb, nourished through the *placenta* and protected within the *amnion*. Through the succeeding months the *foetus* grows until, at due time, the baby is born. For the mother the first signs of pregnancy may be the absence of a menstrual *period*, the onset of *morning sickness* and an urge to urinate more frequently. Pregnancy can be confirmed by a pregnancy test (which detects a particular hormone in the womanís urine), and further tests (*amniocentesis* after the 16th week, *chorionic villus sampling* or ultrasonic scanning) may be made if desired. It is important that a mother stays healthy – infections constitute a risk to the child – and takes only prescribed drugs (avoiding excess alcohol and cigarette smoking). The motherís body changes: the breasts enlarge and become tender, and the womb expands with the baby; there may be backache, headaches and constipation. In later stages the baby may be felt moving around. At about the 36th week, *lightening* occurs, a sign that *labour* is about four weeks away. Finally, contractions of the womb lead to *childbirth*.

pregnancy test Any of the many tests to determine whether or not a woman is pregnant. Some proprietary tests for use at home depend on detection of the presence of the hormone *chorionic gonadotropin* in the urine. Most tests are not reliable, however, if carried out earlier than a week after the first missed menstrual *period*.

premature birth Birth of a baby before the full term of *pregnancy* (generally before the 37th week), or of one that weighs less than 5 pounds (2,5000 grams). Premature babies are cared for in Special Care Baby Units (SCBUs). Small babies born at or near full term are described as "small for dates".

premedication Dual-purpose combination of drugs administered to a patient a short time before he or she is taken to an operating theatre for surgery. Mildly sedative, it also dries up the secretions of the mouth and air passages.

premenstrual syndrome Collection of symptoms that may be experienced by a woman before the onset of each menstrual period. Such symptoms include tiredness, headaches, abdominal tenderness or bloating and clumsiness. Some women also report depression or irascibility and emotional unease (premenstrual tension). Symptoms usually disappear as soon as menstruation starts. Treatment may involve *diuretic* drugs (to stimulate urination) and preparations of *progesterone* (one of the "female" hormones); *antidepressants* may also be prescribed. Many women gain relief from supplements of essential fatty acids, such as evening primrose oil.

premolar In an adultís *dentition*, either of the two teeth between the *canines* and the *molars*. (A childís milk or deciduous teeth do not include any premolars.)

prepatellar bursitis Inflammation of the *bursa* at the front of the kneecap (patella); a common name for it is housemaidís knee. Treatment is with anti-inflammatory drugs. See *bursitis*.

prepuce Foreskin, consisting of the short, tapering, cylindrical length of skin that covers the head (glans) of the *penis*. Glands on its inner surface lubricate the sensitive glans penis underlying it. Removal of the prepuce is *circumcision*. The term is used also for a fold of skin surrounding the *clitoris*.

presbyopia Longsightedness as an effect of aging, involving difficulty in focusing the eyes on nearby objects because the *lens* has become less flexible. The defect can be corrected by wearing *glasses* or *contact lenses*.

prescription Written instruction from a doctor to a pharmacist or chemist for the preparation and supply of specified medication to a named patient.

presenile dementia General name for *dementia* with characteristics of senility occurring before old age. See *Alzheimer's disease*.

presentation Position of a baby just before, and during, childbirth. The headís appearance first from the birth canal signals a "cephalic presentation"; buttocks first a "breech presentation"; the side first, a "transverse presentation". Any presentation other than cephalic may require obstetric intervention.

pressure sore Another name for a *bedsore*.

prevalence Statistical measure of the overall burden of a particular condition within a population, defined as the total number of those affected, or the total episodes of sickness, either at one time (point prevalence) or over a specified time period, such as one year (period prevalence), for instanc,e the number of people with heart disease per 1,000 of the population (or population at risk, such as adults, or males) per year. See also *Incidence*.

preventive medicine Care and treatment designed to prevent diseases and disorders, as opposed to treating and curing them. ınethods include the improvement and sanitizing of environments, social education, and immunization programmes (using vaccines and antiserums).

priapism Condition in which the penis is persistently erect, in the absence of sexual stimulus. Sometimes painful, priapism results from an obstruction in the veins of the erectile tissue that prevents the blood from flowing away. The obstruction may be caused by a clot or by local infection. Treatment may involve *anticoagulants* or surgery to remove the obstruction.

prickly heat Medical name miliaria, a fine irritant rash that appears on the face, neck, chest and back in very hot weather. It involves mild inflammation of the skin around sweat glands. Some relief may be gained by treatment with calamine lotion or antipruritics.

primigravida Medical description of a woman pregnant for the first time.

proctology Study of the functions, diseases and disorders of the *anus* and *rectum*.

prodromal Indicating that major symptoms are shortly to become evident. The term is used for an initial and perhaps minor symptom or an *aura*.

professional negligence Legal term describing a mistake made by a doctor in the course of treating a patient. An act either of omission or of commission, its results – as implied by this term – are usually serious, and the doctor in question may have to attend a court hearing to answer for it. Doctors found guilty of professional negligence may be struck off the register of practitioners.

progesterone Steroid sex *hormone* that regulates the *menstrual cycle* in women. Secreted by the *corpus luteum* in an *ovary*, it controls the cyclic changes of the uterine lining (endometrium). If fertilization occurs, it sustains the uterus, prevents further ova being released by the ovaries and stimulates tissues in the breasts. During pregnancy it is also produced by the *placenta*. In men a very small amount is secreted by the testes. Progesterone is one of a class of hormones called progestogens, a number of which are now synthesized and used in oral *contraception* or to treat *premenstrual syndrome* (PMS), menstrual disorders or a threatened *abortion*.

prognosis Forecast by a doctor of the future course and outcome of a patientís disease or disorder in view of the patientís general health and capacities, and in view of the treatment prescribed.

prokaryote Cell or organism with no nucleus (or that appears to have no nucleus). Bacteria are prokaryotes. The word is also spelled procaryote.

prolactin *Hormone* produced and secreted by the anterior (front) part of the *pituitary gland* which, in the presence of other hormones, stimulates the production of milk in a motherís breasts after childbirth. In non-pregnant women, prolactin stimulates the *corpus luteum* in an *ovary* to produce the sex hormone *progesterone*.

prolapse Displacement downwards of an organ, commonly to protrude through a body orifice. It is generally caused by weakness in the tissues meant to support the displaced organ. Prolapse (usually only partial) of the *vagina*, *uterus* (womb) or *rectum* are the most common forms. A prolapsed uterus, if untreated, may ultimately protrude between the labia. Symptoms include abdominal pain and urinary incontinence; treatment is usually by surgery. Prolapse of the rectum causes the membranous rectal lining to protrude from the anus; treatment is to replace the prolapsed tissue and, if this proves impermanent, surgery. Prolapsed *haemorrhoids* are more common than a prolapsed rectum.

prolapsed invertebral disc Common name slipped disc, displacement of the central softer portion of the fibrous discs between the *vertebrae*. The pulpy material may pass through the harder layer and cause pressure on adjacent nerves and ligaments, or may protrude through into the spinal canal. Either way, there is pain and muscle weakness; if nerves are affected there may be paralysis and possibly even loss of sensation. The displacement can occur anywhere from the neck down to the lumbar region. Treatment generally includes *analgesics*, spinal manipulation and *antirheumatics*, and may also involve a period of immobilization or a surgical operation.

prolapsed uterus Displacement of the *uterus* (womb) downwards, due to weakness in its supporting tissues, most often due to damage during childbirth. Sometimes the cervix (the neck of the womb) is visible at the vaginal opening; in severe cases, the uterus and vagina may protrude externally through the labia. Symptoms include pain, discomfort and urinary difficulties or incontinence. Treatment usually requires surgery to replace the uterus and shorten stretched supporting ligaments, where necessary also repairing the vagina or narrowing the opening.

prophylactic Any means of preventing a disease or disorder. By extension the term is also used to mean a precautionary measure, and thus occasionally to refer to a contraceptive device such as a condom.

proprietary drugs Drugs marketed under brand names, not the approved or generic names.

proprioceptors Nerve endings that sense changes or events within the body. They transmit information to the brain about muscular activity or joint position, particularly in relation to co-ordinated voluntary movements but also when the body is at rest or to trigger reflex actions. Sometimes they are called proprioreceptors.

prostaglandins Any of a group of *hormone*-like fatty-acid derivatives that occur in many tissues of the body and have multiple functions; many have been synthesized for use as drugs. Natural functions include promoting smooth muscle contraction, such as *peristalsis*; causing uterine contractions (as drugs they are used to induce labour or abortion); involvement in *inflammation* (aspirin and *non-steroidal anti-inflammatory drugs* act to ease inflammation by blocking prostaglandins); and in mucus production in the stomach (so prostaglandins are also used to treat *peptic ulcer*).

prostate cancer A malignant tumour (carcinoma) of the *prostate gland* (the gland lying below the bladder that secretes part of the seminal fluid) in men. It becomes increasingly common with age, is generally slow-growing and may cause no symptoms, although as it enlarges it can cause difficulties with urination and may spread, especially to bone, causing pain. The tumour is dependent on male hormones (androgens) for its growth. Because the tumour increases secretion of an enzyme called prostate specific antigen (PSA), a screening test for PSA in the blood is possible. Treatment, where a tumour is discovered, may include hormone therapy to reduce androgen stimulation, or surgery to remove the tumour or, sometimes, the testicles (to stop hormone secretion).

prostate gland Gland in men that lies beneath the bladder, enclosing the junction of the *urethra* and the *vas deferens*. During *ejaculation* it secretes a fluid which forms part of the *semen* and which is thought to provide a viable environment for *sperm*. The prostate swells with age and may eventually constrict the flow of urine; treatment is usually by surgery to remove part or all of the gland.

prostatectomy Surgical operation to remove the *prostate gland.*

prostatitis Inflammation of the *prostate gland* (the gland lying below the bladder that secretes part of the seminal fluid) in men, often due to bacterial infection. In acute prostatitis symptoms are pain in the groin, and sometimes on urination, with a high temperature. In chronic prostatitis difficulty in urination may progress to complete obstruction, with inability to urinate at all. Acute prostatitis is usually treated with antibiotics. In chronic prostatitis surgery may be necessary to remove the prostate (prostatectomy).

prosthesis Device that in appearance or in function (or in both) replaces a part of the body that is defective or missing. *Dentures*, *hearing aids*, and artificial *pacemakers* are prostheses, but the term is more commonly used of an artificial limb or eye.

protein Organic substance composed of complex molecules comprising chains of *amino acids* linked by *peptide* bonds. Proteins form part of every cell in the tissues of the body, and are also constituents of *hormones*, *enzymes* and other essential secretions. Most are synthesized, according to requirements, by the liver from the products of digestion transported there in the blood (especially *globulin* and *albumin*). A few that cannot be synthesized are taken as entire molecules from digested food. Any excess protein formed may be converted into energy-providing glucose, or energy-storing fat.

proteinuria Presence of protein in the urine, also called *albuminuria*.

protoplasm Basic material that forms the components of a cell, ultimately consisting of *protein* and water; it includes the *cytoplasm* and the *nucleus*.

protozoan Any of a multitude of various kinds of organisms consisting of a single *cell.* Some of these tiny animals live as parasites in humans and can cause diseases such as *amoebic dysentery* and *malaria*.

pruritis Medical term for *itching*.

psittacosis Disease of birds, especially parrots, which can be transmitted to human beings through inhalation or contact with the birds, their feathers or droppings, or with an infected person. It is caused by a small bacterium called *Chlamydia psittaci*, and is also known as *ornithosis*. Symptoms include fever, cough, headache and muscle pain; a pneumonia-like illness may ensue – the birds, however, often have no symptoms. Treatment is with antibiotics.

psoriasis Common noncontagious skin disease suffered by 1 or 2 in every 100 people. Symptoms are scaly oval lesions upon patches of reddened skin anywhere on – or all over – the body, but especially on the elbows, knees and scalp, often with brittle fingernails. The lesions are neither painful nor particularly irritating, but they are unsightly and may seriously interfere with patientsí lifestyles. The cause is unknown, but it runs in families and there are probably hereditary factors. Once contracted, usually in adolescence, the disease tends to peak and wane recurrently for the rest of the patientís life; periods of complete remission are seldom longer than two years. Stress, injury or prescribed drugs may trigger symptoms. Some affected individuals also develop a particular form of arthritis. Treatment is to alleviate the symptoms as far as possible, and includes ointments and creams, ultraviolet radiation, drugs related to vitamin D and, if the disease leads to psychological problems, some form of counselling. In severe cases stronger drugs including immune suppressants may be used.

psyche Mental aspect of being an individual (as opposed to the physical aspect). Also, the part of the mind studied in *parapsychology*.

psychedelic Causing a change in *perception*. The term usually refers to a drug or mental condition that produces heightened emotions and sensations, with or without *hallucinations*.

psychiatry Study of *mental disorders*, of methods by which to treat or prevent them, and of the relationship between such disorders and each patientís genetic, anatomical and social disposition. Essentially, a psychiatrist treats a *personality*. To do so, he or she may make use of any of the current forms of *psychotherapy*.

psychoanalysis School of *psychology* originated by Sigmund *Freud* and based to a considerable degree on the view that behavioural disturbances stem from a patientís repressed sexual urges during childhood and adolescence. Its classic form involves the technique of free association – verbal reaction by the patient in immediate response to words suggested by the psychoanalyst, indicating long-established associations in the patientís mind – in order to confront the patient with his or her own repressions. A variety of post-Freudian schools of psychoanalysis now dominate the field.

psychology Study of human behaviour in terms both of mental development from birth to maturity (educational psychology) and of what is not normal (as assessed in clinical psychology). There are various schools of psychology, including *gestalt psychology*, *behaviourism*, *psychoanalysis* and ethology.

psychopathy Form of personality disorder in which the patientís total indifference to all other people leads to casually antisocial acts of violence and destruction. A psychopathís self-interest may also prompt considerable cunning in order to avoid identification.

psychopharmacology Study of the drugs that effect mental processes and behaviour (such as *psychedelic* and *psychotropic drugs* and *antidepressants*), and of how they may be used in treatment.

psychosexual development Mental aspect of the processes involved in sexual maturation, paralleling the physical aspect. According to *Freud*, stages of development include an awareness of gender identity (incorporating also the imprinting of sex-role stereotyping) and orientation towards heterosexuality or homosexuality.

psychosis One of a group of serious *mental disorders* in which the patient loses contact with reality, experiencing instead an existence of *delusions* and *hallucinations*, or severely disturbed thought processes, moods or behaviour. They include *schizophrenia*, *manic-depressive illness*, various forms of *paranoia* and organic psychoses (those with evident physical cause, such as drug intoxication or metabolic derangement). Psychiatric treatment is required, sometimes with hospitalization, and usually antipsychotic drugs.

psychosomatic Relating to both mind and body, usually applied to conditions in which physical symptoms are strongly associated with mental stress of one kind or another, an obvious example being tension *headaches*. Many illnesses either arise in response to such stress or flare up during stressful periods; these include *eczema*, *asthma* and *peptic ulcers*, for example. Treatment for such conditions may be more effective if the pressure is also removed, and psychological treatments may reduce symptoms or aid recovery.

psychosurgery Surgical removal of a specific part of the brain in order to relieve severe and persistent pain or some intractable psychological disorder. The most common operation of this type is *leucotomy*. All such operations are irreversible; most have significant side-effects.

psychotherapy Psychological techniques used in *psychiatry* to treat disorders of the mind manifested as behavioural problems or *personality disorders*. Various schools of *psychology* employ their own methodologies, some requiring the patient to lie on a couch and tell all, others relying on the inter-reactions of *group therapy*. Even in the latter, however, the emphasis is always on a close relationship between therapist and individual patient, and on the patientís own personal development of self-understanding to achieve the removal of symptoms.

psychotropic drugs Drugs that affect a patientís mental disposition. Examples include *stimulants* and *depressants*.

puberty Period at the end of childhood during which boys and girls develop the *secondary sexual characteristics* and their organs of reproduction take on the adult functions. The process is regulated through the activity of the *sex hormones*. Girls tend to reach and complete the stage at an earlier age than boys. The full process of maturation – of which puberty is the initial part – is *adolescence*.

pubis Either of the two bones together making up the front half of the *pelvis*; the two meet at the symphysis. Each also forms part of the socket (*acetabulum*) for a thigh bone (*femur*). The term is also used for the skin and pubic hair covering the pubic symphysis above the external *genitalia*.

public health A branch of medicine concerned with the health needs of the population as a whole, rather than of individual patients. It considers disease trends in the community, environmental hazards, communicable diseases, health education and preventive measures, and overall planning and provision of health services. Public health measures also reflect the national interest in public well-being, embodied in Britain by certain laws and regulations concerning infectious disease control and environmental hazards.

pudenda Another term for the external *genitalia*.

puerperal fever Now rare form of *septicaemia* caused by infection of the uterus (womb) or vagina during or just after childbirth (hence the alternative names, childbirth or childbed fever). By extension the term is used of any high fever occurring at this time caused by infections elsewhere in the body. Treatment with *antibiotics* is usually quickly successful.

puerperium Period of about 40 days after *childbirth* for both mother and child. During this time, as mother and child become familiar with each other (particularly as a result of breast-feeding), the motherís womb gradually returns to its normal size; postnatal depression may set in and require medical treatment; and there is often severe fatigue. The end of the period is generally marked by an obstetric postnatal examination.

pulled muscle Common name for a tear in the fibrous tissue of a muscle, *tendon* or *ligament*, generally caused by over-exertion or unusual stress. Symptoms are sharp pain, fading to a dull ache, and stiffness. Treatment is with heat and massage, careful exercise and, possibly, *analgesics* or *anti-inflammatory* drugs.

pulmonary Relating to the *lungs*.

pulse Pumping beat of the blood circulation, as measured in an artery or vein. It varies according to age, overall health, exertion, and the condition of the *heart*, but an average rate is between 60 and 80 beats a minute. The usual location for detecting the pulse is at the radial artery, just above the wrist; another useful location is at the carotid artery in the neck. Minor irregularities in the pulse – even a missed beat – are fairly normal; other irregularities should be diagnosed by a doctor.

pupil Black centre of the *iris* of the *eye*; the hole through which light passes to reach the *retina* via the *lens*. The pupil is dilated or constricted according to how much light is available, through the action of tiny involuntary muscles in the iris.

purgative Substance that promotes *defecation*. A *laxative* is one type.

purpura Rash-like discoloration of the skin caused by haemorrhage within the skin layers. It may be caused by a leak from abnormally weak blood vessels (as may occur with some inherited disorders), a disorder in the blood *clotting* mechanism, vitamin C deficiency (scurvy), or as an aspect of certain infections. Treatment depends on the diagnosis.

pus Thickish yellow-green fluid formed at the site of an infection in localized areas, such as in abscesses or boils. It represents a mixture of live and dead *leukocytes* (white blood cells which counter the infection), fluid and debris that drains from the area of affected tissue, and bacteria.

pustule Tiny *pus*-containing blister or rash-spot on and just under the skin.

pyaemia Presence of pus in the blood, causing dangerous *septicaemia* (blood-poisoning). Usually resulting from an escape of pus from an abscess or wound, the consequence is usually a multitude of internal abscesses throughout the body. Symptoms are violent fluctuations in temperature and, frequently, *jaundice*. Treatment is urgent investigation in hospital for diagnosis, accompanied by large doses of *antibiotics*.

pyelogram X-ray picture of the *kidneys*, taken after the injection of *radio-opaque* dye either into a vein (intravenous pyelogram) or through a fine catheter passed up one or both ureters (retrograde pyelogram).

pyelonephritis Inflammation of both the renal pelvis (the funnel-shaped structure that collects urine from the *renal tubules*) and the rest of the *kidney*. Acute pyelonephritis may be caused by the spread of infection back up from the bladder or through the bloodstream. Symptoms are pain in the lower back and abdomen, high temperature with shivering, vomiting and increased frequency of urination which may be painful in passing. Treatment is with *antibiotics* and plenty to drink, but should also investigate the cause. The chronic form of the condition involves recurrent acute attacks and may eventually result in kidney failure.

pyemia Alternative spelling of *pyaemia*.

pyloric stenosis Constriction of the final part of the *stomach* (*pylorus*) up to the pyloric sphincter, the muscular valve that allows partly digested food through to the next section of the alimentary canal. Such constriction in adults may be caused by a *peptic ulcer* or tumour growth; in infants it is due to a nodule on the pyloric muscle that tends to cause symptoms around four weeks after birth. In either case, consequent obstruction to the passage of food causes persistent vomiting, especially of fluids, and possible distension of the stomach; weight loss and dehydration follows. Diagnosis may involve a *barium meal* (a special X-ray examination of the stomach) or direct vision with an *endoscope* (a fibre-optic tube passed into the stomach). Treatment depends on the cause, and may include ulcer-healing drugs or surgery.

pylorus Final part of the *stomach*, ending at the pyloric sphincter (the muscular valve which leads through into the *duodenum*).

pyorrhoea Former name for *periodontitis*.

pyrexia Medical name for *fever*.

pyridoxine Vitamin B_6. Found in many foods (including meat, eggs and cereals), it is essential for the conversion of amino acids into other protein substances within the body.

Q

Q fever Infectious disease of dairy animals that is transmitted to humans through drinking (untreated) milk, or breathing dust of dried excreta, from infected animals. It is caused by a Rickettsia micro-organism that is neither a bacterium nor a virus but resembles both. Symptoms include high temperature and shivering, aching head and muscles, chest pains and a cough. Treatment is with *antibiotics*, especially tetracycline, and is quickly successful.

quadriplegic Paralysed in all four limbs.

quadruplet One of four children born to the same mother from a single pregnancy. Still rare, the birth of quadruplets is becoming slightly more common through the use of *fertility drugs*.

quarantine Time during which a person exposed to infection is kept completely or partly isolated from others not so exposed, in order to see whether he or she does in fact develop the disease, and thus to confine its spread if he or she does. Different infections require different periods of quarantine, according to their *incubation* periods.

quartan fever Form of *malaria* in which fever attacks recur every fourth day.

quickening First experience by a pregnant woman of the movements of the *foetus* in her womb (uterus). It commonly occurs between the fourth and fifth months of *pregnancy*, although some normal pregnancies go right through to full term without it, or involve quickening in the second or third month.

quinine *Alkaloid* drug derived originally from cinchona bark and once used to prevent or treat *malaria*. Other, synthetic and less toxic drugs have superseded it in that respect, but it is still sometimes used to treat nocturnal cramp in elderly people.

quinsy Abscess in the tissue of the soft palate around the tonsils. It is usually caused by the spread of infection from *tonsillitis*. Symptoms include high temperature, unpleasant-smelling breath, and difficulty and pain in swallowing or even moving the jaw; there may also be earache. Early treatment with *antibiotics* is usually successful; surgical lancing of the abscess may otherwise be necessary. The condition may recur, and a doctor may therefore advise *tonsillectomy*.

quintuplet One of five children born to the same mother from a single pregnancy. Very rare, the birth of quintuplets now generally follows the use of *fertility drugs*.

R

rabies Also called hydrophobia, a dangerous viral infection of the nervous system caught through contact with the saliva of an infected animal (commonly a dog or fox). Symptoms may take from three weeks to a year to appear, and treatment given before they become apparent is usually successful; but once symptoms are present, recovery is unlikely. The symptoms take the form of a high temperature and depression, followed by manic excitement, violent agitation, and *spasms* of the throat that with an overproduction of saliva cause the classic "frothing at the mouth", especially if the patient attempts to drink. Death follows. Treatment before symptoms appear includes isolation of the patient and an intensive course of rabies vaccine injections. Preventive vaccination is available for travellers.

radiation Energy in the form of electromagnetic waves (*infra-red radiation*, visible light, *ultraviolet radiation, X-rays* and gamma rays), radioactivity or heat. Most forms can be either beneficial or harmful according to dosage and the duration of exposure. Some are used medically for diagnosis (X-rays, radioactivity, *PET*); others as treatment (gamma rays, ultraviolet radiation, heat).

radiation sickness Disorder caused by overexposure to radioactivity (in terms of dosage or duration of exposure). High doses within a brief period cause death through damage to the central nervous system. Lower doses may also cause death through blood and bleeding disorders following damage to the bone marrow. Low-dose exposure may cause vomiting, diarrhoea, *conjunctivitis*, hair loss, balance problems and *anaemia*; the *immune system* may be affected, as may *fertility*, and there is a considerably increased risk of later *cancer* and *leukaemia*. Immediate removal from the source of exposure is vital. In severe, acute cases there may be little that can be done other than to treat problems such as burns to minimize symptoms. In the long term, treatment may be given for specific effects, including, sometimes, bone marrow transplant.

radioactivity Emission of energy in the form of alpha, beta or gamma rays as a result of the spontaneous breakdown of the nuclei of specific chemical elements or their *isotopes*.

radiography Use of X-rays (or, technically, any form of electromagnetic radiation) to provide pictures on photographic film or a fluorescent screen of internal structures or organs for diagnosis, or to check on the progress of a treatment.

radio-immunoassay A technique that uses radioactivity to "label" constituents of body secretions in order to measure very low levels in the blood. It can be used for any substance to which *antibodies* can be formed. A known test amount of the substance is labelled with a radioactive "tracer" and allowed to bind with previously prepared antibodies to the substance. The biological sample is then mixed with this preparation and the extent to which it displaces the radioactively labelled material – which represents the level in the sample – is measured. The technique is employed particularly to assay (determine) hormone levels in the blood.

radio-isotope Radioactive *isotope* of a chemical element. Artificial radio-isotopes are formed by bombarding the elements with beams of neutrons. They are used extensively in *radiotherapy* and as the means of "labelling" in *radio-immunoassay*.

radiology Branch of medicine concerned with the use of *radiation* and *radioactivity*.

radiopaque Describing something that absorbs ("stops") *X-rays*, and thus appears white on an X-ray photograph (which is a negative). Iodine and barium salts are the major constituents of radiopaque dyes and "meals" injected or swallowed to help diagnose internal conditions using X-rays.

radiotherapy Treatment of a disease or disorder using *radiation* (including *X-rays* and *radioactivity*). Methods include controlled doses of X-rays and the surgical implantation or injection of radioactive material, for example to treat *cancer* or *rodent ulcers*.

radius Thicker but slightly shorter of the two bones of the forearm, stretching from the elbow (where it articulates with the *humerus*) to the *wrist* (where it articulates with the other forearm bone, the *ulna*, and with the bones of the carpus) on the thumb side. Rotation of the arm and hand is effected by the radius revolving around and across the ulna, supported by the comparatively fixed elbow joint.

Ramón y Cajal, Santiago (1852–1934) Spanish specialist in *histology* whose research into the structure of the brain led to considerable advances in anatomical knowledge of the central nervous system. It was his work which established that the unit element of the nervous system is the nerve cell (neurone). A prolific writer, he was awarded the Nobel Prize in 1906.

rapid eye movement (REM) Descriptive of the periods during *sleep* when the eyes jerk from side to side under closed eyelids, and *dreaming* is in progress. It occurs during "shallow" sleep, between intervals of deep sleep (in which no dreaming takes place).

rash Patch of skin temporarily subject to eruptions or pustules; the effect is an overall reddening of the skin within an area, often accompanied by itching. It is caused by local or general infection, or by an allergy.

Raynaud's disease Spasm of blood vessels in the fingers, and sometimes other extremities, on exposure to cold, causing numbness, tingling, pain and colour changes. Typically, the fingertips turn white, then blue, then red on rewarming. The cause of Raynaudís disease itself is uncertain, but similar symptoms – Raynaudís phenomenon – can occur due to *arteriosclerosis* and various other diseases, certain drugs, or prolonged use of vibrating tools. Very rarely the damage from restricted blood supply is so severe that gangrene ensures. Patients are advised to keep the hands (and feet, ears, or nose if affected) warm whenever possible. Sometimes drugs are given to relieve the blood vessel spasm, and in severe cases surgery to sever the nerves that control the response may be undertaken.

reaction Response of the body or the mind to stimulus. In medicine, the term is used for abnormal sensitivity, as with *allergies* or (in psychology) defence mechanisms.

receptor Sensory nerve cell that conveys information to the brain relating to any of the organs of the *sensory system* (including the sense of balance) or to an internal organ in which there are sensory nerve endings (*proprioceptors*). The term is used also of the specific chemical part of a cell (particularly of the blood) that "locks on" to the equivalent parts of other substances it encounters, such as drugs, hormones or antigens.

recessive In genetics, ineffective in the presence of an equivalent *gene* that has *dominance*. A personís inherited characteristics or "traits" result from the pairing of genes received from the parents. The characteristic defined by a recessive gene is inherited only if the gene it is paired with (its allele) is also recessive.

rectum Final length of the *alimentary canal*, the section of the large *intestine* continuing from the colon and ending in the *anus*. The rectum holds the *faeces* before *defecation*. About half of it lies within the protection of the *pelvis* and the *peritoneum*; the lower section is supported by the muscular tissues of the pelvic floor.

recurrent laryngeal nerve Nerve that controls the muscles of the *vocal cords*. Its fibres, branching from the *vagus nerve* in the neck, travel with the vagus nerve right down into the upper chest before looping back up to the *larynx*. Various other nerves and blood vessels that loop back on themselves are also called recurrent.

red blood cell Blood cell known also as an *erythrocyte*.

reduction In medicine, the putting back of a broken, displaced or dislocated organ in its normal position.

referred pain *Pain* that is felt at a site on or in the body that is not the location of the injury or disorder causing it. The referral of the pain to the second location is the result of the brainís inability to distinguish exactly between specific sites on certain nerve pathways that involve the spinal cord. For example, pressure on a spinal nerve by a prolapsed ("slipped") intervertebral disc may cause intense referred pain in the leg. Other classic referrals include: from the elbow to the little finger; from the diaphragm, gall bladder or liver to the shoulder; and from the lower jaw to upper.

reflex Sudden involuntary response caused by a sensory stimulus. Requiring an emergency reaction to be taken too quickly even for the brain to be directly involved, the sensory information travels only as far as the spinal cord, where motor nerves are immediately actuated. Most reflexes are linked to crude survival necessities – the pain of a pinprick or a cigarette burn will move a personís finger faster than there is time for the brain to command it. For some reflexes, however, there is little apparent justification, such as the *plantar reflex* or the reflex at the knee joint that may be used diagnostically. Some reflex actions can be induced by repetition (*conditioned reflexes*).

reflex arc Neural circuit used in a *reflex* action. Basically it comprises the sensory nerve ending, the nerve pathway to the local spinal nerve, referral to the grey matter of the spinal cord, and the nerve pathway back to take a motor message again via the spinal nerve to the local muscle or gland.

regimen Course of prescribed therapy, perhaps regulating diet and exercise, and perhaps including drug treatment.

regurgitation Bringing up of food or liquid from the stomach at least as far as the throat or mouth. Nausea is not experienced, and the cause is usually *indigestion* through over-hasty consumption. The term is used also by extension for the backward flow of blood in a heart with damaged *heart valves*, possibly resulting in heart failure.

rehabilitation Restoration of a patient to as full a normal life as possible. It may involve encouraging a patient to make the best use of treatments and therapies (including exercise and *prostheses*) with a view to stabilizing a condition that is less than normal, or it may be meant to give a patient social independence following institutionalized treatment.

reinforcement In psychology, any thing or event that confirms an idea, attitude, or (particularly) *conditioned reflex* in a patientís mind. It is often in the form of something that is perceived as a reward (positive reinforcement) or a punishment (negative reinforcement).

rejection In transplant therapy, the progressive destruction of transplanted cells by the *immune system* of a patient who has received a transplant. Such rejection may sometimes be prevented by the use of *immunosuppressive drugs*, at the expense of the patientís resulting vulnerability to infection. In psychology, the refusal of affection where affection might normally be accepted is also called rejection.

rejuvenation Making young again. Recent histology studies have discovered much about the nature of aging, but have yet to find any mechanism for reversing the process altogether. The term is occasionally used to describe a patient, or part of a patient, that has been rendered "as good as new" by treatment.

relapse Return of worsening symptoms after a *remission*.

relapsing fever Recurrent set of feverish symptoms caused by a bacterial disorder carried by lice or ticks. The symptoms last for up to ten days, and the intervals between them are between 24 and 48 hours. They include high temperature with shivering, rapid heartbeat, headaches and pain in the joints, vomiting and a skin rash. From the second attack there may also be *jaundice*. The fever may cause delirium. Treatment is with *antibiotics*, although untreated the symptoms gradually cease.

relaxant Abbreviated form of the term *muscle relaxant*.

relaxation State of rest – either of the whole body, or of individual muscles when not contracting.

REM Abbreviation of *rapid eye movement*.

remedy Means of treating or compensating for a disorder.

remission Period in which symptoms are distinctly reduced or disappear altogether, although they are expected sometime to return.

renal colic Acute kidney pain usually caused by a *kidney stone*.

renal dialysis *Dialysis* by or for the kidneys, often used to describe the function of a kidney machine (see *artificial kidney*).

renal insufficiency Condition in which a damaged or diseased *kidney* cannot cope with the normal flow of blood (including water, salts and impurities) through it. Fluids accumulate in the tissues (oedema), with waste products that may eventually cause poisoning. The condition may be caused by any of many *kidney diseases*, but especially by long-term high blood pressure (*hypertension*), a stone in the ureter, hormonal disturbance, or cancer. Treatment depends on the diagnosis – but must be carried out as an emergency.

renal tubule Very narrow tube that is an element of a nephron, the filtering unit within the *kidney* that discriminates between useful, viable substances for return to the body and waste products for excreting via the ureter and bladder as urine. The renal tubules also regulate *electrolyte* balance.

renin Kidney hormone secreted in response to stress and directly causing a local increase in blood pressure by contracting the blood vessels. It is part of the mechanism for maintaining normal blood pressure within the *kidney*.

rennin Stomach enzyme that coagulates milk in order that its proteins remain in the stomach (for digestion) as long as possible. For this reason, it is important in the digestive system of babies.

repetitive strain injury (RSI) Pain and inability to use part of a limb, due to prolonged overuse, generally involving repeated performance of a particular movement, or sometimes pressure application or weight-bearing on a specific area. It classically affects word-processor operators, and may necessitate a change of job. Treatment may be with rest, strapping to reduce the load on the affected joint, and pain-killers or anti-inflammatory drugs.

replacement surgery Surgical fitting of a synthetic, grafted or transplanted organ or part of an organ to replace one defective or missing. Common examples of such surgery include hip and knee replacements, and various *shunts* that replace diseased veins or arteries. The term does not normally include the fitting of *prostheses*, which are working substitutes, not replacements; some authorities suggest that it should not include transplants either.

repression In psychology (particularly *psychoanalysis*) the deliberate elimination from consciousness of memories and associations that are unpleasant. Such memories and associations, even when successfully repressed, may later manifest themselves in behavioural *neuroses*. One specific aim of a psychoanalyst is to oblige a patient to confront his or her own repressions.

respiration Breathing, the process by which air is drawn through the mouth and nose, down the *trachea* (windpipe) to the bronchial passages and the *lungs*, where in tiny sacs called *alveoli* its oxygen is exchanged for the carbon dioxide in the "exhausted" blood in the narrow alveolar capillaries. The oxygen is then carried in the blood to the *heart*, from where it is pumped to tissues throughout the body. The carbon dioxide is in the meantime exhaled. The whole mechanism is regulated by a respiratory centre in the brain, by the pumping of the heart, but above all by the movement of the *diaphragm* beneath the lungs which is essential to the physical action of drawing breath in and breathing it out. The generation of energy in cells by the oxidation of glucose is known as (aerobic) tissue respiration.

respirator Machine that sustains a patientís breathing either by enclosing the torso and applying alternate pressure and suction to force air in and out of the body (an "iron lung" or cuirass respirator), or by blowing and sucking air along a tube down the patientís trachea (windpipe). A *heart-lung machine* may also be called a respirator, although it has equally important additional functions. The term is used also for a portable breathing apparatus worn to prevent the inhalation of smoke or poisonous gases.

respiratory arrest Cessation of breathing, whether or not accompanied by *cardiac arrest*. Emergency treatment must first diagnose whether an obstruction in the throat or trachea (windpipe) is the cause; any such obstruction must be removed before *artificial respiration* techniques are attempted. In the case of simultaneous cardiac arrest, *cardiopulmonary resuscitation* (CPR) techniques should be immediately started.

respiratory centre Area within the *medulla oblongata* of the *brainstem* responsible for regulating *respiration.*

respiratory disorders Disorders that cause difficulties in breathing. Most are disorders of the *lungs* (including the bronchi and the bronchioles, and the surrounding *pleura*) and *trachea* (windpipe), and are infections – such as *bronchitis*, tracheitis, *pleurisy* or *pneumonia*. Others include *asthma*, damage or disease in the mouth or throat (such as *abscess* or *tonsillitis*), to the ribs, *diaphragm*, or very occasionally to the *respiratory centre* in the brain.

respiratory distress syndrome Set of symptoms caused in a newborn baby if its *lungs* fail to expand fully. It occurs particularly in babies born prematurely or as the second of twins, or whose mothers have *diabetes* mellitus. It causes rapid, shallow breathing resulting from the failure of the *alveolae* to expand, plus the presence of mucus in the lungs. Treatment involves administering oxygen and intravenous fluids; a *respirator* is sometimes used.

respiratory failure Dysfunction of the lungs that results in the failure of oxygenation.

rest Inactivity, a period of relaxation that may be therapeutic (especially, for example, with fractures and inflammations).

resuscitation Bringing back to consciousness, following *respiratory failure, cardiac arrest*, or both. Respiratory failure demands emergency *artificial respiration* once it has been determined that obstruction of the air passages is not the cause; cardiac arrest demands emergency heart massage; both together require *cardiopulmonary resuscitation* (CPR) techniques.

retardation Delay or slowing, often used to mean psychomotor retardation, the general slowing of movement and thought processes seen in patients with *depression*. It is also used as an abbreviated form of the term *"mental retardation"*.

reticular activating system Network of nerve pathways within the *brain* that is responsible for the degree of consciousness at any moment – from full alertness and awareness of the senses, to the relatively unconscious ticking over of sleep.

reticulo-endothelial system Part of the *immune system* made up of cells (phagocytes) that engulf others identified as "foreign" (including worn-out blood cells) in order to neutralize or destroy them.

retina Light-sensitive surface of rod-shaped and cone-shaped cells that lines the inside of the back of the eyeball. Cone cells detect colours, and rod cells light intensity. Sensory information from the network of nerves in the retina is transmitted along the *optic nerve* to the brain and experienced as *vision*. See also *detached retina*.

retractor Surgical instrument that holds a muscle or a flap of skin aside during an operation.

Reye's syndrome A rare disorder with brain inflammation (*encephalitis*) and liver failure, occurring in children. The cause is unknown but it often follows a viral infection and has been linked with the use of aspirin, so it is now recommended that aspirin should never be given to children under the age of 12 without medical supervision. Hospitalization with intensive supervision and drug treatment is usually needed.

Rhesus factor Group of antigens, the presence or absence of which in the blood is used as one way of distinguishing between *blood groups*. Most people have the factor and are thus

Rhesus (Rh) positive; about 1 person in 7 is Rh negative. The *immune system* of Rh negative people who come into close contact with Rh positive blood (perhaps by transfusion or, in a pregnant woman, contact with the babyís blood in the placenta) immediately creates antibodies to the "foreign" blood. If there is then a second occasion of close contact, *rejection* will occur. Such *Rh factor incompatibility* occurs during pregnancy involving a second child with Rh positive blood and an Rh negative mother.

rheumatic fever Complex response by the body to an attack of *tonsillitis* or similar bacterial infection of the upper respiratory tract. Rheumatic fever may also affect the valves of the heart, causing rheumatic heart disease. Symptoms other than those of the original infection include pain and stiffness of the joints (rheumatism), which swell and redden (arthritis) in sequence, and a skin rash with outbreaks of tender nodules. If the heart is affected, there is chest pain and breathlessness. Sometimes there is also inflammation of the brain tissue, resulting in *chorea* (writhing movements of the head and limbs). Despite the severity of these symptoms, lasting effects are uncommon, although heart valve damage may persist. Treatment is with aspirin and rest; a course of *antibiotics* should be continued for some years afterwards.

rheumatoid arthritis Form of *arthritis* that results in deformity through degeneration of the synovial membrane lining the joints, later affecting the bones, tendons and surrounding tissues. The disorder tends to attack joints symmetrically across the body, especially in the fingers, wrists and feet. It is an *autoimmune* condition (meaning that the immune system starts to attack the bodyís own tissues) and is more common is women than men. Most patients possess a characteristic rheumatoid factor revealed by blood tests. The disease often eventually burns itself out, but the deformity remains. Treatment is with a variety of disease-modifying drugs and should be commenced early to avoid deformity. Anti-inflammatory drugs, rest and physiotherapy can also help to alleviate the pain, swelling and stiffness, and *corticosteroids* are sometimes used in flare-ups. Surgery is sometimes required and may include joint replacements.

Rh factor incompatibility Difference between the *Rhesus factors* of a pregnant woman and an unborn child who is not her first. Such incompatibility may result in *haemolytic disease of the newborn*.

rheumatic fever Complex response by the body to an attack of *tonsillitis* or similar bacterial infection of the upper respiratory tract. Rheumatic fever may also affect the valves of the heart, causing rheumatic heart disease. Symptoms other than those of the original infection include pain and stiffness of the joints (rheumatism), which swell and redden (arthritis) in sequence, and a skin rash with outbreaks of tender nodules. If the heart is affected, there is chest pain and breathlessness. Sometimes there is also inflammation of the brain tissue, resulting in *chorea*. Despite the severity of these symptoms, lasting effects are uncommon although heart valve damage may persist. Treatment is with aspirin and rest; a succeeding course of *antibiotics* should be continued for some years afterwards.

rheumatism Any condition that results in pain and stiffness in the muscles and joints.

rheumatoid arthritis Form of *arthritis* that results in deformity of the joints through degeneration of bones, tendons and surrounding tissues; the disorder tends to attack joints symmetrically across the body. The cause is unknown. Treatment is to alleviate the pain, swelling and stiffness as much as possible, and generally includes aspirin or an equivalent, rest, and physiotherapy. Surgery is sometimes resorted to, perhaps to fit a man-made replacement joint. Steroid drugs may be needed to treat acute episodes.

rheumatology Study of the operation, diseases and disorders of joints and their associated tissues.

rhinitis Inflammation of the membranous lining of the nasal cavities, accompanied by a watery discharge (running nose). Causes may be infection (such as a cold), allergy (such as hay fever), or an unknown factor. Treatment depends on the cause.

rhinophyma Form of *rosacea* of the skin on the nose; it causes a reddening and a swelling of the area that may become large and misshapen. Treatment early enough with *antibiotics* may be effective; cosmetic surgery may otherwise be recommended.

rhinoplasty Surgery to correct the shape of the nose.

rhodopsin Pigment within the light-sensitive *rods* of the *retina* of the eye.

rhythm In electroencephalography, regular oscillations in electrical potential corresponding, for example, to alpha waves, beta waves and delta waves generated in the brain. In gynaecology, the cycle between a womanís *menstrual periods* that comprises a time of infertility, one of fertility, and another of infertility. By extension, the method of *contraception* that involves avoiding intercourse at the fertile part of the cycle is called the "rhythm method".

riboflavin (riboflavine) Vitamin B_2. Soluble in water, the vitamin is found in many foods (including meat, green vegetables and milk) and it is important to tissue respiration and general metabolism. Deficiency of riboflavin causes skin and eye disorders.

ribonucleic acid (RNA) Substance found in cells that is important to the synthesis of *proteins*. This process is effected and monitored at the direction of the other cellular acid, *deoxyribonucleic acid* (DNA), by means of varying the sequence of amino acids that make up the RNA molecule chain. The code for the desired sequence, as specified by the DNA in the cell nucleus, is relayed from the nucleus by messenger RNA and acted upon by transfer RNA at a *ribosome*, the site within a cell at which protein synthesis actually takes place.

ribosome Particle occurring singly or as one of a cluster within a cell which represents the site of, and a major contributor to, *protein* synthesis. The process takes place under the direction of *deoxyribonucleic acid* (DNA) as relayed by *ribonucleic acid* (RNA).

ribs Bones that form the protective cage of the chest, enclosing the lungs and the heart, circling horizontally from the spine at the back towards the sternum (breastbone) at the front. There are twelve pairs: the top seven are connected directly, through cartilage, to the sternum; the next three each connect through cartilage to the next rib above; and the last two are attached only to the vertebrae, "floating" at the front but supported by the muscles between the ribs (intercostal muscles).

rickets Condition in children produced by deficiency of vitamin D (*calciferol*), resulting in turn in a calcium deficiency that leads to poor formation or deformity of the bones. Vitamin D deficiency is usually caused either by an inadequate diet or by lack of sunlight, and is particularly common among Asian children. In occasional cases, rickets is due to kidney disease with increased mineral loss in urine. Treatment is to make up the deficiency with vitamin D and calcium supplements. If treatment is early enough, any deformity tends to disappear.

rigor Symptom consisting of shivering and chills as the body temperature rises rapidly. It is common as the initial sign of acute infection. Rigor mortis, on the other hand, is the stiffness that affects a corpse between 3 and about 24 hours after death, as chemical changes affect muscular tissues.

ringworm Fungal infection (tinea) of areas of soft skin, including those covered by hair. Common symptoms are small, red, scaly rings of itching raised tissue. There are several infective organisms, however. One attacks the pubic region; another causes ringworm of the scalp or beard; and another causes *athlete's foot* (which can lead to *cellulitis*). All forms are highly contagious. Treatment is usually with creams, ointments or powders, or with *antifungal* drugs.

RNA Abbreviation of *ribonucleic acid.*

rodent ulcer Form of *cancer* that attacks the soft skin of the face – the tip of the nose, the edge of the ears, eyelids or lips. The initial symptom is the appearance of a spherical nodule that ulcerates and, if left untreated, continues to ulcerate until deeper structures are damaged or destroyed. Early treatment – by surgery or radiotherapy – is usually effective.

rods Light-sensitive cells in the *retina* of the eye that contain *rhodopsin* ("visual purple"), a pigment which in the presence of light breaks down and turns white, only to reform in darkness. The breakdown is detected by neurones (nerve cells) in the retina, and the information is transmitted along the optic nerve to the brain where it is perceived as the degree of intensity of light in *vision*. Each eye contains more than 120 million rod cells.

Rogers, Carl (1902–1987) American psychologist, founder of the school of humanistic psychology. The basis of this schoolís form of *psychotherapy* is to encourage a personal relationship between a patient and therapist that is the antithesis of confrontation or even consultation: an equal and friendly partnership in which it is the patient who decides on the pace of the therapy.

Rorschach test Another name for the *inkblot test* first devised by the Swiss psychiatrist Hermann Rorschach (1884–1922).

rosacea Inflammation of the skin on the face, caused by a disorder of the sebaceous glands that secrete natural oils within the tissues. Symptoms are redness of the skin, and lumps and spots similar to those of *acne* (rosacea is sometimes called acne rosacea). More women suffer from it than men. Its ultimate cause is unknown. Treatment is with *antibiotics*.

roseola infantum A common disease characterized by a rash on the skin of a young child, preceded by high temperature that may cause convulsions. It is caused by a herpes virus, and treatment is to alleviate the symptoms.

roundworm Parasitic *worm* of a group also called nematode worms. Common throughout the world in areas of poor sanitation, types of roundworm include hookworms and *threadworms*. Roundworms cause infestations such as *ankylostomiasis, ascariasis, filiariasis* and *trichuriasis*.

rubella Commonly called German measles, a highly infectious viral infection – contagious even before the appearance of symptoms and for some time after they have gone. The initial symptoms are raised temperature, headache and a sore throat, with swelling of the lymph glands at the back of the neck. The classic rash of reddish pink spots starts on the face and then spreads all over the body. It lasts up to about seven days, and yields natural life-long immunity. Contracted by a pregnant woman in the early stages of pregnancy, rubella can cause severe defects in an embryo, so unvaccinated pregnant women should keep well away from anyone with rubella. There is no cure; treatment is to alleviate symptoms. A vaccine is available and is usually given in infancy along with measles and mumps immunization (MMR vaccine).

rubeola Medical name for *measles*.

rupture Common name for a *hernia*.

S

saccharine Non-calorific, synthetic sweetener far more concentrated than ordinary sugar (sucrose, which contains 4 calories per gram or 120 calories per ounce).

sacroiliac joint Firm connection between the *sacrum* at the lower end of the *spine* and each *ileum* of the *pelvis*, strongly supported by ligaments. The dual joint is capable of a small degree of movement, and takes the weight of the torso and head and transfers it to the pelvis and the legs.

sacrum Part of the *spine* consisting of five fused *vertebrae* between the lumbar vertebrae of the lower back and the *coccyx* ("tail bone"). It is at the sacrum that the spine is attached to the pelvis by the *sacroiliac joint*.

sadism Desire and practice of obtaining sexual pleasure from watching or inflicting pain on others.

safe period Time of infertility in a womanís *menstrual cycle*. Every woman of child-bearing age (unless pregnant) is fertile for only two or three days at *ovulation* half-way between one menstrual period and the next. The safe period thus lasts from about 5 days after one time of fertility until about 5 days before the next, with menstruation itself in the centre. It is during this time that *sexual intercourse* is "safe" and *conception* is least likely. Utilized as the "rhythm method" of *contraception*, the safe period is not particularly reliable because of the difficulty of judging when it occurs, especially in women with irregular menstrual cycles.

saline Containing salt (sodium chloride), used in medicine to describe a sodium chloride solution at the concentration of body fluids – almost one per cent – used as a substitute for *plasma* in transfusions (for example, to treat shock).

saliva Alkaline secretion of the *salivary glands* and mucous membranes of the mouth which lubricates, cleanses, assists sensory perception (of taste) and speech, and begins the *digestion* of carbohydrates. Its main constituents are water, mucus and enzymes.

salivary gland Any of three pairs of glands located behind the mucous membranes of the mouth: the parotid glands (behind the upper back corners of the mouth) and the submandibular glands and sublingual glands (beneath the tongue); the buccal gland (in the cheeks and lips) also contribute. All of them secrete *saliva* following stimuli for salivation (such as the presence of food in the mouth or even merely the smell or thought of food).

Salmonella Genus of rod-shaped bacteria that cause a variety of gastro-intestinal disorders. One species causes the commonest type of *food poisoning* in humans. Other species of Salmonella bacteria are responsible for *enteric fever*, and especially *paratyphoid* and *typhoid fever*.

salpingitis Inflammation of one or both *Fallopian tubes*, generally caused by the spread of an infection (such as a *sexually transmitted disease*) from the *uterus* (womb) or the *vagina*. Symptoms are severe abdominal pain and a vaginal discharge. Treatment with *antibiotics* is usually successful. Chronic salpingitis involves recurrent attacks, and may result eventually in scarring and blockage of the tube; surgery may be required.

sanatorium Hospital specializing in care for convalescent patients, and including therefore not just the means to treat them but also of *rehabilitation*. The term is used also for hospitals dedicated to the care of special types of patients, particularly those dying of old age or of specific diseases (such as AIDS). See also *hospice*.

Sanger, Margaret (1883–1966) American pioneer of *contraception*, the founder and first president of the American Birth Control League, an organization dedicated to the education and information of all women on the subject.

sanitation Provision of hygienic conditions, particularly in connection with food production and preparation, and drainage and sewage disposal.

sarcoidosis Presence of granulomatous lesions and (sarcoid) in the body. Common sites are the lungs, lymphatic system, liver, bone marrow and eyes. Often there are no outward symptoms; those that do appear are local to the lesions. Treatment, following diagnosis, usually involves *corticosteroid* drugs. Most cases recover fully.

sarcoma Malignant tumour (*cancer*) of connective tissue (the supporting tissues – rather than the organs – of the body, such as muscle, fibrous tissue, bone, cartilage and fat). It may occur anywhere in or on the body and spreads rapidly (*metastasis*). Treatment depends on the site but includes surgical removal, where possible, and often *chemotherapy* in case the tumour has spread, sometimes with *radiotherapy*. A sarcoma in a bone may necessitate amputation, although replacement of the diseased bone by a prosthesis may be possible.

saturated fats Fats which, because of their molecular structure, can absorb no additional hydrogen atoms. Animal fats are almost exclusively saturated fats, and are thought to be less healthful in foods than *polyunsaturated* fats.

satyriasis Persistent desire in a man for heterosexual *sexual intercourse*, the male equivalent of *nymphomania*.

scabies Infestation of the skin by the itch mite, which burrows into the skin to lay its eggs. A contagious condition, its symptoms are severe itching and a rash, both caused by an allergic reaction to the mites and their larvae in the skin tissues. Main sites affected are the finger webs, feet, nipples and pubic region. Treatment is with a scabicide drug applied to the whole body except the face: the entire household should be treated. *Antihistamines* may be given to relieve itching.

scanning Any modern technique that assists diagnosis by providing a computer-enhanced picture of a patientís internal organs. Such techniques include *computerized axial tomography* (CAT), *magnetic resonance imaging* (MRI), *positron emission tomography* (PET) and *ultrasound*.

scapula Medical name for the *shoulderblade*.

scar Medical name cicatrix, fibrous tissue marking where a *lesion* has healed. Perfect healing leaves virtually no scar, but as long as healing (or surgical repair) is not perfect, a scar remains, consisting of *connective tissue*. Some scars on the skin become raised or red if the connective tissue in the scar is thickened through tension (*keloid*). Others, internally, may form *adhesions* or sometimes contribute to *sarcoidosis*.

scarlet fever In a mild form known as scarlatina, scarlet fever is a toxic manifestation of infection with haemolytic streptococcal bacteria, which also cause *tonsillitis*. Symptoms are a high temperature, sore throat, headache, vomiting and, sometimes, diarrhoea. A rash spreads from the neck all over the body; the tongue turns white and also has a rash-like covering of spots (strawberry tongue). The condition lasts for about four days – but the patient may be contagious for at least another fortnight. After-effects may include flaking skin and temporary hair loss, and sometimes complications of *otitis* or kidney inflammation. Treatment is with *antibiotics*.

scar tissue Connective tissue that forms a *scar*.

schistosomiasis Also called bilharzia or bilharziasis, a disorder caused by infestation by flukes of the genus *Schistosoma*, contracted by swimming in water contaminated both by human excreta and by the snails that nurture the larvae of the fluke. Penetrating the skin, the flukes travel to the intestine and bladder, mature, then release eggs. The eggs cause *anaemia* and destroy surrounding tissue. Initial symptoms are high temperature, musele pain, skin irritation and coughing. Dysentery, enlargement of the spleen and *cirrhosis* of the liver may follow; tissue damage in the bladder may lead to *cancer*. Treatment is with highly powerful drugs toxic to the flukes (and potentially toxic to the patient); surgery may be necessary to repair tissue damage.

schizoid Describing a *personality disorder* in which there is extreme solitariness and introspection, leading to eccentric behaviour.

schizophrenia Functional *psychosis* in which thought processes are disrupted, delusions and hallucinations deprive the patient of part or all reality, and behaviour may become violently antisocial. Hereditary factors may contribute towards a schizophrenic predisposition, and stress can precipitate exacerbations. Several types or stages have been observed. Simple schizophrenia merely describes a patientís increasing withdrawal into a closed world; paranoid schizophrenia is characterized by the frequency of *delusions*; and catatonic schizophrenia produces overagitated movements and excitement. Treatment is with antipsychotic drugs and intensive support, both psychologically and socially, aiming to reduce the need for hospitalization or institutional care and allow some integration into the community.

Schwann, Theodor (1810–1882) German physiologist who carried out significant research into the mechanisms of digestion, muscular contraction, fermentation and putrefaction. But his major innovation was to propose that animal and vegetable matter was made of cells. The cells that form the myelin sheath around nerve axons are named after him.

sciatica Pain in the area of distribution of the *sciatic nerve*, from the buttock down the back of the leg to the foot. The condition is usually caused by the pinching of the nerve near its junction with the spinal cord, often as a result of displacement (prolapse) of an *intervertebral disc* (and is thus a type of *referred pain* – pain felt at a site distant to the one really affected). The immediate cause may be lifting a heavy weight or twisting suddenly – or there may be some more serious problem. Persistent sciatica should be medically diagnosed. Treatment is with rest and anti-inflammatory drugs until the pain subsides, but persistent symptoms may require surgery.

sciatic nerve Major nerve that supplies the buttock and the back of the upper leg before branching above the knee to supply the muscles and skin of the lower leg.

sclera Outer layer of the eyeball, the fibrous "white of the eye", of which the *cornea* is also part. The material also surrounds the *optic nerve*.

sclerosis Progressive hardening of any tissues of the body.

scoliosis Curvature of the *spine* sideways, caused by congenital deformity, disease of the local bones, nerves or muscles, or long-term bad posture. Treatment depends on the cause.

screening Mass examination of a section of the population (who may all seem perfectly healthy) to check for specific diseases. Such examinations, for example in the form of *cervical smear tests* or mammography, can detect the presence of disease early enough to greatly increase a patientís chances of easy and successful treatment.

scrofula *Tuberculosis* of the *lymph nodes* in the neck. Now rare, symptoms are large local abscesses. Treatment with special drugs is rapidly effective.

scrotum Sac behind the *penis* of a man or boy, containing the *testes*. Its external location provides the cooler temperature required by the *sperm* for fertility.

scurvy Deficiency disorder caused by lack of vitamin C (*ascorbic acid*). It involves a weakening of the walls of the smaller blood vessels, and results in bleeding and bone disorders. Symptoms include lethargy, irritability, joint pain, bruising, and reduced body weight. Treatment is to make up the deficiency.

sea sickness Form of *motion sickness*.

seasonal affective disorder (SAD) Psychological condition in which shorter days and lower light levels give rise to recurrent winter depressions, with low mood often accompanied by general slowing of thought and activity (psychomotor *retardation*), increased need for sleep and carbohydrate cravings. Fluctuations in *melatonin* (the hormone produced by the *pineal gland* in the brain that regulates *circadian rhythms*) levels may contribute. Symptoms usually start at the onset of winter and remit in the spring. Treatment with light therapy to simulate normal sunlight often produces marked relief, but may necessitate sitting in front of a light box for prolonged periods each morning throughout the winter.

sebaceous cyst Fat-containing *cyst* on the skin caused by blockage of a duct normally used by a sebaceous gland. The gland itself swells up, unable to release its oily secretions. Sebaceous cysts can occur on any part of the skin that has hair, especially the scalp. Treatment is by surgical removal.

seborrhoea Skin disorder caused by overproduction of the oily secretion (*sebum*) of the sebaceous glands. The glands themselves swell, especially on the face, and the skin takes on the oily texture that predisposes to *acne*. Scaling of the skin occurs, causing *dandruff*. A similar disorder – seborrhoeic dermatitis – causes the appearance of scaly *plaques* (patches) to occur over the areas of skin where sebaceous glands are most concentrated. In both cases, medicated shampoos may help.

sebum Oily secretion of the sebaceous glands in the hair-covered regions of the skin. It provides a thin, fatty layer over the skin surface that is effective in preventing both the evaporation of water and penetration by bacteria.

secondary sexual characteristics Physical characteristics of adult men and women that appear at *puberty*. The main characteristics in men are facial and pubic hair, and a voice that has "broken"; those in women are pubic hair, menstruation and developed breasts.

secretin Hormone secreted by the *duodenum* as partly digested food enters it from the stomach. It stimulates the secretion of other digestive juices by the pancreas and the liver.

section Either surgical cutting, during an operation; or an extremely thin slice of a subject for microscopic examination.

sedation Process of reducing excitement, of soothing anxiety, and even of encouraging sleep. It is usually achieved using *sedative* drugs.

sedative Drug that causes *sedation* (calming and encouraging sleep) by suppressing certain brain functions. *Hypnotic drugs* and *tranquillizers* (such as benzodiazepines) in doses lower than those required to induce sleep may be given as sedatives to relieve anxiety and tension, although they tend to produce drowsiness and may be habit-forming.

sedimentation rate Measurement of the time taken for the red cells (*erythrocytes*) in a sample of blood, to which an anticoagulant has been added, to sink and form a sediment. A faster rate than normal indicates the presence of an inflammation or a malignancy.

seizure Sudden onset of physically agitating symptoms – perhaps a convulsion (as with epilepsy), or violent shivering (rigor) that may be an initial symptom of various severe infections.

semen Secretion of the male sex glands at *orgasm*. The semen ejaculated from the penis is made up of a vast number of *sperm* and several types of seminal fluid – some produced by the *seminal vesicles*, some produced by the *prostate gland* and some by *Cowper's glands*. The fluid is intended to provide a medium not only for the sperm during *ejaculation*, but also one for assisting the viability of the sperm while travelling up the vagina, through the cervix and the uterus (womb), to the Fallopian tubes.

semicircular canals Three fluid-filled tubular structures in the part of the inner ear called the *labyrinth*. Arranged at right-angles to each other, each tube has an internal hair-cell structure that registers movement of the fluid. Movement in the tubes is thus registered in every plane, and produces sensory information that is central to *balance*.

semilunar valve One of two *valves* preventing backflow of blood from the heart. Of the two, one controls flow to the lungs (at the beginning of the pulmonary artery), the other to the body tissues (via the aorta). Each valve has three flaps (cusps).

seminal vesicle Small, convoluted sex gland that secretes seminal fluid for ejaculation by a man at *orgasm*. There are two vesicles, one at the top end of each *vas deferens* near the *prostate gland*.

seminiferous tubules Fine, convoluted tubes that comprise the main constituent of each *testis*, and in which sperm are formed.

senility State of physical and mental decline occurring in old age. Many factors affect the rate at which such decline becomes apparent, including inheritance, previous health and lifestyle habits. Treatment is directed at improving specific symptoms, for which drugs may sometimes help. In extreme cases, institutional care may be required.

sensation Perception as experienced by a sensory organ and interpreted by the brain. Such perceptions may be of external stimuli – things seen, heard, touched, and so on – or of internal stimuli – emotions, pain, nausea, and so on. All perceptions are conveyed by appropriate nerve pathways and interpreted by specific centres in the brain.

senses Specialized areas of perception, particularly of external stimuli, as experienced by sensory organs and relayed by nerves to the brain for interpretation. The five major forms of external stimulus are experienced through the eyes (vision), nose (smell), mouth and tongue (taste), ears (hearing) and the skin and external mucous membranes (touch), all of which have thousands of receptor cells and associated nerves. Internally, *proprioceptors* register the physical sensations of balance, discomfort, muscle tension, pain and so on. And at a much higher level there are the centres in the brain that interpret the sensations of aesthetic pleasure: sadness, joy and so on.

sensitization Progressive increase in the *immune response*, particularly to an *allergen*. Allergic responses increase with exposure to the allergen because of the ever greater number of antibodies being produced to counteract it.

sepsis Presence and effect of viruses, bacteria and their toxins, leading potentially to infection, inflammation and decay.

septicaemia Blood poisoning, involving the presence of bacteria in the blood circulation (which may gain access through a dirty wound). It is a dangerous condition because the blood travels to all parts of the body. The result may be destruction of whole areas of tissue if emergency treatment is not carried out. Symptoms are fever with rigors, and possibly a rash and abscesses externally and internally. The usual treatment is with large doses of antibiotics.

septum Any body structure that divides or acts as a partition. There is a septum in the heart (between the right and left halves), nose (between the nostrils), brain and scrotum, for example.

serotonin A body chemical, also known as 5-hydroxytryptamine (5-HT), found in many forms of tissue, including the intestinal wall and the blood platelets. It acts as a *vasoconstrictor*, a *neurotransmitter*, and plays a role in *inflammation*. It is believed to be involved in initiating *migraine* headaches, and has a positive influence on mood. Drugs that block the reabsorption of serotonin, so increasing the levels remaining in the tissues (selective serotonin reuptake inhibitors or SSRIs), are used to treat *depression* and elevate mood by boosting brain serotonin levels.

serum Straw-coloured fluid that is the basis of the blood. In effect it is blood without any *blood cells* or any of the *clotting* factors. It may, however, contain specific antibodies and thus be used in a vaccine to confer passive *immunity* to a specific disease. See also *antiserum*.

serum sickness Reaction to the infusion or the injection of an *antiserum*, caused when the bodyís production of antibodies is too slow to cope with the amount of antigenic material introduced. Symptoms may be severe, representing a form of allergy syndrome, but are generally only temporary.

sex Being either male or female, with all their physical and mental associations. This includes an awareness of being one or the other, and the presence of sex organs even before the appearance of outward *secondary sexual characteristics*. Awareness is important; it is possible for somebody to grow up physically as one sex while simultaneously feeling certain (mentally) of being the other. In such people a series of *sex change* operations may alleviate the considerable mental stress. In ordinary life the sexes are often portrayed as having set patterns of behaviour – patterns that may in fact be imposed by society; this is known as sex role stereotyping.

sex change Series of surgical operations to change the outer reproductive organs of an adult from those of one sex to those of the other. It is undertaken only after rigorous psychological assessment, is performed over a number of months if not years, and may never really fully conceal the original physical build of the patient – but may bring considerable mental relief and peace.

sex hormones Steroid *hormones* that confer the physical (and mental) properties of one *sex* or the other, operative in a person from the time the sex glands are formed in the embryo. Male sex hormones, produced mainly by the testes, are *andro ens*; female sex hormones, produced mainly by the ovaries, are *oestrogens* and *progesterone*. It is the increased production of sex hormones in puberty that leads to the appearance of *secondary sexual characteristics*.

sex-linked disorders Hereditary disorders also called *X-linked disorders*.

sexual abuse Maltreatment of a sexual nature, usually referring to sexual exploitation of children. Any sexual contact between an adult and a child is regarded as sexual abuse, as is exposure of a child to sexually explicit language (in a sexualized rather than educational context) or behaviour or to pornography. Sexual abuse frequently co-exists with physical or emotional abuse and is most often perpetrated upon girls (although boys are not immune) by male members of the childís family (see *incest*), particularly those not directly related to the child. It can leave life-long psychological scars as well as exposing the child to *sexually transmitted diseases* and *pregnancy*.

sexual intercourse Sexual activity between two adults, as a result of which one or both may achieve *orgasm* (climax). Heterosexual intercourse (from which *conception* may result) involves the insertion of a manís erect *penis* into a womanís *vagina*, followed by his *ejaculation* of *semen* within her, representing his orgasm. Her orgasm – which may or may not be simultaneous – derives partly from the vaginal sensations of his insertion and partly from friction of the *clitoris*. Other sexual practices include mutual *masturbation*, anal intercourse and oral sex, some of which may be part of a *homosexual* relationship.

sexual medicine Treatment of physical and mental problems relating to sexual intercourse, generally including psychiatric counselling.

sexually transmitted diseases (STDs) Any of a range of infections that may be acquired through *sexual intercourse* or the close body contact involved with it. Formerly called venereal diseases, they are treated by specialists in genito-urinary medicine and include *syphilis* (now less common than previously), *gonorrhoea, nonspecific urethritis*; *chancroid, Chlamydia, trichomoniasis, candidiasis* (thrush), *herpes* genitalis, genital *warts* and *AIDS* (acquired immune deficiency syndrome). Most cause readily apparent symptoms such as a discharge from the *penis* or *vagina*, pain on urination, spots or *ulceration* on the sexual organs or on the mouth or anus. In women, however, symptoms of some infections may be very mild or pass unnoticed, yet consequences of untreated infections can include *pelvic inflammatory disease* and *infertility*. Some types of the *human papillomavirus*, which causes genital warts, have been linked with the development of cervical *cancer*. Syphilis if untreated can lead to severe neurological and other long-term effects. Someone who contracts *HIV* (human immunodeficiency virus), the virus that causes AIDS, may have no symptoms for years, then succumb to various infections due to a damaged immune system, which may ultimately prove fatal. For all STDs, it is essential that all recent sexual partners are treated.

sheath Also called a condom, one of the barrier methods of *contraception*.

shell shock Form of *battle fatigue*.

Sherrington, Charles S. (1857–1952) English neurologist and physiologist whose investigations into reflex actions led to a new understanding of the operation of the nervous system, with particular reference to the function of chemical *neurotransmitters* between *neurones* (nerve cells) at *synapses*.

shinbone Common name of the *tibia*.

shingles Medical name *herpes* zoster, a viral infection of nerve tracts near the skin. It occurs most commonly in older adults, although caused by the same virus that causes *chickenpox* in children. Shingles is characterized by a very sensitive, red, blistering rash over the area of skin in which the nerves are affected – commonly the chest, but sometimes the face and eyes. The blisters fill with *pus*, form scabs, and gradually disappear. Although the symptoms generally decrease of their own accord within four weeks, some effects (especially pain) may continue for months afterwards. Treatment is to alleviate the symptoms as much as possible, and may require strong pain-killers. Antiviral drugs may also be given.

shivering Usually an attempt by the body when cold to get warm, an uncontrollable trembling which, by contracting muscles, generates heat. When caused instead by a rapid rise in internal temperature (thus leaving the skin feeling cold), it is known as *rigor*.

shock Condition of circulatory collapse in which arterial blood pressure is so low as to fail to circulate the blood fully to the tissues. There are several causes: *haemorrhage* reduces the total amount of blood to the body; body fluids may be lost through severe burns, diarrhoea or vomiting; disease or drugs may inhibit the proper functioning of the heart; bacterial invasion or allergic reaction may cause the thin walls of the veins to dilate to such an extent that blood pressure is seriously reduced. Symptoms in all cases are pallor, cold sweat, breathlessness, dilated pupils, and dryness of the mouth. Treatment depends on the cause.

shortsightedness Common name for *myopia*.

shoulder blade Known medically as the scapula, a flattish triangular bone at the shoulder, protecting the back and the top of the ribcage and articulating with the bone of the upper arm (humerus) at a ball-and-socket joint. The collarbone (clavicle) connects the shoulder blade with the breastbone (sternum).

shunt Tube introduced surgically into the body (or occurring as a congenital deformity) that diverts fluid from one duct to another.

Siamese twins Conjoined twins who, when born, are anatomically joined together and have some tissues in common. The less they have in common (and some share only umbilical blood vessels) the better are their chances of independent survival after being surgically separated.

sibling Brother or sister, born of the same parents.

sickle-cell anaemia Hereditary type of *anaemia* that mainly affects people of African or Mediterranean ancestry. Only those who inherit a pair of sickle-cell genes, one from each parent, develop the disease (those with only one gene are carriers, meaning they are themselves healthy but will pass the gene to around half of their children). The condition is caused by an abnormality of *haemoglobin* (the oxygen-carrying molecule) in red blood cells, which causes the cells to be shaped like crescents (rather than discs), a process known as sickling. As a result, the cells have difficulty in circulating through narrow blood capillaries, and tend to be broken down instead, leading to anaemia and *jaundice*. Alternatively, there may be widespread *thrombosis* where the blood cells congregate. As a perhaps unexpected form of compensation, the disease confers immunity to certain forms of *malaria* (a common tropical disease transmitted by mosquitoes). There is as yet no cure, but treatment is possible to alleviate the anaemic symptoms.

side-effects Extraneous symptoms arising from treatment, particularly with a drug. Before any drug is approved for general use, all possible side-effects must be known and evaluated.

SIDS Abbreviation of *sudden infant death syndrome*.

silicosis Form of *pneumoconiosis* caused by long-term inhalation of silica dust. Particularly at risk – though less so since working environments have been improved by law – are quarry workers, sand blasters, boiler descalers and mine workers. The silica erodes the tissue of the lungs, considerably increasing vulnerability to *emphysema*, *pneumonia* and *tuberculosis*.

sinoatrial node Pacemaker in the heart, located in the upper wall of the right *atrium*. Supplied by nerve fibres of the *autonomic nervous system*, the sinoatrial node produces a regular contraction of the atrial muscle about 70 times a minute. Each in turn triggers an impulse that travels to the *ventricles* for contraction there that brings about the rest of the pumping action. If the node malfunctions, an artificial *pacemaker* may be surgically implanted to assist or replace it.

sinus Cavity, filled with air or blood. The air-filled sinuses in the bones of the face (over the eyes and each side of the nose) may sometimes become inflamed and clogged with mucus and pus (*sinusitis*). Blood-filled sinuses occur in the outer covering of the brain (the dura mater) and in certain blood vessels.

sinusitis Inflammation of one or more of the air-filled cavities of the bones of the skull over the eyes and each side of the nose. All of the sinuses connect with the nasal cavity, and an infection there may spread into the sinuses causing an accumulation of mucus and pus, which, until it drains, may give rise to pain and tenderness. The condition often resolves spontaneously, but treatment with nose drops and sometimes antibiotics may be needed. A few cases where this fails may require treatment by minor surgery.

Sjörgen's syndrome A condition in which there is lack of tear fluid and saliva, resulting in dry eyes and mouth, sometimes accompanied by joint problems and other symptoms. It is an autoimmune disorder, meaning that the immune system attacks the bodyís own tissues. Sometimes it occurs in association with other disorders, such as *rheumatoid arthritis*. Treatment is to deal with symptoms, usually including eyedrops – "artificial tears" – and sometimes anti-inflammatory or painkilling drugs for joint pains.

skeletal muscle Also called striated muscle, one of the three types of *muscle*.

skeleton Systematic structure of bones that constitutes the framework of the human body. Comprised mostly of calcium and phosphates, and honeycombed for strength, the bones form the anchorages for all the muscles, tendons and ligaments, carry the weight of the body, protect many of the internal organs, provide most of the means of articulating the joints, and some also are essential to the formation of blood. The whole human skeleton consists of about 206 bones.

skin Largest organ of the body, and one of its toughest tissues. Self-healing, water-resistant, temperature regulating, infection-repelling and, despite that, highly sensitive, it consists basically of two layers. The epidermis (outer layer) is generally covered in another layer of dead cells that continually flake off; the dermis lies underneath. Within the skin there are also thousands of glands – such as sweat glands and sebaceous glands – and beneath it is a layer of fat that can be used as a store of food and water.

skin graft Surgical replacement of the skin in one area of the body with skin from another, generally in the same patient, to repair damage caused by injury (especially burns). The process may take several operations, although modern methods of tissue culture may soon accelerate the technique.

skin test Any medical test that uses the skin as a medium, especially a *patch test*.

Skinner, Burrhus Frederic (1904–1990) American psychologist, founder of the school of psychology known as *behaviourism*.

skull Bony framework of the head and face consisting of 22 bones (8 in the cranium enclosing the brain and 14 in the face and jaw), many of which are joined together in permanent bonds (called sutures). At birth, the large plates of bone forming the top of the skull are not yet rigidly joined; the lines of fusion at the sutures remain mobile and there are two large gaps, the anterior and posterior *fontanelles*, where the various sutures meet. This allows the bones to squeeze together when the babyís head is passing through the birth canal. The sutures then knit together, forming a tight bony seam and closing the fontanelles over the first 18 months of the babyís life.

sleep Period of virtual unconsciousness experienced (and welcomed) by almost everybody regularly every day. Sleep comprises three distinct forms of repose: light sleep (when first asleep), followed by alternating sessions of deep sleep (in which there are no dreams) and *rapid eye movement* sleep (in which *dreaming* occurs), as can be measured in wave patterns on an *electroencephalograph*. Sleep refreshes and seems to be essential for good health; deprivation of sleep slows intellectual capacity appreciably.

sleeping pills Drugs that induce *sleep*. *Barbiturates* were once commonly prescribed for this purpose, but because of the possibility of dependence, other *sedatives* are now used. One effect of such drugs is a reduction in the number and length of periods of *rapid eye movement* sleep. They may also cause daytime drowsiness, especially if taken in combination with alcohol.

sleeping sickness Form of *trypanosomiasis* endemic in tropical Africa.

sleepwalking Known medically as somnambulism, a symptom of stress that generally occurs during childhood, and is often related to going to bed in a strange place. It apparently coincides with *rapid eye movement* sleep, when dreaming normally occurs. During sleepwalking the eyes may be open or closed, and there may be coherent movement of the arms and hands (as well as the feet) – but there is no memory of the activity on waking next morning.

slipped disc Common name for *prolapsed intervertebral disc*.

smallpox Formerly dangerous viral infection generally contracted by direct contact. Symptoms – headache, backache, fever, vomiting and a generalized skin rash – were severe, and if the victim survived he or she had pitted scars on the skin. Smallpox was the first disease for which a vaccine was developed. A global programme of vaccination by the World Health Organization succeeded in eliminating the disease completely (the first such infectious disease to be totally eradicated), and the virus now remains (closely guarded) in only a few research laboratories.

smear test Examination of a collection of cells taken from the body and placed on a microscope slide. The best-known test is for pre-cancer of the cervix (of the womb) – a *cervical smear test*.

smegma Oily secretion of the sebaceous glands on the underside of the *prepuce* (foreskin) of the penis. If it accumulates it condenses and becomes liable to bacterial infection (*balanitis*); proper hygiene therefore demands regular washing.

smell, sense of The ability to detect odours, limited to discriminating between seven basic smells. The main sensory organ is the *olfactory bulb* which relays information from nerve endings in the nasal cavity to the brain via the *olfactory nerve*.

Smith, Hamilton O. (1931–) American molecular biologist who, using a bacterial enzyme to "cut" a strand of *deoxyribonucleic acid* (DNA), first identified fragments of the DNA as having specific genetic properties. He was awarded a Nobel Prize in 1978.

smoking Inhalation of the gases and smoke from burning tobacco. In many ways an addictive habit, smoking ordinarily represents a means of relieving stress or of gaining time to think. However, the *nicotine* inhaled causes the release in the body of *adrenaline*, which in turn causes a rise in blood pressure by narrowing the blood vessels, and encourages the increase of fatty substances in the blood. The carbon monoxide inhaled prevents the full exchange of gases in the lungs, depriving the body of oxygen. And other substances inhaled (such as tar) irritate the mucous membrane lining the bronchial passages and may cause lung *cancer*. Pregnant women and people with heart, blood or breathing disorders should not smoke. It has been calculated that for every person who dies in a road accident, 4 die from smoking-related disorders.

smoking dependency A strong compulsion to continue with the habitual use of tobacco, most often in the form of cigarettes, with intense craving and irritability if it is suddenly withdrawn. Although smoking represents a means of relieving stress or of boosting concentration, it is also linked with the development of many different diseases, including heart disease and various cancers, especially lung cancer. The nicotine inhaled in cigarette smoke – which is the component responsible for dependence on smoking – causes the release in the body of adrenaline, which in turn causes a rise in blood pressure by narrowing the blood vessels, and encourages the increase of fatty substances in the blood. The carbon monoxide inhaled prevents the full exchange of gases in the lungs, depriving the body of oxygen. Other substances inhaled (such as tar) irritate the mucous membrane lining the bronchial passages and may cause *lung cancer*. Pregnant women and people with heart, blood or breathing disorders should not smoke. It has been calculated that for every person who dies in a road accident, four die from smoking-related disorders. A huge number of methods for giving up smoking are available, ranging from counselling and support groups to acupuncture and nicotine substitutes. The latter, available in various forms, give a dose of nicotine without the other harmful ingredients of tobacco smoke, tiding the person over until the habit of smoking is broken. Nevertheless, giving up is extremely difficult and many people take several attempts before they succeed.

smooth muscle One of three types of *muscle*.

snakebite Bite of a snake, resulting in pain and sometimes redness and swelling at the site, with other symptoms according to the type of venom, which, in severe cases, may be fatal. In most of Europe, adders are the only venomous snakes. People who travel in countryside areas where poisonous snakes are common are advised to carry a supply of antivenom. If somebody is bitten, the snake should be identified if possible (or killed and kept) to assist a doctor in prescribing the appropriate antidote.

sneezing Sudden involuntary expulsion of air and mucus through the nose, usually following local irritation (by dust or *rhinitis*).

snoring Harsh, breathy noise caused by the vibration of the soft *palate* when directly over the larynx during *respiration*. It occurs particularly when lying on oneís back asleep with oneís mouth open. A blocked nose encourages snoring.

Snow, John (1813–1858) Queen Victoriaís obstetrician, whose use of chloroform at the birth of Prince Leopold encouraged public acceptance of *anaesthesia*. He was also the first to detect how cholera spreads.

sodomy Anal intercourse.

solar plexus Network (plexus) of nerves and ganglia in the upper abdomen.

solvent abuse Inhalation of the fumes of petrol or other solvents in order to attain a state of mental stimulation approaching euphoria. The practice is addictive and harmful (a type of drug *dependence*), especially to the mucous lining of the nasal cavity.

somnambulism Medical name for *sleepwalking*.

sonography Use of *ultrasound* for diagnostic and therapeutic purposes.

sore External lesion, ulcer or wound.

spare-part surgery Another name for *replacement surgery*.

spasm Involuntary contraction of one or more muscles, either repeatedly or sustained; there may also be pain. The cause may be a local response to some other problem in the area, such as back or neck pain causing secondary muscle spasm; a general neurological disorder; or a temporary response to low blood calcium levels (*tetany*, typically affecting the hands and feet, when it is called carpopedal spasm).

spectacles Means of correcting *vision*, more commonly called *glasses*.

speculum Medical instrument used to hold open a body orifice so that the operator can look inside.

speech Comprehensible sounds, made through the co-ordinated use of various centres in the brain, the appropriate motor nerves, and the muscles of the larynx, mouth, tongue, lips and cheeks.

speech disorder Any disorder limiting the faculty of *speech*. Causes include congenital defects such as deafness and lack of (or disability in) any of the nerves or muscles normally involved in speech. Emotional disorders may disrupt speech even when the organs are functionally perfect, and mental disorders and those that affect the circulation of the blood in the brain (a stroke) may have similar effects or prevent speech altogether, temporarily or permanently. Many speech disorders can be improved by *speech therapy*.

speech therapy Long-term therapy to improve *speech* in a patient who has a *speech disorder*. Most forms of therapy involve some study of *phonation*. When emotional difficulty is inhibiting speech (perhaps causing a stutter), therapy may include some form of distraction while speaking, to improve fluency. In patients who have lost some of the faculty through a stroke, therapy may be based on inspiring the confidence to remember vocabulary and use it in context.

Spemann, Hans (1869–1941) German embryologist whose research into how an embryo develops from fertilized ovum in a Fallopian tube, implants in the uterine lining, and continues growing within the amnion, won him the award of a Nobel Prize in 1935.

sperm Male sex cell produced in the *testis*, conveyed from the *epididymis* up the *vas deferens* to the *seminal vesicles*, from where they are ejaculated through the *urethra* at *orgasm* as part of the *semen*. Each sperm (or, technically, spermatozoon) comprises a rounded head (in which the nucleus is sited), a middle piece (in which the cellular *mitochondria* are enclosed) and a comparatively long, flexible tail. If *ejaculation* takes place inside a womanís *vagina* (in the absence of a contraceptive device), the rhythmic beating of the tail enables the sperm to "swim" through the cervix into the uterus (womb) and – with the help of muscular contractions in the uterine wall – into the Fallopian tubes. There, depending on the coinciding of a time of fertility in the womanís *menstrual cycle*, it may encounter and fertilize an *ovum* in the process of *conception*.

spermatozoon Individual sex cell, generally called a *sperm*. On average, around two hundred million are released within the *semen* at every *ejaculation*. Generally, only one fertilizes an *ovum* at conception.

Sperry, Roger (1913–1994) American biologist and psychologist whose research into the functions of the cerebral hemispheres of the brain gave new understanding to how one hemisphere may in some respects take on the faculties of the other in case of injury. He was awarded a Nobel Prize in 1981.

sphincter Muscular ring that opens or closes the exit of a passage. The two best-known sphincters are in the alimentary canal: the pyloric sphincter (which controls the exit of food from the stomach) and the anal sphincter (the exit from the rectum). The exit from the bladder is also controlled by a sphincter muscle.

sphygmomanometer Traditional instrument for measuring *blood pressure*, consisting of an inflatable sleeve ("cuff") connected to a tube containing mercury with a calibrated scale. The cuff is wound tightly around the arm and then inflated. The pressure applied to the arm restricts blood flow, which is monitored using a stethoscope (pulsating sounds of flow in time with the heartbeat can be heard). When the pressure is such that the blood stops flowing (so the sounds are no longer heard through the stethoscope), the pressure is released slowly until the blood flow is heard to restart, when a reading is taken on the mercury scale. Pressure continues to be released slowly until the sounds muffle or disappear, when another reading is taken. The two readings represent the systolic and diastolic blood pressures (during the active pumping phase and the resting phase of the cardiac cycle, respectively). Machines offering a digital blood pressure read-out are increasingly used instead of a mercury scale.

spina bifida Congenital spinal defect in which one or more *vertebrae* (backbones) fail to develop properly or at all. As a result, a section of the spinal cord is unprotected and may buckle; associated nerves and other tissues may also bulge out of the gap in the spine or be displaced. It is a form of *neural tube defect* (a group of conditions in which the spine fails to develop properly in the foetus), known medically as rachischisis. The condition causes paralysis, potential deformity of areas supplied by affected nerves and incontinence; there may or may not also be mental retardation. The condition is associated with high levels of a protein, called alphafetoprotein, in the amniotic fluid surrounding a developing foetus, enabling its detection by a blood test at around the 16th week of pregnancy, with confirmation by amniocentesis and ultrasound if high levels are suspected. The mother may then be offered a termination of pregnancy. Surgical treatment is possible in some cases. The risk of spina bifida is reduced if the intending mother takes folic acid supplements from before the time of conception.

spinal anaesthesia General term for subarachnoid or *epidural anaesthesia.*

spinal cord Long cord of nerve fibres and nerve cells that runs from its connection with the *medulla oblongata* of the brain at the top, down the centre of the protecting spinal column to about the level of the second lumbar vertebra. From it, at every vertebral junction, pairs of nerves extend across and to all parts of the body. The spinal cord is one of the two elements of the *central nervous system* (the other is the brain), which controls and monitors all aspects of movement and perception. Like the brain, the cord is surrounded by the three membranous *meninges*, and is made up of *white matter* and *grey matter.*

spinal nerves 31 pairs of nerves that leave the *spinal cord* at vertebral junctions to extend across and to all parts of the body, branching as they do so. Every nerve has two roots in the spinal cord – one for sensory information to be relayed to the brain, the other for motor instruction relayed from the brain – although they merge outside the cord.

spinal puncture Diagnostic procedure also called a *lumbar puncture.*

spine Backbone, bony yet flexible structure comprising the 33 *vertebrae* and their *intervertebral discs*, which surrounds and protects the *spinal cord.* The ribcage is attached to the upper half; towards the bottom the spine is supported by the *pelvis*. A vital part of the skeleton, the spineís ability to support the weight of the head and much of that of the torso has allowed *Homo sapiens* to evolve into an upright, bipedal species. Disorders of the spine include *spina bifida, spondylitis, prolapsed vertebral disc* and curvature (*kyphosis, lordosis* or *scoliosis*).

spirochaete Type of bacterium that has or adopts a spiral shape. *Syphilis* is caused by spirochaete.

spleen Organ in the upper left abdomen, located beside the *liver* and beneath the *diaphragm*. Its main purpose is to provide and renew the *phagocytes* of the *reticulo-endothelial system*; it also produces lymphocytes and acts as a blood reservoir. For all these reasons it has an excellent blood supply, and is composed largely of spongy tissue. But all those functions can be fulfilled by other organs, and surgical removal of the spleen (splenectomy) – possibly following injury – seldom causes problems.

splint Rigid strut used to support and immobilize a fracture before or after resetting.

Spock, Benjamin (1903–1998) American paediatrician whose publication of *Baby and Childcare* in 1946 had a worldwide impact for at least two decades thereafter. His political views cost him popularity in the USA in the 1960s.

spondylitis Inflammation of the joints between the vertebrae of the *spine* or between the *sacrum* and *ilium*. A common form is *ankylosing spondylitis*, in which the joints of the spine gradually fuse together. Symptoms are stiffness and back pain. Treatment depends on diagnosis and exact location – either rest or exercise may be prescribed.

spondylosis Degeneration and disintegration of the *intervertebral discs* that normally give the *spine* its flexibility. Symptoms are pain and stiffness that may be accompanied by audible friction of bone surfaces when the spine is bent. Local support may help the condition; surgical collars or belts may prevent muscular *spasm*. Surgery may be necessary, however, if a nerve becomes pinched.

spore Seed-body of a plant or fungus (which may act as an allergen if inhaled), or the reproductive body produced by a micro-organism (such as bacterium).

sports injuries Injuries, sometimes serious, that are accidental in most sports but incidental in others (such as boxing and rugby). Almost every sport represents a risk of muscular strains, psychological stress and minor abrasions. Fitness is therefore essential for the proper enjoyment of any sport.

sprain Stretching or partial tearing of one or more *ligaments* (particularly in the ankle). Treatment includes immediate ice-packs and long-term rest. Full healing may take months.

sprue Disorder of the small intestine that results in the malabsorption of food. It is prevalent in people who move residence from a temperate climate to a tropical one (tropical sprue), and may be caused by *coeliac disease* (called non-tropical sprue in adults), *pancreatitis* or infestation by intestinal *worms*. Symptoms are steatorrhoea, an inflamed tongue and sore mouth, and possibly swelling of the ankles and muscular cramp. Treatment is with a diet high in calories and proteins, but low in cereals (because they contain gluten, which is implicated in coeliac disease).

sputum Commonly called phlegm, mucus coughed up out of the bronchial passages. It may be examined in diagnosis of respiratory diseases or disorders.

squamous cell Flattened "scale-like" cell, of the *epithelium*.

squint Medical name strabismus, a defect in the directional orientation of one eye. It usually arises as a congenital abnormality, but later in life may be caused by weakness in one of the eye muscles or by paralysis of a motor nerve. In mild cases, corrective *glasses* may be worn to correct the fault. Eye exercises may improve muscular co-ordination. In more severe cases – in which double vision may cause giddiness or nausea – surgery may be necessary.

St Vitus' dance Common name for *Sydenham's chorea*.

stammering Also called stuttering, a disruption of the fluency of speech, such that individual syllables may take an extra second or two to emerge, or be immediately and involuntarily repeated. The cause is psychological or educational, not organic; the effect becomes worse with stress. *Speech therapy* can usually help.

stapes Small, stirrup-shaped bone in the middle ear, attached to the membrane of the "window" of the inner ear, and articulating with the *incus*.

Staphylococcus Common type of spherical bacterium that tends to cluster in bunches. Infection with these bacteria causes the formation of *pus*, in abscesses and boils. Toxins produced by them may cause food poisoning. Some have become resistant to *antibiotics*.

starch Carbohydrate common in the diet, particularly in plant foods, such as cereals and root vegetables. During the process of digestion, starch is transformed into the sugar glucose, through the catalysing effect of the enzyme amylase.

Starling, Ernest H. (1866–1927) London professor of physiology who first identified the nature and function of a *hormone*. He also derived Starlingís law, which states that a muscle (especially the heart muscle) increases its force of contraction in proportion to the increase in stretching while at rest.

starvation Dangerous condition of *malnutrition* through having too little (or nothing) to eat. After the body has used up all its resources of energy-giving fats, it begins using up its own proteins, and body weight decreases rapidly. If sufficient fluids are taken, this may continue for up to about four weeks. By then the body may have lost half its weight, and the heart and the nervous system be the only tissues not to have been depleted in some way; permanent tissue damage will have been done.

steatorrhoea Condition in which a patient passes faeces containing an abnormally high proportion of fat. It is caused by a disorder in the intestinal mechanism for absorbing fat in the body and is a symptom of *sprue*. The faeces are pale, and smell offensively.

stenosis Narrowing of a tube or vessel within the body, generally as an abnormality caused by infection, muscle spasm or fatty deposit.

sterility Either an inability to have children; or the complete absence of potentially infective micro-organisms (pathogens).

sterilization Either the process of rendering a person sterile – unable to have children – common methods of which are *vasectomy* for men, and surgically cutting or closing of the *Fallopian tubes* (salpingectomy) in women; or any method to free an enclosed environment or equipment of infective micro-organisms (pathogens).

sternum Breastbone, the flat bone that provides the vertical support at the front of the ribcage, extending from the base of the neck down to just below the diaphragm. At the top, the sternum is connected to each shoulder blade (scapula) by a collarbone (clavicle). In children, the fact that the bone is actually made up of three sections from top to bottom is visible on X-rays; the sternum of a woman is on average about 20 per cent shorter than that of a man.

steroids Naturally occurring compounds that share a similar chemical structure and have powerful effects on the body. The term is most often used of the *corticosteroids, hormones* secreted by the adrenal glands; other natural steroids are the *sex hormones*, bile salts and *cholesterol*. Some have been synthesized and are used in treatment.

stethoscope Instrument that amplifies sounds from inside a patientís body. It is used especially to diagnose disorders of the heart and lungs.

stillbirth Birth of a dead baby (that is a foetus after the 24th week of pregnancy). Many disorders may account for it – but invariably the mother needs special care and counselling for some time afterwards. Birth of a dead foetus younger than this is called a *miscarriage* (or, sometimes, a spontaneous abortion).

stimulant Substance (often a drug) that stimulates the action of part of the body, especially of the brain. *Amphetamines* and caffeine are stimulants. The opposite is a *depressant* – but *antidepressants* are not necessarily stimulants.

sting, insect Injection of poison by an insect, especially a wasp or a bee. Unless the sting causes an allergic reaction, is in a highly sensitive area of the skin, or is multiple, there is usually no danger. The site should be checked to make sure that the sting (poison sac) is not still in the skin; if it is, it should be scraped out with a fingernail or blunt edge, not pulled out or removed with tweezers (which can squeeze more poison into the skin). Ice can soothe any type of sting; sodium bicarbonate solution (for bee stings) or vinegar (for wasp stings) may alleviate the pain.

stitch Pain beneath the base of the ribcage that occurs during exercise, particularly within an hour or so of eating, and particularly if there has been no attempt at breath control. It is a type of *cramp*.

stitches Known medically as sutures, method of closing a cleanly sliced wound by sewing each side of it together. Various materials may be used – especially silk or thin wire – some dissolving altogether, others requiring to be painlessly removed after the wound has healed sufficiently.

Stokes-Adams syndrome Recurrent bouts of loss of consciousness, caused by a lack of sufficient blood pressure in the arteries, resulting from a disorder of the heart, especially of the *pacemaker*. Treatment is generally by surgical implantation of an artificial pacemaker.

stomach First major organ of *digestion* in the alimentary canal, situated at the lower end of the oesophagus. Its walls are flexible, internally covered in a mucous membrane lining which also has many glands that secrete digestive juices – especially *hydrochloric acid* and *pepsin*. Muscles in the walls produce a churning motion that helps to break down the food. Liquids are absorbed through the walls, particularly when the stomach is empty. From the stomach the food passes on through the pyloric sphincter to the *duodenum*.

stomach pump Tube for siphoning out the contents of the stomach, often in cases of poisoning or drug abuse. It is inserted through the mouth and down the oesophagus.

stomatitis Inflammation of the mucous membranes of the mouth, caused usually by local infection or an infection elsewhere in the body. If the salivary glands are also affected, dryness of the mouth may become a problem.

stone Common name for a *calculus*.

stool Alternative word for *faeces*.

strabismus Medical name for a *squint*.

strain Either the overstretching of one or more muscles, leading to pain that may be cured by heat and careful exercise; or a general term for mental stress leading to fatigue.

strawberry birthmark A pink *birthmark* (naevus).

Streptococcus Genus of spherical *bacteria* which tend to group together in strings or chains. A large number of different types exist, many quite harmless to humans. Others, however, cause infections – some serious (*bacterial endocarditis, pneumonia* and *scarlet fever*) – and, occasionally, allergic reactions. One type causes painful inflammation of the throat ("strep throat"). Most streptococcal conditions respond to treatment with antibiotics.

stress Physical or mental overexertion. Physical stress may aggravate an already existing condition or injury. Mental stress – anxiety, grief, constant pain, and so on – may cause not only behavioural problems but physical symptoms, and long-term stress may affect the bodyís hormone balance. Some physical conditions, if not actually caused by mental stress, are certainly made worse by it (such as *peptic ulcer, migraine* and some allergies). Attempts to remove stress are therefore an important part of the treatment of such disorders. Treatment depends on the source of stress, and will usually include attempts to avoid or reduce lifestyle factors that provoke stress and sometimes training in mental coping skills to deal with stress more effectively.

stretcher Litter for conveying an ill patient who cannot walk. At its simplest, it consists of two long poles with canvas slung between, carried by two people. In an emergency, a stretcher can be improvised from two jackets and a pair of broom handles, a wide board or even an old door.

stria Stripe of differently coloured tissue, especially any of the "stretch-marks" on the skin of the abdomen following pregnancy and childbirth. Skeletal *muscle* appears striated in bands when viewed with a microscope.

striated muscle Type of *muscle*, often also called skeletal muscle.

stricture Narrowing of a tube or vessel, potentially causing pressure or blockage in the flow of its contents. Inflammation, injury, muscle spasm, use of drugs, congenital disorder, high lipid level in the blood – any of these may be a cause.

stroke Disruption in the blood flow around part of the brain, caused either by a blood clot (*thrombus*) in an artery supplying the brain (occurring there or carried there by the circulation from elsewhere) or by the bursting of a blood vessel anywhere in the brain. A common result is the sudden *paralysis* of one side of the body; it may be weak and temporary, strong and permanent, or any intermediate form. A stroke is really a symptom of cardiovascular disorder that has a sudden catastrophic effect on the brain; a mild stroke may precede a more serious one – diagnosis and treatment may reduce the chance of the second. The nature of the paralysis that results depends on the area of the brain affected: very often the weakness is only partial but speech may be affected (if the victim is conscious); sometimes there is *incontinence*. Some patients make a full recovery, but others retain a variety of handicaps (including loss of speech or partial paralysis), which improve only very slowly, if at all. An old term for a stroke is apoplexy. Treatment is mostly by *physiotherapy* (and, if necessary, *speech therapy*) to achieve *rehabilitation*. Depending on the underlying cause, drug treatment or occasionally surgery may also be recommended to reduce the risk of a second stroke.

stroke volume Volume of blood pumped into the *aorta* by the left ventricle of the heart at each contraction.

stupor State in which mental and sensory response to external stimuli is very slow or absent altogether.

stuttering Alternative word for *stammering*.

stye Small *abscess* at the base of an eyelash. It is caused by bacterial infection, possibly spread from elsewhere on the face. Symptoms are swelling, redness and pain. Treatment is frequent bathing and, commonly, plucking the affected eyelash.

styptic Astringent substance that stems bleeding. Silver nitrate, alum, alcohol and one form of vitamin K are examples of styptics (or, technically, haemostatics).

subarachnoid Describing the area filled with cerebrospinal fluid between the *arachnoid membrane* and the *pia mater*, two of the three *meninges* that surround the brain and the spinal cord. Within this subarachnoid space are also several large blood vessels. The bursting of one of these blood vessels in the brain (subarachnoid haemorrhage) causes a dangerous condition resembling a *stroke*.

subconscious In *psychoanalysis*, all the memories, feelings and associations that can be recalled to the consciousness (and have not been repressed far deeper into the *unconscious*).

subcutaneous Underneath the dual surface of the skin (the epidermis and the dermis) – but above deeper levels of muscle, and referring commonly to the layer of connective tissue in between. It is a common site for certain types of *injections*.

sublimation In *psychoanalysis*, a sort of compromise in which the urge to fulfil antisocial or unhealthy desires is channelled into activities that are socially acceptable or healthy.

subliminal Under the threshold of conscious attention, but nevertheless received by the sensory system and possibly acted upon unconsciously. For instance, the introduction of an advertising message as one frame in a film or television picture (which is on the screen for too short a time to be consciously seen) is called subliminal advertising (and is banned in most countries).

sudden infant death syndrome (SIDS) Medical name for cot death, the sudden, unexplained death of an apparently healthy infant during the first two years of life. It is most common between two and six months, in premature and bottle-fed babies, those living in poor conditions, and where there has been a previous cot death in the family. Many suspected links have been investigated, including overheating, respiratory failure, allergic reactions, a viral infection (many infants who succumb have had a respiratory infection in the preceding days, although this alone is not severe enough to explain the death) and even parental maltreatment, but the cause remains elusive and research continues. However, one important factor seems to be the babyís sleeping position, as cot death is more common among those laid to sleep on their fronts. Previous advice to do this has now been reversed and it is recommended that parents lay babies on their backs ("back to sleep"), which this has resulted in a considerable fall in cot death *incidence*.

suffocation Prevention of the passage of air in or out of the lungs, leading quickly to unconsciousness and, unless treated, to death. Suffocation may be caused by an obstruction in the throat (choking) or over the mouth. In such cases, emergency treatment may include *tracheotomy*.

suggestion In psychology, the implanting in somebodyís mind of the wish to do, to feel, or to be something. The person may not consciously realize that it has been suggested.

suicide Taking oneís own life. An attempt at suicide is very commonly a cry for help, a gesture of despair that is ultimately intended not to end it all but to produce a change in circumstances. It has been calculated that about one in five of all emergency hospital admissions is for attempted suicide, and that four out of five attempted suicides are relieved to have survived. Many potential suicides have been dissuaded and comforted by counselling from the Samaritans.

sulphonamides Drugs that are particularly effective against bacterial infections; most are administered orally. They are also called sulpha drugs, and are widely used. Some resistant strains of bacteria have, however, been reported following long-term use, and there are occasionally some unpleasant minor side-effects.

sunburn Overheating of the skin by the ultraviolet radiation of the sun. A genuine form of burn, extreme sunburn may cause swelling, blistering and shock symptoms (*heatstroke*). People with fair skin and red hair are more at risk as their skin type is more sensitive. Recurrent sunburn over a long period may cause serious skin disorders and even cancer, and severe sunburn in children increases the risk of malignant *melanoma* in later life. Treatment is to avoid further sun exposure and ease the symptoms with skin lotions.

sunstroke Alternative name for *heatstroke*.

superego In *psychoanalysis*, the part of the mind that approves of right and disapproves of wrong, reflecting the ideals and instructions instilled by parents and teachers, and providing the behavioural goals towards which the *ego* strives.

suppository Soluble capsule containing one or more specific drugs. When inserted into the *vagina* or into the *rectum* through the *anus*, the drugs released have either a local, concentrated effect or a systemic action. For instance, morphine suppositories may be given if the oral route is not possible. Suppositories for use in the vagina are also known as *pessaries*.

suppression Prevention of any activity or of the appearance of symptoms. In psychology, the term is also used for the conscious refusal to acknowledge the existence or effect of an idea that is particularly unpleasant – a form of defence mechanism.

suppuration Formation of *pus* in an infected and inflamed area (such as an abscess or boil). The pus itself is highly infective.

suprarenal gland Another name for the *adrenal gland*.

surgeon Qualified physician who undertakes surgical operations. Basic training is followed by specialized training. In many specialties, the surgeon has to perform as one of a complex and expert team; in others, a surgeon may operate alone, using local anaesthetic.

surgery Both the clinic in which a doctor daily interviews, treats and prescribes for patients, and the branch of medicine that involves operating on and within a patient following one or more surgical incisions. In this latter sense there are many specialties of surgery, including *cardiothoracic surgery, cryosurgery*, dental and *orthodontic* surgery, *gynaecological* and *obstetric surgery, microsurgery, neurosurgery, orthopaedic surgery, paediatric surgery, plastic* and *cosmetic surgery, urogenital surgery* and *vascular surgery*. Operations in many of these disciplines require general anaesthesia and an entire team of trained surgical, nursing and paramedical staff; nevertheless, all surgical operations carry some degree of risk to the patient – whose permission for the operation is therefore a legal requirement.

surrogate Temporary substitute or stand-in, acting on behalf of another. In treatment for sexual problems where a regular partner is not available, a surrogate sexual partner provided by the therapist may help the patient to regain normal sexual functioning. A *surrogate mother* is one who bears a child for another woman or couple to rear.

surrogate mother A woman who offers her services in becoming pregnant and giving birth to a child with the aim that the baby will be handed over after birth to someone else to raise, usually an infertile couple, because the intending mother either cannot ovulate or cannot for some reason bear children herself. The simplest arrangement is where the surrogate conceives through *sexual intercourse* with the womanís partner; such informal agreements are discouraged in the UK. A similar genetic result is obtained when, with or occasionally without medical involvement, the surrogate conceives through artificial insemin tion using the prospective fatherís sperm. Or donor sperm may be used (the baby will then be related to neither of the social parents, that is, those who intend to raise the child). In any of these cases the baby is the genetic child of the surrogate mother: this is known as partial surrogacy. Alternatively, the intending mother may provide her own eggs for *in vitro fertilization*. The resulting embryos are then implanted in the surrogate and if the fatherís sperm are used the baby will thus be genetically related to both social parents – this is known as full surrogacy. Irrespective of the genetic relationship, in English law the birth mother is the legal mother; however, surrogacy is now recognized to the extent that, provided she consents and certain conditions are fulfilled, a legal transfer of parental rights and responsibilities to the social parents may be effected. Payment for surrogacy is illegal in Britain and many other parts of the world.

sutures Medical name for the *stitches* used in sewing up a wound; metal clips may also be used. It is also the medical name for the fibrous junctions of many of the bones of the skull, which knit together only after birth, and resembling a sort of stitching together as if sewn.

swab Absorbent pad, commonly of cotton wool, used to soak up body fluids in cleaning a wound or in collecting material for examination, or to apply dressings. (Those used during surgical operations are usually "labelled" with a radiopaque tab for easy tracing should one be inadvertently left inside a patient.)

swallowing Set of actions mainly by the jaw and the tongue that transfers food or drink from the mouth to the throat and oesophagus. The soft palate closes off the nasal cavity, and the larynx is closed by the *epiglottis*, so that only the alimentary canal remains open and the air passages are closed.

sweat Common name for *perspiration*.

swelling Serious swelling of whole parts of the body is known medically as *oedema*. Local swellings can be caused by an insect bite or sting, infection or an allergic reaction and usually represent symptoms that require medical diagnosis.

Sydenham's chorea Rare disorder caused by an inflammation of blood vessels in the brain that represents an allergic reaction to bacterial infection, especially to *rheumatic fever*. It most commonly attacks children, female more often than male. Symptoms include involuntary jerks of the limbs and contortions of the face (with consequent problems in speech). Treatment is with *antibiotics*, aspirin and bed rest, and may be continued for several months. The condition sometimes recurs. Formerly known as St Vitusí dance, the condition is not related to *Huntington's chorea*.

symbiosis Beneficial relationship between two different kinds of organism, both of which need or enjoy the presence or effect of the other.

sympathetic nervous system Part of the *autonomic nervous system* that responds to emergencies – the need to take immediate and drastic action. It speeds up the heartbeat, raising blood pressure; it cools the skin by sweating; it dilates the bronchi of the lungs, for more oxygen; and it dilates the pupils of the eyes. The increase in the blood pressure causes the *adrenal glands* to secrete *adrenaline*. The release of glucose by the liver also provides extra energy for action. Once the emergency is over, the *parasympathetic nervous system* takes over to "calm things down".

symptom Abnormal feature or perception on or in the body, or in mental attitude and behaviour, that to a patient represents one of the effects of a disorder. Interpretation of symptoms is a chief factor in diagnosis.

synapse Tiny gap between the ending of one nerve *axon* and the next *neurone*. The gap is bridged by chemical *neurotransmitters* in the process of passing on nerve impulses.

syncope Medical term for fainting, a sudden loss of consciousness caused by temporarily inadequate blood supply to the brain. It may be due to injury or severe haemorrhage (bleeding), but is more usually harmless, caused by prolonged standing, especially with overheating, or emotional shock, and the person recovers rapidly and completely. However, fainting for no evident reason or persistent fainting suggests the need for a medical check-up.

syndrome Set of symptoms and signs all associated with one disorder.

synergism Effect of two agents that in combination is more than the sum of the effect of each separately. The term is applied both to the use of certain muscles that work in combination, and to a combination of two or more drugs used simultaneously. A potentially dangerous synergic effect can occur between certain drugs (such as the antidepressants known as MAO inhibitors) and certain foodstuffs, or between certain drugs and alcohol.

synovial membrane Smooth membrane that lines the bones at joints – forming a fluid-filled *bursa* at some – and that covers many of the *tendons*. The membrane secretes its own lubricating fluid (synovial fluid).

synovitis Inflammation of the *synovial membrane*, caused by infection, injury or an arthritic disorder. Treatment depends on cause.

syphilis Contagious *sexually transmitted disease* caused by bacterial infection. Technically there are three stages of syphilis; it is now rare, however, for the third stage to appear, thanks to modern treatments. Primary syphilis involves the formation of a *chancre* (painless ulcer) at the site of the infection, on a mucous membrane (in the vagina, urethra, mouth or anus). It secretes a highly infectious fluid and persists for between two and six weeks before healing spontaneously. Secondary syphilis appears after a further interval of about eight weeks. Symptoms are headache, high temperature, muscle pain, fatigue and a rash. Ulcers form in the site of the infection and are again highly infectious; this stage may last for several months. Tertiary syphilis may affect any part of the body and appear in almost any extreme form – severe heart disease, severe skin or bone disorder, or severe disease of the brain and spinal cord. Symptoms and tissue damage correspond to location. Penicillin forms the basis of all treatments for syphilis, including treatment for those born with the disease (congenital syphilis).

syringe Tube, at one end of which is a fine hollow needle and at the other a plunger attached to a piston within the tube. It is used to inject fluids through the skin or into a vein (a hypodermic syringe), or to draw fluids out. Another type of syringe is used to irrigate cavities such as the ears, rectum or vagina. It is larger, consisting mostly of rubber tubing with a sizeable bulb to provide a pumping action.

systemic Pertaining to the whole body, not specifically any one part.

systole Contraction of the heart muscle, the action which pumps the blood from the ventricle. The relaxation of the muscle is the *diastole*.

T

tabes dorsalis Medical name for tertiary *syphilis* affecting the spinal cord; yet another name for it is *locomotor ataxia*.

tablet Another name for a *pill*.

tachycardia Fast heartbeat. The condition may be caused by exertion, emotion, use of drugs, fever or disease.

talipes Medical name for *clubfoot*.

talus Major bone at the ankle, one of the seven bones of the *tarsus*. It articulates with the bones of the lower leg.

tampon Absorbent pad retained in a body orifice to collect fluids, particularly the cylindrical pad used by menstruating women to contain the menstrual blood.

tapeworm Parasitic *worm* that may infest the intestines. The larvae are consumed in undercooked contaminated beef, pork or fish, and mature into the adult worms once in the intestine. Tapeworms have a hooked head that attaches to the intestinal wall, with a flat, segmented body dangling beneath. Eggs form in the segments, which break off and pass out of the body. The major symptom is the appearance of these segments in the faeces; there may also be abdominal pain. Tapeworms can also cause the formation of intestinal cysts, containing more larvae. Treatment is with antihelminthic (antiworm) drugs.

tarsus Group of seven bones in the ankle and upper foot. The talus is the ankle bone, and the calcaneus is the heel. Beyond the tarsus are the metatarsal bones, which form the arch of the foot.

taste Sensation originating in the mouth that consists of a (usually subtle) combination of sweetness, sourness, bitterness and saltiness. The sense receptors are taste buds that lie grouped around *papillae* on the surface of the tongue, and the sensations they detect are helped by the presence of *saliva* (a dry solid cannot be tasted). The taste buds send impulses along the glossopharyngeal and lingual nerves to the brain, where they are interpreted as taste. Something akin to taste may also be provided by the sense of smell with pungent foods or drinks. The sense of taste can be affected by disorders of the mouth, and it gradually deteriorates as part of the normal aging process.

Tatum, Edward L. (1909–1975) American biochemist who discovered that the genes which make up the chromosomes are each responsible for the formation of one enzyme. He was awarded a Nobel Prize in 1958.

taxis Manual manipulation of displaced bones or internal organs back into their normal positions.

Tay-Sachs disease Hereditary disorder which prevents the metabolism of *lipids* (fatty substances) in the body, thus leading to an accumulation of lipids in the cells of the brain. It causes blindness, spasticity, mental retardation and usually death before the age of five. It cannot be cured, but it can be avoided by genetic testing of parents likely to be carriers.

TB Abbreviation of *tuberculosis*.

tears Watery secretion of the *lacrimal glands* through the tear ducts round the eyes. Slightly alkaline, tears contain both salt and an antibacterial constituent, and they lubricate and protect the cornea of the eye.

teeth Hard structures, rooted in sockets in each jaw, that chop and chew food in the mouth. The main constituent of the teeth is dentine, covered by an external layer of enamel. At the core of each tooth is the pulp, in which there are nerves and blood vessels. Childrenís *deciduous teeth* number 20; an adult may have a full complement of 32 – 8 incisors for cutting, 4 canines for tearing or transfixing, 8 premolars as utility teeth, and 12 molars (including wisdom teeth) for grinding. Poor dental hygiene leads to an accumulation of *plaque* on the teeth, in which bacteria can erode the enamel causing *dental decay* (caries), which in turn results in the pain of toothache if it penetrates the dentine. Brushing the teeth properly prevents plaque, and a toothpaste containing *fluoride* hardens the enamel and reduces the incidence of decay.

teething The time and effect of *teeth* erupting from the gums. By common usage the term is used mainly for the cutting of the *deciduous teeth* in a baby, but it applies also to the coming through of both the adult set of teeth and the later wisdom teeth.

temperament Habitual mental disposition reflecting an attitude to life.

temperature Important gauge of a personís health, measured by a clinical *thermometer*. Normal body temperature (measured under the tongue, in the armpit or in the rectum) is about 37°C (98.4°F) – fractionally higher in the rectum – but everyoneís temperature varies during the day; womenís are further affected by the *menstrual cycle*. Temperature is considered high if it is 1°C (1.8°F) or more above normal, low if that much below normal. A high temperature (fever) is a common symptom of an infectious disease. Extreme departures of temperature from normal (hyperthermia and hypothermia) are dangerous conditions requiring immediate medical treatment.

tendon Tough white band of fibrous tissue that makes up a *collagen* cord connecting a muscle to a bone. Many are covered in sheaths of *synovial membrane*, which reduce friction and increase freedom of movement. Within the fibres are sensory nerve endings registering the degree of stretch (as is made use of in the knee-jerk *reflex*) and blood vessels that enable a tendon to heal rapidly after injury. Ssee also *ligament*.

tennis elbow Painful inflammation of the tendon attachment at the outer side of the elbow after persistent straining of the joint. Generally, treatment is merely with pain-killers and rest; physiotherapy may be helpful and in extreme cases a local injection of steroid drugs may be given into the painful area. Apart from tennis, it can be caused by unaccustomed energetic movement (as perhaps with a screwdriver or a steering-wheel); a condition with similar symptoms is occasionally the result of a pinched nerve.

tenosynovitis Inflammation of the *synovial membrane* covering a *tendon*. Causes may be overexertion, infection or an arthritic disorder; treatment depends on the diagnosis.

tension State of *stress* which may manifest itself as nervous agitation or even unnatural calm. It is a well-known factor, for example, in *premenstrual syndrome*.

teratogen Any agent or process affecting a pregnant woman that causes serious deformity in the foetus. Teratogens include infection with *rubella*, drugs such as thalidomide, and irradiation with X-rays.

tertian fever Form of *malaria* in which attacks of fever occur every third day.

testis Either of the two major, plum-shaped organs within the *scrotum* (also called a testicle). Each is a primary male sex gland, producing *androgens* (male sex hormones) and acting as a reproductive organ. The testes are located in the abdomen before birth, and descend into the scrotum where they are maintained at lower than body temperature (maintaining the testes at a high temperature affects fertility in a man). Internally, within a protective outside "skin", a testis has many convoluted *seminiferous tubules*, in which sperm are formed. Ducts lead from the tubules to an amorphous structure on top of the testis – the *epididymis* – in which the sperm mature. Fluid from the *seminal vesicles* mixes with the sperm to form semen, which travels up the *vas deferens* (sperm duct) at *ejaculation*. Disorders that can affect the testes include *cryptorchidism, epididymitis* (inflammation), *hydrocele* (accumulation of fluid) and, rarely, cancer.

test meal Meal comprising standard types of food in standard quantities to investigate the secretion of digestive juices. Another type of test meal is a *barium meal*.

testosterone Male *sex hormone*, the principal *androgen* produced (particularly at puberty) by the testes under the direction of the *pituitary gland* secretions of *follicle-stimulating hormone* (FSH) and *luteinizing hormone*. It is because of this process that boys take on the *secondary sexual characteristics* of men. Women also have a small amount of testosterone in their bodies, where it determines the pattern of hair growth.

tests Investigatory procedures that are often an essential part of diagnosis, especially when symptoms are complex or unusual. There are many hundreds of medical tests, each specific and ranging from blood tests and biopsies (examination of tissue samples) to a glucose tolerance test (to investigate the functioning of the hormone insulin) and a patch test (to determine possible allergic reactions to various substances applied to the skin). A few require local, or even general, anaesthesia.

test-tube baby (*in vitro* fertilization) Result of the fertilization of a human ovum outside the body of the prospective mother; implantation of the fertilized ovum in the womb (uterus) then leads to a normal pregnancy and childbirth. See *fertilization*.

tetanus Serious bacterial infection contracted by direct contact between the bloodstream and spores of the bacteria in the soil or the bite of an animal (through an open wound). The disease is primarily caused by the toxin produced by the bacteria. Symptoms are initially overall stiffness and nervous agitation. Then high temperature and a rigid immobility of the mouth and face muscles (giving rise to the common name for the disease, lockjaw) may lead to an inability to breathe, severe pain, and convulsions. Emergency *tracheostomy* may be required, with artificial respiration and intravenous injection of fluids. Further treatment is usually with antitoxin and muscle-relaxant drugs. An anti-tetanus vaccine is available and is routinely administered to anybody who has a dirty wound or animal bite unless they have been vaccinated within the previous 5 years.

tetany Condition in which a lack of blood calcium causes muscle *spasms* in the feet, hands and face. The deficiency may be caused by poor diet, *hyperventilation*, or underactivity of the *parathyroid glands*.

thalamus Either of the two central masses within the cerebral hemispheres of the brain. The thalami receive and co-ordinate all the sensory information – except that of the sense of smell – that reaches conscious awareness.

thalassaemia Hereditary form of *anaemia*, common in Mediterranean countries and Africa, caused by a defect in the red (iron-containing) blood pigment *haemoglobin*, which leads to anaemia, spleen enlargement and defects in the bone marrow. Outward symptoms are pallor, breathlessness, fatigue and, sometimes, *jaundice*. Those severely affected have usually inherited the defect from both parents (thalassaemia major), whereas inheritance from only one parent may leave the individual relatively symptom-free, though still able to transmit the abnormality to their children. Thalassaemia may now be diagnosed in the womb, allowing parents the chance to terminate the pregnancy if the foetus is likely to be severely affected. Treatment is to alleviate the symptoms, usually requiring repeated blood transfusions.

therapy Any form of remedial treatment. The adjective is "therapeutic".

thermography Method of recording differences of heat in and on the body, using a special camera sensitive to infra-red radiation given off by the body. Some disorders (such as cancer) cause local anomalies in temperature. This method, showing different temperatures as different colours, makes diagnosis easy. The picture produced is called a thermogram.

thermometer Instrument for measuring temperature – usually a thin cylinder of glass or plastic, containing a narrow column of mercury that can be read against a calibrated scale. There are several kinds. The most common types used in medicine (clinical thermometers) are for insertion under the tongue or in the rectum to measure body *temperature*.

thiamine *Vitamin*, known also as aneurin or vitamin B_1, that is important to carbohydrate metabolism. It is found in many foods – meat, nuts, pulses, brown rice and potatoes – and dietary deficiency is rare in temperate climates. But some disorders (such as *sprue*) or conditions (such as pregnancy or long-term alcoholism) may also lead to deficiency symptoms – muscle disorders through degeneration of the associated nerves – found classically in *beriberi*.

thirst Strong desire to drink, generally as a result of a decreased level of body fluids, sensed internally as an increase in blood sodium and a decrease of potassium in the tissues. Thirst may naturally follow copious sweating, haemorrhage or vomiting, or be a symptom of *diabetes* or *heart failure*.

thoracic duct Major vessel of the *lymphatic* system, which collects lymph from the lower limbs and abdomen and from the left side of the torso, neck and head, to channel it into the blood system through a vein.

thorax Part of the body between the neck and the abdomen, the chest. The adjective is "thoracic".

threadworm Type of *roundworm* that may be parasitic in the human large intestine, also called a pinworm. Female worms emerge from the patientís rectum at night, lay eggs on the skin around the anus, and die. Scratching by the sufferer may cause the eggs to be picked up on the fingers and swallowed – to develop into more worms. Infestation is known as enterobiasis.

thrill Momentary – or very temporary – "switching on" by the body of the *sympathetic nervous system* as a response to high emotion. The actual sensation is caused mainly by a sudden increase in *adrenaline* in the blood.

thrombin Factor in the blood *clotting* mechanism that converts the protein fibrinogen to the thin strands of insoluble *fibrin* on which the *platelets* accumulate to begin the process of healing. Thrombin is an enzyme substance created only in the area of the injury. See also *coagulation*.

thromboembolism Presence of a blood clot that has become detached from its site of origin and travelled around the bloodstream (embolized) to lodge elsewhere. Causes are thus those of *thrombosis*, and symptoms may be similar. However, the most common site for an embolus to lodge is in the lungs (pulmonary embolism); a large embolus here may cause sudden death, smaller ones may cause heart failure or lung symptoms including coughing up blood. Treatment depends on the site but may include giving drugs to dissolve the clot (*thrombolysis*) or, particularly with a pulmonary embolus, surgery to remove the obstruction.

thrombolysis Use of drugs infused into the bloodstream to dissolve a blood clot, commonly after a *myocardial infarction* or pulmonary embolus (see *thromboembolism*).

thrombophlebitis Clotting of blood (*thrombosis*) occurring at the site of an inflammation in the wall of a vein (*phlebitis*). Pregnant women are particularly at risk, and it typically occurs in the leg veins, producing pain, tenderness and swelling, with local redness in the skin if superficial veins are involved. If, less often, deep veins of the calf are involved (see *deep vein thrombosis*), complications include *thromboembolism*. Treatment of superficial thrombophlebitis is with elasticated support of the area, and anti-inflammatory and analgesic drugs. Treatment where deep veins are involved may require drugs to prevent thromboembolism.

thrombosis Presence of one or more blood clots in a blood vessel. It may be caused either by disease or deformity of the blood vessel, or by a disturbance of the blood *clotting* mechanism – or by a combination of both. There may be associated inflammation. The result of thrombosis in an artery is a deficiency in blood circulation to the tissues supplied by the blood vessel. If this is the heart or the brain, symptoms of *myocardial infarction* or *stroke* may follow, and emergency treatment is necessary. If the clot (thrombus) becomes detached from its original site, it may travel (as an *embolus*) around the circulation until it lodges elsewhere – which may be equally dangerous. Treatment depends on diagnosis and location, but may include drugs to dissolve the clot (*thrombolysis*) or, sometimes, surgery.

thrombus Blood clot within a blood vessel. See *thrombosis*.

thrush Common name for the fungal infection *candidiasis*.

thumb Large, two-boned digit on the inner side of each hand. Set at an angle on the hand, it represents a great evolutionary advance in being opposable to the rest of the fingers, allowing extreme delicacy in handling and picking things up. *Dislocation* of the thumb at the joint with the hand is common and painful.

thymus Glandular organ that lies behind the breastbone just above the heart and made up of chamber-like lobes full of *lymphocytes*. Initially a significant part of the *immune system* in children, it grows with the body until puberty, after which it shrinks and seems to have no further function of importance.

thyroid gland Two-lobed endocrine gland in the front of the neck just below the *larynx*, responsible for the production and secretion of three *hormones*. Two of these (triiodothyronine and thyroxine) are vital both for normal physical and mental development and for metabolism in general. The third (calcitonin) is part of the bodyís mechanism to balance blood calcium and phosphate levels. Secretion of these is controlled by the initial secretion of *thyroid-stimulating hormone* (TSH) by the pituitary gland. Deficiency or excess in any of the hormones may have serious consequences. See *hyperthyroidism; hypothyroidism.*

thyroid-stimulating hormone (TSH) *Hormone* produced and secreted by the anterior (front part) of the *pituitary gland*, which in turn regulates the production and secretion of the hormones triiodothyronine and thyroxine by the *thyroid gland*. As a result, any malfunction in the secretion of TSH may lead to *hyperthyroidism* or *hypothyroidism.*

thyrotoxicosis Medical term for the condition resulting from *hyperthyroidism.*

thyroxine Major *hormone* produced by the *thyroid gland.*

tibia Shin bone, the thicker of the two bones that frame the lower leg (the other is the *fibula*). It is also the inner of the two and is jointed at the top with the thigh bone or femur (the joint being protected by the knee-cap or patella) and at the bottom with the talus (at the ankle). It is also connected at both ends with the fibula.

tic Involuntary twitching of a muscle, generally in the face but also possibly in the neck or shoulder. Like stammering, the condition is worsened by stress and is probably caused by a minor psychological disturbance.

tic douloureux Old name for *trigeminal neuralgia.*

tick External parasite that sucks blood through the skin. Related to *mites*, ticks may carry some fairly dangerous infections, such as *relapsing fever, typhus* and *Q fever*, and an individual type of paralysis that may seriously affect breathing.

tincture Form of plant-derived drug in alcoholic solution.

tinea Fungal infection commonly known as *ringworm.*

tinnitus Noises in the ear not caused by external sounds. Often the cause is not discovered, but the condition may result from an excess of *wax*, high blood pressure, infections of the eardrum or inner ear, the use of certain drugs (such as aspirin) or disorders such as *Ménière's disease*. Treatment depends on the cause; any underlying condition should be corrected, if possible, and any hearing loss alleviated with a hearing aid. Otherwise relaxation techniques and masking with a white noise machine may be helpful in reducing the distress caused by the sounds.

tissue Cellular structure of any part of the body. Skin, bone, cartilage, connective tissue, membrane, even blood (consisting of blood cells and plasma together), are all examples of tissues.

tissue bank Carefully listed and categorized collection of *tissue* material, stored in ideal conditions, for use in transplants, grafts and infusions in patients in an emergency. The major form of tissue kept in banks is blood; there are also banks for specific organs. For most, donors are urgently required.

tissue culture Growing in the laboratory of living tissues taken from a donor or patient, and supplied either with an appropriate growth environment and nutrients in order to generate more of the tissue, or with infective organisms in order to note the effect on the tissue. Of the former, particularly useful is the growing of skin tissues for patients with burns. Cultured from samples of the patientís own skin, the new tissue once grafted is most unlikely to suffer *rejection.*

tocopherol Vitamin E, a *vitamin* that seems to contribute to the structure of cells. It is found in many foods, including dairy products, eggs and cereals, and vitamin E deficiency is extremely rare.

toe Any of ten digits, five on each foot. The big toe has two bones; all other toes have three. Together they assist balance and walking.

tolerance Ability of the body to withstand or contain the effect of a stimulus such as pain, noise, heat, or a drug. To many such stimuli, tolerance increases in the body over long-term constant exposure; tolerance levels may then be said to be high. The effect of all drug treatments depends on a patientís low, normal or high tolerance level. High tolerance to an abused drug (such as alcohol or heroin) is a symptom of dependence. Tolerance is not directly related to sensitivity.

tomography Technique in *scanning* that involves the compilation of many cross-sectional "views" of the same part of the body to provide a three-dimensional computer-enhanced picture of that part at any level. A picture derived in this way is called a tomogram, or CT scan (*computerized tomography*).

tongue Muscular organ central to all functions of the mouth (eating, tasting, swallowing and speaking). It lies partly on the floor of the mouth and partly in the throat, but is attached also to the skull near the junctions with the jaw, and to the palate. It is covered with mucous membrane, and the upper surface in the mouth comprises groups of *papillae* and *taste buds*.

tonic Medication taken orally and intended to increase vigour and morale; or describing a state of continuous contraction of a muscle.

tonsillitis Inflammation of the *tonsils* (the bulging tissues at either side of the back of the mouth) that may be caused by bacterial or viral infection. Symptoms are a sore throat, high temperature, headache, and difficulty in swallowing. Young children may additionally suffer stomach cramps and abdominal pain, and are particularly vulnerable to repeated attacks. Treatment depends on diagnosis of the infective organism but concentrates on alleviating the symptoms; antibiotics may be used in cases of bacterial infection. The practice of surgically removing the tonsils (tonsillectomy) is now rare except in cases of excessively recurrent tonsillitis.

tonsils Spongy pads of lymphoid tissue on each side of the throat, above and below the tongue. Part of the *immune* system, they produce antibodies that destroy harmful antigens in the saliva. However, the tonsils are commonly affected by inflammation (*tonsillitis*), especially in children.

tonus State of semi-contraction of a muscle, representing a "normal" state neither fully contracted nor fully relaxed.

tooth See *teeth.*

toothache Pain caused by infection, such as *tooth decay*, or by *teething*.

tooth decay Medical name caries, the bacterial invasion – promoted by sugary and acidic foods and drinks – of the *plaque* (layer of debris) that adheres to the surface enamel of a tooth, and the gradual decomposition of the enamel and erosion of the dentine that comprises the substance of the tooth. Untreated, the destruction of the tooth eventually reaches the pulp, causing toothache, and potentially forming an abscess. Tooth decay can be prevented to a great degree by minimizing intake of sugary foods and fruit drinks, by regular oral hygiene, and by the application of *fluoride* salts (an ingredient of many toothpastes). Dental repair involves the removal of any decay (using a drill), and the stopping up of the resultant hole with a filling material.

torsion Condition of abnormal twisting. Torsion of an intestine, for example, may restrict the blood supply to the parts of the intestine twisted over each other, and cause an *infarction* unless treated urgently.

torticollis Medical name for *wryneck.*

total allergy syndrome Rare condition in which a patient appears allergically sensitive to almost everything. The condition begins gradually as an *allergy* to a few known allergens; the number of allergens then gradually increases, as does the allergic response to each allergen. Eventually the patient may have to live in a self-contained tent of purified air or oxygen, eating sterilized food and drink.

touch, sense of Sensation of pressure on the surface of the skin. The receptors are tiny nerve endings at various levels within the skin, combinations of which help to give an impression of whether the touch is cold or hot, liquid or solid, blunt or sharp, and so on.

tourniquet Tight band or strap wound round a limb above a wound to halt the flow of blood. The technique was once commonly advocated as a first-aid measure to stem blood loss (and prevent possible poisoning from, say, a snake bite). Now, direct pressure on the wound is considered more effective – and less dangerous in unskilled hands, since a tourniquet left on for too long can deprive the limb of blood and result in tissue damage and even *gangrene*. A tourniquet is still used, however, to pump up the veins when a blood sample is taken.

toxaemia Presence of bacterial *toxin* in the blood, resulting from a local bacterial infection. Symptoms are high temperature, nausea and general malaise. Treatment depends upon the infective organism.

toxaemia of pregnancy Dangerous condition of unknown cause that can occur in women in the final stages of pregnancy. Initial symptoms (pre-eclampsia) include high blood pressure, *oedema* in the legs, hands and ankles, and protein in the urine (*albuminuria*). Hospital treatment may be required even at this stage to ensure rest and, if necessary, drugs to reduce blood pressure. Untreated, the condition may worsen into the dangerous symptoms of *eclampsia*, potentially involving convulsions and coma, and increasing the possibility of the death of the foetus in the womb.

toxicology Study of the nature and effects of poisons and toxins.

toxic shock syndrome Serious condition in which shock develops as a result of *septicaemia*. There is sudden collapse of blood pressure, and the patient will be weak, pale and sweaty. It is most often due to infection with streptococcal bacteria developing on a foreign object within the body, particularly a tampon or *intrauterine contraceptive device (IUCD).*

Treatment involves antibiotics and often a drip to rebalance body fluids.

toxin Type of poison produced by an infective organism such as a bacterium. Toxins cause the formation in the body of special antibodies (antitoxins) to destroy or neutralize them. Chemically treated toxins used for vaccinations are called *toxoids*.

toxoid Chemically treated *toxin* that is no longer poisonous within the human body but retains the capacity to cause the formation of antibodies (antitoxins) in the bloodstream. Toxoids may thus be used as *vaccines*.

toxoplasmosis Potentially dangerous condition resulting from infestation by a parasitic protozoan that can use almost any mammal or bird as its host. Human beings ordinarily contract toxoplasmosis by eating undercooked meat that contains the protozoan larvae. Symptoms are usually relatively mild – muscle pains, slight lymph node enlargement – but may sometimes be severe, possibly involving secondary inflammations and, in pregnant women, abnormalities in the foetus or a miscarriage. Treated early, the condition responds quickly to antibiotics.

trace elements Minerals that the body needs daily, or at least regularly, in minute quantities (traces). Examples include copper, zinc, iodine and selenium.

trachea Windpipe, the strong cartilaginous tube down which air passes from the *larynx* to each of the two main bronchial passages leading to the *lungs*.

tracheitis Inflammation of the *trachea*, usually as part of a more general infection of the *larynx*, *bronchi*, *pharynx* or nose.

tracheotomy Creating a hole through the surface of the neck into the *trachea* (windpipe) as an emergency means of restoring *respiration* when there is a total blockage of the air passage in the throat or mouth. Such a blockage may be temporary – perhaps caused by an accident – or permanent, for instance if caused by cancer. In the latter case, the tracheotomy is also permanent, and is accompanied by the surgical implantation of a dual tube into the trachea (tracheostomy), the inner part of which is removable for cleaning.

trachoma Contagious infection of the *conjunctiva* of the eyes, which discharge *pus*. Untreated, the condition eventually spreads to the *cornea* and causes blindness. Treatment with *antibiotics* is generally effective. In advanced cases, corneal surgery may be required.

tract Long, complex system within the body. The term thus applies both to nerve pathways that extend across the body (such as the corticospinal tract) and to sequences of tubes that duct material from one part of the body to another (such as the digestive tract).

traction Outward pulling. The term is used particularly for the steady, gentle pulling on a fracture once reset (reduced) in order that the broken ends align properly, usually achieved by attaching hanging weights over a pulley. But the term can also refer to maintaining a pull on a joint to release a pinched nerve (especially in the spine) or to gently drawing out a baby from the birth canal using forceps.

trance State in which a personís attention is devoted entirely to one mental objective, to the exclusion of external physical stimuli. Trances occur with *hypnosis* and drugs that produce similar suggestivity, with forms of mental disorder, and with deep or religious meditation.

tranquillizers Drugs that calm, soothe and relax, without taking away intellectual capacity. There is a whole range of them to treat anything from minor anxiety to major *psychosis*.

Most have the side-effect of causing drowsiness. Some tranquillizers used to treat major psychoses also cause odd muscular actions, rashes or hormonal imbalance. In the long term, the tranquillizers for minor anxiety may be addictive.

transfusion Careful introduction of closely matched replacement blood, plasma or an equivalent (such as a saline solution) into a patientís bloodstream, to replace blood or fluid loss. The fluid flows slowly by gravity from a raised container down a tube and through a needle inserted into a vein. See also *blood group*.

transplant surgery Surgical operation to replace a defective or missing internal organ with one from a donor (who may be alive or recently dead). Great care must be taken to ensure the closest possible matching of tissues in order to minimize the possibility of tissue *rejection*. Kidney and liver transplants are among the most common; eyes and the heart (or heart-and-lungs) are rarer. Such surgery is now very often successful, but donors are still scarce.

transsexual Describing a person who is convinced that he or she has a body of the wrong sex. Such a conviction in childhood may perhaps be successfully discouraged; but if maturity is reached and the conviction is strong, a *sex change* operation may or may not be advised. Transsexualism is not the same as *transvestism*.

transvestism Desire and practice of wearing clothes of the opposite sex – generaliy of a man to wear womenís clothing – for pleasure and, in many cases (but not all), sexual gratification. It occurs in relation to both heterosexual and homosexual people; a transvestite is not, however, generally *trans-sexual*.

trauma Physical or mental wound.

travel sickness Form of *motion sickness*.

treatment Care, in terms of medication, nursing and any other therapy, designed to cure a disorder. Most forms of treatment are well established and effective. Disorders actually caused by treatment are known as *iatrogenic disorders*.

tremor Involuntary muscular trembling anywhere in the body. There are several types, and a multitude of possible causes (including simply old age). Medical diagnosis should be sought at the onset.

trench fever Type of feverish disease endemic during World War I, now supposed to be a form of *typhus*.

trench foot Also called immersion foot, the death of the surface skin on the foot caused by long-term exposure to freezing water (as happened to many soldiers in the trenches during World War I) and possibly local infection as well. In several cases, *gangrene* may occur. Treatment is as for *frostbite*.

trephination Surgical cutting of a hole in the skull in order to reach tissues beneath; it is also called trepanning. By extension, the word is used also to describe the cutting of a circular hole in other surfaces, such as the cornea of the eye.

trichinosis Disorder that results from infestation by a parasitic *roundworm*. In humans it is contracted by eating undercooked pork containing the wormís larvae. The larvae spread from the stomach internally to the small intestines, where they reproduce. The next generation of worms migrate to the muscles, where they form small, hard cysts. Any of many symptoms may occur, and diagnosis may be difficult. Following diagnosis, however, drug treatment is usually effective.

trichomoniasis Type of sexually transmitted infection caused by a parasitic protozoan. It affects the vagina in women, and the urethra in men, and a discharge is the major symptom in either case. Drug treatment is quickly effective. Another form of the protozoan causes *dysentery.*

trichuriasis Disorder caused by infestation of a parasitic *roundworm* known as the whipworm. In humans it is contracted by eating food contaminated with the wormís eggs, which then hatch and colonize the large intestine. The eggs representing the next generation are then passed out with the faeces. Symptoms are generally mild; there may be slight abdominal pain. Drug treatment is quickly effective.

tricuspid valve Heart *valve* between the right *atrium* and the right *ventricle* that has three flaps (cusps), which shut tightly to prevent backflow into the atrium when the ventricle contracts.

trigeminal nerve Nerve responsible for relaying sensory information from virtually all the front and top of the head to the brain, and for controlling the action of the lower jaw. It has three branches – towards the eyes, towards the upper jaw, and towards the lower jaw – and is also known as the fifth cranial nerve. Irritation of the nerve gives rise to *trigeminal neuralgia*.

trigeminal neuralgia Pain in the region supplied by the *trigeminal nerve*, particularly on one side of the face and triggered by slight movement of the skin (as with chewing or a light touch). The cause is not known but it may be an effect of old age. Drug treatment may be effective; surgery to cut the nerve is a last resort.

triiodothyronine Major *hormone* produced by the *thyroid gland.*

trisomy 21 Another name for *Down's syndrome*.

tropical medicine Branch of medicine that specializes in the diseases and disorders prevalent in tropical regions – such as *malaria* and many parasitic infestations – and in preventive measures for travellers to such regions.

trunk General term for the *thorax* and *abdomen* together considered a single unit of the body. The term is used also for the stem or initial main part of an organ that then branches.

truss Tight support for a *hernia*, usually consisting of a belt to which strapping and a largish pad are attached. Its use may be temporary – until surgery to reduce the hernia can take place – or permanent, if surgery is not applicable.

trypanosomiasis Any of several disorders resulting from infestation by parasite protozoans of the genus Trypanosoma. One such disorder is known as sleeping sickness (or African trypanosomiasis, to distinguish it from another form prevalent in South America), a long-term disease contracted by bites from tsetse flies. Symptoms during the first stage include high temperature with chills, headache, anaemia, enlargement of the lymph nodes, and muscular pain. At this stage, the disease is curable with drugs. After an interval of months or years, the second stage represents the invasion by the parasites of the blood vessels supplying the brain and spinal cord. This causes lethargy and somnolence and, finally, death. In many areas of Africa in the last decade there have been concentrated efforts to eliminate tsetse flies.

tryptophan One of the *amino acids* necessary for growth and development that cannot be synthesized in the body and must instead be obtained from food, especially such protein-rich foods as dairy products, eggs and meat.

TSH Abbreviation of *thyroid-stimulating hormone*.

tuberculin test Any of several variants of a test to determine whether somebody has at any time formed antibodies against *tuberculosis*. In much of Europe it is carried out ten days or so before immunization with *bacillus Calmette-Guérin* (BCG) vaccine, usually at about the age of 12–14 years. There is no point in giving the vaccine if the patient is already immune.

tuberculosis Potentially serious bacillary infection that may attack any part of the body and cause tissue damage. Many Europeans are immunized between adolescence and old age through inoculation with *bacillus Calmette-Guérin* (BCG) vaccine at the age of 12–14 years – but such protection may fail in old age. The primary site of infection is the lungs and associated lymph nodes, at which point the disease may halt temporarily or permanently. It may show no real symptoms or cause weight loss, high temperature and blood in the sputum. If the disorder spreads into the bloodstream, the effects are widespread and may be catastrophic. Diagnosis may be difficult. Treatment with a combination of antibiotics and antituberculous drugs is usually rapidly effective, although the drug course may have to be maintained for many months.

tumour Anomalous growth of cells where there should be none. Some tumours are harmless (benign), while others continue to grow and are liable to have parts that detach and drift elsewhere and start new tumours (termed malignant), through a process called metastasis. Malignant tumours are called *cancers* and are categorized by the type of cells of which they are composed. (Hollow swellings filled with liquid, however, especially on the skin surface, are much more likely to be *abscesses* – filled with pus – or *cysts* – fluid-filled swellings.) Any unexpected lump detected internally (perhaps by *palpation* – examination by feeling) should be immediately diagnosed by a doctor. Treatment depends on the type of tumour but may involve surgery to remove the lump and, for cancerous tumours, radiotherapy or chemotherapy.

tunnel vision Defect of vision in which only the centre of the *visual field* can be brought into focus; the rest of the field is blurred, rather like looking at the world through a kaleidoscopic tunnel. It occurs as a symptom of the second stage of *migraine* or of advanced *glaucoma*.

twins Two children born of the same mother within hours or minutes of each other. Identical twins are the result of the fertilization of a single ovum that splits into two complete *zygotes*; they are inevitably of the same sex, share a single placenta, and their genetic "fingerprints" are virtually the same. Fraternal twins, on the other hand, are the result of the simultaneous fertilization of two ova by two sperm; they may be of different sexes, have a placenta each, and are only as alike as any two *siblings* may be within a family.

tympanum Medical name for the *eardrum*.

typhoid fever Infection of the digestive system caused by a species of *Salmonella* bacteria. Other species cause milder forms of the disease, such as food poisoning or paratyphoid. Typhoid is usually contracted by eating or drinking something contaminated with infected human urine or excreta. The bacteria travel through the wall of the small intestine into the bloodstream, and are carried throughout the body. Symptoms are very high temperature, slow heartbeat, nosebleed and abdominal pain; there is usually a rash on the front of the body. Delirium may follow. Complications may include *pneumonia* or intestinal bleeding. Symptoms abate after a fortnight, and the disease clears by the fourth week. Diagnosis may require culture tests. Treatment is with antibiotics and, if necessary, transfusions. A vaccine is available.

typhus Any of a group of infection caused by a specific micro-organism that produces symptoms of very high temperature, severe headache, nausea, a rash, shock, and delirium. The infective organism is carried by rat fleas, ticks and mites, or lice. Antibiotics are usually successful in treatment; untreated, the diseases are often fatal.

tyrosine One of the *amino acids* found naturally in the body.

U

ulcer Area of erosion that fails to heal, leaving an open sore on the surface of the skin, or a local breakdown in the surface of a mucous membrane like that lining the mouth (aphthous ulcer) or the digestive parts of the alimentary canal (*peptic* ulcer). Causes include local injury, stress or restricted local circulation (as with *bedsores*), and include many diseases and disorders – especially sexually transmitted diseases (*venereal diseases*) and *cancer* (as with *rodent ulcers*). Treatment corresponds to the cause and the site of the ulcer.

ulceration Process forming an *ulcer*.

ulcerative colitis Inflammation and ulceration of the part of the large intestine called the *colon*, and, usually, the *rectum*. It occurs mostly in young adults, without evident cause. Symptoms are attacks of diarrhoea, bleeding from the anus, pain and internal *spasm*. In the long term, the condition may eventually result in *perforation* (rupture) of the intestine, and *peritonitis*. Treatment is generally with specific drugs or *corticosteroids*. Surgery may also be necessary; recurrent bouts may require a *colostomy* (diversion of part of the intestine to open through the abdominal wall into a bag).

ulna Thinner but slightly longer of the two bones of the forearm, stretching from the elbow (where it forms the bony projection of the joint) to the *wrist* (where it articulates with the other forearm bone, the *radius*, and with the bones of the carpus) on the little finger side. Rotation of the arm and hand is effected by the radius revolving around and across the ulna, supported by the comparatively fixed elbow joint.

ultrasound Very high frequency sound waves (of more than 20,000 Hz) used in diagnosis and therapy. For diagnosis the method of use is refined echo-location: sound waves bounced off various tissues are received, analysed and interpreted by computer on a screen, giving a fair picture of the internal condition of a patient. Sound waves are harmless, but cannot penetrate bone (examination of the brain by ultrasound is not feasible); they are especially good at establishing solidity or internal fluidity of growths. Therapeutically, ultrasound can be used to generate soothing and restorative heat in muscles and joints, and to vibrate kidney or other stones into pieces so that they can be removed without surgery.

ultraviolet radiation Electromagnetic *radiation* of short wavelength, beyond the violet end of the visible spectrum. The ultraviolet rays of the sun cause both the production of vitamin D (*calciferol*) in the body and sunburn; overindulgence in either is harmful.

umbilical cord Twisted, flexible, tubular attachment between a *foetus* in the womb and the *placenta* lodged on the uterine lining. Within it are two arteries and a vein; the arteries carry waste products away from the foetus, and the vein delivers nutrients. After childbirth the cord is cut; the end of the cord attached to the placenta is expelled with the *afterbirth*, and the cut end becomes the navel (umbilicus).

umbilicus Navel, site in the centre of the abdomen where the *umbilical cord* was once attached.

unconscious Either describing a state of partial or complete insensibility, or describing the lack of attention to what one is doing or what is happening. The word is also used as a technical term in *psychoanalysis* to mean all the feelings, associations and memories of the mind that have been repressed from conscious recall (as opposed to the *subconscious*, from which feelings, associations and memories can be recalled at will).

unconsciousness State of partial or complete insensibility. Although sleep is technically a time of unconsciousness, the term is generally used of an involuntary condition from which it is difficult, if not temporarily impossible, to rouse a person. Such a condition may result from the use of drugs, blood loss, *anoxia*, or serious disease or head injury. Long-term unconsciousness is usually described as *coma*.

uncus Body structure in the shape of a hook – especially that of the temporal lobe beneath the cerebral hemispheres of the brain.

undescended testicle Feature of *cryptorchidism*.

urea Nitrogen-containing waste product of the body mostly excreted in the *urine*. It is principally formed by the *liver* during the metabolism of *proteins*. Kidney failure can cause an accumulation of urea in the blood circulation (uraemia), which can be dangerous.

ureter One of the two tubes that carry liquid waste products filtered out by the kidneys (*urine*) down to the *bladder*. The multilayered walls of the ureters use *peristalsis* to maintain the flow. The main disorder that can affect a ureter is blockage by a *kidney stone*, causing the painful symptoms of renal *colic*.

urethra Tube that conveys *urine* from the bladder to the outside. In women and girls the urethra is short, ending at an opening between the clitoris and the vagina. In men and boys it is longer because it travels the length of the *penis*, and in addition to discharging urine has also to take in the secretions of the sex glands that combine with sperm to form *semen*. Because the female urethra is shorter, it is more likely to act as a route for infection entering the bladder (for example, causing *cystitis*). Inflammation of the urethra is called *urethritis*.

urethritis Inflammation of the *urethra* (the tube conveying urine from the bladder to the outside), caused by sexually transmitted infection that may be specific (such as *gonorrhoea*) or nonspecific (*nonspecific urethritis*), or by lesser local infection spread, for example, from the bladder (*cystitis*). Symptoms are frequent and uncomfortable urination and a painful discharge. Treatment, following diagnosis, is usually with *antibiotics*.

uric acid Nitrogen-containing waste product of *nucleic acid* metabolism excreted in the *urine*. Uric acid crystals formed by an excess of it in the body may cause *kidney stones*, blood disorders and, accumulating in the joints, *gout*.

urinary tract All the body structures involved in the production and discharge of *urine*: the *kidneys, ureters, bladder* and *urethra*.

urine Liquid waste product of the body, formed in the *kidneys*, conveyed via the *ureters* to the *bladder*, and stored there until discharged through the *urethra*. Composed mainly of water, it also contains *urea, uric acid* and salt, with traces of other substances. Biochemical examination of a patientís urine for unusual constituents (hormones, blood, proteins or sugar, for example) remains a very useful method of diagnosis.

urine test Examination of somebodyís urine for the presence of unusual substances. For example, the presence of sugar (glucose) may indicate *diabetes* mellitus, and certain hormones may confirm pregnancy (see *pregnancy test*).

urogenital system Those parts of the *urinary tract* and the *genitalia* that are usually considered together because of their anatomical proximity or dual function.

urology Study of the operation, diseases and disorders of the *urinary*.

urticaria Also called hives or nettle rash, usually a minor allergic reaction of the skin, involving an itching *rash* or area of round *weals*; occasionally there are also raised lumps or swelling. It is potentially more serious if swelling involves the face around the mouth and throat, a condition called *angio-oedema*, when the airway may be endangered. Symptoms may last from a couple of hours to several days. The triggering factor is usually dietary (particularly shellfish, eggs or strawberries), but may occasionally be an infection. Treatment usually involves *antihistamine* preparations; treatment of angio-oedema may be a medical emergency to restore normal breathing.

uterus Womb, a pear-shaped abdominal organ in women and girls, connected via the *Fallopian tubes* to the top of the *ovaries*, and via the *cervix* to the *vagina*. Part of the reproductive system, it is lined with a layer of specialized cells (endometrium) that after puberty regularly accumulates and is finally shed through the vagina about every 28 days, following the hormonal directions of the *menstrual cycle*. If *conception* occurs, the fertilized ovum (*zygote*) travels along the Fallopian tube and implants in the endometrium, where a *placenta* develops as the interface of the blood circulations of the embryo and mother; the menstrual cycle is temporarily abandoned. As pregnancy advances, the womb expands as necessary while the foetus grows within the *amnion*. At childbirth, uterine contractions of *labour* expel the baby through the cervix and along the vagina.

uvula Small flap of membrane-covered tissue at the back of the soft *palate*. Of no known purpose, it may be a vestigial remnant of a *septum* that once divided the eating apparatus from the breathing apparatus.

V

vaccination Process of immunization using a *vaccine*.

vaccine Preparation of material intended, once in the body, to cause the formation of *antibodies* against a specific disease, thus conferring temporary or permanent active *immunity* to that disease. The material may be made up of live but weakened (attenuated) micro-organisms (as against rabies and smallpox), dead micro-organisms (as against whooping cough and typhoid fever), *toxoids* (as against tetanus and diphtheria) or a genetically engineered substance that mimics part or all of the outer coating of a micro-organism (as is being tested against malaria). Most vaccines are administered through injection; a few are taken orally.

vacuole Space within a cell, containing either a clear form of *cytoplasm*, air, or "captured" extracellular material. It is in vacuoles that some leukocytes (white blood cells) can engulf bacteria or other "foreign" bodies.

vagina Part of the sex organs of a woman or girl, comprising a strong, muscular, membrane-lined tube connecting the *vulva* with the *cervix* of the *uterus* (womb). From birth until the first time of sexual intercourse the outer opening of the vagina is covered by a (usually incomplete) membranous fold called the *hymen* (although the hymen may be broken by vigorous physical activity before that time). At the conclusion of *sexual intercourse*, the vagina conveys *semen* into the womb. For this reason, the vagina is the location for almost all "barrier" methods of *contraception*. The vagina expands considerably during *childbirth*. Disorders that can affect the vagina include *vaginismus, vaginitis* and various *sexually transmitted diseases*.

vaginismus Contraction of the muscles around and of the *vagina*. It may be caused by stress or anxiety, injury or internal *ulceration*, inflammation or infection of the vaginal lining or of the bladder.

vaginitis Inflammation of the *vagina*, causing pain and discharge. It is commonly caused by some change that affects the normally harmless bacteria ordinarily present in the vagina – for example, a new method of *contraception*, having sexual intercourse for the first time or changing sexual partner, or starting a regimen of antibiotics. The bacteria then cause an infection. Vaginitis can occur after the menopause as a result of a lack of female sex hormones. It may also be a symptom of a *sexually transmitted disease* such as *candidiasis* (thrush) or *trichomoniasis*. Treatment depends on the cause but may involve antibiotics or antifungal drugs; often the sexual partner should also receive treatment.

vagotomy Surgical operation to cut part of the *vagus nerve* to treat a *peptic ulcer*.

vagus nerve Tenth cranial nerve, a major nerve that controls much of the *parasympathetic nervous system*. It extends from the *medulla oblongata* of the brainstem all the way down to the upper abdomen via the neck and chest, with many branches (to the mouth, ear, throat, vocal cords, lungs, heart and organs of digestion), a few of which are not directly part of the parasympathetic system.

valve Body mechanism that allows a fluid to flow in one direction only along a tube. Valves occur in the heart, veins, intestines and lymphatic system.

valvular diseases of the heart Disorder connected with the valves of the heart, sometimes caused by deformity through scarring or by constriction or dilation of the opening for some other reason. Scarring can be caused by *rheumatic fever* and may also lead to constriction of the opening on each side of the valve. Any form of valvular disease strains the heart muscle and may eventually result in *arrhythmia* or *heart failure*. Surgery may be necessary to repair or replace a defective valve.

varicella Medical name for *chickenpox*.

varicocele Condition in which *varicose veins* form in the first length of the spermatic cord, the complex tube with its own network of nerves and blood vessels that conveys sperm from the testes to the urethra up by the prostate gland. Causing an enlargement of the *scrotum* on the affected side (usually the left), symptoms are a dull ache that may generally be relieved by wearing a support. But the increased warmth in the area may result in temporary infertility.

varicose ulcer *Ulcer* that forms as a complication of *varicose veins* because of the reduced blood circulation in the region.

varicose veins Distended and twisted veins, blue when close to the skin surface, caused through internal pressure – for instance on the pelvic veins during pregnancy – damage to the *valves* that would normally control the blood flow. There may be some hereditary predisposition. They occur most commonly in the legs, where damage to the valves and veins may cause *phlebitis* and venous *thrombosis*, but are also found fairly often at the anus (as *haemorrhoids*). Symptoms, apart from appearance, are pain and local swelling. Complications such as *phlebitis* may occur. Treatment consists largely of supportive pressure, the artificial creation of thrombosis in the vein to occlude it (sclerotherapy), or surgery to repair or remove it.

variola Medical name for *smallpox*.

vas deferens Sperm duct, one of the two tubes that conveys *sperm* in semen from the *testes* up to the *urethra*. Movement of the semen is brought about by contractions of the muscular walls of the ducts.

vasectomy Surgical cutting and tying of each *vas deferens* (sperm duct) to create infertility in a man without reducing *libido*, as an increasingly popular means of birth control. A small incision is made on each side of the scrotum, and the resultant scars are tiny.

vasoconstriction Narrowing of a blood vessel, especially an artery, through the contraction of the tiny muscles in the vascular walls. Part of the mechanism that controls *blood pressure*, the process is regulated by a specialized centre in the brain (the vasomotor centre). Vasoconstriction naturally increases blood pressure; the opposite is *vasodilation*.

vasoconstrictor Drug that causes the constriction of the blood vessels, especially arteries, thus raising *blood pressure*. Such drugs work either locally (by local application, as in nasal decongestants) or generally (as used to maintain blood pressure during surgical operations, or to control shock). In dentistry a vasoconstrictor may be added to a local anaesthetic to extend its effect.

vasodilation Widening of a blood vessel, especially an artery, through the relaxation of the tiny muscles in the vascular walls. Part of the mechanism that controls *blood pressure*, the process is regulated by a specialized centre in the brain (the vasomotor centre). Vasodilation (also called vasodilatation) naturally reduces blood pressure; the opposite is *vasoconstriction*.

vasodilator Drug that causes the widening of blood vessels, especially arteries, thus reducing *blood pressure*. Such drugs almost all work specifically either on the heart (to relieve *angina pectoris*) or on the blood vessels of the limbs (for example to relieve chilblains), and are administered orally or by injection. Most, in large doses, cause unpleasant side-effects.

vasomotor Control of the tiny muscles in the walls of the blood vessels, especially the arteries. Such muscles are under the control of the vasomotor centre in the *medulla oblongata* of the *brainstem*, itself regulated by the overall requirements of the *sympathetic* and *parasympathetic nervous systems*.

vasopressin Another name for *antidiuretic hormone* (ADH).

vector Animal or insect that carries and transmits the micro-organisms that cause infection, usually without itself contracting the disease.

vegan See *vegetarianism*.

vegetarianism Dietary regimen that avoids the consumption of animal or fish meat. Some vegetarians do however eat shellfish; many eat animal-derived products such as eggs, milk and other dairy produce. Vegetarians belonging to the school of strict vegetarianism that forbids consumption of any animal or fish products whatever are known as vegans.

vein Blood vessel in the circulatory system that returns blood to the heart. All veins except one convey deoxygenated blood, from which the tissues have taken oxygen and nutrients, back to the heart (the right atrium) for pumping on to the lungs to be reoxygenated there. The exception is the pulmonary vein, which takes the newly oxygenated blood from the lungs to the heart (the left atrium) for pumping around the body. The walls of veins are triple-layered but thinner than those of the *arteries* (which have to withstand more pressure). There are many more veins than arteries in the body, and they are proportionally larger and contain more *valves*. Common disorders that can affect or involve veins include *haemorrhoids* (piles), *phlebitis, varicocele* and *varicose veins*.

vena cava Either of the two large *veins* that convey deoxygenated blood into the right atrium of the heart for pumping to the lungs and reoxygenation. The superior vena cava returns blood from the head and arms; the inferior vena cava returns blood from the rest of the body.

venereal disease Older term for *sexually transmitted disease*.

venereology Obsolete term for genitourinary medicine.

venom Any *poison* injected into somebody by an animal, such as an insect (bees, hornets and wasps), snake, an arachnid (including scorpions) and even some species of fish. All venoms in composition and effect are specific to the creature involved; antidotes may require to be equally specific. See also *sting, insect; snakebite*.

ventilation Maintaining an airflow. In medicine the term particularly applies to maintaining the flow or air in and out of the respiratory system, and to optimizing the exchange of gases within the *lungs*. A device or machine to effect this is called a ventilator (especially if the patientś respiratory system is completely paralysed) or *respirator*.

ventral Relating to the front of the body or of an organ, as opposed to the *dorsal* (rear) aspect.

ventricle Either of the two lower chambers of the *heart*, both of which pump blood out and away. The right ventricle receives deoxygenated blood from the venous system through the right atrium and pumps it towards the lungs for reoxygenation; the left ventricle receives newly oxygenated blood from the lungs through the left atrium and pumps it out to the body via the aorta. The term is used also for any of the four brain cavities filled with cerebrospinal fluid – two lateral ventricles, one in each cerebral hemisphere; a third between them; and the fourth in the hindbrain, connected with the centre of the spinal cord. All four intercommunicate through narrow channels.

ventricular fibrillation Breakdown of the rhythmic pumping action of one or both *ventricles* of the *heart*, a catastrophic stage reached following an increase of the beat within the ventricle to a rate out of phase with the overall heartbeat. The result is *cardiac arrest*, requiring emergency treatment. Its most common cause is *myocardial infarction. Atrial fibrillation* is not necessary so life-threatening.

ventricular flutter Slight *arrhythmia* in the beating of the *ventricles* of the heart; it represents a lesser form of *ventricular fibrillation*.

venule Narrow branch of a *vein*.

verruca Also called a plantar wart, a type of *wart* that occurs on the soles of the feet. Projecting from the skin surface, verrucas are naturally subject to great pressure on standing and walking, and may become callused over and cause pain. They are also highly contagious, to the extent that epidemics. Treatment is to remove them by freezing, application (under careful medical supervision) of caustic solutions, cauterization or surgery.

vertebra Bony segment of the vertebral column that makes up the *spine*, enclosing the spinal cord and protecting the junctions of the cord with the spinal nerves. There are 33 vertebrae: from the top, 7 cervical (in the neck), 12 thoracic (at the back of the chest), 5 lumbar (in the lower back), 5 fused to form the *sacrum*, and 4 more fused to form the *coccyx*. Each vertebra consists of an almost cylindrical body, in which – down to the second lumbar vertebra – the spinal cord is enclosed, and from which spread seven bony projections (processes) that act both to link adjacent vertebrae and as the bases for nervous and muscular attachments. Discs of fibrous connective tissue (*invertebral discs*) separate the vertebrae and give the spine its flexibility. Disorders that can affect the vertebrae include *scoliosis, spina bifida, spondylitis* and slipped disc (*prolapsed intervertebral disc*).

vertebral column Basic skeletal structure that forms the *spine*.

vertigo Extreme dizziness, in which the immediate environment is perceived to be spinning round at high speed or tilting at an angle. The result of a disorder of the mechanism that regulates *balance* (in the inner ear or the auditory nerve and its centre in the brain), it may be caused by infection, low or high blood pressure, or drug abuse. The disabling effect may be accompanied by nausea and, occasionally, other difficulties in vision and hearing. Medical diagnosis is essential. Treatment depends on the cause but may include drugs to alleviate the symptoms.

Vesalius, Andreas (1514–1564) Belgian anatomist who compiled a classic descriptive book on the subject, based largely on his dissections of executed criminals. Published in 1543, the book became the standard reference work on anatomy for at least the next two centuries.

vesicle Small container of watery fluid. The term thus describes not only blisters containing *serum*, as occur in chickenpox and following burns, but also any sac or bladder containing clearish liquid – such as the seminal vesicles at the top of the *vas deferens* (which store seminal fluid), the gall bladder and the urinary bladder.

vestibule Small cavity that leads on to a larger one. The term is applied particularly to the middle part of the inner ear which leads on to the bony *labyrinth*.

villus Tiny finger-like projection on a mucosal surface, one of the many thousands that extend the absorptive surface area and providing a means of either absorbing substances (as in the small intestine), or of maintaining adhesion (as do the chorionic villi, between the placenta and the uterine wall).

virilism Set of symptoms that in a woman effect *masculinization*.

virology Study of *viruses*, the diseases and disorders they cause, and the symptoms involved. It is a branch of microbiology.

virulent Potentially causing severe symptoms, or of a particularly poisonous nature.

virus Tiny infective entity, consisting only of a strand of *ribonucleic acid* (RNA) or *deoxyribonucleic acid* (DNA) and an outer protein coat, which infects by invading a cell and using the cellís material to replicate itself. Many viruses invade only specific cells of the human body, although the effect may be general. A few cause no symptoms unless some triggering factor acts as a catalyst. Antibiotics, which are very effective against other forms of infection, are normally quite ineffectual against viruses – although a number of viral infections can be prevented by *vaccination* and some respond to antiviral drugs. Viral infections include *AIDS* (acquired immune deficiency syndrome), *chickenpox*, the common *cold, herpes, influenza, measles, mumps, poliomyelitis, rabies, rubella, shingles, smallpox, typhus* and *yellow fever*.

viscera All the organs inside the chest and (particularly) the abdomen.

vision Combination of the organs of sight (the *eyes* and the *optic nerves*) and the interpretation of the brain to produce a coherent coloured, three-dimensional picture of the environment. Difficulties in achieving a good focus through the *lens*, clarity through the *cornea* or lens, or distinction between colours and shades through the *cones* and *rods*, or in using both eyes simultaneously to see the same object, may be caused by congenital defect, aging, injury or disease. Many such defects can be corrected by wearing *glasses* or *contact lenses*.

visual field Area within the *vision* of one or both eyes, centred on the object that is actually being looked at. A white object at the edge of the visual field is perceived better than a neutral-hued one there, because the sensitivity of the *retina* increases towards the centre. The visual field may thus be said to vary with varying brightness and colours within the same overall view.

vital capacity Maximum amount of air a person can exhale after previously inhaling as much as possible. The volume may be measured using a spirometer.

vital statistics Technically, statistics to do with birth, life and death within an area of population. Birth rate, child mortality rate, life expectancy and overall death rate are all subjects of vital statistics (sometimes called biostatics).

vitamin Substance vital to the metabolic functions of the body, generally effective even in minute amounts. Most are obtained in food; some are synthesized within the body using various internal processes. Vitamin A (retinol) maintains healthy skin and mucous membranes, and is good for night vision; it is found in dairy products, some fruit and vegetables, eggs and fish oils; excess intake is toxic. Vitamin B_1 is *thiamine*; vitamin B_2 is *riboflavin*; vitamin B_6 is *pyridoxine*; vitamin B_{12} is *cyanocobalamin*; other members of the vitamin B complex are *niacin, folic acid, pantothenic acid* and *biotin*. Vitamin C is *ascorbic acid*; vitamin D is *calciferol*; and vitamin E is *tocopherol*. Vitamin K is found in two forms, phytomenadione (in vegetables) and menaquinone (in meat); in humans it is essential to blood clotting, and a deficiency can cause a haemorrhage. Vitamins are categorized as either fat-soluble or water-soluble: A, D, E and K are fat-soluble, C and the B complex are water-soluble. Many vitamins can be stored in the body for several weeks before replenishment is necessary.

vitamin deficiency Any of the several disorders caused by the lack of *vitamins*, now comparatively rare in the Western world. Deficiency of vitamin A can cause *xerophthalmia*. Deficiency of some of the vitamin B complex can be serious – especially of vitamin B_{12} (*cyanocobalamin*) and *folic acid* (both potentially causing anaemia or peripheral neuritis) – although deficiency simply does not occur of *biotin* and *pantothenic acid*. Scurvy results from vitamin C (*ascorbic acid*) deficiency; rickets or brittle bones from vitamin D (*calciferol*) deficiency; and blood disorders from vitamin E (*tocopherol*) and vitamin K deficiency. In all cases, treatment is to make up the deficiency.

vitiligo Condition in which patches of surface skin lose all *melanin* (skin pigment) pigmentation, and become white. Beginning anywhere in the body, the patches may expand to cover most of it – or may gradually disappear as pigmentation is somehow restored. It is an *autoimmune disease* (one in which the immune system attacks the bodyís own tissues) that especially affects dark-skinned races. Treatment with drugs and ultraviolet light may help, especially if the patient has darker skin colouring. In other cases camouflage make-up is often recommended.

vitreous humour Non-refractive jelly-like substance that fills the eyeball between the *lens* and the *retina*.

vocal cord One of two adjacent flaps of muscular tissue that lie across the *larynx*. Together they regulate the flow of air through the gap between them (the glottis), and vibrate to produce the sounds of speech. Fine control of the air flow enables the raising or lowering of pitch or volume of sound; the sound may then be refined by the action of the tongue, mouth and lips. The nerves serving the cords are a branch of the *vagus nerve*.

voice Characteristic pitch and intonation of speech, as produced by the *vocal cords* and refined by the tongue, mouth and lips.

vomiting Known medically as emesis, the involuntary expulsion through the mouth (and sometimes the nose) of food and digestive juices from the stomach. A symptom of many disorders, it is effected by a muscular reversion of *peristalsis*, some authorities say a *reflex* action, although it is actually regulated by a vomiting centre in the brain (which can be affected by drugs). A drug to instigate vomiting is called an *emetic*; one that prevents it is an *anti-emetic*; and the sensation that vomiting is imminent is *nausea.*

voyeurism Desire and practice of obtaining sexual pleasure by secretly watching others as they undress, when they are naked, or when they are indulging in sexual activity.

vulva External *genitalia* of a woman or girl, consisting of the two pairs of *labia*, with their associated glands, the *clitoris*, the urethral opening, and the opening of the *vagina.*

vulvitis Inflammation of the *vulva*. The most common cause is fungal or bacterial infection, such as *candidiasis* (thrush), which has symptoms of itching and pain. Other causes range from the pressure of tight underwear to general skin disease, *diabetes* mellitus or *sexually transmitted disease*. Treatment corresponds to diagnosis, but commonly involves antibacterial or antifungal drugs.

W

wart Columnar growth on the skin. Usually painless, harmless and small, warts constitute the first type of (usually benign) tumour definitively known to be caused by a virus, the *human papillomavirus*. Pigmented or not, they may appear virtually anywhere on the skin – but particularly on the hands, elbows and knees – and may disappear as quickly and spontaneously. Some around the genital region are sexually transmitted, and some types of the papillomavirus that cause genital warts are linked with the development of cervical *cancer*. Others on the soles of the feet (*verrucas*) may be painful because of the pressure constantly put on them. Treatment is generally only necessary for genital warts and verrucas, although it may be administered elsewhere for cosmetic purposes. Removal of a skin wart is by application of caustic solutions (available over-the-counter), or by cauterization or freezing under medical supervision. Genital warts require specialist treatment and regular smear tests thereafter.

Wassermann reaction test Blood test to detect antibodies to the infective micro-organism that causes *syphilis*; if present, the patient has the disease.

wasting Degeneration and disintegration of the cells of organs and tissues due to aging, *deficiency disorders*, prolonged disuse or disease. Under specific conditions it is known also as *atrophy* or *marasmus*.

water bed Water-filled mattress which, because it adapts and conforms to a patientís body resting on it, is less likely than normal beds to cause *bedsores*.

Watson, James D. (1928–) American biologist instrumental in determining the molecular structure of *deoxyribonucleic acid* (DNA) together with Maurice Wilkins and Francis Crick. All three men were awarded a Nobel Prize in 1962.

wax Substance secreted by bees, used medically in ointments and as a *styptic*. A similar substance, called cerumen, is produced in humans by glands in the outer part of the auditory canal of the *ears* for protection and for trapping dust particles.

weal Raised area of inflamed skin, caused by rubbing, scratching, lashing or an allergic reaction.

weaning Stage in the early life of a baby at which the diet is changed, either from breast-feeding to bottle-feeding, or from milk and milk-based variants to puréed solids such as fruit and cereals.

weeping wound Wound from which *serum* (blood *plasma* from which the blood *clotting* factors have been used up) leaks, often caused by accidentally stretching the newly forming skin over the wound. (*Pus* leaking from a wound is *suppuration*, which indicates *sepsis* that requires treatment.)

weight Physical heaviness of a person, in many respects a measure of health. Normals apply to age, height, build, and sex, and over so many contributory factors there is as a result a wide range of variant normals. Consequently, in general only people who are seriously above or below their appropriate normals are considered to have weight problems. The main reason for such problems is simply eating too much (leading to *obesity*) or too little – for which there may be a psychological factor (as with overeating through stress, or underеating through *anorexia nervosa*). However, there are many physical diseases and disorders that can cause obesity (such as heart, liver or kidney disorders) or abnormal thinness (such as diabetes mellitus, tuberculosis or cancer). In most cases, correct diet may be the best treatment.

wen Common name for a *sebaceous cyst.*

wet nurse Lactating woman employed to breast-feed another motherís child.

whiplash injury Injury (usually minor and of temporary effect) to the spine and its muscular and nervous attachments at the neck, caused by a sudden forwards movement of the body that leaves the neck and head behind – as in a car seat when the car is hit from the rear. There may be a momentary *blackout* followed later by a stiff neck and pain in the muscles of the neck and back. Medical diagnosis is advisable to check for further injury.

white blood cell Type of cell known medically as a *leukocyte*.

white matter One of the types of *nerve fibres* that make up the *central nervous system* (the brain and the spinal cord). In the brain it surrounds the *grey matter*, and is white because of the greater number of *myelin*-covered fibres it is composed of.

whitlow Alternative term for paronychia.

whooping cough Medical name pertussis, a potentially serious bacterial infection of the membranous lining of the throat and bronchial passages, most common in young children. Symptoms appear in two stages: first there are the catarrhal symptoms of a heavy *cold* in which the dry, breathless cough after which the disease is called becomes more pronounced; then there are paroxysms of coughing, possibly with bleeding from the nose and mouth, and vomiting – complications such as pneumonia may arise from this stage. Eventually the paroxysms subside and the symptoms gradually vanish, but full recovery may take several months. Drug treatment during the first stage may prevent the onset of the second; treatment otherwise is isolation and drugs to alleviate the symptoms. Vaccination is available, and is commonly administered (with vaccines against *diphtheria* and *tetanus* in the combined *DTP* vaccine) in three stages to infants in their first year of life.

Wiesel, Torsten (1924–) American neurological biologist whose researches into vision in collaboration with David Hubel led to them both being awarded a Nobel Prize in 1981.

Wilkins, Maurice H.F. (1916–2004) New Zealand biophysicist instrumental in determining the molecular structure of *deoxyribonucleic acid* (DNA) together with James Watson and Francis Crick. All three men were awarded a Nobel Prize in 1962.

Wilson's disease A congenital deficiency of the protein that carries copper in the blood, leading to copper deposits in the body which in turn cause liver and brain disease. The patient may have *jaundice*, mental retardation and parkinsonism (see *Parkinson's disease*), and often has a characteristic brown ring in the eyes. Drug treatment to mop up excess copper can prevent mental retardation and other symptoms if started early enough.

wind Also called *flatulence*, presence of air and other gases (flatus) in part of the alimentary canal. Wind in the stomach may emerge through the mouth as a belch; wind in the intestines may emerge through the anus.

windpipe Common name for *trachea*.

wisdom teeth Four large *molar* teeth that erupt, one at the back of each side of each jaw, after adolescence. Their size and shape may cause problems in *dentition*, and extraction of one or more may be necessary.

withdrawal Set of physical and psychological symptoms that a person who is dependent on an addictive drug undergoes if he or she fails to maintain the dosage. Physical symptoms may include nervous agitation, sweating, tremors and vomiting; psychological symptoms may include loss of the sense of well-being that the drug used to guarantee, and subsequent depression (see *dependence*). To a minor degree, a *hangover* represents a similar combination of withdrawal symptoms.

withdrawal method Known medically as *coitus interruptus*, one of the least satisfactory forms of *contraception*.

womb Common name for the *uterus*.

worms Parasitic infestation by any of various types of primitive legless animals, particularly by a type that attacks the intestines. Symptoms may include diarrhoea, abdominal pain and sometimes fever; untreated infection may lead to *anaemia*, *malabsorption* of food and complications such as intestinal ulcers, liver abscesses or lung disease. There are three main types of parasitic worms: *roundworms* (including hookworms and threadworms), *tapeworms* and *flukes*. Infestation by roundworms and tapeworms is mainly of the intestines, although tapeworms can also affect the liver. Flukes tend to infest the blood vessels, bladder, liver or lungs. Treatment in all cases is with *anthelminthic* (worm-killing) drugs or, if necessary, surgery.

worry Another word for *anxiety*.

wound Injury that penetrates the skin and causes bleeding on the surface; thus both accidents and surgical operations result in wounds. By extension, a wound also describes tissue damage even where the skin is not broken, as with a *bruise* or an internal injury caused by a blow.

wrist Medical name carpus, the joint that allows the hand to move independently of the arm. It consists of eight bones, four of which articulate with the two bones of the forearm (*radius* and *ulna*) and four which articulate with the bones of the hand (the metacarpals). The bones are covered in membrane and ligaments, and the whole joint is arched over with a thick band of connective tissue called the retinaculum. One painful disorder involving the wrist is *carpal tunnel syndrome*.

wrist drop Paralysis of the forearm muscle that controls the *wrist*, so that the wrist remains limp and the hand is "dropped". It is caused by damage to the radial nerve in the upper arm (as may occur with lead poisoning).

writer's cramp *Cramp* and stiffness of the muscles in the thumb and first two fingers of the hand, following an unusually prolonged session of use (as in knitting, sewing or writing). The usual treatment is to rest the hand.

wryneck Medical name torticollis, a painful condition in which *spasm* of the muscles in the neck causes the head to assume a twisted or leaning position. It may take time to develop if caused by local irritation of the nerves or by a congenital disorder – in which case treatment is usually by surgery. An acute condition may be caused by cold or trauma, and can be successfully treated with heat and rest.

X

xanthoma Small, yellowish lump or *plaque* in the skin, usually a symptom of a high level of *cholesterol* in the blood. Xanthomata consist of deposits of fat within the skin and occur particularly on the eyelids. They may also occur internally, on the *tendons* of the hands and feet.

X-chromosome Type of *sex chromosome*. The pairs of sex chromosomes in women and girls are both X-chromosomes (those in men and boys consist of one X-chromosome and one *Y-chromosome*). Disorders associated with anomalies of the sex chromosomes include Turnerís syndrome (in which somebody has the combination XO – that is, only one sex chromosome) and Klinefelterís syndrome (in which somebody has the combination XXY – that is, an extra X-chromosome). Both usually result in infertility.

X-linked disorders Also called sex-linked disorders, genetic (hereditary) disorders deriving from the presence of a recessive *gene* on the *X-chromosome* which in men and boys is not paired with a corresponding gene in the shorter *Y-chromosome*. In women 0 who have two X-chromosomes – the recessive gene can be paired with a dominant gene, so they do not have the disorder but they remain carriers and their male children may inherit. The classic example is *haemophilia*.

xenophobia Form of *neurosis* in which there is an overpowering and unreasoned terror (*phobia*) of strangers and foreigners.

xeroderma Condition in which the skin surface is abnormally dry and may be rather rough. Causes are aging, sunburn, or a hereditary disorder present from birth known as ichthyosis. Creams and lotions are generally effective treatment.

xerophthalmia Deficiency disorder that produces increasing dryness of the *cornea*, *conjunctiva* and *tear* ducts of the *eyes*. Untreated, the cornea may eventually become opaque, effectively blinding the patient. The cause is lack of vitamin A (retinal. Treatment is to make up for either deficiency.

X-rays Form of electromagnetic *radiation* that penetrates softer human tissues but is absorbed (stopped) by harder ones – a fact that, recorded on photographic film or displayed on a fluorescent screen, greatly assists diagnosis of internal disorders. The diagnostic use of X-rays is called *radiography*; treatment with X-rays is one type of *radiotherapy*. Overexposure to X-rays can be harmful.

Y

yawning Involuntary action involving opening the mouth wide (almost always after taking a deep breath), holding the breath briefly while depressurizing the *Eustachian tubes*, and gradually but forcefully exhaling. What this sequence achieves, or is intended to achieve, is not fully understood but it is often associated with fatigue or boredom, particularly after prolonged inactivity. Some authorities describe it as a *reflex* action.

yaws Bacterial disease commonly infecting children in tropical areas of poor sanitation. The bacterium – a *spirochaete* related to the one that causes syphilis – attacks the body through wounds or abrasions on the skin. Symptoms include high temperature and pain, followed by ulcerative swellings on the lips, elbows, buttocks and knees. The swellings generally then heal, and an interval of some years may elapse before the next stage occurs. At that time, further ulcerative swellings break out and may seriously affect underlying organs and bones. Treatment is with *antibiotics*, particularly penicillin, and is effective.

Y-chromosome Type of sex *chromosome* found only in men and boys, in whom it is paired with an *X-chromosome* (women and girls have two X-chromosomes). There may be *recessive genes* on the X-chromosome whose effects are not cancelled by dominant genes on the Y-chromosome (giving rise to *X-linked disorders*).

yeast Single-celled fungus of the Saccharomyces genus. There are many species. Some are toxic; some cause disease, such as *candidiasis* (thrush); and some are very useful in promoting fermentation (as making bread, wine and beer). Yeasts are also used commercially for producing vitamin B supplements.

yellow fever Acute viral infection relatively common in tropical Africa and South America. The virus is carried by mosquitoes and attacks kidney and liver tissues. Initial symptoms are high temperature with shivering, headache and other pain, vomiting, confusion and *photophobia*. There may then be a short period of remission before the onset of *jaundice* (causing yellow skin from which the disease gets its name), internal haemorrhaging and protein in the urine. *Heart failure*, *encephalitis*, coma and death may follow. There is no treatment other than to alleviate symptoms. It is fatal in about 5–10 per cent of cases. People who live in areas where the disease is endemic may have some resistance to it; for others a vaccine is available.

yoga Meditational practice involving physical exercises and breath control, designed to promote physical and mental vitality.

Z

zinc Metallic element essential to the body as a *trace element*. Various zinc salts are used in medical treatment, although most are toxic if taken orally. Zinc oxide, zinc acetate, zinc stearate and zinc sulphate are antiseptic astringents; a suspension of zinc carbonate is *calamine* lotion; zinc chloride is a major constituent of the cement used by dentists to fill teeth; and zinc undecenoate is an antifungal agent.

zoonosis Any infectious disease of animals (or insects) that can be transmitted to humans. Such diseases include *anthrax, brucellosis, cowpox, dengue fever*, some forms of *encephalitis, Lassa fever, malaria, ornithosis, plague, Q fever, rabies, toxoplasmosis, bovine tuberculosis, typhus*, and some kinds of *worms*.

zygomatic arch Horizontal arch of bone forming the cheekbone, sometimes called the zygoma. An extension from the zygomatic bone which makes up part of the *orbit* (eye socket), it curves round to the temporal bone, so helping to protect the hinge joint of the jaw.

zygote Product of *conception*, an *ovum* that has been fertilized by a *sperm*.

Medical Terminology

Most important words in common use in medicine – and many in biology – are listed and defined in the main A to Z section of this book. Of course there are also thousands of others, which are less common and therefore less familiar. The meanings of most of these can be deduced from a knowledge of the linguistic elements, particularly prefixes and suffixes, of which they are built up. For example, the meaning of *cholecystitis* can be deduced by knowing that *chole* = gall or bile, *cyst* = bladder, and *itis* = inflammation (therefore *cholecystitis* = inflammation of the gall bladder).

The following table lists word elements with their meanings and an example of usage.

Word element	**Meaning**	**Example of usage**
a-, an-	lacking, without	*acrania* = lacking a skull*anoxia* = lacking oxygen
a-, ab-, abs-	away from, not	*atoxic* = not poisonous*abortion* = not born
ad-	towards	*adrenal* = towards the kidney
aden-, adeno-	gland	*adenitis* = inflammation of a gland*adenoma* = glandular tumour
-aemia	blood	*anaemia* = lacking blood
aer-, aero-	air	*aerobic* = living in air
-aesthesia	feeling	*anaesthesia* = lacking feeling
-agogue	producing	*galactagogue* = producing milk
-algesia, -algia	pain	*analgesia* = without pain*neuralgia* = nerve pain
all-, allo-	other	*allotropy* = existing in other forms
amb-, ambi-, amphi-	both sides	*ambidextrous* = able to use both hands*amphicrania* = two-sided headache
amyl-	starch	*amylase* = enzyme for digesting starch
ana-	up	*anastasia* = inability to stand up
andro-	male	*androgen* = male hormone
angi-, angio-	blood vessel	*angiigitis* = inflammation of a blood vessel
ante-	before	*antenatal* = before birth
anti-	against	*antibiotic* = against life
apo-	from, opposed	*aposia* = opposed to drinking
-ase	enzyme	*amylase* = enzyme that breaks down starch
arter-, arterio-	artery	*arteriosclerosis* = hardening of an artery
arth-, arthro-	joint	*arthritis* = inflammation of a joint
auto-	self	*autograft* = graft of oneís own tissue
bi-, bis-	two	*bicuspid* = two-cusped*bisexual* = attracted to both sexes
bili-	bile	*biliary* = pertaining to bile
blasto-	germ-plasm	*blastocyst* = ball of germ cells
blephar-	eyelid	*blepharitis* = eyelid inflammation

-bolus	lump	*embolus* = lump inside
brachi-, brachio-	arm	*brachialgia* = pain in arm
brachy-	short	*brachycephalic* = short-headed
brady-	slow	*bradycardia* = slow heartbeat
bronch-, broncho-	bronchial tubes	*bronchitis* = inflammation of the bronchi
caco-	bad, ill	*cacosmia* = sensing a bad smell that others do not
capsul-	tissue envelope	*capsulitis* = inflammation of the eye lens
carcin-, carcino-	cancer	*carcinoma* = epithelial cancer
card-, cardio-	heart	*myocarditis* = inflammation of the heart muscle
cata-, cath-	down	*catabolism* = breaking down (foodstuffs)
-cele	cyst, swelling	*hydrocele* = swollen with fluid
cent-, centi-	hundred	*centigrade* = on a scale of a hundred
cephal-, cephalo-	head	*cephalgia* = pain in the head
cerebro-	brain	*cerebration* = brain function
cervic-, cervico-	neck	*cervicitis* = inflammation of the neck of the womb
-chalsia	relaxing	*achalsia* = lack of relaxation
cheil-, cheilo-	lip	*cheilosis* = sore, swollen lips
cheir-, chiro-	hand	*cheiralgia* = pain in hand
chol-, chole-	bile, gall	*cholelithiasis* = having gallstones
chondr-, chondro-	cartilage	*chondritis* = inflammation of cartilage
chord-, chordo-	spinal cord	*cordotomy* = cutting of the spinal cord
chrom-, chromo-	colour	*chromatopsia* = abnormal colour vision
chron-	time	*chronic* = long-lasting
-cide	death	*bactericide* = agent that kills bacteria
circum-	around	*circumoral* = around the mouth
cirrho-	wasting	*cirrhosis* = wasting of an organ (liver)
co-, com-, con-	together	*coagulation* = sticking together*commensal* = living together*confluent* = merging together
coel-, coelo-	abdomen, cavity	*coelioscopy* = examining the abdomen through an endoscope
col-, colo-	colon	*colitis* = inflammation of the colon
colp-, colpo-	vagina	*colpotomy* = cutting into the vagina
conch-	nose, shell	*conchotomy* = artificial opening into the nose
conio-	dust	*pneumoconiosis* = lung disease caused by dust
contra-	against	*contraception* = preventing conception
copr-, copro-	faeces	*coprophobia* = fear of faeces
cord-, cordo-	cord	*cordectomy* = removal of the vocal cords
cortico-	cortex	*corticosteroid* = hormone of the adrenal cortex
cost-, costo-	rib	*intercostal* = between the ribs
cox-, coxo-	hip	*coxalgia* = pain in the hip

crani-, cranio-	skull	*craniometry* = measuring the skull
cryo-	freezing	*cryosurgery* = destroying tissue by freezing
crypt-, crypto-	hidden	*cryptorchidism* = failure of the testicles to descend into the scrotum
cubit-, cubito-	elbow	*cubital fossa* = hollow at the front of the elbow
cuta-, cuti-	skin	*subcutaneous* = under the skin
cyst-, cysto-	bag, bladder	*cystitis* = inflammation of the bladder
-cyte, cyto-	cell	*leukocyte* = white blood cell
dacro-, dacryo-	tears	*dacryocystitis* = inflammation of the lacrimal sac
dactyl-	fingers, toes	*dactylitis* = inflammation of the fingers or toes
de-	removal or loss	*demineralization* = loss of minerals from the bones or teeth
dec-, deca-	ten	*decalitre* = ten litres
deci-	tenth	*decibel* = tenth of a bel
demi-	half	*demilune* = half-moon shaped
dent-, denti-, dento-	teeth	*dentate* = having teeth
derma-, dermo-, dermato-	skin	*dermatitis* = inflammation of the skin
dextro-	right	*dextrocardia* = with the heart on the right
di-	two	*dimorphic* = having two forms
dia-	across, through	*diathermy* = heating through
dipla-, diplo-	double	*diplopia* = double vision
dis-	absence, apart, double	*disinfect* = free from infection*dislocation* = out of place*disarticulation* = separation of two bones at a joint
disco-	disc	*discoidectomy* = removing an intervertebral disc
dorsa-, dorso-	back	*dorsalgia* = back pain
duodeno-	duodenum	*duodenectomy* = removing the duodenum
dys-	abnormal, difficult	*dyslexia* = difficulty in reading
ec-, ecto-	outside	*ectoparasite* = parasite that lives on the skin
-ectomy	cutting, removal	*tonsillectomy* = removal of the tonsils
-emesis	vomiting	*haematemesis* = vomiting blood
en-, endo-, ento-	inner, within	*entropion* = inward-turning eyelid*endothelium* = lining of the womb*entopic* = within the eye
enter-, entero-	intestine	*enteritis* = inflammation of the intestine
ep-, epi-	above, upon	*epidural* = upon the dura (membrane)
erythr-, erythro-	red	*erythrocyte* = red blood cell
-esthesia	feeling	*anaesthesia* = without feeling
eu-	well	*euphoria* = well feeling

ex-, exo-	out	*exhale* = breathe out*exophthalmos* = protruding eyes
extra-	beyond, outside	*extra-uterine* = outside the womb
fibro-, fibros-	fibre	*fibrositis* = inflammation of fibrous tissue
fore-	before, in front of	*foreskin* = prepuce
-form	shape	*cruciform* = cross-shaped
-fuge	cause to leave	*febrifuge* = agent that reduces fever
galact-, galacto-	milk	*galactocele* = cyst containing milk
gastr-, gastro-	stomach	*gastritis* = inflammation of the stomach
-gen, -genic	origin, production	*oncogenic* = tumour-forming
geria-, geronto-	old age	*geriatric* = concerning old age
gingiv-, gingivo-	gums	*gingivitis* = inflammation of the gums
gloss-, glosso-	tongue	*glossitis* = inflammation of the tongue*glossopharyngeal* = concerning tongue and pharynx
glyc-, glyco-	sugar	*glycaemia* = sugar in the blood
-gnosia, -gnosis	knowledge	*prognosis* = forecast
-gogue	make flow	*galactogogue* = agent that causes milk to flow
gon-, gono-	seed, semen	*gonorrhoea* = sexually transmitted disease
gonad-, gonado-	ovary, testicle	*gonadotropic* = stimulating ovary or testicle
gonio-	angle	*gonioscopy* = examining the angle in the eye
gony-	knee	*gonyocele* = fluid on knee
-gram	record, tracing	*sonogram* = record made using sound
-graph, -graphy	recording	*cardiography* = recording the heartbeat
gyn-, gynae-	female	*gynaecomastia* = breast development in a male
haem-, haemato-, haemo-	blood	*haemoptysis* = spitting blood
hemi-	half	*hemicrania* = one-sided headache
hepat-, hepato-	liver	*hepatitis* = inflammation of the liver
heter-, hetero-	different, other	*heterocellular* = made of different cells
hidr-	sweat	*bromhidrosis* = smelly sweat
hist-, histo-	tissue	*histology* = study of tissues
holo-	all	*holistic* = concerning the whole body
homo-, homoeo-	same	*homosexual* = attracted to the same sex
hydr-, hydro-	fluid, water	*hydrocephalus* = fluid on the brain
hyper-	excess, over	*hypertension* = high blood pressure
hypno-	sleep	*hypnotic* = causing sleep
hyp-, hypo-	too little, under	*hypotension* = low blood pressure
hyster-, hystero-	womb	*hysterectomy* = removal of the womb

iasis	condition, state	*amoebiasis* = infected with amoebae
iatro-, iatry	medical treatment	*iatrogenic* = arising from treatment*psychiatry* = treatment of the mind
ideo-	mental activity	*ideomotor* = motor action evoked by an idea
idio-	peculiar to	*idioventricular* = affecting or peculiar to the ventricle
-ify	become, form	*ossify* = become bone
ileo-	ileum (intestine)	*ileostomy* = removal of the ileum
ilio-	ilium (hip)	*ilio-inguinal* = concerning the hip and the groin
infra-	beneath	*infrapatellar* = below the knee-cap
inguin-, inguino-	groin	*inguinal hernia* = rupture in the groin
inter-	between	*intercostal* = between the ribs
intra-, intro-	into, within	*intrauterine* = within the womb
ir-, irid-, irido-	iris	*iritis* = inflammation of the iris
isch-, ischo-	suppressed	*ischaemia* = inadequate blood flow
ischi-, ischio-	of the ischium	*ischiorectal abscess* = abscess between the rectum and the ischium
iso-	equal, singular, uniform	*isodactylism* = all fingers the same length
-itis	inflammation	*arthritis* = inflammation of a joint
-ize	become, form	*keratinize* = become horny
juxta-	near	*juxtaspinal* = close to the spine
karyo-	nucleus	*karyogenic* = forming a nucleus
kerat-, kerato-	cornea, horn	*keratitis* = inflammation of the cornea*keratoderma* = horny skin
kin-, kine-	movement	*hyperkinetic* = overactive movement
koil-, koilo-	concave	*koilonychia* = having concave nails
labi-, labio-	lip(s)	*labiodental* = concerning the lips and the teeth
lact-, lacto-	milk	*lactorrhoea* = excessive milk flow
laparo-	abdomen	*laparotomy* = cutting into the abdomen
laryng-, laryngo-	larynx	*laryngitis* = inflammation of the larynx
latero-	side	*lateroversion* = turning to one side
-lepsy	attack	*narcolepsy* = attack of sleepiness
lepto-	small, thin	*leptodermic* = thin-skinned
leuc-, leuco-, leuk-, -leuko	white	*leucocyte* = white blood cell
lingu-, linguo-	tongue	*linguodental* = concerning the tongue and teeth
lip-, lipo-	fat	*lipoma* = fatty tumour
lith-, litho-	stone (calculus)	*lithotomy* = removal of a stone (by cutting)
lob-, lobo-	lobe	*lobotomy* = cutting into a lobe (of the brain)

-lysis	breaking down	*haemolysis* = breaking down of blood (cells)
macro-	large	*macrophage* = large scavenger cell
mal-	bad, poor	*malabsorption* = poor absorption (of food)
-malacia	softening	*osteomalacia* = softening of bones
mamma-, mammo-	breast	*mammography* = X-raying the breast
mani-, manu-	hand	*manubrium* = hand-shaped part of the breastbone
mast-, masto-	breast	*mastitis* = inflammation of the breast
med-, medi-, medio-	middle	*mediocarpal* = concerning the middle of the wrist
mega-	large	*megacolon* = enlarged colon*acromegaly* = enlarged bones and features
melan-, melano-	black	*melanocyte* = pigment-producing cell
mening-, meningo-	membranes of the brain/spinal cord	*meningitis* = inflammation of the (brain) meninges
men-, meno-, menstru-	menstruation	*menarche* = age of onset of menstruation
mes-, meso-	middle	*mesomorph* = somebody of medium build
met-, meta-	beyond, change	*metatarsals* = foot bones beyond the tarsals*metaplasia* = abnormal change in a tissue
-meter	measurer	*spirometer* = instrument for measuring lung volume
metr-, metro-	womb	*endometrium* = womb lining
micro-	small	*microvilli* = small villi
mio-	less, smaller	*miotic* = causing the pupil to contract
mon-, mono-	one, single	*monorchidism* = having one testicle
morph-	form, shape	*morphology* = scientific study of form
-motor	causing movement	*oculomotor* = controlling eye movement
muc-, muco-	mucus	*mucopurulent* = containing mucus and pus
multi-	many	*multipara* = having had two or more children
my-, myo-	muscle	*myalgia* = pain in muscle
myce-, myco-	fungus	*mycosis* = disease caused by a fungus
myel-, myelo-	marrow	*myelitis* = inflammation of bone marrow
myxa-, myxo-	mucus	*myxoma* = tumour of mucous tissue
narco-	stupor	*narcotic* = causing drowsiness
nas-, naso-	nose	*nasopharynx* = nose and pharynx
necro-	death	*necrosis* = death of tissue
neo-	new	*neoplasm* = abnormal growth of new tissue
nephr-, nephro-	kidney	*nephritis* = inflammation of the kidney
neur-, neuro-	nerve	*neuralgia* = pain in a nerve
nitr-, nitro-	nitrogen	*nitrobacteria* = bacteria that break down ammonia

noct-	night	*noctambulation* = sleep-walking
non-	no, not	*nonocclusion* = bite in which teeth do not meet
nucl-, nucleo-	nucleus	*nucleic acid* = chemical in the cell nucleus
nyct-, nycto-	night	*nyctophobia* = fear of the dark
nymph-, nympho-	clitoris, labia, female sexuality	*nymphomania* = excessive female sexual desire
ocul-, oculo-	eye	*oculofacial* = concerning the eye and the face
odont-, odonto-	tooth	*orthodontic* = straightening teeth
odyn-, odynia-	pain	*pleurodynia* = pain in the wall of the chest
oestro-	stimulation	*oestrogen* = female sex hormone
olig-, oligo-	few	*oligomenorrhoea* = scanty menstrual flow
-oma	tumour	*sarcoma* = tumour of connective tissue
omo-	shoulder	*omodynia* = pain in the shoulder
onco-	tumour	*oncology* = study of tumours
onych-, onycho-	nail	*onychophagy* = nail-biting
oo-	egg, ovum	*oogenesis* = egg production
oophor-, oophoro-	ovary	*oophorectomy* = removal of an ovary
ophthalm-, ophthalmo-	eye	*ophthalmoscope* = instrument for looking into the eye
opisth-	backwards	*opisthotonus* = arched back position
opti-, opto-	eye, vision	*optic nerve* = nerve from eye to the brain*optometer* = instrument for measuring refraction of the eye
orchi-, orchid-, orchido-, orcho-	testicle	*monorchidism* = having only one testicle
ortho-	straight, normal	*orthopnoea* = breathing only when upright*orthoptics* = realigning vision
os-, oss-, osteo-	bone	*osteoclasis* = remodelling of bone (during growth or after fracture)
-osis	diseased state	*nephrosis* = kidney disease
-ostomy	opening	*colostomy* = making an opening in the colon
ot-, oti-, oto-	ear	*otitis* = inflammation of the ear
-otomy	cutting	*tracheotomy* = cutting into the windpipe
ov-, ovi-, ovo-	egg, ovum	*ovulation* = release of an egg (ovum)
ovar-, ovario-	ovary	*ovariectomy* = removal of an ovary
oxy-	oxygen	*oxyhaemoglobin* = compound of oxygen and haemoglobin
pachy-	thick	*pachyotia* = thick ears
paed-, paedo-	child	*paediatrics* = treatment of children
palat-, palato-	palate	*palatitis* = inflammation of the palate

pan-, panto-	all, whole	*pandemic* = epidemic in a whole population
pancreat-	pancreas	*pancreatin* = digestive juice from the pancreas
par-, para-	alongside, beyond	*paranormal* = beyond normal experience
-paresis	weakness	*myoparesis* = muscular weakness
-parous	giving birth	*multiparous* = having several children
path-, -path, patho-, -pathy	disease, illness	*pathology* = study of (causes of) disease*psychopath* = somebody with a disordered mind
pector-	breast, chest	*angina pectoris* = pain in the chest
pelvi-, pelvio-	pelvis	*pelviotomy* = cutting of pelvic bones
-penia	lack, shortage	*leucopenia* = lack of white blood cells
-pepsia, pepti-	digestion	*dyspepsia* = indigestion*peptic ulcer* = stomach ulcer
per-	through	*perfusion* = pouring a liquid through
peri-	around	*pericardium* = membrane surrounding the heart
periton-	peritoneum	*peritonitis* = inflammation of the peritoneum
-pexia, -pexy	fixing in place	*orchidopexy* = fixing of an undescended testicle
phaco-, phako-	lens	*phacocele* = rupture of the eye lens*phakitis* = inflammation of the eye lens
-phage, phago-, -ophagy	eating	*bacteriophage* = virus that attacks bacteria*phagocyte* = scavenger (engulfing) cell*onychophagy* = nail-biting
phall-, phallo-	penis	*phallodynia* = pain in the penis
pharyng-	pharynx, throat	*pharyngitis* = inflammation of throat
phil-, -philia	love	*paedophilia* = sexual desire for children
phleb-, phlebo-	vein	*phlebitis* = inflammation of a vein
-phobe, -phobia	fear	*photophobia* = dislike of strong light
-phonia, phono-	sound	*phonocardiograph* = instrument for recording heart sounds
phot-, photo-	light	*photopsia* = seeing flashes of light
-phylac, -phylaxis	protection	*prophylaxis* = preventive treatment
physio-	nature, physiology	*physiotherapy* = treatment using exercises
physo-	air, gas	*physometra* = air or gas in the womb
plasia-,	formation	*hyperplasia* = excess tissue growth
plasm-	blood, cytoplasm	*plasmacytoma*_= tumour of the plasma cells
-plasty	plastic surgery	*labioplasty* = plastic surgery of the lips
-plegia, -plexy	stroke, paralysis	*paraplegia* = paralysis of the lower body
pleur-, pleuro-	lung membranes	*pleurisy* = inflammation of pleural membranes
pluri-	more, several	*plurinuclear* = having several nuclei

pneu-, pneumo-	lung	*pneumonitis* = localized lung inflammation
pod-, podo-	foot	*podarthritis* = inflammation of joints in the foot
polio-	grey matter	*poliomyelitis* = inflammation of grey matter of spinal cord
poly-	many	*polydactyly* = having extra fingers (or toes)
post-	after, behind	*postnatal* = after birth
pre-	before, in front	*premenstrual* = before menstruation*premolar* = in front of the molar (teeth)
pro-	before, on behalf	*prolactin* = hormone released before milk flow
proct-, procto-	anus, rectum	*proctalgia* = pain around the anus
prost-, prostato-	prostate	*prostatectomy* = removal of the prostate gland
proto-	first	*protodiastole* = period after the end of systole, before the start of diastole (in the cardiac cycle)
pseud-, pseudo-	false	*pseudocyesis* = false pregnancy
psych-, psycho-	mind	*psychogenic* = originating in the mind
pulmo-, pulmono-	lung	*pulmonary hypertension* = raised pressure within lung blood vessels
py-, pyo-	pus	*pyoarthritis* = pus in a joint
pyel-, pyelo-	kidney	*pyelogram* = kidney X-ray
-pyresis, pyreto-, pyro-	fever	*antipyretic* = agent that reduces fever
rachi-, rachio-	spine	*rachiodynia* = spinal pain
radi-, radicul-	root	*radiculitis* = inflammation of a nerve root
radio-	radiation	*radiograph* = image produced by X-rays
re-	again, back	*re-infection* = infection for a second time
ren-, reno-	kidney	*adrenal* = gland on top of the kidney
retin-, retino-	retina	*retinitis* = inflammation of the retina
retro-	backwards, behind	*retroversion* = tipping backwards (of womb)
rhin-, rhino-	nose	*rhinoplasty* = surgery to reshape the nose
-rrhage, -rrhagia	flow (outwards)	*haemorrhage* = bleeding*menorrhagia* = excessive menstruation
-rrhaphy	join, suture	*tarsorrhaphy* = stitching the eyelids together
-rrhoea	discharge, flow	*diarrhoea* = watery faeces*pyorrhoea* = flow of pus
sacchar-	sugar	*saccharine* = a sweetening agent
sacr-, sacro-	sacrum	*sacroiliac* = concerning the sacrum and ileum
salping-	(Fallopian) tube	*salpingectomy* = cutting of a Fallopian tube
sapr-, sapro-	putrefaction	*saprophyte* = organism that feeds on dead and putrefying tissue
sarc-, sarco-	flesh, muscle	*sarcoma* = fleshy tumour

schisto-, schizo-	cleft, split	*schistocephalic* = with a split skull
scler-, sclero-	hard	*scleroderma* = hardening of the skin and other fibrous tissue
-sclerosis	dryness, hardening	*arteriosclerosis* = hardening of arteries
-scope, -scopy	see, view	*endoscope* = instrument for examining inside the body
seba-, sebo-	fatty secretion	*seborrhoea* = excessive secretion from the skin
semi-	half	*semilunar* = crescent-shaped
-sepsis, septic-	decay, putrefaction	*antisepsis* = against infection*septicaemia* = blood poisoning (by bacteria)
sero-	serum	*serology* = study of antibodies in blood
sial-, sialo-	saliva	*sialolith* = stone in a salivary duct
sider-, sidero-	iron	*sideropenia* = iron deficiency
sinistr-, sinistro-	left	*sinistrocular* = left-eyed
soma-, somat-	body	*somatalgia* = pain in the body
spasmo-, spasti-	spasm	*spasmolytic* = agent that relieves spasm
spermo, spermato-	sperm	*spermaturia* = sperm in the urine
sphyg-, sphygmo-	pulse	*sphygmomanometer* = instrument for taking blood pressure
spin-, spina-	spine	*spina bifida* = cleft spine
splanchn-	intestine	*splanchnic nerves* = nerves supplying the abdominal organs
splen-, spleno-	spleen	*splenomegaly* = enlargement of the spleen
spondyl-, spondylo-	vertebra	*spondylitis* = inflammation of the joints of the spine
-stasis	stationary, stagnant	*haemostatic* = agent that stops blood flow
steato-	fat	*steatorrhoea* = passage of fat in the faeces
steno-	constricted	*stenothorax* = narrowing of the chest*stenosis* = narrowing of a duct or canal
sterco-	faeces	*stercolith* = stone made of dried faeces
stereo-	three-dimensional	*stereopsis* = three-dimensional vision
stern-, sterno-	sternum	*sternotomy* = cutting through the breastbone
steth-, stetho-	chest	*stethoscope* = instrument for listening to sounds in the chest (and elsewhere)
-sthenia, -sthenic	active, strong	*myasthenia* = lack of muscular strength
-stoma, stomat-, -stomosis, -stomy	mouth, opening	*stomatitis* = inflammation of the mouth*colostomy* = opening into the colon
sub-	under	*subcutaneous* = under the skin

super-, supra-	above, in excess	*superlactation* = excess milk production*suprarenal* = above the kidney (adrenal)
sym-, syn-	together, with	*symphysis* = place where bones join together*synarthrosis* = fibrous union of a joint
tacho-, tachy-	fast, speed	*tachycardia* = fast heartbeat
tars-, tarso-	ankle/foot,	*tarsalgia* = pain in the ankle or instep*tarsitis* =
eyelid		inflammation of the eyelid edge
-taxia, taxy-	voluntary movement	*ataxia* = unsteady movement
tel-, tele-	distant, far, end	*telangiitis* = inflammation of the smallest blood vessels
ten-, teno-	tendon	*tendinitis* = inflammation of a tendon
thalam-, thalamo-	thalamus	*thalamotomy* = cutting into the thalamus
thalass-, thalasso-	sea	*thalassaemia* = Mediterranean anaemia
-therapy	treatment	*radiotherapy* = treatment with radiation
therm-, thermo-	heat	*thermoplegia* = heatstroke
thio-	sulphur	*thiodotherapy* = treatment with sulphur and iodine
thorac-, thoraco-	chest	*thoracotomy* = surgically opening the chest
thrombo-	blood clot	*thrombophlebitis* = clotting following inflammation of a vein
thyro-	thyroid	*thyromegaly* = enlargement of the thyroid gland
-tomy	cutting, separating	*vagotomy* = cutting of the vagus nerve
-tonia, -tonic	tension	*myotonia* = inability to relax a muscle
tonsill-, tonsillo-	tonsils	*tonsillectomy* = removal of the tonsils
tox-, toxico-	poison	*toxicosis* = poisoning
trache-, tracheo-	trachea	*tracheoscopy* = viewing inside of the windpipe
trans-	across, through	*transorbital* = through the eye socket
tricho-	hair	*trichology* = study of hair
troph-, -trophy	nourishment, development	*trophoblast* = tissue that forms the placenta and connects with the maternal blood supply*atrophy* = lack of growth, wasting
tub-, tubo-	tube	*tubectomy* = removal of a Fallopian tube
tympan-, tympano-	eardrum	*tympanitis* = inflammation of the eardrum
ultra-	beyond	*ultrasound* = high-frequency sound waves
uni-	one	*unicellular* = single-celled (organism)
urethr-, urethro-	urethra	*urethritis* = inflammation of the urethra
-uria, urino-	urine	*haematuria* = blood in the urine*urinogenital* = concerning urinary and genital

uter-, utero-	uterus	*uterodynia* = pain in womb
uvul-	uvula	*uvulitis* = inflammation of the uvula
vagin-	vagina	*vaginismus* = spasm in the muscles of the vagina
vas-, vasi-, vaso-	vessel, sperm duct	*vasoconstrictor* = agent that narrows blood vessels*vasectomy* = cutting of the sperm duct(s)
vene-, veno-	vein	*venepuncture* = puncture of a vein
venter-, ventro-	abdomen	*ventrocystorrhaphy* = stitching of bladder to the abdominal wall
vesic-, vesico-	bladder	*vesicovaginal* = relating to the bladder and vagina
vir-, viro-	virus	*viraemia* = viruses in the blood
xanth-, xantho-	yellow	*xanthoma* = yellow (fatty) skin lesion
xer-, xero-	dry	*xeroderma* = dry sin
zoo-	animal	*zoophobia* = fear of animals

Calorie Content of Foods and Drinks

A calorie is a unit of heat energy, equal to the amount of heat needed to raise the temperature of 1 gram of water through 1 degree Celsius (or centigrade). In measuring the energy content of foods, dietitians prefer to use the kilocalorie (= 1,000 calories), by convention written as Calorie (with a capital C), although many books about food do not preserve this subtle distinction and omit the capital C. Another unit is the kilojoule (1 kilojoule = 4.186 Calories). Calorie contents are given for raw or boiled vegetables or fresh fruit, raw or cooked without sugar, unless indicated otherwise. For ease of calculation, all figures are rounded to the nearest whole number.

Food/drink	**per 100 gm**	**per ounce**
Almond *See* Nuts		
Anchovy (canned)	195	55
Apple	35	10
juice	43	12
Apricot		
fresh	25	7
dried (uncooked)	180	50
dried (stewed)	64	18
canned (in syrup)	105	30
Arrowroot	355	100
Artichoke		
globe	7	2
Jerusalem	18	5
Asparagus	18	5
Aubergine	14	4
Avocado pear	210	60
Bacon		
lean (boiled)	140	40
lean (grilled)	175	50
lean (fried)	460	130
fatty (boiled)	320	90
fatty (grilled)	425	120
fatty (fried)	495	140
Bamboo shoots	35	10
Banana	70	20
Barley, pearl (boiled)	125	35
Beans		
baked (canned in sauce)	64	18
broad	46	13

Beans (*cont.*)		
butter	92	26
French	7	2
haricot	88	25
red (kidney)	88	25
runner	18	5
soya	405	115
Bean sprouts	35	10
Beef		
corned	210	60
lean (grilled)	210	60
lean (roast)	265	75
fatty (roast)	350	100
minced	175	50
oxtail (stewed)	88	25
steak	195	55
Beefburger	265	75
Beer (per half pint)		
bitter	90	
brown	80	
lager	75	
light	75	
mild	75	
stout	100	
Beetroot	42	12
Biscuits		
cream	440	125
crispbread	335	95
dry	440	125
shortbread	495	140
sweet	550	155
Black pudding *See* Sausages		
Blackberry	25	7
Blackcurrant	25	7
juice (unsweetened)	50	14
Bran (wheat)	210	60
Brawn	160	45
Brazil nuts *See* Nuts		

Bread (loaf)		
brown	230	65
low-calorie	140	40
white	230	65
wholemeal	210	60
Bread (rolls)		
brown	280	80
soda	265	75
white	280	80
wholemeal	210	60
Bread sauce	105	30
Breakfast cereals		
(unsweetened)	355	100
Broccoli	18	5
Brussels sprouts	18	5
Butter	760	215
Cabbage	18	5
Cakes		
fruit	335	95
Madeira	390	110
scones	370	105
Scotch pancakes (drop scones)	280	80
sponge	300	85
Carrot	18	5
Cashew nuts *See* Nuts		
Cauliflower	11	3
Caviar (black)	210	60
Celeriac	14	4
Celery	3	1
Cereals *See* Breakfast cereals		
Cheese		
Brie	315	90
Blue (Danish)	370	105
Blue (Stilton)	460	130
Caerphilly	355	100
Camembert	300	85
Cheddar	405	115
Cheshire	335	95

Cheese (*cont.*)		
Cottage	88	25
Cream	440	125
Dolcelatte	335	95
Edam	315	90
Feta	195	55
Gorgonzola	405	115
Gouda	300	85
Leicester (red)	425	120
Mozzarella	335	95
Parmesan	405	115
Processed (spread)	300	85
Wensleydale	405	115
Cherry	35	10
glacé	210	60
Chestnuts *See* Nuts		
Chicken		
roast	210	60
roast (skinned)	140	40
Chicory	16	3
Cider (per half pint)		
dry	95	
sweet	140	
Chips *See* Potatoes		
Chocolate		
drinking (cocoa)	355	100
milk	550	155
plain	510	145
Cockles *See* Shellfish		
Coconut		
desiccated	600	170
fresh	350	100
milk	18	5
Cod		
boiled/poached	90	25
fried (in batter)	195	55
roe (fried in crumbs)	175	50
Cod liver oil *See* Oil		

Coffee (per cup, black,		
unsweetened)	0	0
For white add 10, for sweetened		
add 25 per spoonful of sugar		
Coley (boiled/steamed)	70	20
Corn-on-the-cob	125	35
Cornflour	355	100
Corn oil *See* Oil		
Courgette	7	2
Crab (boiled)	125	35
(canned)	88	25
Cranberry	14	4
Cream		
double	440	125
half	125	35
single/soured	210	60
whipping	335	95
Crispbread *See* Biscuits		
Crisps *See* Potatoes		
Cucumber	11	3
Currants (dried)	245	70
Custard (egg/powder)	115	33
Damson	35	10
Dates (dried, stoneless)	260	70
Dogfish (rock salmon; fried in		
batter)	265	75
Dripping	880	250
Duck		
roast	335	95
roast (skinned)	195	55
Eel (fried)	250	70
Egg		
boiled	140	40
fried	230	65
poached	240	45
Endive	11	3
Figs		
dried (uncooked)	210	60

Figs (*cont.*)		
dried (stewed)	125	35
raw	60	11
Fish fingers		
fried	230	65
grilled	175	50
Flounder	53	15
Fruit salad (canned/dried)	105	30
Gammon *See* Bacon (lean)		
Gelatine	335	95
Gherkins	18	5
Goose (roast, skinned)	320	90
Gooseberries	35	10
Grapefruit		
raw	11	3
canned (in syrup)	60	17
juice	35	10
juice (sweetened)	60	11
Grapes		
black	50	14
white	60	17
Gravy (from browning)	280	80
Greengage	42	12
Grouse (roast, skinned)	175	50
Guinea-fowl	105	30
Haddock		
fillets, steamed	70	20
fried	175	50
smoked, steamed	105	30
Hake (steamed)	88	25
Halibut (steamed)	105	30
Ham (lean, boiled)	195	55
Ham and pork (chopped and canned)	265	75
Hare (stewed)	140	40
Hazelnuts *See* Nuts		
Heart		
lamb	195	55
ox	175	50

Herring		
bloater (grilled)	175	50
fillet (fried)	230	65
kipper (grilled)	210	60
roe (fried)	245	70
Honey	280	80
Horseradish		
raw	53	15
sauce	210	60
Ice cream	175	50
Jam	265	75
Jelly	53	15
Kidney (fried)	160	45
Kohlrabi	7	2
Lager *See* Beer		
Lamb		
breast (roast)	390	110
chops (grilled)	280	80
leg (roast)	265	75
shoulder (roast)	300	85
Lard	880	250
Leeks	35	10
Lemon curd	280	80
Lemon (with peel)	14	4
juice	7	2
Lemon sole		
steamed	90	25
fried (in crumbs)	180	50
Lentils	105	30
Lettuce	18	5
Liqueurs (per measure)		
Benedictine	90	
Cherry brandy	50	
Cointreau	85	
Crème de Menthe	80	
Drambuie	85	
Pernod	80	
Tia Maria	75	
Lime juice	105	30

Liver		
fried	245	70
stewed	195	55
Liver sausage *See* Sausages		
Lobster (boiled)	40	12
Loganberries		
canned	53	15
stewed	14	4
Low-fat spread	355	100
Luncheon meat	315	90
Lychees (canned)	70	20
Macaroni *See* Pasta		
Mackerel		
fired	195	55
smoked	320	90
Mandarin oranges (canned)	53	15
Mangoes		
fresh, raw	53	15
canned	70	20
Margarine	760	215
Marmalade	265	75
Marrow	7	2
Marzipan	440	125
Mayonnaise	705	200
Melon	18	5
Milk		
buttermilk	53	10
condensed (sweetened)	320	90
evaporated (unsweetened)	160	45
goatís	70	20
powdered	495	140
semi-skimmed	53	15
skimmed	35	10
whole	65	18
See also Cream		
Mincemeat *See* Beef		
Mint sauce (sweetened)	105	30
Muesli	370	105

Mulberries	35	10
Mushrooms		
fried	210	60
raw	7	2
Mussels *See* Shellfish		
Mustard and cress	3	1
Nectarines	53	15
Noodles *See* Pasta		
Nuts		
almonds	600	170
brazils	620	175
cashews	550	155
chestnuts	175	50
hazels	390	110
peanuts	565	160
walnuts	530	150
Oil		
cod liver	880	250
corn (maize)	900	255
olive	920	260
peanut	880	250
soya bean	880	250
sunflower	880	250
wheatgerm	880	250
Okra	18	5
Olive oil *See* Oil		
Olives (with stones)	88	25
Onions		
boiled/raw	18	5
fried	355	100
Orange juice		
fresh/unsweetened	36	10
sweetened	53	15
Oranges	36	10
Oysters *See* Shellfish		
Parsley	18	5
Parsnips	53	15
Partridge (roast)	210	60
Passion fruit	18	5

Pastry		
choux	320	90
flaky	565	160
short	530	150
Pasta (boiled)	125	35
P té	335	95
Peaches		
canned	88	25
dried (raw)	210	60
dried (stewed unsweetened)	70	20
fresh	35	10
Peanut butter	620	175
Peanut oil *See* Oil		
Peanuts *See* Nuts		
Pearl barley *See* Barley, pearl		
Pears		
canned	70	20
fresh	35	20
Peas		
canned/processed	88	25
dried/split (boiled)	105	30
fresh/frozen	70	20
Peppers (red or green)	21	6
Pheasant (roast)	210	60
Pickles		
onions	18	5
piccalilli	35	10
sauerkraut	18	5
sweet	140	40
tomato chutney	160	45
Pigeon (roast)	230	65
Pilchards (canned)	125	35
Pineapple		
canned	88	25
fresh	42	12
juice (canned)	53	15
Plaice		
steamed	88	25
fried in crumbs	230	65

Plums		
canned	70	20
stewed (unsweetened)	35	10
Pomegranate	70	20
Pork		
chops (grilled)	250	70
crackling	670	190
leg (roast)	280	80
Porridge (unsweetened)	42	12
Port *See* Wines		
Potatoes		
baked	105	30
boiled	88	25
chips	250	70
crisps	530	150
instant mashed	70	20
roast	160	55
sauté	175	50
Prawns	105	30
Prunes (stewed unsweetened)	70	20
Pumpkin	7	2
Quail (roast)	70	20
Rabbit (stewed)	175	50
Radishes	14	4
Raisins	250	70
Raspberries		
canned	88	25
stewed (unsweetened)	25	7
Redcurrants	18	5
Rhubarb (unsweetened)	7	2
Rice (boiled)	125	70
Rice pudding (canned)	88	25
Rock salmon *See* Dogfish		
Roe (fried)		
cod	210	60
herring	250	70
Rosehip syrup	230	65
Sago (boiled)	125	35
Salad cream	355	100

Salami *See* Sausages		
Salmon		
canned	140	40
smoked	140	40
steamed	195	55
Salsify	18	5
Sardines (canned)		
in oil	335	95
in tomato sauce	175	50
Sausages		
beef (fried/grilled)	265	75
black pudding (fried)	300	85
bratwurst (boiled)	265	75
chipolata	230	65
liver sausage	300	85
pork (fried/grilled)	320	90
salami	495	140
saveloy	265	75
white pudding	440	125
Saveloy *See* Sausages		
Scallops *See* Shellfish		
Scampi		
boiled	105	30
fried (in crumbs)	300	85
Scones *See* Cakes		
Scotch pancakes *See* Cakes		
Semolina (boiled)	125	35
Semolina pudding	140	40
Shellfish		
cockles	53	15
mussels	88	25
oysters	53	15
whelks	88	25
winkles	70	20
Sherry *See* Wines		
Shortbread *See* Biscuits		
Shrimps		
boiled	125	35
canned	88	25

Skate (fried in batter)	195	55
Soda bread *See* Bread		
Soft drinks		
bitter lemon	53	15
cola	53	15
ginger ale	35	10
lemonade	35	10
soda water	0	0
tonic water	35	10
Sole, lemon *See* Lemon sole		
Soya bean oil *See* Oil		
Soya beans *See* Beans		
Soy sauce	18	5
Spaghetti *See* Pasta		
Spinach	31	9
Spirits (per measure)		
brandy	50	
gin	50	
rum	50	
vodka	50	
whisky	50	
Sprats (fried)	390	110
Spring greens	11	3
Spring onions	18	5
Sprouts, Brussels *See* Brussels sprouts		
Squid		
fried in batter	195	55
steamed	88	25
Stock cube	88	25
Strawberries		
canned	88	25
fresh	25	7
Suet	830	235
Sugar (all types)	390	110
Sultanas	250	70
Sunflower oil *See* Oil		
Sunflower seeds	530	150
Swede	18	5

Sweetbread, lamb (fried)	230	65
Sweetcorn		
canned	70	20
fresh/frozen	105	30
Sweet potatoes	88	25
Sweets		
boiled	350	100
fudge	440	135
gums (sweetened)	335	95
peppermints	390	110
toffee	425	120
See also Chocolate		
Syrup		
golden	300	85
maple	250	70
Tangerines	35	10
Tapioca (boiled)	125	35
Tea (per cup, without milk, unsweetened)	0	0
With milk add 10, with sugar add 25 per spoonful		
Tomato juice, canned	14	4
Tomato sauce	105	30
Tomatoes	18	5
Tongue	210	60
Treacle, black	250	70
Tripe (stewed)	105	30
Trout (steamed)	88	25
Tuna (canned in oil)	280	80
Turnip	18	5
Turkey		
roast	175	50
roast (skinned)	140	40
Veal		
fried (in crumbs)	210	60
roast	230	65
Vegetable oils *See* Oils		
Venison (roast)	195	55
Vermouth *See* Wines		

Vinegar	4	1
Walnuts *See* Nuts		
Watercress	18	5
Water melon	18	5
Wheatgerm	355	100
Wheatgerm oil *See* Oil		
Whelks *See* Shellfish		
White pudding *See* Sausages		
Whitebait (fried)	530	150
Whiting (steamed)	70	20
Wholemeal bread *See* Bread		
Wines (per glass)		
campari	115	
port	75	
red, dry	80	
red, sweet	95	
rosé	85	
sherry, dry	50	
sherry, medium	65	
sherry, sweet	80	
vermouth, dry	60	
vermouth, sweet	75	
white, dry	75	
white, sparkling	90	
white, sweet	100	
Winkles *See* Shellfish		
Worcestershire sauce	70	20
Yam	125	35
Yoghurt		
flavoured	88	25
natural	53	15
Zucchini	11	3

Vitamins and Minerals in Foods

Vitamin	Sources	Action in the body
Vitamin A (retinol; precursor: carotene)	Fat-soluble vitamin found in animal fats, eggs, dairy produce, fish liver oil, liver, green leafy vegetables, carrots.	Necessary for night vision, healthy skin, and healthy mucous membranes. Deficiency causes night blindness, dry eyes and skin; excess causes hair loss, peeling and yellow skin.
Vitamin B complex		
Vitamin B_1 (thiamine)	Water-soluble vitamin found in yeast, wholegrain cereals, pulses, peanuts, liver, kidney, potatoes.	Necessary for normal carbohydrate metabolism, nerve function and digestion. Not stored in body. Deficiency causes digestive disorders, beriberi.
Vitamin B_2 (riboflavin)	Water-soluble vitamin found in yeast, eggs, milk, green vegetables, liver, kidney.	Necessary for normal carbohydrate and protein metabolism, growth and healthy mucous membranes. Deficiency causes cracked lips, skin disorders, over-sensitivity of eyes to light.
Vitamin B_6 (pyridoxine)	Fish, liver, wholegrain cereals, milk, pulses.	Necessary for growth and amino acid metabolism. Deficiency causes convulsions in children, anaemia and nerve disorders in adults.
Vitamin B_{12} (cyanocobalamin)	Water-soluble vitamin found in liver, kidney, dairy products; absent in vegetables.	Necessary for the formation of red blood cells. Deficiency causes pernicious anaemia.
Biotin	Abundant in liver and yeast. Formed by bacteria in intestines.	Necessary for energy release from carbohydrates and fats, and for healthy skin. Deficiency rare.
Folic acid (folacin)	Yeast, liver, kidney, mushrooms, green leafy vegetables.	Necessary for growth of red blood cells and cell division. Deficiency causes fatigue and anaemia.
Niacin (nicotinic acid)	Yeast, wholegrain cereals, liver, kidney.	Necessary for cell metabolism, fat synthesis, healthy skin. Deficiency causes pellagra.
Pantothenic acid	Yeast, liver, eggs, wholegrain cereals. Formed by bacteria in the intestines.	Necessary for enzyme action in cells. Deficiency (rare) may cause skin disorders.

Vitamin C (ascorbic acid)	Water-soluble vitamin found in citrus fruits, tomatoes, fresh vegetables.	Necessary for growth and repair of skin and other tissue. Deficiency causes scurvy.
Vitamin D (calciferol)	Fat-soluble vitamin found in butter, fish, liver oils, eggs, yeast. Formed in the skin by action of sunlight.	Necessary for absorption of calcium and phosphorus, and for formation of bones. Deficiency causes rickets in children, and osteomalacia in adults.
Vitamin E (tocopherol)	Fat-soluble vitamin found in vegetable oils, eggs, green vegetables. Formed by bacteria in the intestines.	Necessary for cell membrane stability, may be involved in fertility. Deficiency makes red blood cells liable to rupture.
Vitamin K (phytomen-adione)	Green leafy vegetables, vegetable oils. Formed by bacteria in the intestines.	Necessary for normal blood clotting. Deficiency causes bleeding, especially in babies.
Minerals		
Calcium	Milk and cheese, fish, green leafy vegetables, beans.	Necessary for the structure of bones and teeth. Extra needed by children and pregnant and lactating women. Deficiency causes rickets in children and osteomalacia in adults.
Iron	Meat, liver, green leafy vegetables, pulses.	Necessary for haemaglobin and red blood cells. Deficiency causes anaemia.
Trace elements	Tiny amounts of certain metallic elements such as iodine, magnesium, selenium and zinc, perform various functions in the body and are essential to health. They are abundant in a normal balanced diet, and deficiency disorders involving them are very rare.	

Major Drug Types

Drugs can be assigned to various categories, according to their mode of action. Some of the categories overlap, depending on the basis of their definition, and a few types have more than one name (for example, antineoplastic and cytotoxic both describe anti-cancer drugs).

Drug type	Application/use	Example
Amoebicidal	Prevention/treatment of disorders caused by amoebae (such as dysentery).	Chloroquine, metronidazole.
Anaesthetic	Deadening sensation, generally or locally.	General: halothane, nitrous oxide, thiopentone. Local: lignocaine.
Analgesic	Relief of pain (without affecting other senses).	Aspirin, codeine, paracetamol.
Antacid	Neutralizing stomach acid.	Aluminium hydroxide, magnesium trisilicate, sodium bicarbonate.
Anthelminthic	Prevention/treatment of disorders caused by worms.	Mebendazole, piperazine.
Anti-allergic	Most anti-allergic drugs are *Antihistamines* or *Corticosteroids*. They also include mast cell stabilizers.	Sodium cromoglycate.
Antianginal	Antianginal drugs include *Beta-blockers*. They also include calcium antagonists.	Nicardipine, verapamil.
Antiarrhythmic	Treatment of fast/irregular heartbeat.	Amiodarone, digoxin.
Anti-asthmatic	See *Bronchodilator*; *Mucolytic*.	
Antibacterial	Treatment/prevention of bacterial infection.	Aminoglycosides, sulphonamides.
Antibiotic	Treatment of bacterial or fungal infections.	Ampicillin, penicillin, tetracyclines.
Anticancer	See *Cytotoxic*.	
Anticoagulant	Inhibiting blood clotting mechanism.	Coumarin, heparin, warfarin.
Anticholinergic	Treatment of muscle spasm in the intestines, reducing secretions, dilating the pupils.	Atropine, dicyclomine hydrochloride.
Anticonvulsant	Controlling convulsions (such as in epilepsy).	Clonazepam, phenobarbitone.

Antidepressant	Treatment of depression. See also *MAO inhibitor*.	Fluoxetine, trimipramine.
Antidiarrhoeal	Treatment of diarrhoea.	Codeine, kaolin.
Anti-emetic	Treatment/prevention of nausea and vomiting.	Promethazine, hyoscine.
Antiepileptic	See *Anticonvulsant*.	
Antifungal	Treatment of disorders caused by fungi.	Griseofulvin, imidazoles.
Antihistamine	Treatment of allergy; also used as *Anti-emetic* and *Sedative* drugs.	Chlorpheniramine, promethazine.
Antihypertensive	See *Beta-blockers*; *Vasodilators*.	
Antimalarial	Treatment/prevention of malaria.	Chloroquine, pyrimethamine.
Antineoplastic	See *Cytotoxic*.	
Antiparkinsonian	Treatment of Parkinsonism.	Levodopa.
Antiperspirant	Prevention of perspiration.	Aluminium chloride.
Antiprotozoal	See *Amoebicidal*; *Antimalarial*.	
Antipyretic	Treatment of fever.	Aspirin, paracetamol.
Antirheumatic	Treatment of rheumatism.	Aspirin, phenylbutazone.
Antiserum	*Vaccine* produced in animals.	
Antispasmodic	Antispasmodics include *Bronchodilators* and *Anticholinergics*.	
Antithrombotic	See *Anticoagulant*.	
Antitubercular	Treatment of tuberculosis.	Ethambutol, isoniazid.
Antitussive	Suppression of cough.	Codeine, pholcodine.
Antivenin	Treatment of venomous bites.	Specific to animal.
Antiviral	Treatment of (certain) viral infections.	Aciclovir, idoxuridine.
Antipsychotic	Treatment of psychosis.	Butryophenones, thioxanthenes.
Anxiolytic	See *Tranquillizer*.	
Appetite suppressant	Treatment of obesity.	Lipase inhibitors, methylcellulose.
Beta-blocker	Treatment of angina and hypertension.	Acebutolol, propranolol.

Bronchodilator	Treatment of bronchial spasm (as in asthma).	Fenoterol, salbutamol.
Calcium antagonist		See *Antianginal.*
Chelating agent	Treatment of heavy metal poisoning.	Penicillamine, calcium disodium, edetate.
Contraceptive	Prevention of conception.	Oestrogen, progestogen.
Corticosteroid	Treatment of allergy, inflammation/rheumatism	Hydrocortisone.
Cytotoxic	Treatment of cancer.	Busulphan, fluorouracil.
Decongestant	Treatment of nasal congestion.	Ephedrine.
Diuretic	Treatment of oedema.	Frusemide, thiazides.
Emetic	Stimulation of vomiting.	Ipecacuanha.
Expectorant	Treatment of cough by thinning mucus.	Diphenhydramine hydrochloride.
Fungicidal	See *Antifungal.*	
Globulin	See *Vaccine.*	
Haemostatic	Treatment of haemorrhage.	Ethamsylate.
Hormones	Treatment of endocrine disorders; also used as *Contraceptives.*	Adrenal: hydrocortisone; Gonads: androgens, progestogens; Growth: somatropin;Pancreas: insulin;Pituitary: vasopressin;Thyroid: carbimazole, liothyronine.
Hypnotic	Inducement of sleep or unconsciousness.	Flurazepam, nitrazepam.
Hyperglycaemic	Controlling lack of blood glucose.	Diazoxide.
Hypoglycaemic	Controlling excess blood glucose (in diabetes mellitus).	Insulin.
Hypolipidaemic	Controlling lipids (such as cholesterol).	Benzafibrate, nicotinic acid.
Hypotensive	See *Beta-blocker.*	
Immunoglobulin	See *Vaccine.*	
Immuno-suppressant	Suppression of immune system.	Azathioprine, cyclosporin.

Laxative	Stimulate defecation.	Bisacodyl, magnesium citrate.
MAO inhibitor	Treatment of severe depression.	Moclobemide, phenelzine.
Mast cell stabilizers		See *Anti-allergic*.
Muscle relaxant.	Relaxation of muscles.	Dantrolene, diazepam.
Narcotic	Relief of severe pain.	Morphine.
Pediculicide	Treatment of infestation with lice.	Carbaryl, permethrin.
Scabicide	Treatment of infestation with mites.	Benzyl benzoate, malathion.
Spermicide	Killing sperm. See also *Contraceptives*.	Nonoxinol-9.
Stimulant	Stimulation of the brain.	Amphetamine, caffeine.
Sympatho-mimetic	Stimulation of the heart muscle.	Adrenaline, dopamine.
Tranquillizer	Treatment of anxiety, insomnia, nightmares.	Diazepam, lorazepam.
Vaccine	Conferring of immunity. Antisera are prepared using animals, immunoglobulins using humans; they may contain live or dead pathogens, or bacterial toxins.	Specific to the disease.
Vasoconstrictor	Causing contraction of blood vessels (raising blood pressure).	Metaraminol
Vasodilator	Causing widening of blood vessels (lowering blood pressure).	Prazosin, thymoxamine.

Average Heights and Weights of Children

The following table gives the average heights and weights of children throughout their growing period from birth to age 20 years. Because the timing of the growth spurts before and during puberty often vary from person to person, heights within 5 per cent and weights within 10 per cent for boys and up to 25 per cent for girls (of the averages given) are usually considered to be normal.

BOYS

Age (years)	Height cm	(in)	Weight kg	(lb)
Birth	58.0	(22.8)	4.0	(8.8)
2	85.0	(33.5)	12.0	(26.5)
4	101.5	(40.0)	16.5	(36.4)
6	107.5	(42.3)	20.0	(44.1)
8	115.0	(45.3)	24.5	(54.0)
10	134.0	(52.8)	30.0	(66.1)
12	144.0	(56.7)	36.0	(79.4)
14	157.0	(61.8)	45.5	(100.3)
16	169.0	(66.5)	55.5	(122.4)
18	175.0	(68.9)	64.0	(141.1)
20	175.0	(68.9)	66.5	(146.6)

GIRLS

Age (years)	Height cm	(in)	Weight kg	(lb)
Birth	58.0	(22.8)	3.0	(6.6)
2	83.0	(32.7)	11.5	(25.4)
4	98.5	(38.5)	16.0	(35.3)
6	111.0	(43.7)	20.0	(44.1)
8	123.0	(48.4)	23.5	(51.8)
10	134.0	(52.8)	30.0	(66.1)
12	144.5	(56.9)	39.5	(87.1)
14	155.0	(61.0)	46.0	(101.4)
16	161.5	(63.6)	55.0	(121.2)
18	164.5	(64.8)	59.0	(130.0)
20	164.5	(64.8)	59.5	(131.1)

Ideal Body Weight of Adults

The following table lists ideal body weights (measured without clothes) for various heights (measured without shoes). Because most of the population is slightly overweight, actual average weights are usually 5 to 10 kg (11–22 lb) heavier. Also, the weights are given for somebody of average build aged 25 years. People of heavy or slight build may be about 5 kg heavier or lighter. Most medical authorities allow an additional 0.5 kg (approx. 1 lb) for each year of a personís age up to age 40 – but no additional weight thereafter.

ADULTS

Height cm	(in)	Men kg	(lb)	Women kg	(lb)
145.0	(57)	47.9	(105.5)	46.0	(101.5)
147.5	(58)	49.7	(109.5)	47.2	(104.0)
150.0	(59)	52.4	(115.5)	48.5	(107.0)
152.5	(60)	53.1	(117.0)	49.4	(109.0)
155.0	(61)	55.3	(122.0)	51.0	(112.5)
157.5	(62)	56.7	(125.0)	52.4	(115.5)
160.0	(63)	57.8	(127.5)	53.5	(118.0)
162.5	(64)	59.2	(130.5)	55.3	(122.5)
165.0	(65)	61.0	(134.5)	57.2	(126.0)
167.5	(66)	62.1	(137.0)	58.5	(129.0)
170.0	(67)	64.9	(143.0)	60.3	(133.0)
172.5	(68)	66.7	(147.0)	62.1	(137.0)
175.0	(69)	68.3	(150.5)	64.0	(141.0)
177.5	(70)	71.4	(157.5)	65.5	(144.5)
180.0	(71)	72.6	(160.0)	67.6	(149.0)
182.5	(72)	74.6	(164.5)	69.2	(152.5)
185.0	(73)	76.2	(168.0)	71.4	(157.5)
187.5	(74)	78.0	(172.0)	73.3	(161.5)
190.0	(75)	80.7	(178.0)	75.3	(166.0)

Weights and Measures

In English medical texts, weights and other measures may be stated in Imperial Units (called Customary Units in the United States) – inches, ounces, pints, and so on – or in Metric Units (known scientifically as SI Units) – centimetres, grams, millilitres, and so on. Similarly, temperatures may be stated in degrees Fahrenheit or degrees Celsius (which is the same as centigrade). The following tables list factors that can be used to convert from one system of units to the other.

Imperial into Metric

Length:	*To convert*		*Multiply by*
	inches	to millimetres	25.4
	inches	to centimetres	2.54
	inches	to metres	0.254
	feet	to centimetres	30.48
	feet	to metres	0.3048
	yards	to metres	0.9144
	miles	to kilometres	1.6093
Area:	square inches	to square centimetres	6.4516
	square feet	to square metres	0.0929
	square yards	to square metres	0.8316
	square miles	to square kilometres	2.5898
	acres	to hectares	0.4047
	acres	to square kilometres	0.00405
Volume:	cubic inches	to cubic centimetres	16.3871
	cubic feet	to cubic metres	0.0283
	cubic yards	to cubic metres	0.7646
	cubic miles	to cubic kilometres	4.1678
Capacity:	fluid ounces	to millilitres	28.5
	pints	to millilitres	568.0
	pints	to litres	0.568
	gallons	to litres	4.55
Weight:	ounces	to grams	28.3495
	pounds	to grams	453.592

	pounds	to kilograms	0.4536
	pounds	to tonnes	0.0004536
	tons	to tonnes	1.0161

Metric into Imperial

Length:	*To convert*		*Multiply by*
	millimetres	to inches	0.03937
	centimetres	to inches	0.3937
	centimetres	to feet	0.032808
	metres	to inches	39.37
	metres	to feet	3.2808
	metres	to yards	1.0936
	kilometres	to miles	0.6214
Area:	square centimetres	to square inches	0.1552
	square metres	to square feet	10.7636
	square metres	to square yards	1.196
	square kilometres	to square miles	0.3861
	square kilometres	to acres	247.1
	hectares	to acres	2.471
Volume:	cubic centimetres	to cubic inches	0.061
	cubic metres	to cubic feet	35.315
	cubic metres	to cubic yards	1.308
	cubic kilometres	to cubic miles	0.2399
Capacity:	millilitres	to fluid ounces	0.0351
	millilitres	to pints	0.00176
	litres	to pints	1.760
	litres	to gallons	0.2193
Weight:	grams	to ounces	0.0352
	grams	to pounds	0.0022
	kilograms	to pounds	2.2046
	tonnes	to pounds	2204.59
	tonnes	to tons	0.9842

Temperature

To convert a Fahrenheit temperature to Celsius, subtract 32 and multiply by 5/9 (= 0.556).

To convert a Celsius temperature to Fahrenheit, multiply by 9/5 (= 1.8) and add 32.

The following table lists equivalents:

oF	oC		oC	oF	
0	-17.8		0	32	– Water freezes
10	-12.2		5	41	
20	- 6.7		10	50	
30	- 1.1		15	59	
32	0	– Water freezes	20	68	
40	4.4		25	77	
50	10.0		30	86	
60	15.6		35	95	
70	21.2		36	96.8	
80	26.7		37	98.6	– Normal body temperature
90	32.2		38	100.4	
95	35.0		39	102.2	
96	35.6		40	104	
97	36.1		45	113	
98	36.7		50	120	
99	37.3		60	140	
100	37.8		70	158	
105	40.6		80	176	
110	48.4		90	194	
212	100	– Water boils	100	212	– Water boils